Harvard Graphics® for Windows Made Easy

Harvard Graphics® for Windows Made Easy

Mary Campbell

Osborne McGraw-Hill

Berkeley New York St. Louis San Francisco
Auckland Bogotá Hamburg London Madrid
Mexico City Milan Montreal New Delhi Panama City
Paris São Paulo Singapore Sydney
Tokyo Toronto

Osborne **McGraw-Hill**
2600 Tenth Street
Berkeley, California 94710
U.S.A.

For information on software, translations, or book distributors outside of the U.S.A., please write to Osborne **McGraw-Hill** at the above address.

Harvard Graphics® for Windows Made Easy

Copyright © 1992 by McGraw-Hill, Inc. All rights reserved. Printed in the United States of America. Except as permitted under the Copyright Act of 1976, no part of this publication may be reproduced or distributed in any form or by any means, or stored in a database or retrieval system, without the prior written permission of the publisher, with the exception that the program listings may be entered, stored, and executed in a computer system, but they may not be reproduced for publication.

234567890 DOC 998765432

ISBN 0-07-881790-0

Information has been obtained by Osborne **McGraw-Hill** from sources believed to be reliable. However, because of the possibility of human or mechanical error by our sources, Osborne **McGraw-Hill**, or others, Osborne **McGraw-Hill** does not guarantee the accuracy, adequacy, or completeness of any information and is not responsible for any errors or omissions or the results obtained from use of such information.

Publisher
Kenna S. Wood

Acquisitions Editor
Elizabeth Fisher

Associate Editor
Scott Rogers

Technical Editor
Paul Sevigny

Editor
Janis Paris

Proofreaders
Linda Medoff
Louise Sellers

Indexer
Susan DeRenne Coerr

Quality Conrol Specialist
Bob Myren

Computer Designer
Jani Beckwith

Cover Design
Bay Graphics Design, Inc.

Contents

Acknowledgments	....	xix
Introduction	....	xxi

1	**Overview and Basic Features**	1
	Package Overview	2
	Terminology	3
	Choosing the Best View for Working	4
	Analytical Slides	7
	Text Slides	11
	Organization Chart Slides	13
	Chart Galleries	14
	Drawing and Symbols	14
	ScreenShow	16
	Templates and Backgrounds	16
	Import and Export Features	17
	The Basic Package Features	17
	Starting Harvard Graphics	18
	Quitting Harvard Graphics	18
	Getting Help	19
	Mouse Versus Keyboard	19
	Menu Selections	21
	Using Dialog Boxes	23
	Output	25

	Saving Files	25
	Changing Directories	26
	Changing Defaults	27
2	**Outlining a Presentation**	**29**
	A Look at the Outliner	30
	Switching from the Slide Editor to the Outliner	32
	Making the Outliner the Default View	34
	Using the Outliner to Create a Presentation	34
	Completing a Title Chart	35
	Creating Bullet Charts	36
	Creating Placeholders for Other Charts	37
	Saving a Presentation	38
	Printing the Presentation	38
	Closing and Reopening a Presentation	39
	Revising a Presentation	41
	Moving a Topic	41
	Copying and Deleting Topics	42
	Adding a Topic	45
	Splitting a Topic in Two Parts	45
	Collapsing and Expanding the View	47
	Creating a Slide Summary	48
	Reorganizing Your Presentation Slides	49
	Resetting the Default View to the Slide Editor	49
3	**Creating Text Charts**	**51**
	Getting Started	53
	Different Types of Text Charts	55
	Using Chart Galleries	56
	Creating a Chart from the Gallery	56
	Viewing Other Gallery Options	57
	Creating a Bullet Chart with a Gallery Option	58
	Checking the Spelling for Charts	59
	Spell Checking Options	60
	Checking the Current Bullet Chart	61

Other Text Chart Creation Options	63
Creating Another Title Chart	63
Looking at Two New Bullet Charts	65
Using Data Forms to Create Table Charts	68
Creating a Three-Column Table Chart	70
Working with the Slide Editor to Create and Enhance Charts	74
Moving from Slide to Slide	74
Selecting Text	75
Using Text Boxes	76
Moving Text	77
Size, Color, Style, Font, and Placement of Text Entries	78
Changing the Chart Palette	81
Text Chart Fonts	83
Other Text Styles	84
Chart Appearance Attributes for Specific Chart Types	86
Using the Slide Editor to Create a Free-Form Chart	88

4 Learning XY Chart Basics with Bar Charts — 91

Getting Started	93
Adding Information to the Chart	96
Adding Data Series	96
Revising the Titles	98
Adding Legends	100
Changing Data	102
Altering Data Values	102
Reorganizing Data	103
Inserting and Deleting Rows and Columns	104
Moving an Entire Row or Column of Data	105
Changing the Order of the Series	106
Organizing a Series Differently	108
Printing Your Charts	113
Output Options	114
Changing Margins	114

Setting Up Your Print Device	114
Printing Your Data Charts	116
Different Types of Bar Graphs	116
Bar Chart Styles	116
Other Bar Chart Options	119
Creating an Overlap Bar Chart	120
Creating a Stacked Bar Chart	121
Creating a 100% Bar Chart	122
Creating a Step Bar Chart	122
Creating a Paired Chart	125
Other Bar Chart Enhancements	127
Changing Fill Options	128
Changing the Chart Frame	132
Changing Gridlines	133
Changing 3D Options	133
Changing Text	134
Adding a Data Table	135
Checking Your Spelling	137

5 Additional XY Data Chart Options 139

Getting Started	140
More Options for XY Charts	142
Entering the Data to Look at New Display Options	143
Changing the Line Thickness	145
Using Markers for Data Points	147
Changing the Line Style	149
Changing the Line Fit Option	150
Changing the Way Data Series Are Shown	151
Mixing Display Types	152
Hiding Data Series	153
Adding 3D Effects to Line Charts	154
Creating a Cumulative Chart	156
Changing the Legend	156
Changing the Axes	160
Adjusting Grid Lines	165
Adding Data Labels	166

Showing a Goal Range	....	167
Area Charts	....	168
Creating an Area Chart	....	168
Adding a 3D Effect	....	170
High/Low/Close Charts	....	170
Creating a High/Low/Close Chart	....	172
High/Low/Close Chart Options	....	175
Including Other Chart Types	....	177
Using Calculations	....	179
Arithmetic Formulas	....	180
Using Keywords in Formulas	....	183

6   Creating Pie Charts 189

Getting Started	....	189
Setting the Slice's Appearance	....	193
Selecting Colors	....	193
Selecting Fill	....	194
Cutting Pie Slices	....	195
Displaying Multiple Pies	....	195
Adding a Second Pie	....	196
Adding Pie Chart Labels	....	199
Creating Another Multiple Pie Chart Slide	.....	201
Options for Multiple Pies	....	202
Proportionally Sized Pies	....	202
Linking Pies	....	203
Enhancing the Pie's Appearance	....	206
Displaying Pies as Columns	....	206
Sorting Pie Slices	....	207
Changing the Pie's Starting Angle	....	208
Changing the Pie Size	....	210
Setting the Size of Slice Pointers	....	211
Changing Options for 3D Charts	....	211
Legends for Pie Charts	....	212
Selecting Label Display	....	213

7   Creating Organization Charts 217

Getting Started	....	219

Adding an Organization Chart to a Slide	221
Additions to the Organization Chart	223
Adding More Levels	224
Adding a Staff Position	226
Organization Chart Changes	226
Changing the Boxes	226
Last Level Options	229
Changing the Text Style	229
Changing Your View of an Organization Chart	231
Collapsing and Expanding Your View	232
Creating a Slide Summary	233
Responding to a Reorganization	233
Changing Entries	234
Adding an Entry	235
Changing the Location of an Entry	235
Deleting a Subordinate	236
Converting a Bullet Chart to an Organization Chart	237

8 Using Drawing, Symbols, and Other Enhancements **241**

Getting Started	244
Adding Text and Objects in the Slide Editor	247
Adding Objects	248
Creating a Chart and Adding Annotations with Draw	250
Adding More Objects	252
Modifying Objects	255
Selecting Objects	255
Grouping Objects	255
Moving Objects	256
Sizing Objects	259
Changing Object Attributes	259
Selecting Color and Fills	261
Deleting Objects	262
Copying Objects	263
Adding Symbols	265

	Other Changes	267
	Rotating and Flipping Objects	268
	Aligning Objects	271
	Looking Closer at a Drawing	273
	Adding Special Effects	273
	Creating Multiple Charts with Symbols	276
9	**Enhancing Your Presentations**	**277**
	Getting Started	278
	Editing an Existing Presentation	278
	Reordering Slides	279
	Deleting Screens from a Presentation	280
	Adding ScreenShow Effects	282
	Setting Defaults for the ScreenShow	282
	Setting Options for Individual Charts	283
	Using Special Effects	284
	Setting the Display Time	286
	Signaling the Next Slide	287
	Trying ScreenShow Effects	287
	Using HyperShow Features to Control the Presentation Order	288
	Defining the Key to Activate the Link	289
	Defining the Destination Slide	290
	Changing Default Key Assignments	291
	Trying HyperShow Links	292
	Creating a Menu of User Choices	293
	Building a Chart in Stages	296
	Outputting Presentations	299
	Using Plotters and Film Recorders	299
	Using the Autographix Service	300
10	**Using Templates, Backgrounds, and Styles**	**303**
	Getting Started	304
	Working with Backgrounds	307
	Editing a Background	307
	Adding a Stamp	308
	Changing Existing Elements	308

	Applying an Existing Background	309
	Creating Templates	310
	Adding Symbols	313
	Applying a Template to a Chart	315
	Using a Template When You Create a New Slide	315
	Changing the Default Templates	317
	Using Styles	318
	Saving a Presentation Style	318
	Applying a Presentation Style	319
11	**Importing and Exporting Data**	**321**
	Importing Lotus Data	323
	Taking a Look at the 1-2-3 Data	323
	Importing the Entire Worksheet	325
	Importing a Selected Portion of the Worksheet	327
	Creating a Warm Link	328
	Transposing Rows and Columns	330
	Importing ASCII Data	332
	Creating a DDE Link	334
	Exporting Slide Images	335
	Exporting an Image for a Slide	336
	Exporting Image Files for a Presentation	337
	Exporting a Presentation Outline	338
12	**Customizing Harvard Graphics**	**341**
	Customizing with Color Palettes	342
	Chart Colors	342
	Custom Colors	345
	Editing a Color Palette	345
	Customizing Preference Settings	347
	Customizing with Macros	350
	Recording a Macro	350
	Executing a Macro	356
	Entering Data	358

A	**Installing Harvard Graphics**	**359**
	Installing Harvard Graphics	359
	Hardware Requirements	360
	Backing Up Your Disks	360
	Installing Harvard Graphics on	
	Your Hard Disk	361
	Using Supplemental Drivers	362
B	**Using Windows**	**365**
	Starting Windows	366
	Exiting Windows	366
	The Windows Interface	367
	The Program Manager	369
	Menus in Windows	369
	Opening Applications	370
	Switching to a Window	371
	Positioning and Sizing Windows	372
	The Windows File Manager	375
	Deleting Files	376
	Formatting a Disk	377
	The Windows Print Manager	378
C	**Symbols Files**	**381**
D	**Harvard Graphics Speed Keys**	**395**
	Speed Keys	395
	Functions Performed by Speed Keys	396
E	**Harvard Graphics Movement Keys**	**399**
	Index	403

Acknowledgments

I would like to thank the following individuals for their contributions to this book:

Margaret Campbell for checking the keystrokes in all the examples to ensure that they worked correctly.

Liz Fisher, Scott Rogers, Janis Paris, Jani Beckwith, Linda Medoff, Louise Sellers, and Hannah Raiden at Osborne/McGraw-Hill for all of their help.

Helen Kendrick at Software Publishing for providing the needed beta software.

Paul Sevigny for his technical review of the manuscript.

Introduction

Harvard Graphics is the best-selling graphics presentation package. It supports the creation of both text and analytical charts. Business users find that the features of this package allow them to communicate their goals and ideas in a more persuasive format. The package supports many customization options and allows the automation of charts with macros or templates. The graphs can be output to a printer, plotter, or 35-millimeter film. It is also possible to create a slide show with graph images. Symbols included with the package allow the creation of professional-looking output, custom tailored to your need. The drawing features allow additional flexibility in chart modification. In addition to freehand drawing, Harvard Graphics for Windows supports flipping, rotating and magnifying images, as well as making it easy for you to sort the slides in your presentation or organize it in outline format.

Harvard Graphics for Windows Made Easy is designed to meet the needs of the new Harvard Graphics for Windows user. You will find everything you need, from simple installation instructions to step-by-step examples, to create all types of charts and more sophisticated features like templates and macros.

If you have not installed Harvard Graphics on your machine, start with Appendix A for step-by-step instructions that will ensure your success.

If you have already installed Harvard Graphics for Windows on your system, you can start with Chapter 1 to learn about the wide variety of chart types that you can create with Harvard Graphics for Windows. After completing the overview chapter, feel free to select whichever chapter will help you complete the task you are working on. If you want to learn about all the features of the product, you can proceed through the chapters from the beginning and add new skills with each chapter you complete. Although the sequential approach ensures that you will learn about all aspects of the product, feel free to jump ahead at any time if you need a feature in a later chapter.

If you have already mastered the basics of Harvard Graphics, you will still find this book beneficial. Since most users initially master the features on a trial-and-error basis, there are probably many features that you have not used. You can learn about these additional options by proceeding sequentially through the chapters. You can also use the table of contents to help you select topics you want to add to your basic skills set.

Organization of This Book

This book is organized into 12 chapters and 5 appendixes. Each chapter is structured to be completed in a single session. As you finish each chapter you will have added a new presentation-building skill. Each chapter is self-contained, so you can complete the later chapters without the need for entering the exercises in the early chapters.

Chapter 1 provides a perspective on the features offered by Harvard Graphics. You are shown a variety of analytical and text charts created with the product, and can use these images to help you select the chart type you want to use in your presentations. Unlike the other chapters, it is not designed for hands-on practice.

Chapter 2 introduces you to the Outliner. You can use it when you are brainstorming to put together ideas for a presentation. It is also a good place to put together bullet charts that list your main points.

Chapter 3 allows you to create text charts for slides or transparencies that you can use in your presentations. The bullet and table chart examples are included.

Chapter 4 introduces the XY Chart form for the entry of information to a bar chart. The various components of a graph, such as the X- and Y-axes, are introduced. The use of different X-axis types and their effect on a graph area are also discussed. Other enhancements to the basic bar graph are covered, and a completed graph is saved and printed.

Chapter 5 provides an opportunity to look at three new chart types. In addition to the basic line and area charts, you can create a high/low/close graph.

Chapter 6 teaches you how to create a pie chart that gives a different perspective than the other graph types. Pie charts are ideal for showing the components of a whole, whether it is budget dollars, sales units, or head count. The examples provide an opportunity to create and print a pie graph and to use options such as color, removing a slide, 3D, and linking.

Chapter 7 makes it easy to create an organization chart after reorganization. This chapter provides examples for entry, editing, and printing of an organization chart.

Chapter 8 shows you how to use the Slide Editor view and drawing features, even if you are not an artist. Geometric shapes, arrows, and lines can be added to the screen automatically.

Chapter 9 teaches you how to use ScreenShow effects that make a presentation even more professional looking.

Chapter 10 shows you how to create a template to create many similar slides. You will also learn about using backgrounds and styles in this chapter.

Chapter 11 provides some techniques for sharing data between Harvard Graphics and other programs.

Chapter 12 provides a reference for techniques that help you customize Harvard Graphics. You will also learn how to use the Windows Recorder to capture keystrokes for replay at a later time.

Appendix A provides the instructions you may need if Harvard Graphics for Windows is not already installed on your machine. Appendix B provides an overview of important Windows concepts and procedures. Appendix C shows you what each symbol in the various symbol files looks like. This appendix is a handy reference when you want to select a symbol and do not know which file it is in. Appendix D provides a quick reference to speed keys. Appendix E is a reference of the movement keys and how they perform.

The Command Card provided at the back of this book will show you all the toolbox tools available from the Slide Editor view, in addition to the most commonly used pull-down menus available from the main menu.

Conventions Used in This Book

Several conventions have been used throughout this book to expedite your mastery of Harvard Graphics and make the learning process as easy as possible.

- Entries that you must make to duplicate examples in this book are shown in boldface within numbered steps.
- The word "choose" is used to indicate a choice you must make from a Harvard Graphics for Windows menu. The word "select" is used to indicate dialog box options you need to select.
- The word "type" is used to indicate information you must type from the keyboard.
- Uppercase letters are used for all file names, although you may use either upper- or lowercase letters in your entries.

1

Overview and Basic Features

Business graphics are not new. For years smart managers have realized it is possible to project a professional image and present a better message with the aid of graphs and charts. Studies indicate that people can absorb more information from a graph than an array of numbers and that they can retain it for a longer time.

Realizing the advantages of graphics came at a significant cost as recently as a few years ago. A manager had to contact a graphic artist or an individual in the company's graphics department to arrange for the appropriate presentation materials. Few presentations were constructed in less than several weeks, which often meant that the graphics materials arrived the afternoon before a big presentation. The cost ranged from several hundred to several thousand dollars, depending on the size and complexity of the charts required.

Today graphics still offer the same advantages, but the costs have decreased dramatically for individuals who use Harvard Graphics. In only hours you can create slides that add emphasis and clarity to your presentations. Once your raw data is recorded on the Harvard Graphics Data Forms, you can make changes in just a few minutes. All the variety you need to create an interesting presentation is present, with all types of analytical and text charts as well as drawing capability. Symbol files provided with the package even allow you to create logos and high-interest additions to your charts without the need for any artistic talent.

Harvard Graphics supports output to all of the popular printer and plotter devices. In addition, it allows interface to many of the popular film recorders to create 35-millimeter film images directly. You can also use the ScreenShow feature provided with the package in combination with a large screen monitor as an effective presentation vehicle.

This chapter will give you an overview of the package features. This allows you to focus on the chapters that provide information on an immediate need you may have to create a specific type of slide. Following the overview is an introduction to the basic features of all applications. This will provide you with basic skills for running the package, and from then on you can skip from chapter to chapter as you need skills to present your information in new ways.

Package Overview

Harvard Graphics is one of the most popular graphics packages because of its ease of use and wide variety of slide types. Charts and graphs are created on a blank slide capable of displaying any type of chart, graph, or drawing. Harvard Graphics is easy to use because it employs a straightforward menu system with options selectable by keyboard or mouse. Features are selected by clicking the mouse, using the keyboard to make a menu selection, or using the speed keys. Default selections allow you to create a slide quickly without a need to choose size and layout options unless you want to customize the slide. This means that your initial focus can be on defining and entering your data. Harvard Graphics for Windows provides new options for enhancing slides as well as a streamlined approach to tasks that were available in earlier releases.

To make it easy to create and manage your slide presentations, Harvard Graphics provides three different views that you can work with. Some tasks such as saving a copy of the presentation can be completed from all views. Other tasks such as changing the axis labels can only be completed from a specific view. This means that there are some menu selections common to all

Chapter 1: *Overview and Basic Features* 3

three views, whereas other menu options are unique to one view. You can move from view to view of your data by choosing the desired view from the View menu. You can also click the various view icons as shown at the upper-right edge of Figure 1-1, which presents the Slide Editor view.

Terminology

The variety of charting options makes this package suitable for creating all types of written and visual slide presentations. All output created by the package is referred to as *slides*. It is common to refer to some of the more analytical charts as *graphs*. The slides that contain text are frequently referred to as *charts* although you will want to keep in mind that each is placed on a slide and that slides can contain charts, graphs, drawings, and additional text. The entire orientation of Harvard Graphics for Windows revolves around working with slides to create a presentation, although you will find the terms slide and chart used interchangeably throughout this book. Whether you want

Figure 1-1.   *Graph terminology*

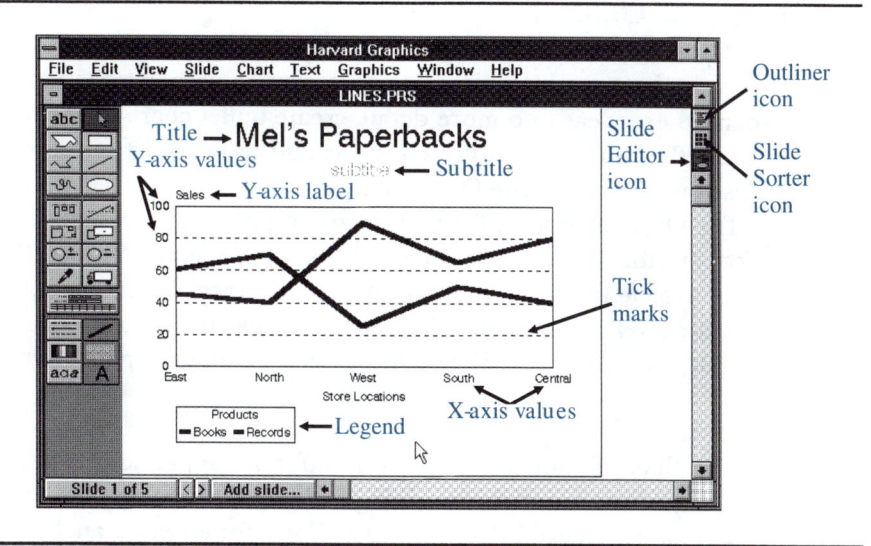

analytical charts, word charts, a varied symbol library, or drawing capability, this one package can meet your needs.

Harvard Graphics supports object-oriented graphics to ease transfer between the file formats of other programs. This means the package can be defined as a vector-based graphics package, as opposed to a bitmapped package. *Vector-based* packages create their images from lines and curves, whereas *bitmapped* packages are dependent on individual pixels or dots on the screen. A vector-based package offers one advantage over bitmapped graphics. The vector graphic image is composed of a series of objects—symbols, boxes, lines, arrows, and text. Any of these objects can be changed without affecting anything else in the chart. It is also much easier to alter the size of a particular object on the screen with vector-based packages.

Choosing the Best View for Working

Most packages provide only one way to work with your information. Harvard Graphics for Windows provides three. The three different views are the Outliner, the Slide Editor, and the Slide Sorter. Each is uniquely suited for different types of tasks.

Using the Outliner

If you are brainstorming to put together a presentation, the Outliner offers the best working view. It allows you to record your ideas. You can expand these ideas into more detail, create bullet charts that list key points, put together an organization chart, or add other chart types to any of the slides you create with the Outliner view.

The Outliner is ideal for getting an overview of a presentation. You can look at just the slide titles or see all of the detail. Figure 1-2 shows the Outliner with both slide titles and bullet detail on the screen. Indentation makes it easy to see the level of each entry. At any time you want to work more closely with one slide, you can use the Slide Editor icon at the upper right to switch the view.

Using the Slide Editor

The Slide Editor provides two different appearances depending on whether you are entering or editing slide data or making enhancements to the basic slide. Figure 1-3 shows a Data Form for entering analytical informa-

Figure 1-2. *Outliner window*

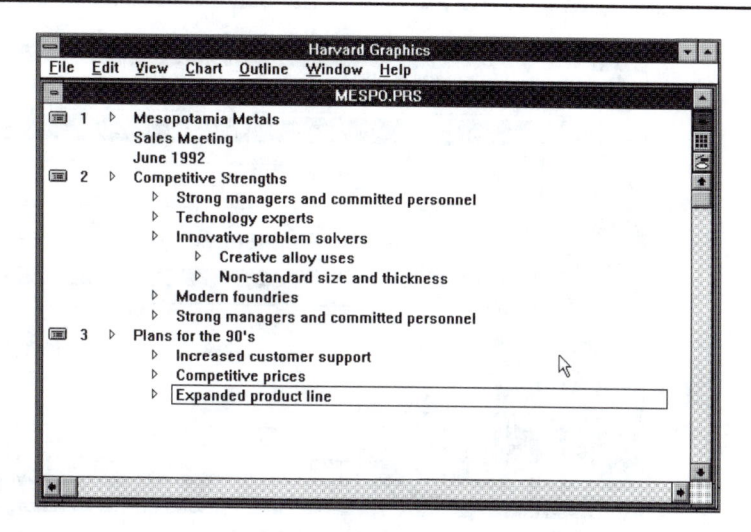

tion. Your Data Form will have a different appearance depending on which type of chart you are placing on the slide. When you are finished entering data you can choose OK from the bottom of the Data Form or press CTRL+F4.

The Slide Editor screen that appears when you finalize your data entry displays the slide as well as a toolbox as shown in Figure 1-4. You can use the tools in the toolbox to add drawing to the slide, to add text in any location, or to color and size the slide objects. If you prefer you can use the menu to invoke most toolbox options as well as other chart enhancements. If at any time you need to change the data used to create the chart you can move back to the Data Form easily.

Using the Slide Sorter

The Slide Sorter is like having a light tray to use in arranging 35MM slides. Harvard Graphics Slide Sorter view is useful for reorganizing your presentation. You can see a picture of each slide on the tray. It is easy to reorder the slides from this view. It is also the view of choice if you want to delete several slides.

Figure 1-3. *Data Form for entering an XY chart*

Figure 1-4. *Slide Editor*

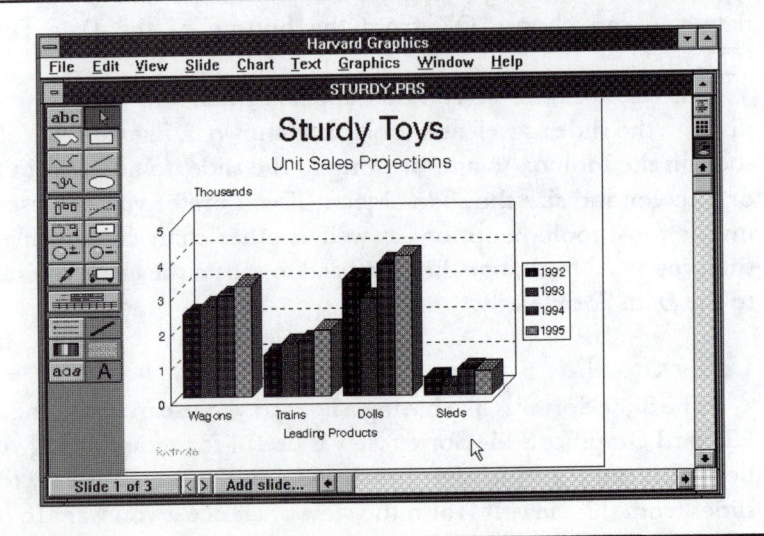

Chapter 1: *Overview and Basic Features* 7

You can preview your slides with jackets around them or without. The sample Slide Sorter screen shown in Figure 1-5 does not have jackets around the slides. If you need to take a close-up look at the data for any slide while working in the Slide Sorter all you need to do is switch to the Slide Editor view.

Analytical Slides

Analytical slides display numeric data in a form that is easier to understand than reviewing the raw numbers. Harvard Graphics creates slides containing many types of analytical charts including bar charts, pie charts, and line charts. Reading through detailed sales figures for a product can leave your head spinning, and you may end up with no clear picture of the success of the product. On the other hand, presenting the information in summary form on a slide shows an upward or downward sales trend at a glance.

Figure 1-5.   Slide Sorter

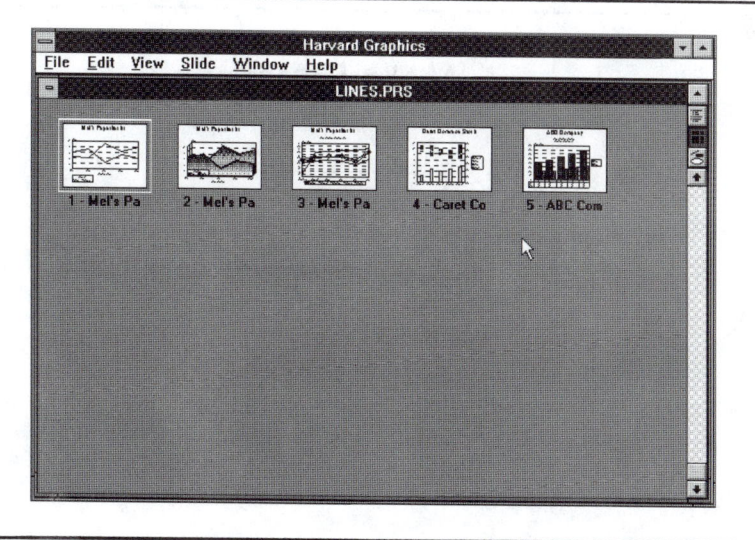

Chart Basics

Harvard Graphics provides support for analytical slides of many different sizes and shapes. The various options for these slides are commonly referred to as charts, as in bar chart and pie chart. Regardless of the type chosen, values to be shown on a slide are stored in a series, and each value represents one data element to be recorded on the slide. For example, a series can contain the 1992 sales figures by product (each of the data elements within the series represents the sales of one product in 1992).

Tick marks (little lines extending from an axis) can add accuracy to your interpretation of the values shown in the slide. Most of the charts shown on these slides are prepared using a vertical Y axis and a horizontal X axis, as shown in Figure 1-6. The X axis is used to show products, years, or other groupings for the data being measured. Each entity measured is shown by a point along the X axis marked with an X-axis label. The Y axis is used to measure quantity, such as sales amount, head count, number of automobiles, or bushels of wheat produced. Harvard Graphics provides options that control the scale used to label the measurements on the Y axis.

Figure 1-6.   *Line chart*

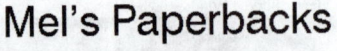

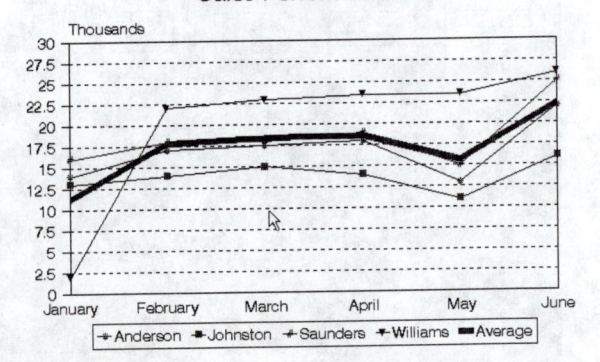

Titles can be used to label the axes and at the top of the slide to describe the data presented. Harvard Graphics allows for a title line and a subtitle line on the Data Form. You can use (CTRL)+(ENTER) to add another line to these entries but you may need to select a smaller text size to add these additional lines. Legends distinguish one series from another when multiple series are shown on a slide. Footnotes provide you with an option for providing further information about a slide or an element of a slide. You can also use the Text tool in the Slide Editor to add text to any location on a slide.

Types of Analytical Slides

Although Harvard Graphics provides a wide variety of slide types, your selection depends on the type of data you want to show on the slide. As you gain more experience with the package, you will get better at selecting the best slide type to present your message. The chapters of this book that discuss various types of charts offer suggestions to help you make these decisions.

When you tell Harvard Graphics that you want to add a slide, you can select a slide type from a chart gallery. If you prefer, you can indicate the type of slide you want to create and make all the customizing changes yourself. You can choose from a text chart, pie chart, vertical bar chart, organization chart, or drawing using the radio buttons in the Add Slide dialog box.

Pie and XY charts are the two options for analytical slides that help your audience analyze the data presented. XY charts include all the slide options that create a chart using the X and Y axis. XY slides include Vertical bar, Horizontal bar, Line, Area, High/Low/Close, and Scatter options. Pie charts include many options without using an X or Y axis.

Vertical and horizontal bars are two popular types of XY charts. They consist of one or more sets of bars, the length of which is controlled by the data in the series. Bar charts are an excellent choice for presenting data that has changed over time, such as sales volume, the number of customers, or the number of retail outlets. The most basic type of Vertical bar chart, which you can create in only a few minutes, is shown in Figure 1-7.

The options and enhancements for bar slides make this one type seem as if it were actually many types. When you want to show data grouped by year, an overlapped bar chart can place the value for each series in a given year within the same group. A stacked bar chart places the values in each series atop the values from the corresponding previous series. Other enhancements,

Figure 1-7.   *Bar chart*

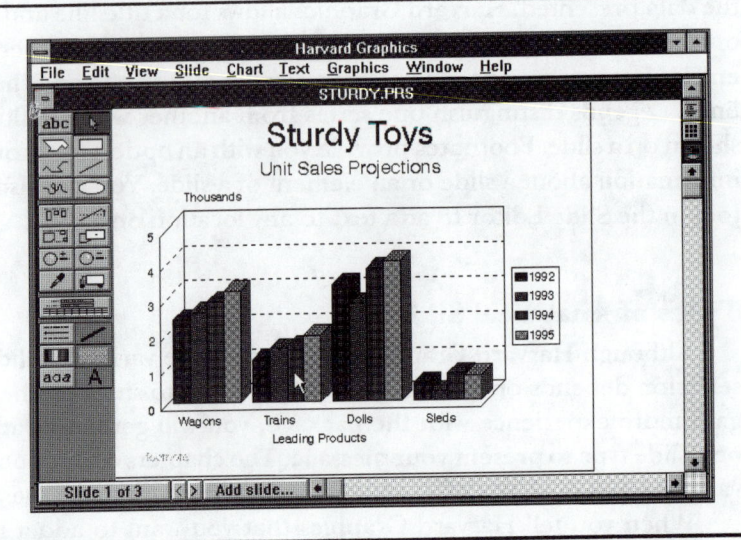

like a 3D effect, can be used to improve aesthetics or to draw attention to product sales increases or decreases.

High/low/close slides are the perfect way to chart stock and bond prices over time. These charts provide a way to show up to four series of data in one high/low/close slide. At a glance you can see if the opening price of the stock or commodity has held relatively constant, while the high and low values may vary considerably. You will appreciate the ability to change the Y-axis starting values, because it normally is not possible to show the data effectively if 0 is used as the minimum value shown on the scale. Figure 1-8 shows the effectiveness of a high/low/close selection combined with displaying a series as a bar in presenting market data. This chart shows you how you can include additional series of data, such as display of volume for each day.

Line charts are another type of XY chart that allows you to show a trend in your data over time. If you have a large number of data points, a line chart can prove to be a better choice than a bar chart, since each data point does not require a bar. Line charts can also be smooth, as in a trend line chart. The connection between the points in the line can take on a zigzag appearance if a curved line is not used for the chart.

Figure 1-8. *High/low/close chart*

[Chart: Caret Common Stock — High/Low, Close, Open, Volume for August 1–5]

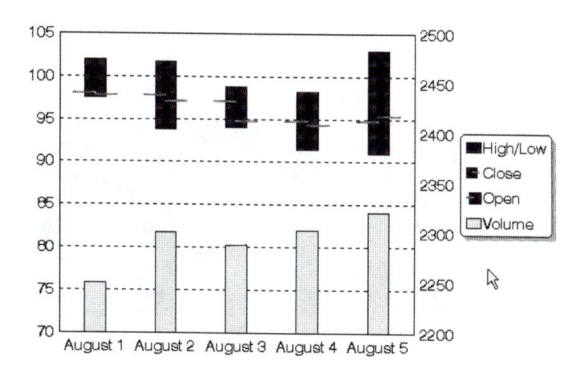

Area graphs are created in the same way as line charts except the area underneath the line is filled with a pattern or color. Area charts are striking in appearance and can be used in combination with other graph types, such as a line chart. For example, in Figure 1-9 total cost is represented as an area chart and salary costs are shown as a line.

Pie charts are ideal when you want to communicate what part of a whole each series value is. Although pie charts do not use an X- and Y-axis, it is easy to create a simple pie chart. You can also enhance a pie by cutting a pie slice and pulling it away from the pie, and even linking it to a column chart as shown in Figure 1-10.

Text Slides

Text slides are word charts. They may be highlights from your presentation, a few important statistics, the names of several good books, or the steps defined to complete a project, to name a few choices.

Figure 1-9.   Area/line chart

Mel's Paperbacks

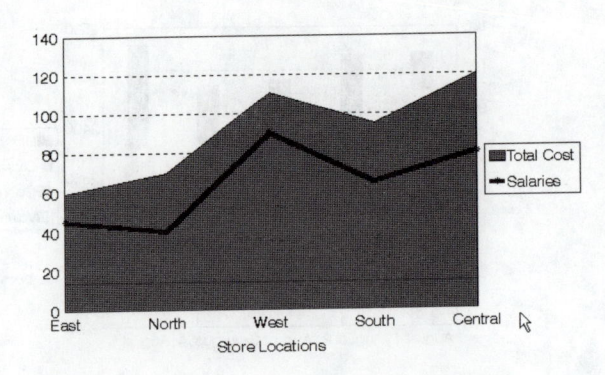

Figure 1-10.   Pie chart linked to a column

Industry Sales

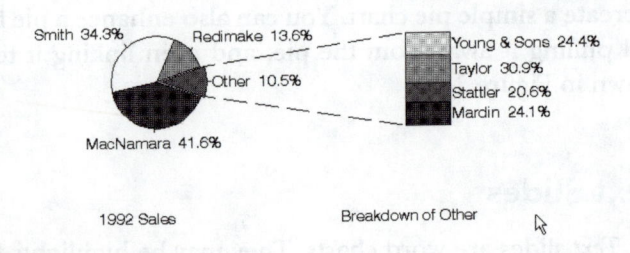

Chapter 1: *Overview and Basic Features* 13

Harvard Graphics provides several types of text slides. Title slides allow you to create a title page for a report or a title page for a presentation. Bullet slides allow you to enter a series of short items or phrases. In a bullet slide, a special symbol is used to the left of each entry. Figure 1-11 shows a bullet slide with two different styles of bullets. Table slides allow you to place data on the screen in a clean columnar fashion and can have from 2 to 24 columns. You might use a table slide to report results by salesperson. The name could be placed in the first column and the results in rows immediately thereafter.

Organization Chart Slides

Organization charts consist of boxes with the names of individuals or organizational units inside each box. A hierarchical structure is normally presented to portray relationships, as in the chart for Mesopotamia Metals found in Figure 1-12.

Figure 1-11. *Bullet chart*

International Representatives

- François Monet
  - France
  - Holland
- Margaret Müller
  - Germany
  - Switzerland
- Klauss Weiß
  - Austria
  - Spain

Figure 1-12. *Organization chart*

Mesopotamia Metals
Organization Chart

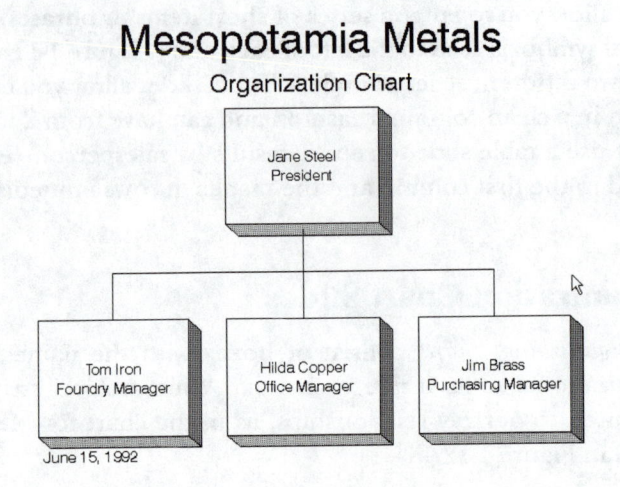

Jane Steel
President

Tom Iron
Foundry Manager

Hilda Copper
Office Manager

Jim Brass
Purchasing Manager

June 15, 1992

Chart Galleries

Harvard Graphics for Windows provides a selection of predefined styles for each type of slide. The selection of predefined styles for any slide type is called a *chart gallery*. Rather than selecting a slide type and defining all the options, you can save time by choosing the gallery option after selecting the slide type you want. Figure 1-13 shows the gallery of options available to you for a vertical bar slide.

Drawing and Symbols

Even if you are not an artist, the Harvard Graphics drawing features can improve your presentations. The Slide Editor provides a toolbox of options to assist you as you attempt to enhance a chart with drawing options. You can

Figure 1-13.   *Chart gallery*

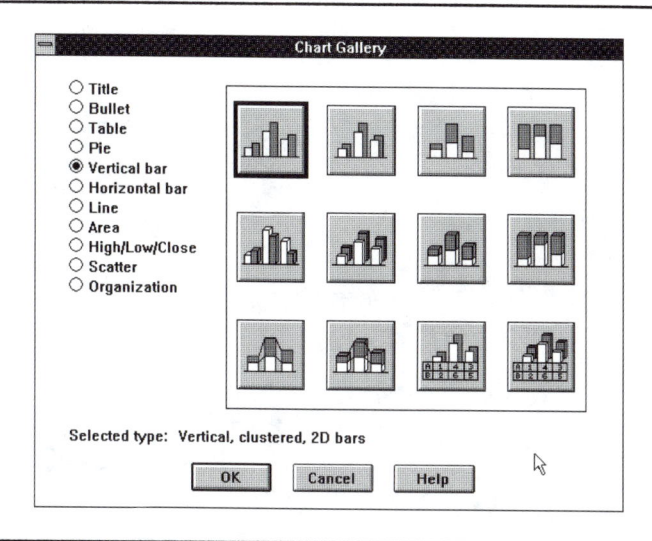

use the Slide Editor tools to create straight-line charts such as PERT (Program Evaluation and Review Techniques) diagrams to assist you with project management activities. PERT charts diagram a sequence of activities that need to be completed on a project. You can also create drawing slides that provide a free-form approach to slide creation.

The Slide Editor tools can add emphasis to a particular line on an existing slide. With just a little artistic talent, you can add a small drawing to a slide. Or the library of hundreds of symbols allows you to call up professional-looking symbols and add them to your slide. Features for moving and sizing these symbols make them easy to incorporate. Figure 1-14 is a distribution diagram that shows the flow of a product from the source of the raw material to the final delivery of the end product. The symbols on this slide are easier to comprehend than a slide created with words, and it took less than 10 minutes to create because it is composed of symbols from the Harvard Graphics symbol library. You can use Slide Editor features to flip, rotate, and magnify charts, or to include free-hand drawings, arcs, and polygons.

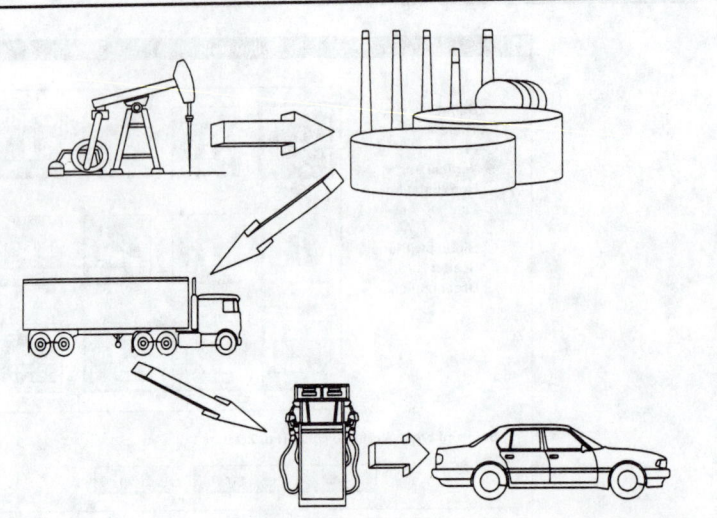

Figure 1-14. *Distribution diagram*

ScreenShow

ScreenShow features allow you to display a slide show on your computer screen. You can add transition effects that control how one screen replaces another and determine the time that slides remain on the screen. The names of transition options such as Fade, Blinds, Wipe, Scroll, and Iris indicate how the transition from one screen to another can be handled. Shows can be viewed from beginning to end, or you can start anywhere in the middle.

HyperShow features further enhance a ScreenShow by allowing you to add buttons that control progress through a ScreenShow or start another application. Effectively, these buttons allow you to interract with the needs of your audience by altering the presentation while it is in process.

Templates and Backgrounds

A *template* is nothing more than a chart type and a set of options that you define ahead of time. It is useful if you must create many similar charts. You can use your templates every time you create a new chart or just occasionally when you need a specific version. Templates can control the chart type, font selection, point size, the location of titles, the slide background, and the color palette used among other things.

A *background* is the area behind a slide. It is like a clear sheet of mylar that you can lay the slide on. You can add a border or graphic image to this background and then use it for all the slides in your presentation.

Import and Export Features

With Harvard Graphics you can import data from Lotus 1-2-3, Microsoft Excel, or delimited ASCII files as used in databases. You can even use named ranges in your Excel and 1-2-3 files and access these ranges from Harvard Graphics. You can establish links to worksheet data to have the latest information automatically show in your slides once you open the presentation containing them. You can also use clip art created with may other packages, or send text and graphics to word processing software or desktop publishers to be refined.

The Basic Package Features

At this point it is assumed that your software package is installed and you are ready to explore the preliminary features of the package. If you have not as yet installed your package, turn to Appendix A, "Installing Harvard Graphics," and complete the steps in the simple installation procedure.

In this chapter you will learn how to use the mouse with the package, how to save a file, and how to change default settings. Some keyboard techniques will also be included but since a mouse is required for the package and many tasks are easiest with a mouse, the primary emphasis will be on mouse instructions. You will continue to use these skills as you proceed through the book. You may feel you do not need to try the instructions presented in these sections, but you will find that you master the package in a shorter period of time if you actually try the examples here.

Starting Harvard Graphics

To start Harvard Graphics you must have Windows active in your machine. You will need to double-click the icon for Harvard Graphics. This means two quick presses of the left mouse button in rapid succession with the mouse pointer on the Harvard Graphics icon. If you installed the package with the default options, this icon will be in the Windows Applications program group. If this window (or the window of whichever group you added Harvard Graphics to) is not open, you must open it to select Harvard Graphics.

After you start the package, the Harvard Graphics title screen displays briefly and is then replaced by a window with a limited set of options—primarily for allowing you to create a new presentation or to open an existing one:

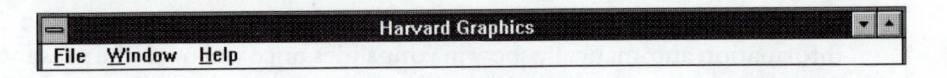

```
┌─────────────────────── Harvard Graphics ───────────────────────┐
 File  Window  Help
```

Quitting Harvard Graphics

When you are ready to end your Harvard Graphics session, you can choose Exit from the File menu. You can make these selections from the menu by moving the mouse pointer to File in the menu at the top and dragging down through the pull-down menu that is displayed, until you get to Exit and then releasing the mouse. Or click on the File menu and then click on Exit to leave the program. If you would prefer to use the keyboard, pressing (ALT)+(F) will activate the File menu. You can always use the (ALT) key plus the underlined letter from the menu bar to pull down the menu. After the pull-down menu is displayed, you can use the (ARROW) keys to highlight the desired selection and press (ENTER) to finalize your selection. Alternatively, you can type the underlined letter in the menu selection to select it. A shortcut approach to most menu options is represented by the speed keys that display at the right side of the pull-down menu. You can type the shortcut key sequence to eliminate the need for activating the menu bar and choosing an option from a pull-down menu. The speed key makes your selection automatically. For example, you can create a new presentation by choosing New

Chapter 1: *Overview and Basic Features*   19

presentation from the File menu or simply pressing CTRL+N. If you attempt to exit without saving, a warning message reminds you that you have not saved your presentation after making changes.

Getting Help

The F1 key is known as the Help key and provides information on the features of the package right on your screen. If you are looking at a screen that offers you options, pressing F1 displays a screen that describes the task you need to complete. You can also select a specific dialog box option *before* requesting help to access help on a specific option. This type of help is referred to as *context-sensitive help* because the package attempts to supply exactly the information you need. You will learn more about the Help feature later in this chapter.

Mouse Versus Keyboard

Harvard Graphics *requires* you to have a mouse to make full use of the package. Many tasks support the use of either the mouse or the keyboard but a few—such as the tools in the Slide Editor—require you to use a mouse. For tasks that support either, you can access all options regardless of which approach you choose. The factors that determine your selection are your preference and the tasks before and after the desired action. For example, if you are typing on a Data Form you might find it just as easy to use the keyboard to move to another field on the form rather than using the mouse. If you are a fast typist, or your desktop is cluttered, you may prefer to use the keyboard as much as possible, rather than attempting to roll your mouse over books, papers, and coffee cups. Remember, though, that the mouse can be easier to use since there are not as many options. You simply click, double-click, or drag with the mouse to accomplish any task, whereas the keyboard keys take on different actions depending on what task you are working on.

Throughout this book, directions are provided for keyboard entry of data. Other directions tell you to choose a menu option or select a dialog box option. You can use either the mouse or keyboard approach but the underlined letter in each menu choice makes it easy for you to use the keyboard approach if you prefer it. Other than completing a text entry, you will find the mouse to be the method of choice for the dialog box.

Keyboard Specifics

If you have used the keyboard to work with other packages, you will find the transition to Harvard Graphics easy. Although some of the keys may have new functions, many have the same function as in other programs and are somewhat intuitive.

Making a mistake is no problem with Harvard Graphics. If you select the wrong menu from the menu bar, press (ESC) and select again. If your selection results in the display of a dialog box on the screen requesting more information, you cannot use (ESC) to back out of your request. You will need to select the Cancel command button in the dialog box to eliminate the effect of your erroneous request. You can move the mouse pointer to this button and click it to select Cancel. If you type a character incorrectly, press (BACKSPACE).

Many of the keyboard keys are self-defining—you know when you press them the effects they will have. The (↑) key, for instance, moves you up one line. Other keys such as (CTRL)+(END) behave a little differently depending on whether you are entering a slide title, data for an analytical chart, or text in a text chart. You will find a complete list of key actions in Appendix E, "Harvard Graphics Movement Keys."

Speed Keys

Harvard Graphics for Windows supports the use of speed keys to activate features quickly. You can use a speed key rather than making a series of menu selections. For example, you can save a chart by pulling down the File menu and choosing Save. To use the speed key option to accomplish the same task, all you need to do is press the (CTRL)+(S) key combination. Other speed key options are shown in Appendix D, "Harvard Graphics Speed Keys."

Mouse Actions

A mouse is a device that you roll across the desktop to select objects or commands on the screen. The buttons on the top of the mouse are pressed to activate certain features. Harvard Graphics uses the left mouse button to make selections. The right mouse button is not used as frequently but can be used to undo a menu selection, although it has no effect once a dialog box is displayed. This means that you can press the left mouse button to select an option from the menu bar or pull-down menu and the right mouse button to back out of the last menu command you requested as long as it did not result in the display of a dialog box.

It is important to note that a mouse must be installed before it is operational. If your mouse is not working, check the installation instructions in Appendix A for directions.

Menu Selections

The Harvard Graphics menu bar varies by the view you are working in. The menu bar shown previously is presented when you first start the package.

This menu bar gets you started with a new presentation or allows you to open an existing one. Other limited menu selections are also available.

If the Data Form of the Slide Editor is active you need menu options that expedite your entry and editing. The menu bar shown below meets these needs when you are entering data for a vertical bar chart:

```
Harvard Graphics
File  Edit  View  Data  Window  Help
```

Once you have finished entering your data and move to the Slide Editor screen, the menu bar shown below appears. Note that the Edit data pull-down menu activated from the Chart menu is additionally displayed here to illustrate a pull-down menu:

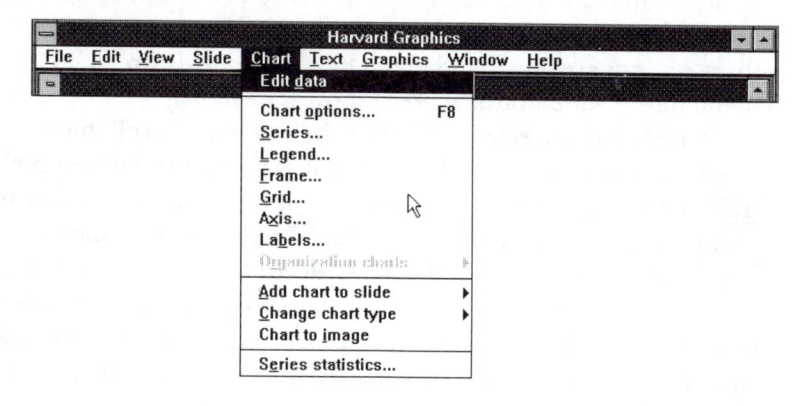

```
                       Harvard Graphics
File  Edit  View  Slide  Chart  Text  Graphics  Window  Help
                         Edit data
                         Chart options...        F8
                         Series...
                         Legend...
                         Frame...
                         Grid...
                         Axis...
                         Labels...
                         Organization charts
                         Add chart to slide      ▶
                         Change chart type       ▶
                         Chart to image
                         Series statistics...
```

This menu provides options for enhancing the slide with text and graphics as well as changing some of the chart elements.

When you work in the Outliner you will see this menu bar:

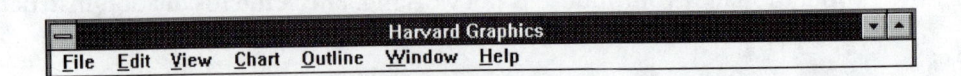

```
                        Harvard Graphics
File   Edit   View   Chart   Outline   Window   Help
```

The Outliner menu bar provides options for editing the entries and reorganizing the outline.

The Slide Sorter lets you rearrange the slides in your presentation. This is the menu bar you will see at the top of the Slide Sorter window:

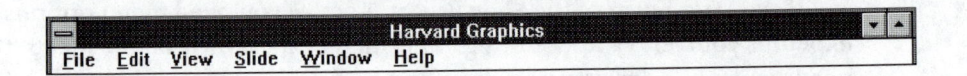

```
                        Harvard Graphics
File   Edit   View   Slide   Window   Help
```

When you select a menu bar option, Harvard Graphics displays a pull-down menu of more specific options. Options displayed in faded text are not currently available and cannot be selected. When you select a menu option, Harvard Graphics takes one of several actions. It may execute your request immediately, although more likely it will display a submenu or a dialog box to allow you to refine your selection. An ellipses (...) following a menu option indicates that a dialog box will be displayed next. An option followed by an arrow head pointing to the right indicates that a submenu will display. All these options are illustrated in the Edit data pull-down menu (from the Chart menu in the Slide Editor screen) shown previously.

To make menu selections using the mouse, you roll the mouse across the work surface to position the highlight. The mouse buttons act the same as (ENTER) and (ESC). Once your selection is highlighted you can press the left mouse button to make the selection. Press the right mouse button if you decide you want to back out of the selection.

At any time during the graph definition process, you can switch between the mouse and the keyboard without altering any of the work you are doing. The choice is intended to be a matter of convenience that allows you to mix and match entries and selections.

Chapter 1: *Overview and Basic Features* 23

Using Dialog Boxes

Dialog boxes are a convenient way to define all of your needs to Harvard Graphics in one concise form. When you make a menu selection followed by an ellipses, a dialog box will display as shown in Figure 1-15, which represents the Chart Options dialog box in the Slide Editor. Dialog boxes allow you to specify additional options. You can move from option to option by either pressing (TAB) or clicking the mouse on the option you want. Pressing (ENTER) tells Harvard Graphics that you are finished with the dialog box and selects whichever command button is highlighted. Unless you have changed the default selection, this will be the OK button—which tells Harvard Graphics to proceed with the selections you made in the dialog box.

The various options frequently are referred to as *fields,* since they contain one piece of important information for the current task. A variety of ways are used to define your selections in different fields. A close-up look at Figure 1-15 will supply examples of most of the options.

The "Chart orientation" field at the top of the box provides two options, Vertical and Horizontal. These options can be selected with the radio buttons

Figure 1-15.   *Chart Options dialog box*

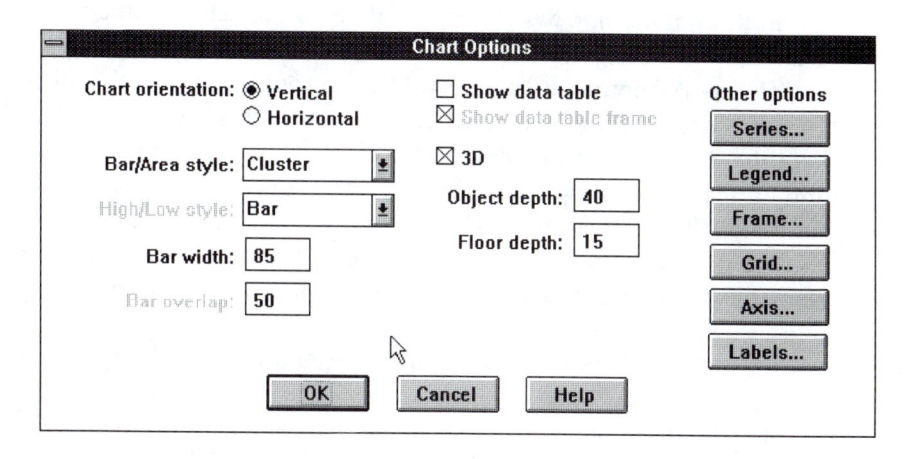

next to them. The filled radio button is the option currently selected. Radio buttons indicate that the options are mutually exclusive. If you click the dot for Horizontal, it will be the current selection for the "Chart orientation" field. There is no way to select both options at the same time since selecting one radio button ensures that none of the others are selected.

The Bar/Area style field is activated with the down arrow next to the field. You can click this arrow to activate a drop-down list box. This is a box of selections, any one of which can be selected by clicking it. To conserve space, these options are not displayed all the time. (Note that some menu choices and dialog boxes also have *list* boxes, which are always displayed; for instance, a list of filenames will appear whenever you ask to open an existing presentation.)

The "Bar width" field uses a text box for your entry. You can click this box to make it active and then type an entry in this field to represent the bar width you want to use. The "Bar overlap" text box is dimmed and will not accept an entry at this time since overlapping bars is not an option based on the other selections made in this dialog box.

The 3D field is represented by a check box. If the box contains an X, the option is in effect. You can change the current status of a check box by clicking it: a box without an X will gain one, whereas if the box currently contains an X, it will be removed. Check boxes are not mutually exclusive and you can place X's in as many as needed to represent your request.

Buttons at the side of the window allow you to activate other dialog boxes. The ellipses on the buttons indicate that their selection will display a dialog box.

The special command buttons at the bottom—OK, Cancel, and Help—will end the current definition, at least temporarily. Both OK and Cancel eliminate the dialog box from view with OK processing your dialog box entries and Cancel eliminating the entire request. Help only temporarily eliminates the dialog box, allowing you to look at as many help windows as needed. When you are finished with Help, choose the E_xit command from its F_ile menu to return to the dialog box exactly where you left off. Or press (ALT)-(F4) for a quick way to exit Help.

Another method for defining your needs through a dialog box is a series of selection boxes. This was shown in the Chart Gallery boxes earlier in the chapter in Figure 1-13. Click a selection and then click on the OK command button at the bottom of the dialog box. This method is also used for other options such as color selection.

Output

Harvard Graphics has conveniently organized the File menu to make it easy to create either printer output or a file for exporting information to another program. Information on the various output devices and definitions of the default setups are found in Appendix A, "Installing Harvard Graphics." In this appendix, you will learn how to define output devices.

Your monitor is your output device if you create a ScreenShow. The quality of your output depends on the type of monitor and graphics adapter you have. For example, a monochrome monitor cannot display color. You can choose from a wide variety of color monitors and graphics adapters. They vary in the number of pixels or dots per inch used to create the image. For instance, an EGA monitor consists of a pixel grid that is 640 dots by 350 dots, whereas a VGA monitor has 640 by 480 pixels. Some film recorder devices will only be able to produce output of the same quality level as the monitor.

Saving Files

When you create a presentation you will want to save it. The first time you save the presentation you must supply a name for it. You should choose Save as from the File menu to display a dialog box for entering your filename. If you forget and choose Save instead, Harvard Graphics still presents you with the Save As dialog box, which requests a name for the file. You must enter a filename in accordance with DOS rules. The name should consist of from one to eight characters with no spaces or special symbols except the underscore. When you select the OK command button at the bottom of the box, Harvard Graphics appends .PRS to the filename that you entered when saving your presentation.

Once a presentation has been saved to disk once, it is easier to save it to disk under the same name. All you need to do is choose Save from the File menu. Harvard Graphics automatically takes the current version of the presentation and uses it to replace the version of the file currently on disk. Pressing the (CTRL)+(S) speed key is a shortcut that provides the same result as these two menu selections. Although this command is a quick convenience, it is also dangerous if you want to save your presentation under a different name. You are not prompted before the file is replaced. The burden is on you to remember to choose Save as from the File menu when you want to save the presentation under a new name. My recommendation would be to save the file under the new name as soon as you start your modifications rather than waiting to complete the process and risk accidentally choosing the Save command.

Not only can you save the file under a new name, you can also save it to a different directory by choosing Save as from the File menu. If you want to save a file in a disk directory other than the current directory, type the entire path name when you enter the filename. If the current directory is C:\HGW\PRES and you want to save the current presentation as BARS in the subdirectory SLESMEET, you must change the name of the directory in the Save As dialog box.

Once you save a file, you have a permanent copy of it on disk. You can use the File menu's Open command or the CTRL+O speed key to open a presentation at any time. After you specify the name of the file, this command brings the file into memory and allows you to work with it. Files remain in memory until you exit Harvard Graphics or tell Harvard Graphics to close the file. You can use the Window menu to switch back and forth if you have several open presentation files.

Changing Directories

Changing the storage location for one or two presentations is a simple process. When you need to change the location for a file, it is easy to make the change in the Save As dialog box. If you find yourself changing the location with each presentation file you save, however, you should change the drive and/or the directory permanently. The directory you use must exist at the time you make the change. If you need to establish a new directory, you can use Window's File Manager or the DOS MD command to create the directory. You can change the storage location of your charts by following these steps:

1. Choose Preferences from the File menu. The dialog box shown in Figure 1-16 is displayed.

Chapter 1: *Overview and Basic Features* 27

Figure 1-16. The File menu's Preferences dialog box

```
                            Preferences
        Default presentation style: d:\HGW\STYLE\default.sty
               Main dictionary file: d:\HGW\winus.lex
            Personal dictionary file: d:\HGW\winuser.lex
              Default data directory: d:\HGW\PRES\
       Default style / palette directory: d:\HGW\STYLE\

        Default view for new presentation: Slide Editor
       Default view for open presentation: Slide Editor
                  Measurement units: Inches
       Import / export ASCII character set: Multilingual (CP 850)

        ☐ Show jackets in Slide Sorter
        ☒ Prompt to update data links

              [ OK ]   [ Cancel ]   [ Help ]
```

2. Change the "Default data directory" field to the drive and directory you want to use.

   You can select the text in this box and press (DEL) to remove it or click the text at the location where you want to make a change and then type additional characters, using the (BACKSPACE) or (DEL) key to remove unwanted text.

3. Select OK to finalize the change.

Changing Defaults

Figure 1-16 also shows the other default options that can be changed. You can access these changes at any time with selections from the Preferences dialog box. Your changes remain in effect for the current session and subsequent sessions.

2

Outlining a Presentation

Harvard Graphics for Windows provides an Outliner that makes it easy to organize your presentations. You can jot down your ideas as slide titles in the Outliner and reorganize them with the Slide Sorter as your plan evolves. You can use the Outliner to brainstorm and plan your entire presentation yet create entries that will be part of the presentation later. You can continue by adding substance to the basic outline and creating charts directly from the Outliner. You can create title charts to introduce sections of a presentation as well as bullet charts to present your main ideas. Both types of charts can be entered directly on the Outliner screen. For example, you can create organization charts that show employees and their duties from the Outliner and then add data or table charts at a later time.

   The Outliner is nothing more than a view of your presentation. It is not the default view for a presentation but should be the selected option when you need an overview of an existing presentation or when planning a new presentation. In this chapter you will learn how to make the Outliner the default view as well as how to create title and bullet charts from the Outliner. You will learn how to add slide titles that remind you to add charts at a later time. You will learn how to print the data in a presentation and how to control the level of detail that appears onscreen. You will also learn how to organize presentations and save and retrieve them for use at a later time.

A Look at the Outliner

When you create an outline with a word processor or a pencil and paper you enter topics with subtopics beneath them. The subtopics provide additional detail or information about the topic. The Outliner uses the same building blocks for outlining a presentation. Within each slide you create you can enter a series of topics and subtopics. The titles you enter for each slide and the *next level of entries beneath the title* are topics. Lower levels are subtopics. Each level is indented to show the relationship to the item above it. Your current position within the Outliner is marked by a box around the entry. A text cursor within this box marks your place when you are typing. Figure 2-1 shows the Outliner with text entered for several slides. The box around Mesopotamia Metals indicates the current place in the Outliner. This box will be referred to as a highlight. You will create a duplicate of these Outliner entries in a few minutes.

Like other Harvard Graphics views, the Outliner provides a scroll bar that you can use to move around the screen. Since the Outliner focuses on an entire presentation rather than one slide, the scroll bar is used to move from top to bottom in a presentation. You can click the arrows at the top and bottom of the scroll bar—or slide the scroll box within the bar to look at different parts of the presentation. You can use the mouse to activate each menu at the top of the screen; or you can use the (ALT) key to activate it, highlight the desired selection in the pull-down menu, and press (ENTER). The icons above the vertical scroll bar represent the Outliner, Slide Sorter, and Slide Editor. You can click them at any time for a different view of the current presentation. These icons (which are shown in Figure 2-1) are enlarged in Table 2-1.

Chapter 2: *Outlining a Presentation* 31

Figure 2-1. Outliner screen with data

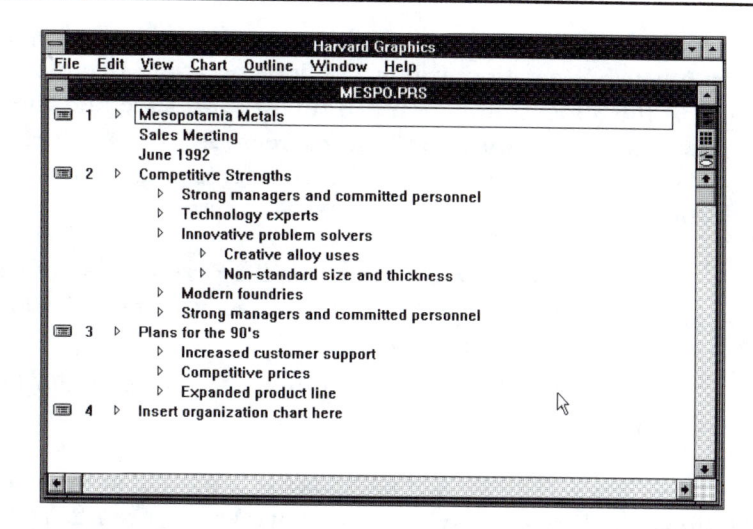

Table 2-1. View Option Icons

Icon	View Option
	Outliner icon
	Slide Sorter
	Slide Editor

Switching from the Slide Editor to the Outliner

Unless you change your default settings for Harvard Graphics when you start a new presentation, you will be looking at the Data Form for a single slide in the Slide Editor. You can finalize this slide and then choose the Outliner icon from the Slide Editor screen. After starting Harvard Graphics, follow these steps to create a new presentation and switch to the Outliner:

1. Choose New presentation from the File menu. As a shortcut you can simply press CTRL+N instead of activating the File menu and then choosing New presentation.
2. Select the Title radio button and then select the OK command button.

The Data Form for a title slide in a presentation currently named Untitled-1 will appear and look something like Figure 2-2. Your display may differ slightly since the name of the presentation depends on how many others you have already created. Harvard Graphics names each new presentation Untitled with the next sequential number appended to the end.

3. Select the OK button at the bottom of the Data Form to finalize the slide without additions.

The Slide Editor appears and provides icons in the upper-right corner for each of the view options. You can click these icons or select the desired view from the View menu.

4. Click the top icon, which is the Outliner icon.

This activates the Outliner as shown in Figure 2-3. The Outliner only shows the initial information from the first slide consisting of a slide number, an icon, and dimmed text marking the location for the title. Different types of slides will have different types of icons.

Chapter 2: *Outlining a Presentation*

Figure 2-2.   *Data Form for a title chart*

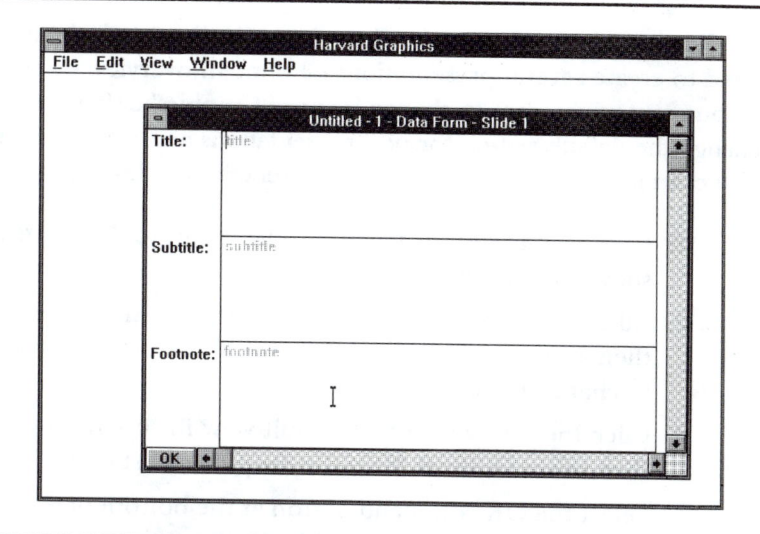

Figure 2-3.   *Initial Outliner screen*

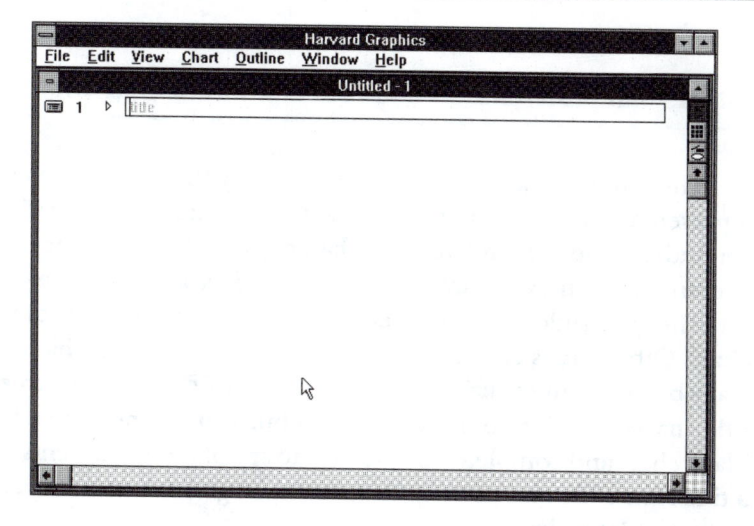

Making the Outliner the Default View

You can always change the view to the Outliner with the icon, but if you need to create several presentations or want an overview of existing presentations, you might want to change Harvard Graphics' default settings. You can change the default setting for new presentations and existing ones separately. You can make this change with File Preferences by following these steps:

1. Choose Preferences from the File menu to display the dialog box shown in Figure 2-4.
2. Click the arrow next to "Default view for new presentation," and then select Outliner from the drop-down list box (that will appear) to change the default to Outliner.
3. Click the arrow next to "Default view for open presentation," and then select Outliner from the drop-down list box.
4. Select the OK command button at the bottom of the dialog box.
    All presentations will have the Outliner view as their default unless you change File Preferences again. This change will affect the current Harvard Graphics session as well as new sessions.

Using the Outliner to Create a Presentation

The Outliner can help you organize your thoughts as you start planning a presentation. You can use it to create the details for your slides or insert a reminder to add them later. You can copy and move topics as you begin a presentation, and you can even collapse and expand your view of the entries.

The first slide that you create in a presentation is automatically a title chart. Other slides created after the first slide are blank charts that automatically become bullet charts when you press (ENTER). You can create additional title charts as well as other chart types but you will need to add them to the blank chart and complete a Data Form to specify their contents. You can enter a title for a slide and nothing else, and then go back and add a chart to these slides at a later time.

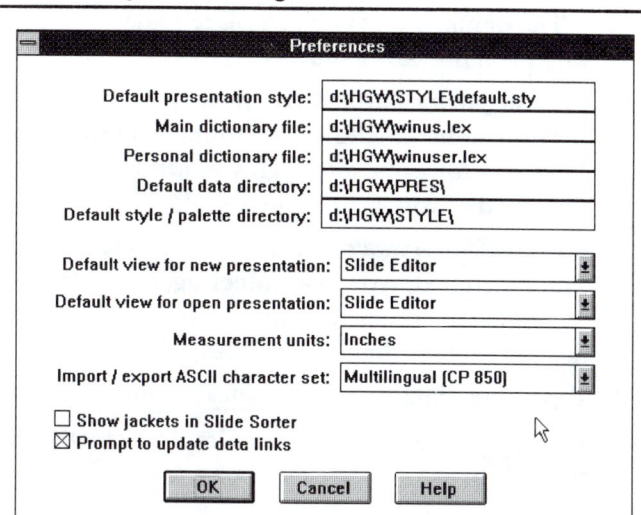

Figure 2-4.   *File Preferences dialog box*

Completing a Title Chart

A title chart is used to introduce a presentation or a section of a presentation. It displays the title for a slide in large letters and optionally allows you to enter a subtitle and footnote for a chart. The first chart in any new presentation is automatically established as a title chart unless you add bullet items.

You can add other title charts as section separators within the presentation. You might also restrict your entry to a slide title when you want to create a placeholder slide to which you will add data at a later time. Although this slide is not a title chart per se (its only entry is a title), it provides a marker where another chart type will be added later.

For now, let's finish the first slide from the presentation started earlier in the chapter. Later in the chapter you will learn another procedure for creating a title chart further on in a presentation. Your screen should look like Figure 2-3 as you begin to make entries for a title chart slide with these steps:

1. Type **Mesopotamia Metals** over the dimmed text that reads title.
   The dimmed text acts as a placeholder, it will not print or display when you preview a slide.
2. Choose <u>S</u>how subtitle & footnote from the <u>O</u>utline menu.
   This command allows you to make both entries since it adds an extra line for each, although you can choose to enter text for only the one that you want.
3. Press (ENTER) to move to the next line (subtitle) that has been added with faded text, type **Sales Meeting**, and then press (ENTER).
   You can also click the dimmed footnote text entry to move to the next line rather than press (ENTER).
4. Type **June 1992** and press (ENTER). A line for a bullet appears.
5. Press (ENTER) to have Harvard Graphics create the number and icon for slide 2.

Creating Bullet Charts

Bullet charts allow you to list main topical ideas and subtopics. To make sure slides are as readable as possible you will want to keep your entries short and use parallel grammatical construction for your entries. This means if your first entry is "Triple sales" your next entry might be "Double customer base" to ensure that numerical adjectives start each entry. Of course, you can use nouns, verbs, or modifiers (any part of speech), but it is best to use the same format for each bullet entry. You will also want to limit the number of bullets on each chart to between six and eight entries to present a manageable amount of information on each slide.

Use the (TAB) key when you want to indent a bullet to the next level and (SHIFT)-(TAB) when you want to back up one level.

Tip: *Although Harvard Graphics allows you to create nine levels of bullets, try not to exceed four to maximize the readability of the completed chart.*

The Mesopotamia Metals presentation will contain two bullet charts. Later you may want to add more topics or subtopics to the charts. Follow

Chapter 2: *Outlining a Presentation* 37

these steps to create a bullet chart of "Competitive Strengths" and another for "Plans for the 90's":

1. Type **Competitive Strengths** and press (ENTER).
2. Type **Technology experts** and press (ENTER).
3. Type **Innovative problem solvers** and press (ENTER).
4. Press (TAB), type **Creative alloy uses**, and then press (ENTER).
5. Type **Non-standard size and thickness**, press (ENTER), and then press (SHIFT)+(TAB).
6. Type **Modern foundries** and press (ENTER).
7. Type **Strong managers and committed personnel** and press (ENTER) twice to create an icon and number for slide 3.
8. Type **Plans for the 90's** as the title and press (ENTER).
9. Type **Increased customer support** and press (ENTER).
10. Type **Competitive prices** and press (ENTER).
11. Type **Expanded product line** and press (ENTER) twice.

Your presentation consists of a title chart and two bullet charts. With the addition of a placeholder as a reminder of work to be done later, your first presentation is almost complete.

Creating Placeholders for Other Charts

You can continue to create bullet charts by following the instructions used in the previous examples. Although you can also add other types of charts from the Outliner, for now all you will do is add a placeholder where you want to put a chart at a later time. One type of chart that you can add later is an organization chart to show the personnel working in key positions and the reporting hierarchy. To add these placeholders all you need to do is type a reminder as the chart title. To add a reminder for the organization chart, type

Insert organization chart here.

There is no need to press ENTER to add bullets beneath the title. If you wanted to add additional blank charts for later additions you could press ENTER twice but since you do not need to add another slide to the current presentation this will not be necessary.

Saving a Presentation

Each presentation you create is saved as a separate file on disk. You can later open these presentation files and access any of the slides they contain. The first time you save a presentation, choose Save as from the File menu. You must supply a name consisting of one to eight characters and then press ENTER or select OK. Harvard Graphics adds the filename extension .PRS to the name that you type before storing your data on disk. Subsequent saves can be accomplished by choosing Save from the File menu without typing a filename. Of course, you can always save another copy under a new name by choosing Save as from the File menu. To save the presentation for Mesopotamia Metals follow these steps:

1. Choose Save as from the File menu to display the dialog box shown in Figure 2-5.
2. Type **MESPO** and press ENTER.

You now have a permanent copy of the presentation on disk even if your system crashes. If you make additional changes you will need to decide whether to update the MESPO.PRS file on disk or save the updated copy under a new name.

Tip: Harvard Graphics does not prompt you before overwriting the file when you choose Save from the File menu. The responsibility is yours to ensure that you do not overwrite the current copy of a file that you want to leave unchanged.

Printing the Presentation

You can print your presentation as either one slide per page or as handouts with a default setting of three slides per page. To request a printout,

Chapter 2: *Outlining a Presentation*

Figure 2-5.   File Save As dialog box

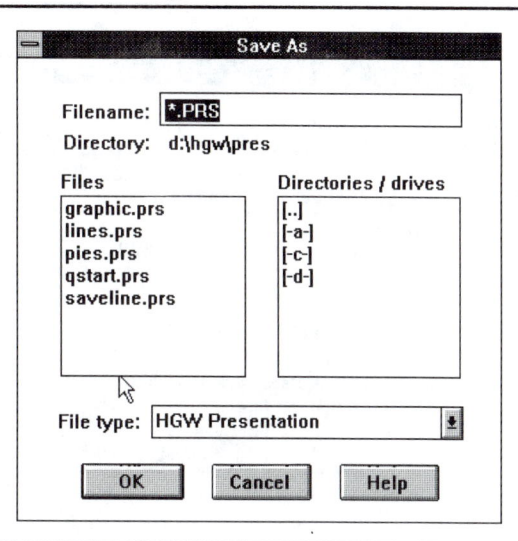

you will need to use the Print command on the File menu and complete a dialog box. Follow these steps to print the current presentation:

1. Choose Print from the File menu to display the dialog box shown in Figure 2-6.
2. Select Slides to print one slide per page or Handouts to print three slides per page.
3. Select All next to Slides to print your entire presentation, or select Range and specify a beginning and ending slide in the From and To text boxes on the right side of the box.
4. Select OK to begin printing.

Closing and Reopening a Presentation

Harvard Graphics allows you to create a presentation and leave it open on the screen while you work on a new presentation. This is a good strategy

Figure 2-6.   Print dialog box

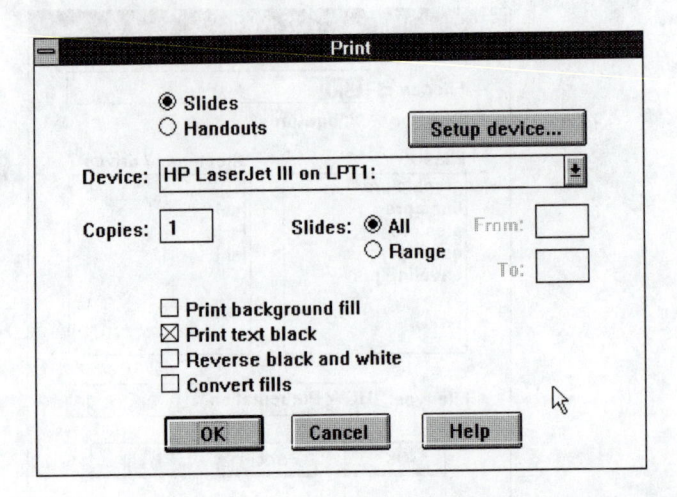

if you plan to review the existing presentation as you create the new one. In later chapters you will even learn how to copy slides from one presentation to another. If you do not plan to refer to the presentation, it is better to close it. This frees up the memory used, makes Harvard Graphics run more efficiently, and eliminates the risk that you could accidentally change a presentation. You can use the Close command in the File menu to close a presentation and the Open command to reopen it or another presentation. Follow these steps to close MESPO then reopen it:

1. Choose Close from the File menu.

    Since you just saved the presentation, Harvard Graphics does not prompt you about saving it again. The presentation is closed, and if no other ones are open, the screen shows a limited menu that allows you to open another presentation, change preference settings, and perform other limited tasks.

2. Choose Open from the File menu.

3. Highlight the file named MESPO and press (ENTER) to reopen the presentation.

Revising a Presentation

There are many changes that you can make to a presentation once you get the basics down. You can revise slides by changing the order of topics, adding new topics, or deleting ones that no longer seem appropriate. You can also revise the level of detail shown for an entire presentation. You will make some changes to the MESPO presentation, but you will save the changed version under a new name. If you are concerned that you will accidentally overwrite a version, you can take the precautionary step of saving it now under a new name. If you decide to do that, you would:

1. Choose Save as from the File menu.
2. Type **MESPO9** and press (ENTER).
   Now when you select save, the changed version will automatically update MESPO9—not MESPO, which you will need in its original form in a later chapter. Or choose any other name you prefer.

Moving a Topic

As you plan a presentation you may decide to give more or less emphasis to a topic or change the order of topics. To move a topic to a new location, move the mouse pointer to the icon for the item. Press the left mouse button and hold it down while dragging the item to a new location. A pointing hand appears as you move the object and a line appears as you move the item above or below another entry. When the line indicates the location you want to move the object to, release the mouse button.

You can change the level of an existing topic by changing its indentation. The (TAB) key will indent a topic further, making it a subtopic of the preceding topic. The (SHIFT)+(TAB) keys together will remove a level of indentation, making it the same level as the preceding topic. Follow these steps to make changes to slide 2 in the presentation:

1. Move the mouse pointer to the icon for "Strong managers and committed personnel."
2. Drag this entry up until a line appears above "Technology experts" and release the mouse button.
3. Move the highlight to "Creative alloy uses."
4. Press (SHIFT)+(TAB) to remove the indentation from this entry.
   Harvard Graphics moves this entry and places it on the same level as "Innovative problem solvers." These changes are reflected in Figure 2-7.

Copying and Deleting Topics

To delete or copy a topic or subtopic to a new location within a slide, you need to select it first. The procedure for selecting an object is to click to the

Figure 2-7. Slide 2 after moving several items

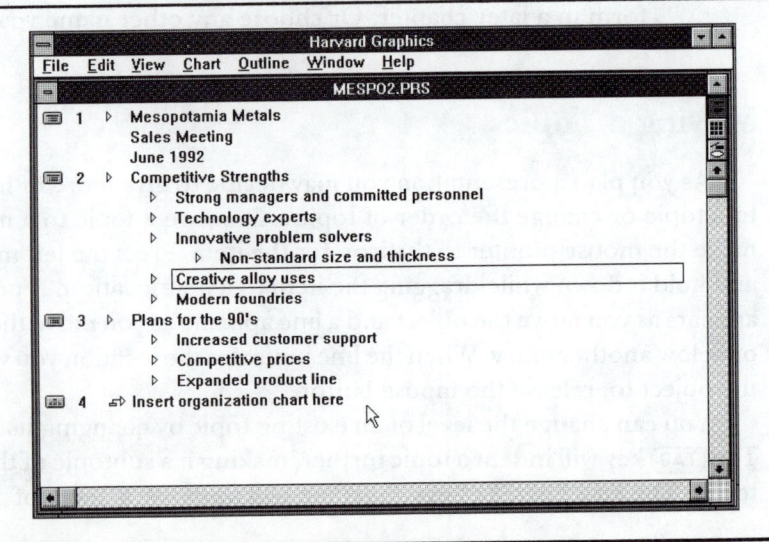

Chapter 2: *Outlining a Presentation*

left of the object's icon. To select a contiguous group of objects, click to the left of the top icon. Drag down from this icon to form a rectangle including all the other icons to be included. You can press the (DEL) key to delete the selected icons or you can choose to copy them to a new location.

To copy entries, you will use the Windows Clipboard available to all windows applications. This Clipboard is nothing more than a special area in memory accessed by all applications. You can temporarily store a segment of text or other entries on this Clipboard. You can copy the text from the Clipboard to the current application or another application. To perform these tasks with the Clipboard, you will use the Copy and Paste commands on the Edit menu. If you have used other Windows applications, you are already familiar with these commands. You can copy from one presentation to another if you have multiple presentations open. You can switch between presentations with the Window menu by selecting the number next to the presentation you want to activate.

Try out the Copy option now on slide 3 by following these steps:

1. Choose New presentation from the File menu.

    The new presentation is opened and assigned the number 2 unless you had more than one other presentation open.

2. Choose 1 from the Window menu, which will reactivate your original presentation.

3. Move the mouse pointer to the left of the bullet for "Plans for the 90's" in slide 3 and drag the mouse pointer until a rectangle includes this bullet.

    When you release the mouse this bullet as well as the subordinate entries beneath it are selected as shown in Figure 2-8.

4. Choose Copy from the Edit menu.

    This places a copy of the slide text on the Windows Clipboard without affecting the slide.

5. Choose 2 from the Window menu.

    This activates the new presentation.

6. Choose Paste from the Edit menu to copy the contents of the Clipboard to the new presentation.

    A new slide containing the contents of the Clipboard is created as shown in Figure 2-9.

Figure 2-8.   *Selected bullets items*

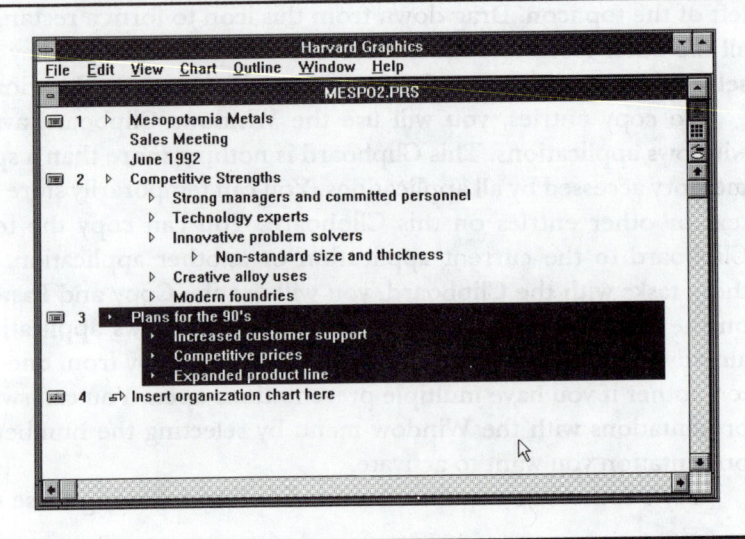

```
┌─────────────────────────────────────────────────────────┐
│                    Harvard Graphics                  ▼ ▲ │
├─────────────────────────────────────────────────────────┤
│ File  Edit  View  Chart  Outline  Window  Help          │
├─────────────────────────────────────────────────────────┤
│ ─                         MESPO2.PRS                    │
│  ▤  1  ▷  Mesopotamia Metals                            │
│            Sales Meeting                                │
│            June 1992                                    │
│  ▤  2  ▷  Competitive Strengths                         │
│              ▷  Strong managers and committed personnel │
│              ▷  Technology experts                      │
│              ▷  Innovative problem solvers              │
│                  ▷  Non-standard size and thickness     │
│              ▷  Creative alloy uses                     │
│              ▷  Modern foundries                        │
│  ▤  3  ▸  Plans for the 90's                            │
│              ▸  Increased customer support              │
│              ▸  Competitive prices                      │
│              ▸  Expanded product line                   │
│  ▤  4  ↵  Insert organization chart here                │
│                                                         │
└─────────────────────────────────────────────────────────┘
```

7. Choose <u>C</u>lose from the <u>F</u>ile menu to close the new presentation.
8. Choose No when prompted about saving the presentation (since we will not be working with this file again).

    Your original presentation will automatically become the active window when the new one is closed.

Figure 2-9.   *New presentation with copied entries*

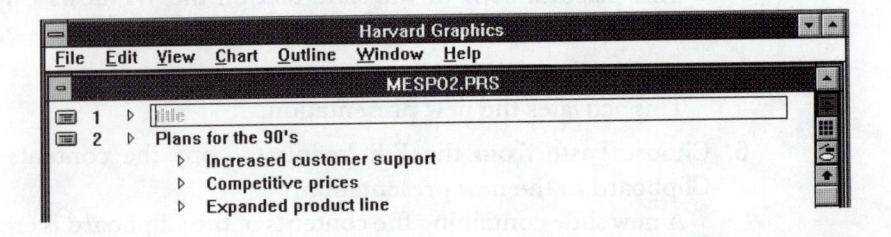

```
┌─────────────────────────────────────────────────────────┐
│                    Harvard Graphics                  ▼ ▲ │
├─────────────────────────────────────────────────────────┤
│ File  Edit  View  Chart  Outline  Window  Help          │
├─────────────────────────────────────────────────────────┤
│ ─                         MESPO2.PRS                    │
│  ▤  1  ▷  title                                         │
│  ▤  2  ▷  Plans for the 90's                            │
│              ▷  Increased customer support              │
│              ▷  Competitive prices                      │
│              ▷  Expanded product line                   │
└─────────────────────────────────────────────────────────┘
```

Adding a Topic

Harvard Graphics is always ready for you to insert new topics within the space limitations established for a slide. All you need to do is move right above where you want the new entries to be inserted and press ENTER. You may have to use TAB and SHIFT+TAB to adjust the indentation of the new entry.

Try this now with slide 3 by adding some new topics at various levels:

1. Position the highlight on the first bullet entry in slide 3, "Increased customer support," and press ENTER. The bullet entry is at the same level as the preceding entry and must be indented to enter a subtopic.
2. Press TAB, type **24 hour phone support**, and then press ENTER. The new bullet is at the same level as your last entry.
3. Type **Technical support teams**.
4. Click the last bullet in slide 3, "Expanded product line," to move the highlight there, or use your arrow keys to move the highlight.
5. Press ENTER to add a new bullet and type **Employee training program**. The revised slide will look like Figure 2-10.

Splitting a Topic in Two Parts

When you create bullet charts there are several important points that can make your charts more readable. You may want to limit each bullet entry to one thought or item, and ensure that the length does not exceed 20 to 25 characters. When you completed the entry for "Strong managers and committed personnel," both rules were broken—and the bullet item displays on two different lines if you print or preview the chart. You could shorten the line by eliminating some adjectives, but the text still covers two different topics. A better approach might be to split the topic into two parts. You can insert a new bullet, select part of the lengthy entry, and move it to the new bullet. You will use the Cut command in the Edit menu to move selected text from an item and store it temporarily on the Windows Clipboard. You can use Paste to place the Clipboard information in a new location. Follow these steps:

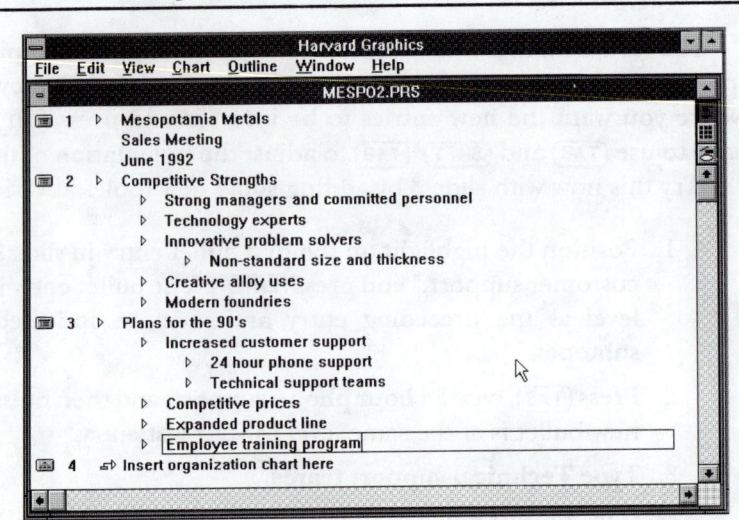

Figure 2-10.   *New topics and subtopics*

```
┌─────────────────── Harvard Graphics ───────────────────┐
│ File  Edit  View  Chart  Outline  Window  Help          │
├─────────────────────── MESP02.PRS ──────────────────────┤
│  ▣  1  ▷  Mesopotamia Metals                            │
│            Sales Meeting                                │
│            June 1992                                    │
│  ▣  2  ▷  Competitive Strengths                         │
│               ▷  Strong managers and committed personnel│
│               ▷  Technology experts                     │
│               ▷  Innovative problem solvers             │
│                     ▷  Non-standard size and thickness  │
│               ▷  Creative alloy uses                    │
│               ▷  Modern foundries                       │
│  ▣  3  ▷  Plans for the 90's                            │
│               ▷  Increased customer support             │
│                     ▷  24 hour phone support            │
│                     ▷  Technical support teams          │
│               ▷  Competitive prices                     │
│               ▷  Expanded product line                  │
│               ▷ │Employee training program│             │
│  ▣  4   ⇨  Insert organization chart here               │
└─────────────────────────────────────────────────────────┘
```

1. Move the highlight to "Strong managers and committed personnel" in slide 2 and press (ENTER) to add a new bullet beneath it.

2. Select "and committed personnel" as shown in Figure 2-11.

    You can select text by moving the mouse pointer to the first character, and then clicking and dragging across the text until it is all highlighted.

3. Choose Cut from the Edit menu to remove the selected text from the first bullet.

4. Move the highlight to the new bullet and choose Paste from the Edit menu.

5. Press (HOME) and the (DEL) key five times to remove the first five characters then type a capital **C** to produce the display shown in Figure 2-12.

Figure 2-11.   Selected text within a bullet

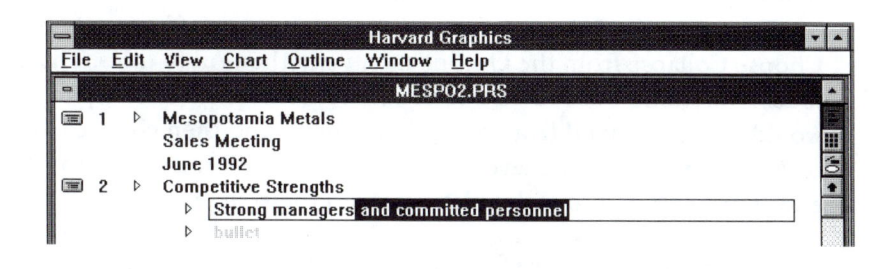

```
                        Harvard Graphics
File  Edit  View  Chart  Outline  Window  Help
                        MESP02.PRS
   1  ▷  Mesopotamia Metals
         Sales Meeting
         June 1992
   2  ▷  Competitive Strengths
            ▷  Strong managers and committed personnel
            ▷  bullet
```

Collapsing and Expanding the View

In a lengthy presentation you might want to hide the display of subtopics to get a quick overview of the presentation order. Fortunately, it is quick and easy to change the level of detail that is displayed. You can choose the expanded display (the default) or two different levels of consolidation.

The first level of consolidation affects only the current or selected topics. This option is selected by choosing Collapse from the Outline menu and then Topic. This selection hides only subtopics. If you have only one level of bullet

Figure 2-12.   Text split between two bullets

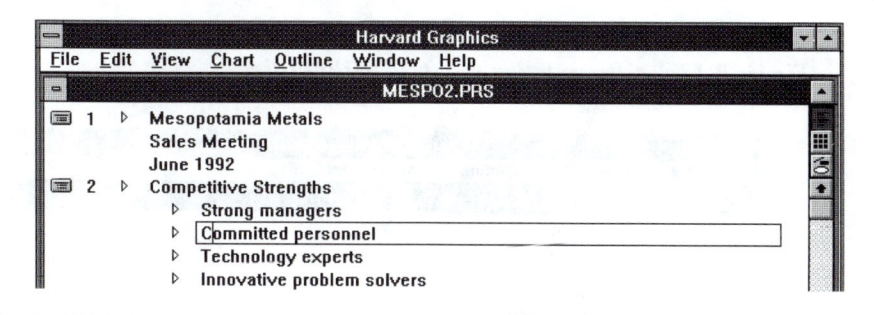

```
                        Harvard Graphics
File  Edit  View  Chart  Outline  Window  Help
                        MESP02.PRS
   1  ▷  Mesopotamia Metals
         Sales Meeting
         June 1992
   2  ▷  Competitive Strengths
            ▷  Strong managers
            ▷  Committed personnel
            ▷  Technology experts
            ▷  Innovative problem solvers
```

entries on your charts, making this selection will not change it since this option only hides the second level and further.

The second of the two consolidation options affects an entire slide. Choose Collapse from the Outline menu and then All to titles. This selection hides everything but the title of the chart. To expand the display again you would choose Expand from the Outline menu and then choose either Topic or All depending on the level of expansion you want. Let's try to collapse an entire presentation to slide titles now with these steps:

1. Choose Collapse from the Outline menu.
2. Choose All to titles to create a display that matches Figure 2-13.
3. Choose Expand from the Outline menu.
4. Choose All to return the presentation to its original display format.

Creating a Slide Summary

As you plan a presentation you might have an area where you have a significant amount of expansion from your initial entries. You can use the slide summary feature to create a separate slide from each topic in an existing slide. Each topic below the title for the slide becomes a slide itself. You can add titles to these and expand them as much as you want. If you were to later remove the slide summary feature, all the added detail would be placed back in the original slide. You use the Make slide summary and Remove slide

Figure 2-13.   Presentation collapsed to slide titles

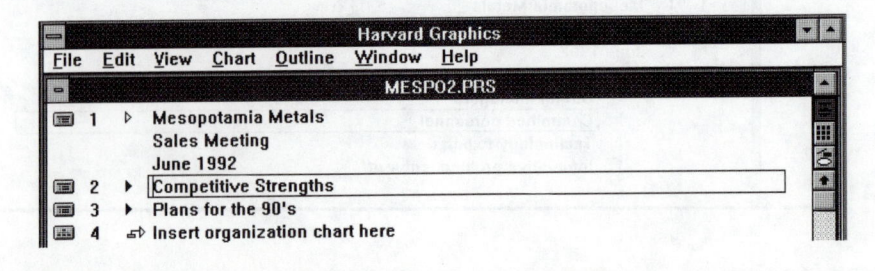

```
                         Harvard Graphics
 File  Edit  View  Chart  Outline  Window  Help
                           MESP02.PRS
     1  ▷  Mesopotamia Metals
            Sales Meeting
            June 1992
     2  ▷  Competitive Strengths
     3  ▷  Plans for the 90's
     4      Insert organization chart here
```

Chapter 2: *Outlining a Presentation* 49

summary commands in the Outline menu to make these changes. Try this with the current presentation now:

1. Move the highlight to "Competitive strengths" in slide 2 in the presentation.
2. Choose Make slide summary from the Outline menu.
   Your display changes and slides 2 through 8 now contain the information from the original slide 2 as shown in Figure 2-14.
3. Choose Remove slide summary from the Outline menu.
   The presentation returns to the original 4-slide display.

Reorganizing Your Presentation Slides

The Slide Sorter is the view you need to use to reorganize your slides. The thumbnail sketch that the Sorter provides for each slide makes it easy to change the order of slides. All you need to do is drag slides to the desired location. Follow these steps to learn the basic reordering procedure:

1. Choose Slide Sorter from the View menu or click the Slide Sorter icon.
2. Drag the image for slide 1 to the right of the image for slide 3. A small slide icon will show the proposed location that will be used for the slide when you release the mouse button.
3. Choose Close from the File menu and select No when prompted about saving the revised presentation (we will not use these changes again).

Resetting the Default View to the Slide Editor

At the beginning of the chapter you set the default view to the Outliner. You can keep that view and switch to other ones with the View menu or the various view icons but since the next several chapters focus on individual slides you will want to work from the Slide Editor. Follow these steps to change the default back to the Slide Editor:

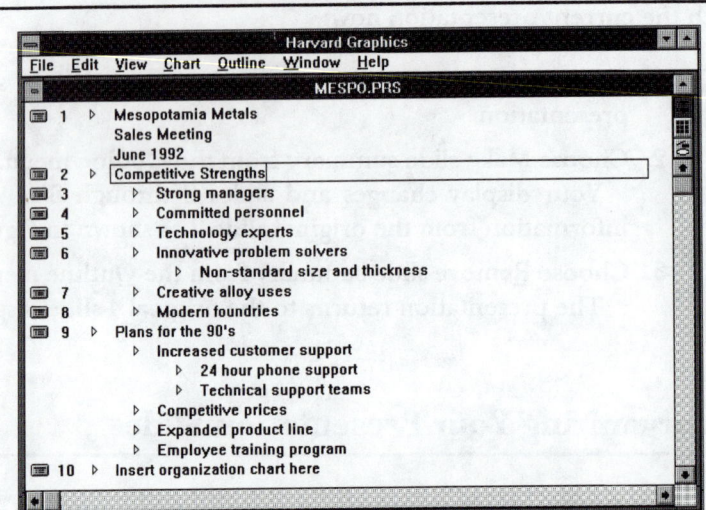

Figure 2-14. *Slide summary created from slide 2*

```
                        Harvard Graphics
 File   Edit   View   Chart   Outline   Window   Help
                           MESPO.PRS
   1   ▷  Mesopotamia Metals
          Sales Meeting
          June 1992
   2   ▷  Competitive Strengths
   3      ▷  Strong managers
   4      ▷  Committed personnel
   5      ▷  Technology experts
   6      ▷  Innovative problem solvers
             ▷  Non-standard size and thickness
   7      ▷  Creative alloy uses
   8      ▷  Modern foundries
   9   ▷  Plans for the 90's
          ▷  Increased customer support
             ▷  24 hour phone support
             ▷  Technical support teams
          ▷  Competitive prices
          ▷  Expanded product line
          ▷  Employee training program
  10   ▷  Insert organization chart here
```

1. Choose Pre_f_erences from the _F_ile menu.
2. Click the arrow next to "Default view for new presentation," and then select Slide Editor from the drop-down list box to change the default to Slide Editor.
3. Click the arrow next to "Default view for open presentation," and then select Slide Editor from the drop-down list box.
4. Select the OK command button at the bottom of the dialog box.

3

Creating Text Charts

Although text charts lack some of the pizzazz of analytical charts that show numerical data in bars, lines, or pie chart circles, they are often the backbone of a presentation. As you saw when creating the examples for the Outliner in Chapter 2, these charts provide the key introductory points for a presentation. You can also use text charts to summarize some of the data presented in analytical charts and display conclusions at the end of a presentation.

Text charts can serve a useful purpose for both the speaker and the audience. For the audience they provide a reinforcement of the speaker's main points. Since learning can be increased by stimulating both the senses of hearing and sight, audiences often retain information better when verbal presentations are accompanied by visuals.

An experienced speaker will often find that notes are not necessary when key points are summarized in text charts. There is no need for fumbling with cards or losing one's place in pages since the speaker can be guided by the contents of the text charts. The final product from Harvard Graphics can be produced as a 35-millimeter slide or a transparency so professional-quality output is possible.

Harvard Graphics supports many types of text charts beyond the title and bullet charts you have used, so you should be able to select a chart type that meets your needs and adds needed variety to a presentation.

Text charts are easy to create, and there are some techniques that you will find helpful in preparing all types of text charts. Figure 3-1 shows a basic chart designed much like a conventional memo. As such, it is a little too busy for a demonstration. The chart in Figure 3-2 was made for the same presentation but was streamlined to show phrases rather than sentences using the bullet chart form introduced in Chapter 2. This chart also incorporates more white space and uses a combination of upper- and lowercase letters rather than all uppercase.

As you look through the examples in this chapter, you will learn other techniques to help you create the best text charts possible. You will explore other forms of text charts as well as further customization options for the basic chart types you have already used.

In this chapter, you will also learn how to use Harvard Graphic's spelling check to make sure your presentation is as professional as possible.

Figure 3-1.   Text chart with busy design

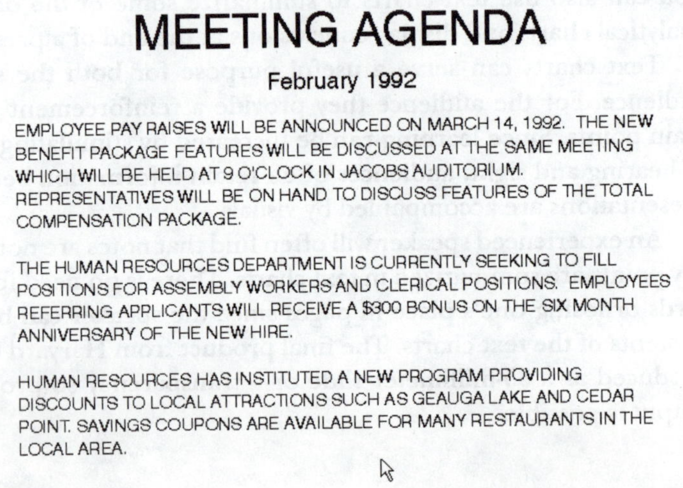

MEETING AGENDA
February 1992

EMPLOYEE PAY RAISES WILL BE ANNOUNCED ON MARCH 14, 1992. THE NEW BENEFIT PACKAGE FEATURES WILL BE DISCUSSED AT THE SAME MEETING WHICH WILL BE HELD AT 9 O'CLOCK IN JACOBS AUDITORIUM. REPRESENTATIVES WILL BE ON HAND TO DISCUSS FEATURES OF THE TOTAL COMPENSATION PACKAGE.

THE HUMAN RESOURCES DEPARTMENT IS CURRENTLY SEEKING TO FILL POSITIONS FOR ASSEMBLY WORKERS AND CLERICAL POSITIONS. EMPLOYEES REFERRING APPLICANTS WILL RECEIVE A $300 BONUS ON THE SIX MONTH ANNIVERSARY OF THE NEW HIRE.

HUMAN RESOURCES HAS INSTITUTED A NEW PROGRAM PROVIDING DISCOUNTS TO LOCAL ATTRACTIONS SUCH AS GEAUGA LAKE AND CEDAR POINT. SAVINGS COUPONS ARE AVAILABLE FOR MANY RESTAURANTS IN THE LOCAL AREA.

Chapter 3: *Creating Text Charts* 53

Figure 3-2. *Improving the appearance of the text chart*

Meeting Agenda
February 1992

Compensation package
    Pay raises
    New benefit package

Hiring needs
    Assembly workers/clerical positions
    $300 bonus opportunity for referrals

Employee discount program
    Geauga Lake/Cedar Point
    Restaurants

Getting Started

    This chapter focuses on the use of the Data Form and Slide Editor for entering and changing text chart information. You will learn to use the Chart Gallery to select from the many variations possible. You will find that creating all varieties of text charts is easy. You simply enter your information on the Data Form and then change basics, like size and placement of the information, with the Slide Editor.

    Follow these steps to create the first screen in a presentation when the Slide Editor is the default view:

1. Choose New presentation from the File menu. An Add Slide dialog box appears. Select OK.

2. Select Title. Your screen will look like Figure 3-3 where the Data Form for a title chart is displayed. This screen has three sections—top, middle, and bottom. You can make entries on any or all of the lines in each section.

3. Type **High Performance, Inc.** and then press (TAB) to move to the next section of the Data Form.

4. Type **Achievement Awards** and then press (TAB) to move to the next section of the Data Form.

5. Type **February 15, 1992**. Then select OK.

6. Press (F2) to view the entries.

7. Press (ESC) to have Harvard Graphics display your entries in the Slide Editor. In the Slide Editor, you will see the tool box of options, duplicated on the command card in this book, that allows you to easily change basic chart entries.

    For now we will save the presentation with this chart and look at adding another chart as our next step.

8. Choose Save as from the File menu, type **TEXT**, and press (ENTER) to save the presentation with its first chart.

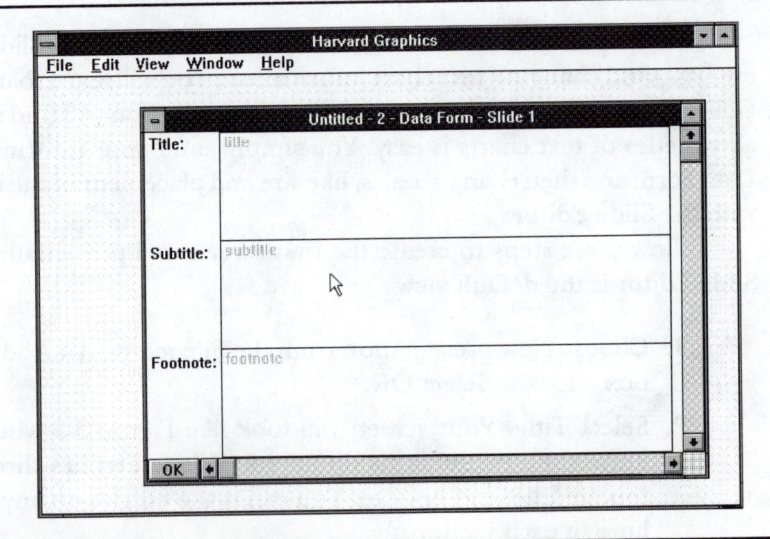

Figure 3-3.   *Title chart Data Form*

You can see that it is just as easy to create a text chart from the Slide Editor as from the Outliner. In eight steps, you have entered all the data to create a presentation with a three-line title chart and saved a copy of the chart to disk.

As you learn a few new options you will find that another step or two allows you to make dramatic changes to the appearance of the chart.

Different Types of Text Charts

Any chart that consists primarily of characters is considered to be a text chart in Harvard Graphics. In addition to the title and bullet charts, Harvard Graphics also provides table charts that have a columnar organization of the data—like the chart shown in Figure 3-4.

With Harvard Graphics, you can also enter text on a drawing screen in what is commonly referred to as a free-form chart. There are no predefined formats for this type of chart, and you can make up your own rules for where the data goes.

Figure 3-4. *Table chart*

Innovative Marketing
New Products in 1992

Product	Date Introduced	Developer
Quick-Rol	February 15	High Tech
Sof-Tex	March 10	Textiles Unlimited
Heat-Away	June 22	Kool King
Seal R More	August 1	Work Savers
Sports Score	November 3	Broadcasters
Time Save	December 22	Efficiency Experts

A different Data Form is used to enter each type of chart. The forms are tailored to the type of entries that you will make for each type of chart. After entering your data on these forms you can use the tools provided by the Slide Editor to change the appearance of a chart. These changes can be small, such as using a different size text or more elaborate embellishments like the drawings and symbols you will learn about in Chapter 8, "Using Drawing Symbols and Other Enhancements."

Using Chart Galleries

A *gallery* is a predefined chart option. When you are specifying the type of chart you want to use, you can choose from a gallery of examples that customizes each chart type. Because you can select a visual image from a gallery, you can select the look that most closely matches your needs without having to define your exact requirements. Once you select the appearance you want to achieve, you can enter data and produce a slide without making customizing selections. You will want to make the galleries part of your repertoire as you proceed since they offer you so many options in a minimum of time. Although galleries were available in earlier releases of Harvard Graphics, there are some differences with Harvard Graphics for Windows. You will want to read this section even if you have used galleries before.

Galleries allow you to build sophisticated charts with a minimum of effort. The use of gallery selections also ensures compatible color schemes, allowing you to create an entire presentation with a consistent appearance.

Creating a Chart from the Gallery

When you create a chart, all you need to do is select Chart Galleries from the Add Slide dialog box after selecting the type of slide that you want to create. You can look at the gallery options for the chart type you selected. Figure 3-5 shows the gallery chart options for a bullet chart. The eight sections

Chapter 3: *Creating Text Charts*

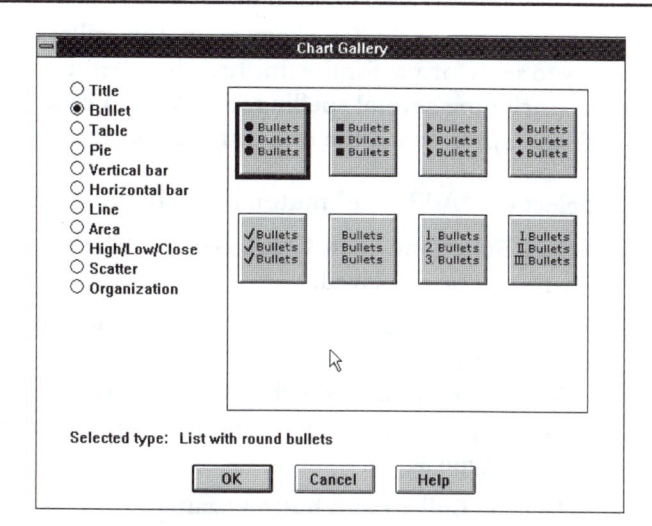

Figure 3-5.   *Gallery of options for a bullet chart*

of the screen each represent a gallery option. Other chart types may provide a different number of options. Select the option that appeals to you most by clicking it with the mouse and selecting OK, or by pressing (TAB) followed by the Spacebar to move to your selection and pressing (ENTER) to select OK.

You can begin entering data on the Data Form. The customized selections needed to create the chart's special appearance have already been entered by your previous selections.

Viewing Other Gallery Options

There are galleries for every type of Harvard Graphics chart available from the Add Slide dialog box. You can click any other chart type while a gallery is displayed to see the gallery options for a different chart type. Each gallery offers a family of related options.

Creating a Bullet Chart with a Gallery Option

When you create a bullet chart from the gallery, you will have an opportunity to see a format for the finished chart before entering data. Follow these steps (including several spelling mistakes) to create a bullet chart that uses a different symbol than the one you previously used:

1. Select the "Add slide" button at the bottom of the window.
2. Select Bullet and then Chart Gallery. The chart gallery for bullet charts will be displayed.
3. Select the Title radio button to see the gallery change to the options for title charts.

    You can continue selecting chart types until you find an appearance that you like, or you can return to a previous gallery by selecting its chart type again.

4. Select the Bullet radio button again.
5. Select the second bullet chart option (square bullets) in the first row of selections and then select OK.

    The Data Form for the bullet chart is displayed. It looks like the screen shown in Figure 3-6. It does not appear any different onscreen than if you had created a bullet chart with the default symbols. You must preview or print the slide to see the square bullet symbols. First let's enter some data.

6. Move to the title area and type **Aardvark, Inc.** and press (ENTER).
7. Type **Staff Meeting** and press (ENTER) twice.
8. Type **Discuss hiring needs** and press (ENTER) twice to leave a blank line after the bullet.
9. Type each of the following bullets with the spelling mistakes shown, pressing (ENTER) twice after each bullet except the last one:

    Assign temporary constructin parking

    Revew current projects

    Request voulenteers for charity

    Discuss compny picnic

Chapter 3: *Creating Text Charts* 59

10. Select OK and then press (F2) to view the chart that contains the square bullets and your data, as shown in Figure 3-7.
11. Press (ESC) to display the Slide Editor screen.

Tip: *You do not have to worry about running out of space for new slides in a presentation. Each presentation can contain as many as 400 slides.*

Although you have completed the chart, it would not make a very good impression in a presentation since the spelling errors would distract from the message of the chart. Before exploring additional bullet chart options you need to learn to check the spelling of your text charts since even a single misspelled word destroys the professional image you want to project.

Checking the Spelling for Charts

The Harvard Graphics spelling check option actually provides checks beyond incorrect spelling. It looks for numbers that are punctuated incor-

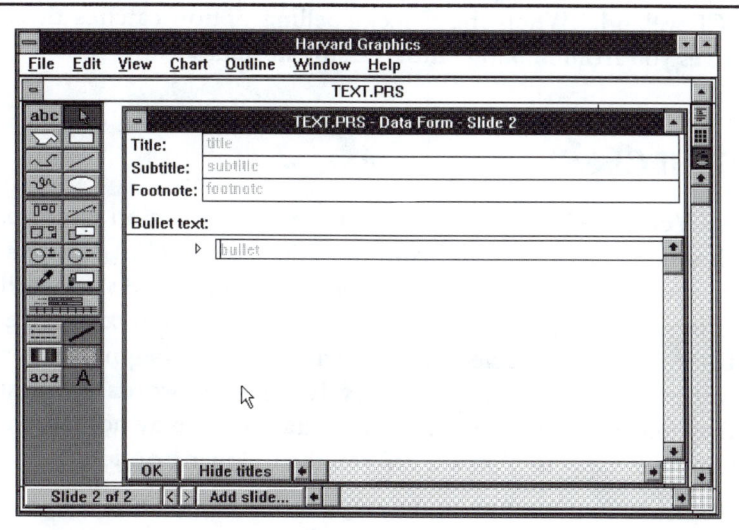

Figure 3-6. *Data Form for a bullet chart*

Figure 3-7.   Bullet chart with square bullets

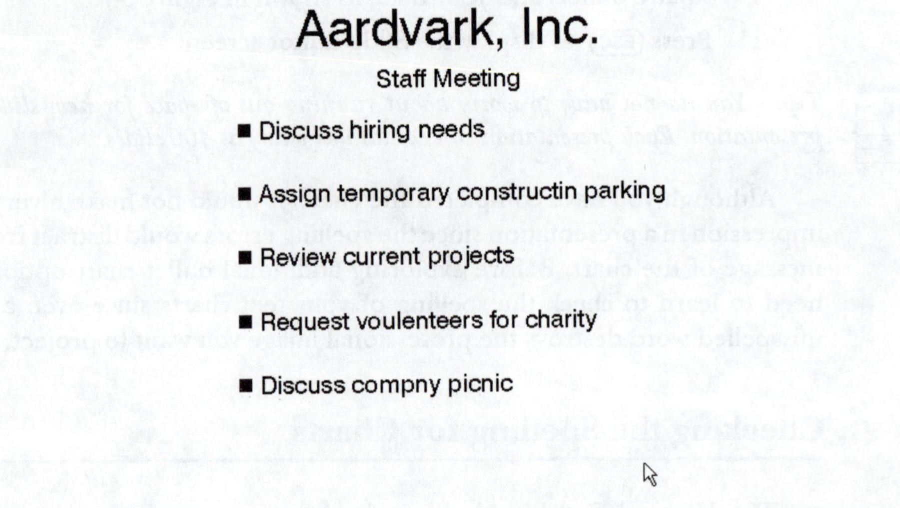

Aardvark, Inc.
Staff Meeting

- Discuss hiring needs
- Assign temporary constructin parking
- Review current projects
- Request voulenteers for charity
- Discuss compny picnic

---

rectly, such as 9,45.90. It looks for repeated words, as in "The Year of the the Tiger." Words with probable incorrect capitalization are also marked, as in "CLeveland." When the Check spelling option catches these oversights, it saves you from making embarrassing mistakes.

Spell Checking Options

You can check the spelling on one slide or in an entire presentation by choosing Check spelling from the Edit menu. Select "This slide" or "Entire presentation" to control the scope of the check. To skip words in all capital letters, such as acronyms, place an X in the check box "Ignore words in ALL CAPS." When you select OK, Harvard Graphics begins checking and stops at words that are not in its dictionary. It flags these words as "questionable" since they may be misspelled or their capitalization may not match what Harvard Graphics expects. You are offered the following options:

Chapter 3:   *Creating Text Charts*   **61**

Ignore	Used when a word is spelled correctly. This option ignores Harvard Graphics' suggestion that there is a problem.
Replace	This option uses the word that displays in the Replacement list box as a substitute for the word. Used after selecting a word from the Suggestions list box, this option first places the word in the Replacement box, and (if you confirm it) supplants the word in the text. Note that you can edit the word while it is in the Replacement box.
Add to dictionary	Adds the questionable word to your personal dictionary. This option should be used for proper names or special terms that you will use frequently. Once words are added to a personal dictionary, Harvard Graphics checks this dictionary as well as its main dictionary before flagging a word as questionable.
Stop checking	Cancels spelling check.
Help	Offers help on spelling check.

Harvard Graphics also checks for repeated words. It allows you to keep a double word or eliminate it by selecting "Remove word" or "Ignore word."

Checking the Current Bullet Chart

Since text charts offer so much potential for spelling mistakes, you will want to try the spelling check feature for yourself and use it on every presentation that you create. Such checking can prevent costly mistakes in output.

Follow these steps to correct the errors in the current slide and then make the necessary corrections:

1. Choose Chec<u>k</u> spelling from the <u>E</u>dit menu and then select "This slide" and OK.

Harvard Graphics highlights "Inc.", the first word in the slide that contains a potential misspelling, as shown in Figure 3-8. The Correct Spelling dialog box displays a list of potential corrections and offers the choices discussed earlier. Since this word is currently spelled correctly and is part of the company name, you may not want to have it appear as a questionable word in subsequent spelling checks, so add it to your personal dictionary.

2. Select "Add to dictionary."

    Harvard Graphics adds "Inc." to your personal dictionary and proceeds with its checking. Next Harvard Graphics highlights "constructin."

3. Select "construction" from the Suggestions list box and then select Replace.

    As soon as you select a suggestion, it is placed in the Replacement box and used to replace the word in text when you select Replace.

4. "Voulenteers" is the next questionable word highlighted, but none of the suggestions can be used.

5. Click the Replacement text right in front of the letter "l" and then press (BACKSPACE) to delete the letter "u".

6. Click the Replacement text right before the "n", press (BACKSPACE) to delete "e", and then type **u**.

    The replacement text now reads "volunteers."

7. Select Replace.

    The word "compny" is highlighted next.

8. Highlight "company" in the list box and then select Replace.

    Harvard Graphics displays a message that the spelling check is complete.

9. Select OK.

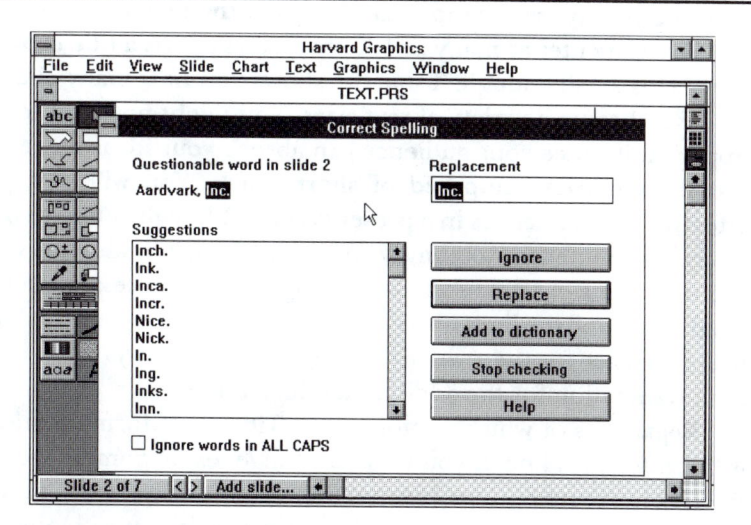

Figure 3-8. *Questionable spelling highlighted*

Other Text Chart Creation Options

You will want to look at creating a few more charts in the current presentation, which will allow you to try a few more gallery selections as well. After completing these charts we will shift our focus to the Slide Editor's enhancement options.

Creating Another Title Chart

Title charts can be used for more than the beginning of a presentation. They can be used as dividers to segment your presentation when you have several major areas to cover. Each new area may start with another title chart. An entry placed in the top section of the Title chart form will automatically be larger than the text placed in either of the other two sections of the chart, allowing you to use the top area to present the theme for the new section.

You can enter as many as 100 characters across a title chart if the size of the text is small enough. Table 3-1 shows you how many characters can fit across a chart in a variety of text sizes. You might not want to approach the upper limit, since your audience can absorb your ideas more quickly if you use short entries composed of short words. You will find phrases more effective than sentences in a presentation. Although you have been taught to always use sentences to convey written and spoken ideas, if you attempt to use them on a chart you will be adding many unnecessary words. Also, you need not use all the lines on a chart. Blank lines improve readability and often make it easier for the reader to focus. You can always add another chart to the presentation for the additional information.

Regardless of which section of the Title chart form you use, the default is to center each line. If you want to change text alignment, you must look at the text attribute options covered later in this chapter or use a chart gallery to alter the appearance for you. In this example you will look at placing the

Table 3-1.   *Character Sizes and the Number of Character Spaces Used*

Character Size	Number of Characters Across
20	12
15	15
12	19
10	23
8	28
6	38
4	55
2	100

footnote closer to the subtitles. You will alter this chart again later to resize the subtitle and footnote. Follow these steps:

1. Select **A**dd slide from the **S**lide menu.
2. Select Title and then select Chart Galleries.
3. Select the third example in line 1 (Title, Subtitle, Footnote; Centered) and then select OK.

The Data Form looks the same as your first Title chart. You will not see the change until after entering your data.

4. Type **Effective Time Management** and press (TAB).
5. Type **Reduce meetings** and press (TAB).
6. Type **Eliminate paperwork**, select OK, and then press (F2) to display a chart like Figure 3-9.
   Later you can make changes to the size of the last text entry if you wish.

Looking at Two New Bullet Charts

You will want to create a few more bullet charts for practice. The two charts in this section offer a look at a new format for bullets and the addition of special characters with the text you type. You can use the techniques learned in the second example any time you need to type text regardless of the chart type that you are creating.

Creating a Numbered List

Sometimes you want to emphasize the order of steps in the information presented. A numbered list can help reinforce the sequence of activities by putting a number to the left of each item in the list. Harvard Graphics adds sequential numbers for you automatically when you change the default bullet

Figure 3-9.   *Creating another title chart*

Effective Time Management
Reduce meetings
Eliminate paperwork

symbol to use numbers. You will learn how to make this change through the Slide Editor later, but for now all you need to do is select the gallery option for either Arabic or Roman numbers to have Harvard Graphics make the change.

Follow these steps to change the bullet style and enter a new chart:

1. Select **A**dd slide from the **S**lide menu, select Bullet, and then select Chart Galleries.
2. Select the third option on line 2. Then select OK.
3. Move to the Title line on the Data Form and type **Product Testing Phases**.
4. Move to the first bullet and type **Laboratory trials** and press (ENTER) twice.
5. Type **Limited customer sites** and press (ENTER) twice.
6. Type **Full beta program** and press (ENTER) twice.
7. Type **Final testing with gamma release** and then select OK.

Chapter 3: *Creating Text Charts* 67

If your screen image is too small to display OK, you can maximize the display in order to be able to select it—or use CTRL+F4 instead of clicking OK.

8. Press F2 to view the chart, which looks like Figure 3-10.
   This chart, with its numbers indicating a sequence, looks completely different than the last one.
9. Press ESC.
10. Choose Save from the File menu to update the TEXT.PRS file.

Using Special Symbols

Special symbols are character representations beyond what you see on your keyboard. They may be foreign characters, monetary symbols other than the dollar sign, arrow heads, or symbols used for bullets. You can use them anywhere you enter text, including bar chart axes titles and legends. Harvard Graphics supports the entry of these special ANSI (American National Standards Institute) symbols by entering a special combination of keys. You must press ALT then type a zero from the numeric keypad and while still

Figure 3-10.   *Bullet chart as a numbered list*

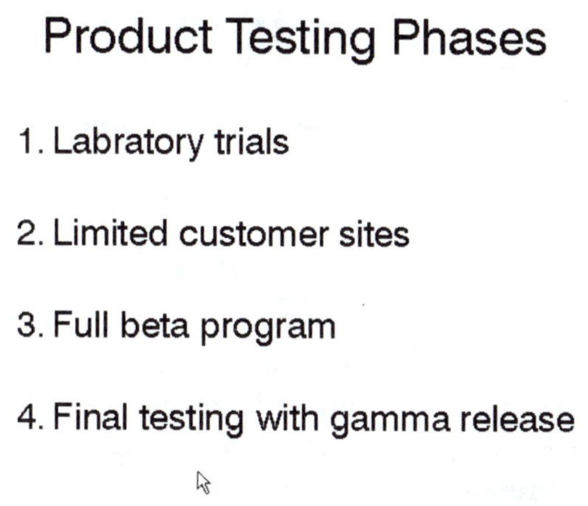

Product Testing Phases

1. Labratory trials

2. Limited customer sites

3. Full beta program

4. Final testing with gamma release

holding down (ALT), type the three-digit code from Table 3-2 that corresponds to the character that you want to add. A little practice will make this clearer.

To practice adding special symbols to a chart, follow these steps to create a chart listing international representatives for a company:

1. Select <u>A</u>dd slide and then select Bullet. Select OK.
2. Type **International Representatives** for the title, and then press (ENTER) three times.
3. Type **Fran** but *do not* press (ENTER). The next letter you need requires a special symbol. Press (ALT) and while holding it down type **0231** from the numeric keypad. (This is the entry for ç cedilla.)
4. Continue typing **ois Monet - France** and press (ENTER) twice.
5. Type **Margaret M**, press (ALT), and type **0252** from the numeric keypad (ü umlaut). Type **ller - Germany** and press (ENTER) twice.
7. Type **Klaus Wei,** press (ALT), and type **0223** from the numeric keypad (the German sharp ß). Type **- Austria** and then press (ENTER) twice.
8. Type **Wilhelm B** and press (ALT)+**0246** (a short way to express this key press) from the numeric keypad (ö umlaut). Type **-Switzerland** and then press (ENTER) twice.
9. Type **Jos** and press (ALT)+**0233** to create the é acute. Type **N** then press (ALT)+**0250** (ú acute) followed by (ALT)+**0241** (ñ tilde). Complete the entry by typing **ez - Spain**. Select OK.
10. Press (F2) to preview the chart, which now looks like Figure 3-11.
11. Press (ESC) to return to the Data Form.

Using Data Forms to Create Table Charts

Table charts allow you to display several entries in a table format. The table chart is a chart that is divided into columns and rows. This chart type is useful for presenting the actual numbers used in other charts that you may include in a presentation. The rows and columns of a table chart allow you to show relationships between data.

Chapter 3: *Creating Text Charts*

Table 3-2.   Special Symbols Codes

Code	ANSI Character	Code	ANSI Character	Code	ANSI Character
160		192	À	224	à
161	¡	193	Á	225	á
162	¢	194	Â	226	â
163	£	195	Ã	227	ã
164	¤	196	Ä	228	ä
165	¥	197	Å	229	å
166	¦	198	Æ	230	æ
167	§	199	Ç	231	ç
168	"	200	È	232	è
169	©	201	É	233	é
170	ª	202	Ê	234	ê
171	«	203	Ë	235	ë
172	¬	204	Ì	236	ì
173	"	205	Í	237	í
174	®	206	Î	238	î
175	-	207	Ï	239	ï
176	°	208	Ð	240	ð
177	±	209	Ñ	241	ñ
178	²	210	Ò	242	ò
179	³	211	Ó	243	ó
180	ʼ	212	Ô	244	ô
181	µ	213	Õ	245	õ
182	¶	214	Ö	246	ö
183	·	215	×	247	÷
184	,	216	Ø	248	ø
185	¹	217	Ù	249	ù
186	º	218	Ú	250	ú
187	»	219	Û	251	û
188	1/4	220	Ü	252	ü
189	1/2	221	Ý	253	ÿ
190	3/4	222	þ	254	þ
191	¿	223	ß	255	ÿ

Figure 3-11.   *Bullet text chart with special symbols*

International Representatives

- François Monet - France

- Margaret Müller - Germany

- Klauss Weiß - Austria

- Wilhelm Bö - Switzerland

- José Núñez - Spain

Harvard Graphics for Windows provides a unique new approach for entering table chart data on a mini-spreadsheet form. The form corresponds to a small corner of a spreadsheet, such as 1-2-3. The form is labeled with column headings consisting of the letters A-Z and AA-AE for a total of 31 columns. The rows are numbered from 1 to 100. You can uniquely identify the intersection of each row and column, called a cell, by specifying first the column and then the row location, although you are unlikely to use all these locations when creating your table charts.

Creating a Three-Column Table Chart

A three-column chart can be an effective way to present the exact sales figures and regions for the top five sales personnel or showcase the results of your top three divisions. You can enter as many as 100 lines and 24 columns in a table chart, although you will want to limit your entries to fewer lines (unless your presentation will be effective with very small characters).

Chapter 3: Creating Text Charts

You can press TAB to move one column to the right or ENTER to move down one row. HOME moves to the first cell in the current row and CTRL+HOME to the first cell in the first row. The END key moves the highlight to the last cell containing data in the current row. You can also use the arrow keys to move from row to row and column to column. Once you start entering data in a cell, you are in Edit mode.

Edit mode changes the way that these keys respond. TAB still moves you one cell to the right but first it finalizes you entry. ENTER finalizes and moves down one cell. HOME moves to the first character on the line and END moves to the end of your entry and the right and left arrow keys move one character at a time within your entry.

As you type an entry for the current cell marked by the highlight, you can enter as many as 255 characters. The characters will appear on the Edit line as you type and they will be placed in the cell when you finalize the current entry. A marker (>) is used to indicate a data length that extends beyond the column width. Later, you will learn to change a column width to accommodate this situation. You can split an entry into two lines by pressing CTRL+ENTER. A split vertical bar (¦) is used to indicate this action in the cell, although you will not see the data on two lines until you preview or print the chart.

Follow these steps to create a chart showing new products in 1992 and their date of introduction:

1. Select <u>A</u>dd slide, and then Table, followed by OK.

    The Data Form with the entries you will be making looks like Figure 3-12.

2. Move to the Title area, type **Innovative Marketing**, and press ENTER.

3. Type **New Products in 1992** and press ENTER twice.

4. Type **Product** and press ENTER.

5. Continue to enter these product names in the first column, pressing ENTER after each:

    Quick-Rol
    Sof-Tex
    Heat-Away
    Seal R More

Sports Score
Time Save

6. Press CTRL-HOME and then TAB.

7. Complete these entries, pressing ENTER after each:

   Date Introduced
   February 15
   March 10
   June 22
   August 1
   November 3
   December 22

8. Press CTRL-HOME once and TAB twice to move to the top of column 3.

9. Type **Developer** and press ENTER.

Figure 3-12.   Data Form with table chart entries

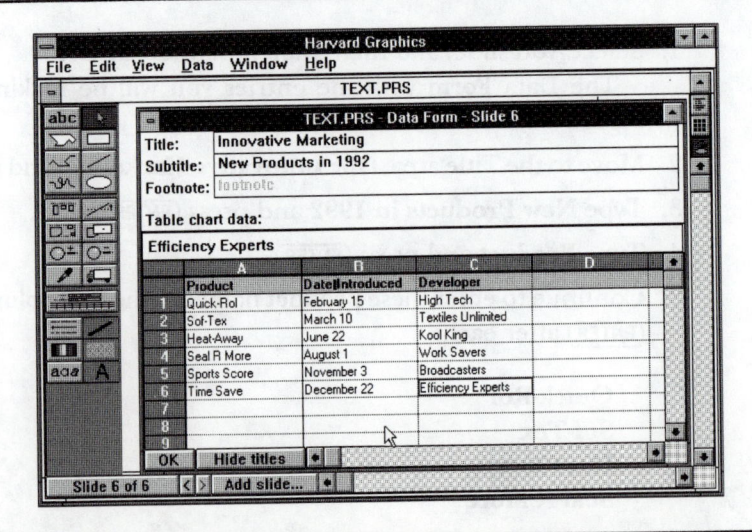

Chapter 3: *Creating Text Charts* 73

10. Complete the entries in column three by typing these entries and pressing (ENTER) after each one:

    High Tech
    Textiles Unlimited
    Kool King
    Work Savers
    Broadcasters
    Efficiency Experts

11. Press (F2) to show the chart that appears in Figure 3-13.
12. Press (ESC) and then choose Save from the File menu.
13. To make another copy of the presentation that you can alter, choose Save as from the File menu and type **TEXTX** as the filename.

Tip: *You can insert or delete rows or columns by moving the cursor to the insertion or deletion location and choosing Insert or Delete (these appear from the Data menu).*

Figure 3-13. *Completed table chart*

Innovative Marketing
New Products in 1992

Product	Date Introduced	Developer
Quick-Rol	February 15	High Tech
Sof-Tex	March 10	Textiles Unlimited
Heat-Away	June 22	Kool King
Seal R More	August 1	Work Savers
Sports Score	November 3	Broadcasters
Time Save	December 22	Efficiency Experts

Working with the Slide Editor to Create and Enhance Charts

The menu at the top of the Slide Editor screen provides a full range of options for customizing the text in your charts. Many of these menu actions can also be invoked through the icons represented in the toolbox to the left of the chart shown on the Slide Editor screen. You will learn how to use these features to change text attributes, text location, text alignment or justification, and bullet attributes. You will also learn how to alter the column width for table charts. You will use the Slide Editor to add two new charts to your presentation as you create a table chart and a free-form chart from the Slide Editor.

There are a few techniques that you will use as you make changes with the editor. These are moving from slide to slide, selecting text, and using text boxes. You will want to take a quick look at these basic techniques before exploring change options.

Moving from Slide to Slide

As your presentation grows you need to be able to move quickly from slide to slide to make changes. If you need to move more than one slide away from the current slide, you will want to click the "Go to" button in the lower-left corner of the window. This is the button that reads Slide n of x, where n is the number of the current slide and x is the total number of slides in the presentation.

Once you click this button, the "Go to" dialog box appears. You can type the slide number that you want to "Go to" or use the horizontal scroll bar in this box to move to another slide. This scroll bar works the same way as the vertical scroll bar does on the Data Form and the Outliner.

If you only need to move to the next or previous slide you can use the arrows next to the "Go to" button on the Slide Editor window. Clicking these arrows moves you one slide at a time in the direction indicated by the arrows.

Try the "Go to" feature now with these steps:

1. Click the "Go to" button at the bottom of the screen.

Chapter 3: *Creating Text Charts*

2. Type **6** and press ENTER.
    Slide 6 is displayed in the Slide Editor.
3. Click the "Go to" button.
4. Drag the scroll box to the left to slide 1.
5. Click OK to display slide 1.

Selecting Text

Text must be selected as a first step to changing it. When you select text, you will select a block of it. You can change the entire block that you select or just a portion of it. If you are working with a bullet chart that contains a title and five bullet entries initially entered via the Data Form screen, you will have two text blocks that you can select. The first block contains the title for the slide and the second block contains the bullet entries. You can select either block by selecting any character within the block. This means that to select the title, you can click any character of the title; and to select the five bullet entries, you can click any character from any of the bullet entries. The handles that appear on your screen at the edges of the block indicate what is selected.

Look at the toolbox on the Slide Editor in Figure 3-14 and find the Selection tool, shown below:

With it, you can move to the left of a text block and drag a box around the text to select it. Once you have the box around the desired text, release the mouse button and handles will appear around the selected text block.

If you only want to work with part of a text block, after selecting it, press CTRL+E or select the Text tool, shown below:

Click the first character to select and drag the mouse to the last character that you want to include. The selected characters are highlighted within the box.

Using Text Boxes

Text boxes provide an editing feature for large or small blocks of text. You can select the Text tool to work with a text box. The text block will appear in the text box when you click the Text tool. Once the Text tool is selected, you can move from text box to text box on a slide by pressing the up and down arrow keys. The default is to show a ruler with the box to make it easier to set tabs, change justification, or edit the contents of the box. Refer again to Figure 3-14, which shows a text box with a ruler. The icons are used to set tabs and change justification. The set of icons on the left are used for tabs and the group on the right are used for justification. To turn off the ruler you would choose Show text ruler from the Text menu.

You can insert text with a text box by moving the cursor to the point where you want to insert characters and begin typing. To delete a section of

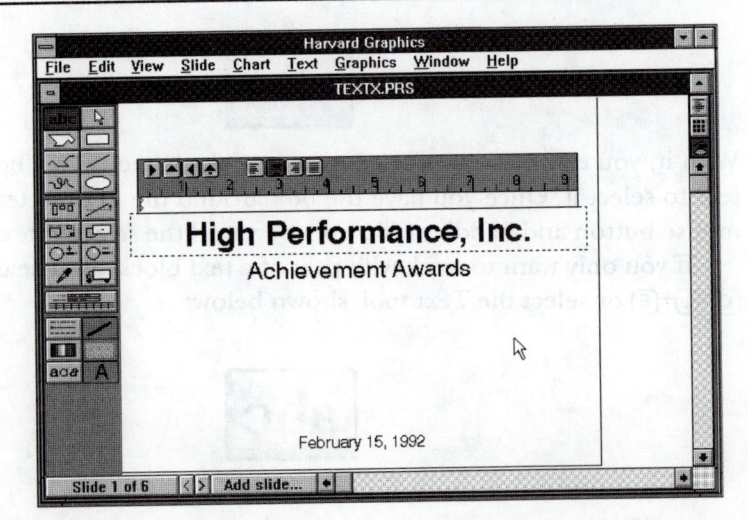

Figure 3-14.   Text box with a ruler

Chapter 3: *Creating Text Charts* 77

text within a box, click the first character and drag the mouse to the last character. Then press (SHIFT)+(DEL) to place the text on the Clipboard, or choose Clear from the Edit menu to eliminate it without adding it to the Clipboard.

To display a text box around the title in slide 1, follow these steps:

1. With the Selection tool active, drag a box around the title. When you release the mouse button, handles will appear.
2. Select the Text tool.
3. Press (↓).

The text box moves to the next text object in the chart. Click the window to the right of the chart to unselect the text.

Tip: *You can also use the other Clipboard commands with selected text.* (CTRL)+(INS) *(Edit Copy) and* (SHIFT)+(INS) *(Edit Paste) can be used to copy text to the Clipboard and paste it to another location.*

Moving Text

You can relocate text easily with the Selection tool. You can also add blank lines to a chart's Data Form to add more space between entries.

Moving Text with the Selection Tool

All you need to do to move text is to select it and drag it to a new location. Try this now with the subtitle for slide 1:

1. Click the Selection tool again.
    The default is Tool Lock, which keeps a tool active after you use it—so you need to choose the Selection tool again since the Text tool was the last tool used.
2. Drag a box around the subtitle.
    Handles appear around the subtitle text.

3. Move the mouse pointer until it is inside the bounds of the handles and looks like four arrow heads pointing in all four directions.
4. Drag the text box down until the top of the dotted box forms a base for the subtitle text on the screen. The text is relocated and is still selected.
5. Drag a box around the footnote entry for a date.
6. Drag the date box up beneath Achievement Awards.
7. Click to the right of the slide to unselect the footnote.

Changing Line Placement

Spacing text in the title chart is also important. You can control some of the spacing with blank lines. These lines are added by pressing (ENTER) without making an entry on the line. If you need two lines in the top section and two lines in the middle section, you might consider placing your entries in the first and third line of the top section and the first and third line of the middle section. This alternative adds important space between the lines of text.

Size, Color, Style, Font, and Placement of Text Entries

Although the content of your message is most important, its appearance is a vital factor in how you convey your message. The correct placement and size of text can highlight information for the reader and present a professional image. Also, the size of the characters affects both the number of characters and the number of lines that will fit on a chart. With Harvard Graphics it is easy to change the size of the text and alter its placement on your output.

Changing Text Size

Each type of text chart has its own default character size in different lines of the chart. Text sizes are measured in points with one point equal to 1/72 of an inch. Harvard Graphics supports text sizes from 4 to 512, although most sizes used are closer to the lower end of the range. Figure 3-15 shows some sample text sizes. Typically, titles and subtitles are larger than detail lines, and

Chapter 3: *Creating Text Charts* 79

Figure 3-15. *Various point sizes*

This is 12 point

This is 24 point

This is 36 point

This is 48 point

footnote lines are the smallest of all the defaults. The default text size settings for a title chart are 48 for the title, 36 for the subtitle, and 24 for a footnote. Reducing the size of any entries much below 24 makes it difficult to read these entries from a distance. You can increase the size of the text or even choose to make sections the same size. To change the size of any text, first select it. Choose Size from the Text menu and then select a size from the seven options presented. You can look at the current size setting before picking a new one. You must specify the actual point size you want to use yourself after choosing All attributes from the Text menu.

Follow these steps to change the size of the footnote text in slide 1:

1. With the Selection tool active, select the footnote text.
2. Choose Size from the Text menu.
3. Select 36 to make the footnote the same size as the subtitle.

Your chart will look something like the one in Figure 3-16.

4. Click to the right of the slide to unselect the footnote.

Changing Text Color

The default text color for each section is different, but you can change the color for any element to either a numbered chart color or a custom color. When you use chart colors, the colors of the various chart elements can change as you substitute a different palette of colors. Although this is a more advanced technique, you will sometimes want to create a custom look for your presentations and prefer colors other than the default. Later you will learn more about working with palettes, which are a full range of complementary color selections.

For now the important point is that when you select a color number, it will be affected by the current palette. Custom colors are not affected by the selection of a palette and will always remain the same. If you assign a custom red to a title, the title will remain red regardless of the current palette selection, whereas the selection of a chart color that currently appears as red

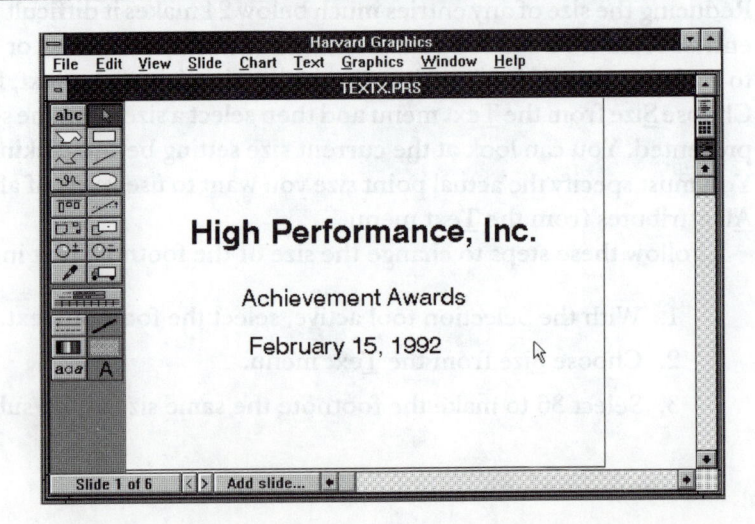

Figure 3-16. Title chart with changes

Chapter 3: *Creating Text Charts* 81

may not remain red if the palette is edited or if a new palette is used. To set the color of a section of text, select the text, chose Color from the Text menu, and then select a chart or a custom color.

To change the color of the title on the next chart follow these steps:

1. Click the arrow to move to the next slide.
    Colors 1 and 2 are assigned to the title and subtitle. You will make the title the same color as the subtitle by making it color 2.
2. Click the title.
3. Choose Color from the Text menu.
4. Select color number 2. Now both chart components are the same color.

Tip: You can use the Eyedropper tool, shown below, to transfer text attributes to other text. This includes size, color, font, and style. Select the text with the desired attributes and click the Eyedropper with the (↑) (the eyedropper will expand into two eyedroppers, each with an arrow), select the text to be changed, move the mouse pointer to the Eyedropper and drag to the right to select the Eyedropper with the (↓).

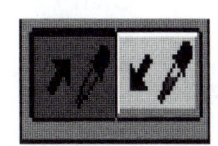

Changing the Chart Palette

A palette is a complete set of color selections. All the colors in a palette blend well together, and that makes it easy to select good color combinations. As mentioned, Harvard Graphics palettes have two sets of colors, chart colors and custom colors. When you select a palette, a background color and a primary set of other colors is selected. Table 3-3 provides a list of the palette options supported by Harvard Graphics. Some are for specific output devices. You will generally want a dark background if you plan to view your charts on screen and a white background for printed output. If you do not have a color print device and you primarily want to create output for printing, you will want to select one of the monochrome palettes to be able to see the final appearance. You will learn more about palettes in Chapter 12, "Customizing Harvard Graphics."

Table 3-3.   Palette Options

File	Background	Colors
DEFAULT.PL	White	Blacks/browns
MONOW.PL	White	Monochrome
MONOB.PL	Black	Monochrome
1BLU.PL	Dark blue	Blues
2BLU.PL	Dark blue	Blue/green
3BLU.PL	Dark blue	Blue/gray
4BLU.PL	Dark blue	Blue/red/gray
5BLU.PL	Dark blue	Red/gray/yellow
6BLU.PL	Dark blue	Green/blue
7GRY.PL	Gray	Red/gray/orange
8RED.PL	Red-black	Red/green
9CYN.PL	Cyan	Blues
10GRY.PL	Gray	Gray/yellow
11WHI.PL	White	Blacks/browns
12WHI.PL	Ivory	Black/brown/red
13WHI.PL	White	Black/brown/blue
HR1BLU.PL	Dark blue	Blues
HR2BLU.PL	Dark blue	Blues
HR3BLU.PL	Dark blue	Blue/brown/gray
HR4BLU.PL	Dark blue	Blue/gray/orange
HR5BLU.PL	Dark blue	Red/orange/gray
HR6BLU.PL	Green-black	Green/blue
HR7GRY.PL	Gray-black	Red/gray/brown
HR8RED.PL	Red-black	Red/green/brown
HR9CYN.PL	Light blue	Blue/red
HR10CYN.PL	Gray	Blue/red
HR11WHI.PL	White	Black/brown/blue
HR12WHI.PL	Ivory	Black/brown/red
HR13WHI.PL	White	Black/brown/blue
PLOTTER.PL	White	Black/blue/red

Chapter 3: *Creating Text Charts*

When you choose a new palette, each chart element assigned a color number will find its number in the new palette. Chart objects with custom colors are not affected by palette changes. Follow these steps to change the chart palette:

1. Choose Color palette from the Slide menu.
2. Choose Apply.
3. Select a palette.
4. Select "This slide" or "Entire presentation" to control the impact of the change.
5. Select OK.

Text Chart Fonts

A font is a set of characters in a consistent typeface. Just as a change in your voice inflection conveys a different message to your audience, changing the font in your chart can present a different slant to the information your message contains. The default Swiss font is clear and striking. The Swiss style might be an appropriate choice for presenting a marketing plan. On the other hand, if you are doing a presentation on architecture in the Middle Ages, you might prefer the look of an elaborate Gothic font.

Harvard Graphics supports several different types of fonts. The Bitstream fonts are listed first in the menu of font options. They are ideal for screen presentations since they can be rotated, flipped, or stretched—although they print more slowly than other fonts. After the Bitstream fonts, you will find a list of hardware fonts and fonts for Windows. These are all marked with bullets. They print faster than the Bitstream fonts and are ideal for printed presentation. If you stretch, rotate, or flip these fonts, Harvard Graphics will substitute a Bitstream font for the font that you selected.

To change the font for text, select the text, and then choose Font from the Text menu. Select the font desired from the menu or dialog box presented. A dialog box is used when you have more than 25 font options available. If you want your font change to affect the entire presentation, you need to choose Change presentation font from the Slide menu and then select the desired font. Try a font change for slide 2 by following these steps:

1. Choose Select all from the Edit menu. This selects the entire chart.
2. Choose Font from the Text menu.
3. Choose Geo Slab from the Font menu. The entire chart uses the new font as shown in Figure 3-17.
4. Click another location to unselect the entire chart.
5. Click the text for the Title.

Other Text Styles

You can change the text style in any graph, but such changes are even more significant in text charts because all you have are words to convey your message. You can use features like underlining and italic to emphasize a particular entry.

Figure 3-17. Bullet chart with Geo Slab font

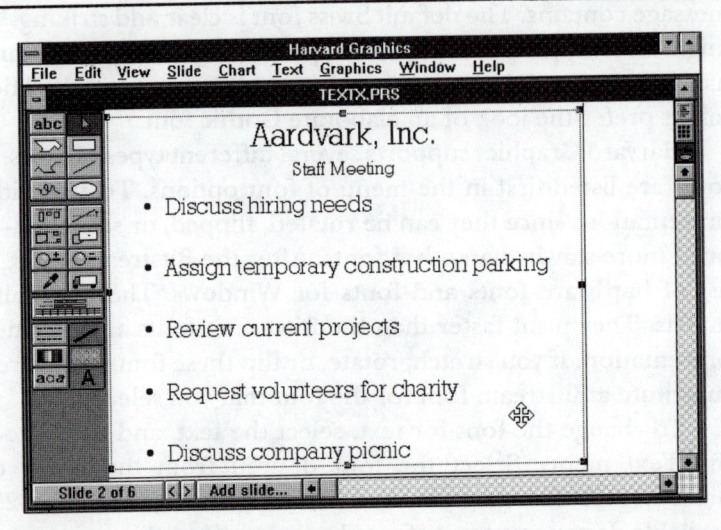

Chapter 3: *Creating Text Charts*

The basic features for changing text style work the same whether you are working on an analytical chart or a text chart. You select text, and then choose Style from the Text menu. You can pick from such styles as Normal, Bold, Italic, Underline, and Strikethrough.

Making Text Bold

You can try making the title text bold while it is still selected from the last example:

1. Choose Style from the Text menu.
2. Choose Bold from the Style menu. The Title text is changed to bold. You can always choose Undo from the Edit menu if you do not like the change.

Changing Text Justification

Another option is to change the position of the text within the lines of a text box. The default for title charts is to center each entry, but you can use left, right, or full justification for any or all of the lines on a title chart. After selecting the text box that you want to change, you can use the icons in the box. The four right-most icons on the top line of the ruler provide the easiest means of change since clicking the one that shows the desired alignment will immediately change it. You can also choose Justify from the Text menu and then select the desired justification from a menu of options. This is the best approach when you want to change multiple entries but not the entire chart.

Follow these steps to change the justification for the table chart you created in slide 6:

1. Click the "Go to" button, type a 6, and select OK.
2. Select the table.
3. Choose Justify from the Text menu.
   This is the easiest approach since the Text Box will not change the entire table in one step. You could choose Select all from the Edit menu and then use the Text box to change everything—but this option changes the Title and subtitle, which you do not want to alter.

Chart Appearance Attributes for Specific Chart Types

There are two additional options specific to one chart type that you will want to add to your repertoire of skills at this time. These are the ability to change the appearance of table charts and the ability to alter the bullet characters used with bullet charts.

Appearance Options for Table Charts

There are a number of quick changes that you can make to your table charts. You can have the amount of data in any cell in a row determine the row height. To make this change, choose Chart options from the Chart menu. This will display the Table Chart Options dialog box shown in Figure 3-18. Click "Fit row height to largest cell" and then select OK to make this change.

The labels at the top of the chart in the first row are shown horizontally. You can choose to change these labels to a vertical display with one of the two other "Text orientation in the first row" options shown in the dialog box.

The same dialog box provides a selection for Grid that opens another dialog box of options. When you make this selection you can make selections for the following:

Displaying a frame around the table
Displaying grid lines after the first row
Displaying grid lines after other rows
Displaying grid lines after the first column
Displaying grid lines after other columns
Extending grid lines into the first column or row

Each option is provided through a check box or radio button.

You can also change the grid line marker width and color. This change is made by choosing one grid line or the entire table. After selecting Line attributes from the Graphics menu, select a style from a drop-down list box or choose a new thickness from the options displayed.

Changing the Bullet Character

The Chart Galleries for bullet charts present only some of the options for bullet characters. You can use any keyboard character for your bullet charac-

Chapter 3: *Creating Text Charts* 87

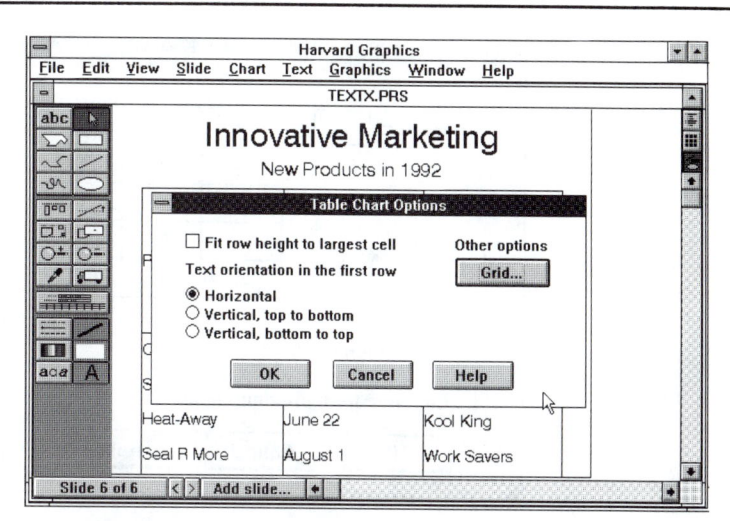

Figure 3-18. *Dialog box for table chart options*

ter or any of the special ANSI characters discussed earlier. You can set the bullet symbol for a level in a bullet chart or for a single bullet item. To change all the bullets at a level, select the entire bulleted list. If you want to change only one bullet you must proceed by selecting the Text tool and clicking the one bullet to change.

Either way, your next step is to choose Set bullet attributes from the Text menu. The Bullet Attributes dialog box appears. This box displays the current bullet symbol for the first four levels (all levels after this continue to use the same symbol as that used in the fourth level), the font, color, size, and distance from text that the bullet is placed. You can change any of the options shown. After clicking the bullet or level that you want to change, the Bullet Symbol dialog box, shown in Figure 3-19, appears. You can select a symbol or numeric representation, or use the (ALT)+0*nnn* option discussed earlier where you enter a three-digit code that corresponds to the character that you want. Go back and look at Table 3-2 for some ideas about appropriate special settings.

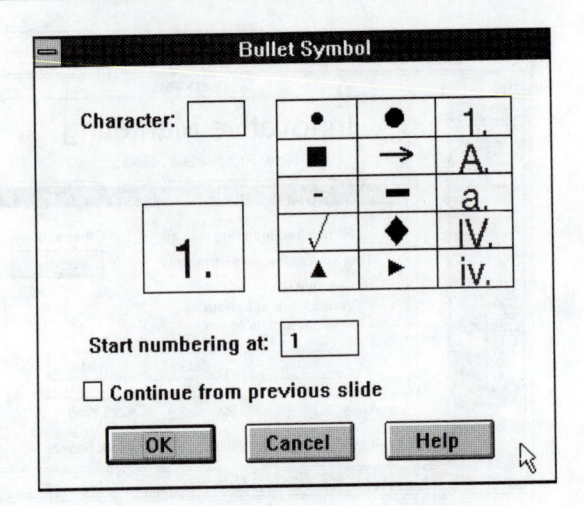

Figure 3-19.   *Bullet symbol dialog box*

Using the Slide Editor to Create a Free-Form Chart

The charts you have looked at so far have all placed elements in a predefined location. You can create text charts where you make all the rules for text placement and sizing. These charts are called free-form charts since they do not follow a form. Free-form charts are created by adding a drawing chart to a slide and then using the Text tool to add the desired text. Follow these steps to create a free-form chart containing two quotations:

1. Select **A**dd slide to add the seventh slide to the presentation.
2. Select Drawing and OK.
3. Click the faded Title text and then choose the Text tool.
4. Type **Favorite Quotes** and then click below the title.
5. Choose **S**ize from the **T**ext menu and then select 36.
6. Click the area where you want to begin typing (to the left, just below the title) and type **In politics stupidity is no handicap.** Press (ENTER).
7. Press (TAB) six times and then type **Napoleon**.

Chapter 3: *Creating Text Charts* 89

8. Press (ENTER) and then type **In politics the choice is constantly between two evils.** Press (ENTER) again.
9. Press (TAB) six times and then type **John Morley**.

Your chart will look like Figure 3-20.

10. Choose Save from the File menu to resave TEXTX.PRS.
11. Choose Close from the File menu.

Tip: *You can also get a head start on a free-form chart by creating another chart type from the gallery and choosing "Sample chart data" from the "Add chart" dialog box, which appears when you select Add slide. The data will serve as a placeholder, and you can use the Slide Editor to put in your own entries.*

Figure 3-20. *Free-form chart*

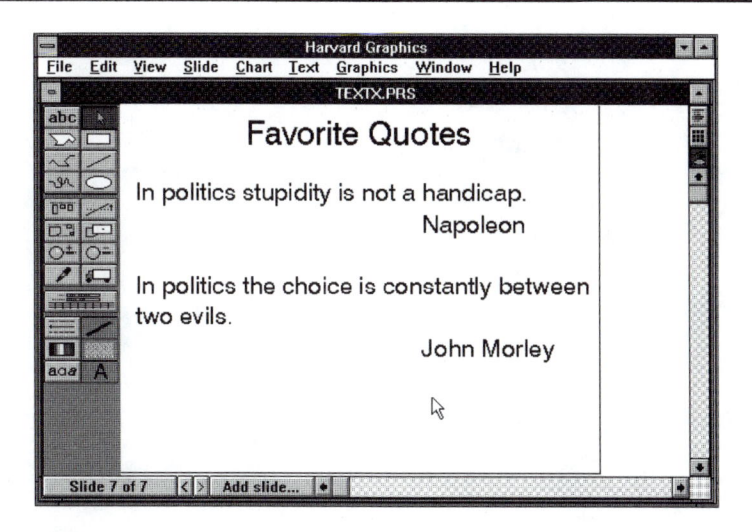

4

Learning XY Chart Basics with Bar Charts

XY charts are charts created using a horizontal X axis and a vertical Y axis. The X axis is normally used to show data by product, month, or division. The Y axis shows quantity measurements such as units sold, dollars, or headcount. These charts are often referred to as data charts since they are used to present a graphic picture of your data.

Harvard Graphics supports a variety of XY charts with bar charts being one of the most popular styles. Bar charts consist of a series of vertical or horizontal bars that represent your data. The length or height of each bar is determined by the quantity entered for each piece of information, so it is easy to make relative comparisons between data values.

Bar charts allow you to present relationships in data for several time periods and to show several categories of data in one chart. The colors or patterns you use to differentiate the bars can make a dramatic statement to your audience, which will help convey your message. The bold statement made by a bar chart allows your audience to absorb many important pieces of information from the chart with a minimum of discussion.

You might find a bar chart to be a persuasive way to present the increase in sales for your territory over a two-year period. Bar charts are also an excellent means of emphasizing the differences in a series of data. If certain products are contributing more to company profits than others, a bar chart that presents profit data for several product offerings over a period of time can make this point clear to your audience.

Bar charts use an X axis and a Y axis to create the basic form for the chart. As shown in Figure 4-1, the horizontal X axis is used to show the classifications you established for your data, if you create a vertical bar chart. The vertical Y axis always measures the quantity when bars are shown vertically. Adding X- and Y-axis titles will make it clear to anyone looking at your graph what classifications and units of measure you have selected. X-axis label names allow you to mark each point on the X axis.

In this chapter you will learn to enter data and then create a bar chart in only a few minutes. After completing this basic chart, you will build on its format to create more sophisticated charts. You will have an opportunity to add data to the graph as well as try stacked bars, horizontal bars, and other customization options.

Figure 4-1.   Bar chart with major components labeled

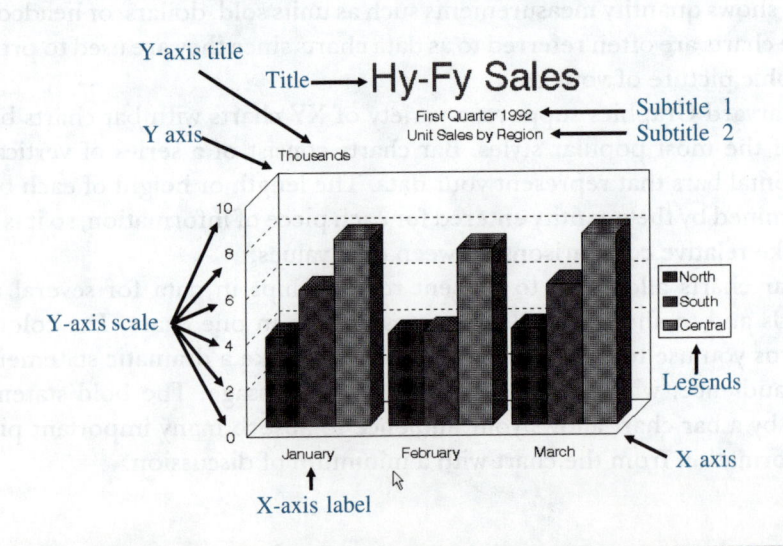

Chapter 4: *Learning XY Chart Basics with Bar Charts* 93

Getting Started

Figure 4-2 shows a bar chart that you can create with only a few minutes of work. A title and subtitle appear at the top of the chart. The one series of data on the chart represents sales figures for the four top products sold by Sturdy Toys during 1992. The data series has no legend or description since the titles make it clear what the data on the chart represents.

Follow these steps to enter the data and display the chart:

1. Choose New presentation from the File menu.
2. Select "Vertical bar" and then select OK.
    The Data Form shown in Figure 4-3 is displayed. Although this form allows you to choose many different data types for the X-axis labels, Names are the default. This means that you do not need to make any change to the form. You will enter the names of products or other classifications along the X axis.
3. Use the (↑) or click the faded title text to move to the Title entry.

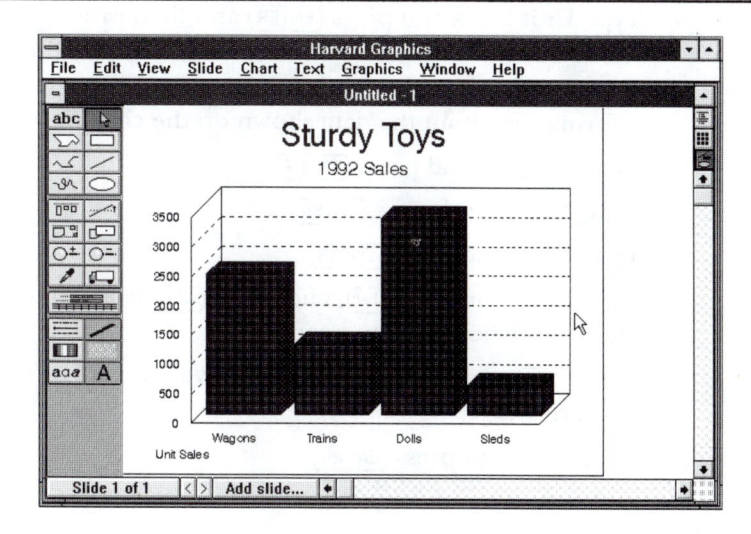

Figure 4-2.   *Quick bar chart for 1992 data*

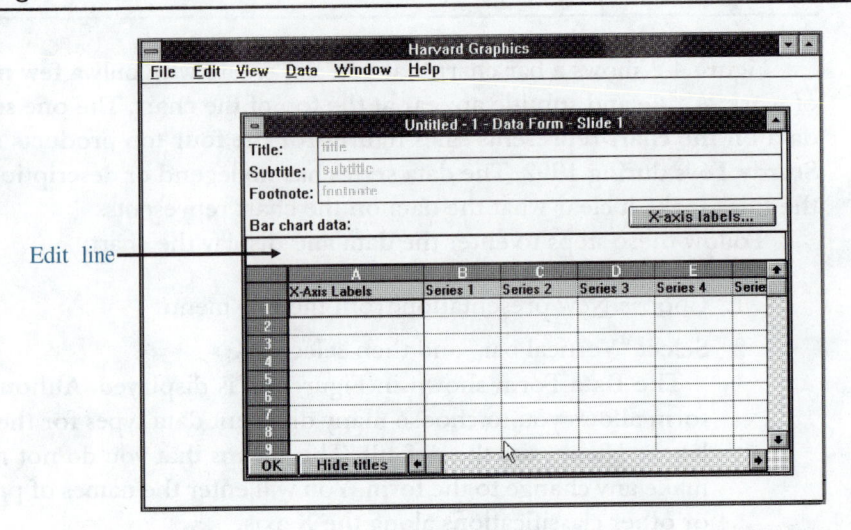

Figure 4-3.   Bar chart Data Form

Edit line ──▶

4. Type **Sturdy Toys** and press (ENTER).

5. Type **1992 Sales** and press (ENTER).

6. Type **Unit Sales** and press (ENTER) and then press (↓).

    The Footnote field is normally used to specify the source for the data presented on the chart, but you can also use it to specify other information about the data shown on the chart.

7. Type **Wagons** and press (ENTER).

8. Type **Trains** and press (ENTER).

9. Type **Dolls** and press (ENTER).

10. Type **Sleds**, press (ENTER), and press (CTRL)+(HOME) to move back to the X-axis labels column heading.

11. Press (TAB) and then press (↓) to move the cursor to the first entry for Series 1.

12. Type **2395** and press (ENTER).

Chapter 4: *Learning XY Chart Basics with Bar Charts* 95

13. Type **1200** and press (ENTER).
14. Type **3350** and press (ENTER).
15. Type **500** and press (ENTER).
    The completed XY Chart form should match Figure 4-4.
16. Select OK and then press (F2) to view the chart with its default of 3-dimensional bars. Press (ESC).
    Since there is only one data series shown on the chart, there is no need for a legend and you can remove the legend display.
17. Choose Legend from the Chart menu and then select "Show legend" to remove the X that indicates the option is selected. Select OK.
18. Press (F2) to create a graph like Figure 4-2 on your screen.
19. Press (ESC) to return to the Slide Editor.
20. Choose Save as from the File menu and then type **STURDY** and press (ENTER).

Figure 4-4.   *Completed Data Form*

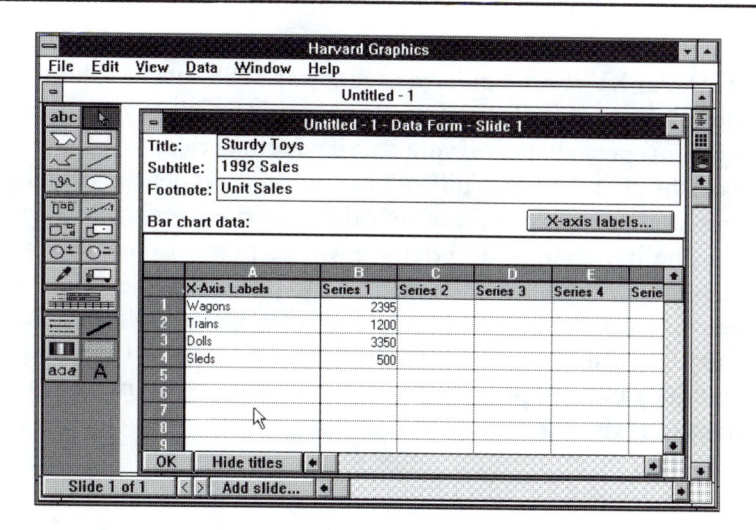

Although there were many steps to complete before seeing the chart, most of the steps were needed to enter the data. The actual menu selections needed to create the chart were few. Now that you see how easy it is to represent your data in chart form, you should be ready to enhance your reports and presentations with bar charts. Let's look at some of the additional enhancements you can make.

Adding Information to the Chart

Even though you saved the chart, it is still in memory. You can continue to make changes to it and save the enhanced version along with the rest of your presentation under the same or a different filename. You can add more data series and descriptive information, like legends, that describe each series. You can also revise the titles to reflect the addition of new data.

Adding Data Series

Harvard Graphics allows you to enter as many as 16 series of data on one chart. An XY chart can have as many as 1023 sets of values for these series. However, in normal circumstances you will find that you cannot create a clear graphic representation of your data if you come close to the limit. With too many bars, the chart becomes difficult to interpret and defeats your initial purpose of presenting a clear picture of your data that does not require close analysis.

The bar chart is an effective way to present data that represent actual sales, and it is also an effective way to present projections, especially when there are projected increases or decreases in sales volumes. To minimize data entry you can use the data entered for the first chart as a projection of 1992 unit sales and add projected sales figures for several more years. Follow these steps to revise the bar chart:

1. Select Edit data from the Chart menu.

Chapter 4: *Learning XY Chart Basics with Bar Charts*

2. Press CTRL+HOME, press TAB twice, and then press ↓ to move to the column for Series 2 in the row for wagons so you can add more data.

3. Type the following numbers, pressing ENTER after each, to supply sales projections for 1993 for the products listed:

   Wagons   2600
   Trains   1500
   Dolls   2800
   Sleds   250

4. Press CTRL+HOME, press TAB three times, and then press ↓ to move where you will make your first entry for Series 3.

5. Type the following numbers, pressing ENTER after each, to supply sales projections for 1994:

   Wagons   2900
   Trains   1600
   Dolls   3800
   Sleds   750

6. Press CTRL+HOME, press TAB four times, and then press ↓ to move to the first entry for Series 4.

7. Type the following numbers, pressing ENTER after each, to supply sales projections for 1995 for the products listed:

   Wagons   3200
   Trains   1900
   Dolls   4000
   Sleds   700

8. Your Data Form should now match Figure 4-5.

9. Press F2 to view the chart with the three additional series.

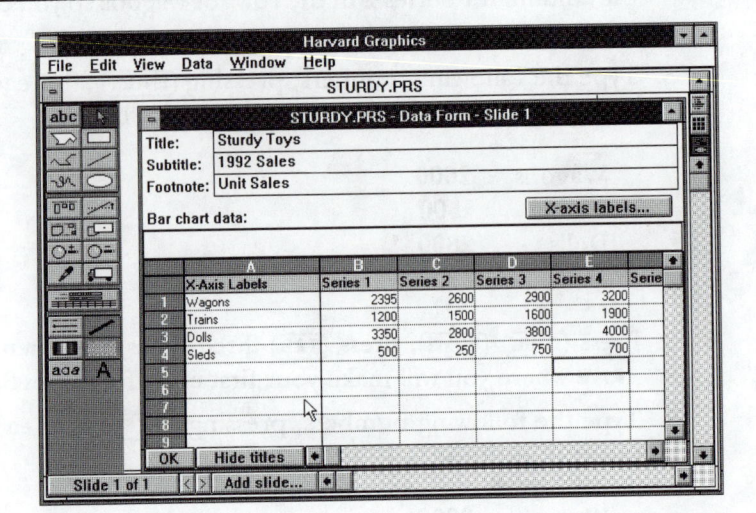

Figure 4-5.   Adding data to the original bar chart

The extra data has been added, but additional work is needed to revise the titles and to add legends that allow you to show the meaning of each set of bars.

Revising the Titles

When the titles were initially entered, the chart was used to present sales data for the current year. The revised data represents projected sales volume and needs to have the title entries changed to accurately reflect the contents of the chart.

You also can add titles to the vertical axis (the Y axis) or change existing Y-axis titles. The chart has only one Y axis so you will enter the axis title as the Y1-axis title.

Adding information in fields that you have not used is easy because all you need to do is move to the field and complete your new entry. Revising existing entries requires a little more work. If you are doing a complete

Chapter 4: *Learning XY Chart Basics with Bar Charts* 99

replacement, clear the old data and then type the new. If you are only replacing part of an entry you can select the part that you do not want before clearing. If you are inserting additional text, move to where you want to add it and begin typing. Everything you type for a title, subtitle, or footnote is inserted at the insertion point.

Follow these steps to revise the subtitle and footnote entries:

1. Press (ESC) to return to the Data Form.
2. Use (↑) to move to the subtitle field and select the current entry, 1992 Sales.
3. Choose Clear from the Edit menu.
4. Type **Sales Projections** and press (ENTER).
5. Select the footnote text and then choose Clear from the Edit menu.
    Next you will change the Y-axis label to indicate the data is shown in units rather than using a footnote to provide this information.
6. Click OK to go to the Slide Editor screen and then choose Axis from the Chart menu.
7. Click after the s in Thousands (Harvard Graphics will present this unit to you) for the Y1 Title.
8. Type **of Units**, click OK, and then press (F2) to view the altered chart. Notice the new subtitle and Y-axis title on the chart.

The titles of the chart have been revised to more clearly describe the contents of the chart. You can work with the chart to further refine its appearance by experimenting with different ways of displaying the same information. For instance, the information presented in the Y-axis label could just as easily be displayed in the Subtitle field if the Title field is expanded to include "Unit Sales Projections."

After you make the following changes, you will notice a little more balance in the distribution of information on the chart.

1. Press (ESC) to return to the Slide Editor screen.
2. Choose Axis from the Chart menu and then click to the right of Thousands in the Y1 title that you just revised.

3. Press (DELETE) until "of Units" is removed.

    You want to leave the word "Thousands" since this text indicates that the values along the Y axis are thousands, not ones. If you delete the entire Y-axis label, people viewing the graph would not be sure whether values along the Y axis represent ones, thousands, or millions.

4. Click the X-Axis Title field and then type **Leading products**.
5. Select OK.
6. Choose Edit data from the Chart menu.
7. Move the mouse pointer in front of Sales in the Subtitle field. Click the mouse, type **Unit**, and then press the (SPACEBAR).

    Since Harvard Graphics for Windows inserts text any time you type it, there is no need to press the (INSERT) key. In fact, unlike in many other DOS programs, this key has no effect.

8. Press (F2) to view the chart.

Adding Legends

Any time you show more than one series of data in a bar graph, you must add legends to describe the data displayed in each series. If you turn the legend display back on, Series 1 through Series 4 will display in the legend area, but this will not provide any meaningful information about what data is contained in each series.

You can add legends for each data series through entries on the XY Chart form. Follow these steps to add the years 1992 through 1995 as legends for the chart data series:

1. Press (ESC) to return to the Data Form.
2. Move to the legend cell for Series 1 that was deleted earlier.
3. Type **1992** and press (TAB).
4. Type **1993** and press (TAB).
5. Type **1994** and press (TAB).
6. Type **1995** and then select OK.

Chapter 4: *Learning XY Chart Basics with Bar Charts*

7. Choose Legend from the Chart menu at the top of the Slide Editor screen.
8. Select "Show legend" and then select OK.
9. Press (F2) to view the chart. Your screen should match Figure 4-6.
10. Press (ESC).
11. Press (CTRL)+(S) to save the presentation with the updated information for slide 1.

    (CTRL)+(S) is a speed key. *Speed keys*, which you will learn more about in subsequent chapters, are key combinations that you can press to quickly perform a routine operation. You can use speed keys to save and get charts, print charts, and perform other operations. You can use either the speed key or the command to obtain the same results. You must be especially careful with (CTRL)+(S). Although it can save you time, it automatically updates the file

Figure 4-6.   Graph with legends and titles entered

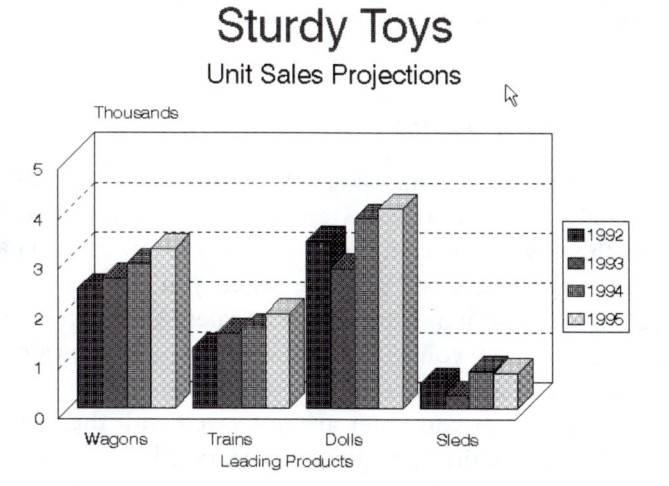

without asking you if you want to use a different name or furnishing any other prompt.

The data in the chart you just created is ideal for focusing on the growth within each product line because it makes it easy to compare sales for wagons for each year. But the organization of the data in series by year does not facilitate comparing the total sales for 1992 against the total sales in 1995. To make this comparison you must organize your data differently. In the next section you will look at organizing your data points and series in a different sequence as well as changing the entire data structure to create series by product rather than by year.

Changing Data

Changing data can be as simple as typing a new number. It can also be more complicated if you choose to reorder the points along the X axis or the order of the series shown on the graph. Harvard Graphics' access to the Windows Clipboard makes these tasks as easy as possible. When combined with features that allow you to add and delete rows and columns, you will soon be an expert with sequencing data.

Altering Data Values

As you enter new data values, the charts that contain them are updated immediately. As soon as you view the chart on the Slide Editor screen or preview the way it will print, the new value appears in the chart. In effect, this feature provides "what-if" graphics when you are working with a task like projecting headcount or future product sales. Although calculations have not been covered as yet, you will find that you can update calculations to reflect the change in a data value referenced by a formula.

New values that you enter are not saved with the presentation data on disk until you specifically request that Harvard Graphics save the data. This means that you can make changes without worrying about losing the original entries that you stored to disk. If you wish to save your new entries, it does

Chapter 4: *Learning XY Chart Basics with Bar Charts*   103

mean that you will be responsible for saving the presentation containing the chart to disk.

Changes within the data itself work a little differently than changes to titles. If you move the highlight or cursor to a table cell, you can type a new entry and it will replace the old entry rather than be added to it. If you want to insert text you must move to the cell and then click the edit line at the location where you want to insert or delete text, and then make your change.

To see how easy it is to make a change, follow these steps to update the projected sales data for sleds:

1. Choose Edit data from the Chart menu.
2. Move to the 1995 entry for sleds.
3. Type **950**.
4. Press (F2). Notice that the new data is immediately reflected in the height of the bar for sleds in 1995.
5. Press (ESC) to return to the Data Form, and type **700** as the entry for sleds in 1995; this returns the entry to its original value.
6. Choose Save from the File menu to update the presentation file STURDY.PRS.
7. Choose Save as from the File menu then type **STOCKS** and press (ENTER) to provide a second copy of the presentation that currently contains only one slide.

    You can enter any meaningful name for your files. The name STOCKS was chosen under the assumption that other stocks would be evaluated and charts created for them within this presentation.

You can continue to make changes to as many fields, titles, and legends as you want. The next time you draw the chart on the screen, it will be updated for each of the entries you have made.

Reorganizing Data

You can make some changes to the order of the data shown on your chart. This allows you to correct for an entry omission, create a more aesthetic graph, or arrange the series or X data entries in alphabetical order.

You can change either the order of the data points on the X axis or the order of the series. Changing the order of the X-axis data points normally is appropriate only with a data type of Name, as used in the current example. When you begin creating charts with other data types, such as years, months, or days, changing the order of the data point entries is not appropriate unless you accidentally entered them in the wrong order.

The procedure you use depends on whether you want to change the order of the data points or the series. Remember to think of the data points as rows and the series as columns. This makes it easy to keep the two types of changes separate.

The technique that you will use is basically the same for both series and data points. You will add a blank row or column where you need it on the Data Form and then move data to this new location. You can delete any blank rows or columns you no longer need after moving the data. We will take a look at the commands used for inserting, moving, and deleting and then apply these commands to the data for the current chart.

Inserting and Deleting Rows and Columns

If you want to move a data series or set of data values from one location on a Data Form to another, you need a blank row or column to store the data. Rows and columns you no longer need should be deleted from the Data Form. The two procedures are very similar.

To insert a row or column you must:

1. Click a row number or column letter.
2. Choose Insert from the Data menu (accessible only from the Data Form).
3. Choose Row or Column from the Insert menu.

Follow these similar steps to delete one or more adjacent rows or columns:

1. Click a row number or column letter.
2. Choose Delete from the Data menu.
3. Choose Row or Column from the Delete menu.

The row or column will be deleted even if it contains data.

If you want you can try a few of these options on your own without risk. When you are finished, choose Close from the File menu and select No to discard the presentation without resaving it. Next, choose Open from the File menu and select STURDY to reopen the file. You will work with the STURDY file knowing that even if you accidentally lose data you have another file named STOCKS with your important information stored.

Moving an Entire Row or Column of Data

The first step in moving a row or column of data to a new location is selecting the row or column of data to be moved. You can click the row number or column letter in the Data Form to select the row or column. After the data is selected you can choose Cut from the Edit menu to remove the row or column of data and place it on the Clipboard. You can select the new location and then use Paste from the Edit menu to copy the data from the Clipboard to its new location.

Reordering the X-Axis Data Points

You can use the techniques just discussed in combination to change the presentation order of data points within a bar graph. You can move the data for the current data point forward or backward in the data point list. When the data point is moved in the list, the data from each series that corresponds to the data point is moved within the table (the program assumes you will be moving an entire row of data).

After looking at the graph in Figure 4-6 you might decide that the graph would be more visually appealing if you order the X data points from the highest to the lowest selling product. Although it may be difficult to differentiate between products where sales figures are close, you can still achieve the effect you are striving for if you position them by appearance.

Try these steps to order the graph so that the largest selling product displays first:

1. Move to the row containing Wagons, choose Insert from the Data menu, and then choose Row. A blank row is inserted at the top of the Data Form.

2. Select the row containing the Dolls data points by clicking the row number.
3. Choose Cut from the Edit menu.
    The X data point Dolls and the data associated with it disappear from the Data Form. The row formerly occupied by the Dolls data is now blank.
4. Click the row number for the blank row at the top of the form. Choose Paste from the Edit menu. The Dolls data points now take the place of the blank row.
5. Click row 4, the blank row, and then choose Delete from the Data menu.
6. Press (F2) to display the graph.
    As shown in Figure 4-7, the data points in the display have been reordered to display the data for dolls first.
7. Press (ESC) to return to the Data Form.
8. Press (CTRL)+(S) to save the presentation.

It was necessary to save the presentation again in order to save a copy of the presentation with the X data points in the new sequence. If you need the chart both the old way and the new way, you can save the presentation with a different name or select the first slide and copy it to another slide and then make the changes.

Changing the Order of the Series

Changing the order of the series in the chart uses the same procedure, except now you will be working with columns. You must add a new blank column and use this location to reposition a series.

Although you are more likely to need this type of change when you use products, divisions, or cities as a series, you can use it with the year entries to display them in reverse order, with 1995 shown first and 1992 shown last. To accomplish this change, follow these steps:

1. Select column B containing the 1992 data.

Chapter 4: *Learning XY Chart Basics with Bar Charts*

Figure 4-7. *Changing the order of the data points*

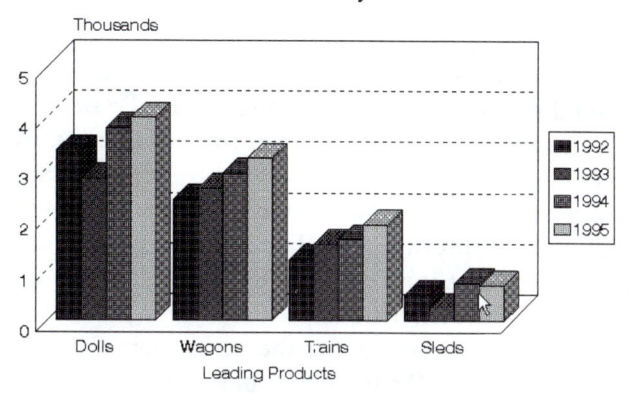

<img: Sturdy Toys Unit Sales Projections bar chart showing 1992-1995 data for Dolls, Wagons, Trains, Sleds>

2. Choose Insert from the Data menu and then choose Column.
   A new blank column is added and all the column letters for 1992 are adjusted up by one.
3. Select column F containing the 1995 data.
4. Choose Cut from the Edit menu.
5. Select column B and then choose Paste from the Edit menu.
6. Select column C and then choose Cut from the Edit menu. Select column F and then choose Paste from the Edit menu.
   This action places 1992 data at the end of the list and leaves two more columns to swap.
7. Select column E containing the 1994 data and then select Cut from the Edit menu. Select column C and then select Paste from the Edit menu.
8. Select column E and then select Delete from the Data menu.
9. Select OK and then press (F2) to look at the chart with the series shown in reverse order. Your chart will display 1995 through 1992.

10. Press ESC.
11. Press CTRL+S as a speed key approach to requesting a save.

Organizing a Series Differently

When you created the sales projection chart for 1992 to 1995, you organized the series by year. You can present the same data with a different slant if you organize it so that each product is a series, with the points along the X axis representing the years 1992 through 1995. Switching to a stacked bar display makes it easy to look at the total sales in a given year. It is important to decide before entering your data which organization structure you want to use, because there is no easy way to change the data from one structure to the other without reentering it.

If you use the products for the series names, you may want to use a different entry for the X data points, like a time period. You can choose from any of the options in Table 4-1 when you select your X data type. Selecting one of the new data types will also allow you to specify a starting entry, an ending entry, and an increment. Evenly spaced values can be generated automatically, thus saving you a significant amount of entry time. Table 4-1 shows some examples of acceptable entries for each of the optional fields and the series of X data values that Harvard Graphics would generate.

The data shown in Figure 4-8 is identical to the data entered in the earlier data form, except it is organized in series by product name. Follow these steps to enter the data for the new chart:

1. Select Add slide.
2. Select "Vertical bar." Select OK.
3. Select X-axis labels to display an X-Axis Labels dialog box similar to the one shown in Figure 4-9.

    The dialog box shown in Figure 4-9 already has a format of Year selected. This causes some of the text that might be faded on your screen to show in a darker color since it is an option for a Year format but not for the default format Names.

4. Select Year from the Format list box by clicking on it.

Table 4-1. Example Entries

X Data Type	Starting	Ending	Increment	Entries
Names	N/A	N/A	N/A	Boston...New York; Computers...Monitors
Numeric	10	100	10	10, 20, 30,...100
	0	5	.5	0, .5, 1, 1.5,...5
Day	MON	FRI	1	MON, TUE,...FRI
	Sunday	Friday	1	Sunday...Friday
Week	2	10	2	2, 4, 6, 8, 10
Month	June	December	1	June, July,...December
Quarter	First	Fourth	1	First, Second, Third, Fourth
Year	92	97	1	92, 93, 94, 95, 96, 97
	1992	1998	2	1992, 1994, 1996, 1998
Month/Day	Sept 1	Sept 29	7	Sept 1, Sept 8,...Sept 29
Month/Year	Jan 92	Jun 92	2	Jan 92, Mar 92, May 92
Year/Month	92 Jan	92 Mar	1	92 Jan, 92 Feb, 92 Mar
Month/Day/Year	1/1/92	2/28/92	7	1/1/92, 1/8/92,...2/26/92
Day/Month/Year	1/10/92	5/10/92	1	1/10/92, 2/10/92, 3/10/92, 4/10/92, 5/10/92
Year/Month/Day	1992 Jan 1	1992 Jan 3	1	1992 Jan 1, 1992 Jan 2, 1992 Jan 3
Quarter/Year	1/92	4/92	2	1/92, 3/92
Year/Quarter	92-Q1	92-Q4	1	92-Q1, 92-Q2, 92-Q3, 92-Q4
Time	9:00 AM	1:30 PM	90	9:00 AM, 10:30 AM, 12:00 AM, 1:30 PM
Time/Day	9 AM Mon	12 PM Wed	6	9 AM/Mon, 3PM/Mon, ...9 AM/Wed

Figure 4-8.　*Data organized by product*

Figure 4-9. 　*Selecting a format for X-Axis Labels*

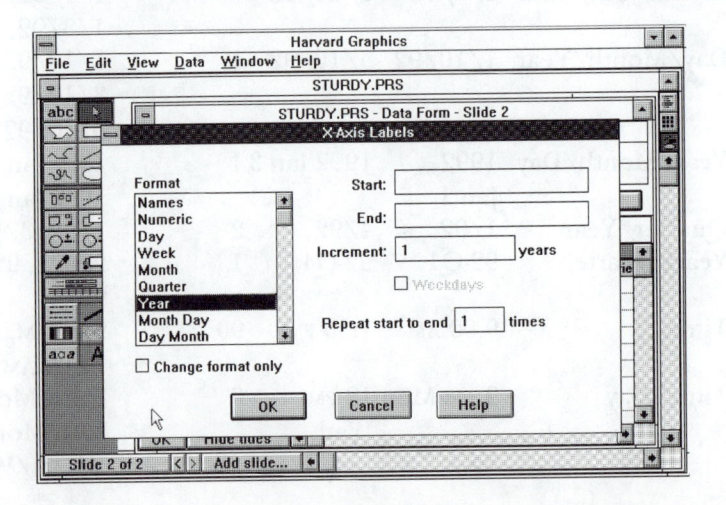

5. Type **1992** in the Start field and press (TAB).

    Harvard Graphics displays a default end year of 1996 to provide a five-year spread, but this is not what you want, so you will need to type an entry for the End field.

6. Type **1995** in the End field and press (TAB).
    The default increment is exactly what you need, 1.

7. Press (ENTER) to select OK with the Increment field set as 1.

    Note the years for the X data points have been entered for you. (Although these entries saved just a few keystrokes compared to entering each of the X data values directly on the Data Form, other X data types, like Day and Month, offer even greater time savings.)

8. Move to the Title field with (↑) and then type **Sturdy Toys** for the Title field and press (ENTER).

9. Type **Sales Projections** and press (ENTER).

10. Type **Management Projections** and press (CTRL)+(ENTER) to split the footnote into two lines. Type **Based on average industry growth** for line 2 of the footnote, and then move to the Legend for Series 1 box by pressing (TAB).

    You can use multiple lines for a footnote or subtitle, although you might need to reduce the text size and alter the placement of these entries later.

11. Enter the following legends, pressing (TAB) after each, except the last entry.

    Dolls
    Wagons
    Trains
    Sleds

    It would be possible to enter a legend and then enter the data values for that column—or to enter all the legends and then all of the data. The advantage of entering X-axis labels and legends first is that it provides a framework for data entry, although it does require a few extra keystrokes.

12. Press (SHIFT)+(TAB) three times (to move three cells to the left) and then press (↓).

13. Enter the following data as the entries for Series 1 for doll sales, pressing (ENTER) after each to move to the next row in the column.

    3500
    2800
    3800
    4000

14. Press (CTRL)+(HOME) and then press (TAB) twice to move to the column for Wagons. Press (↓).

15. Complete the following entries, pressing (ENTER) after each:

    2395
    2600
    2900
    3200

16. Press (CTRL)+(HOME), press (TAB) three times, and then press (↓) to move to the column for Trains.

17. Complete the following entries, pressing (ENTER) after each:

    1200
    1500
    1600
    1900

18. Press (CTRL)+(HOME), press (TAB) four times, and then press (↓) to move to the column for Sleds.

19. Type the following, pressing (ENTER) after each entry but the last:

    500
    250
    750
    700

20. Select OK and then select the Footnote text and drag the text down slightly.

Chapter 4: *Learning XY Chart Basics with Bar Charts* 113

21. Select Size from the Text menu and select a text size of 12 for the footnote text.
22. Press F2 to display the graphshown in Figure 4-10.
23. Press ESC.
24. Press CTRL+S to save the presentation with the new slide.

Printing Your Charts

Although data charts make an even more impressive display on the screen than do text charts, there are times when you want to print them and incorporate them into reports and other printed material. You can then use some of the features covered in Chapter 3 to enhance your text entries on the chart; for instance, using a different font or style. There are several options you can use to change the way the current presentation is printed. These options are selected after choosing the Setup command from the File menu.

Figure 4-10.   *Chart based on new data entered*

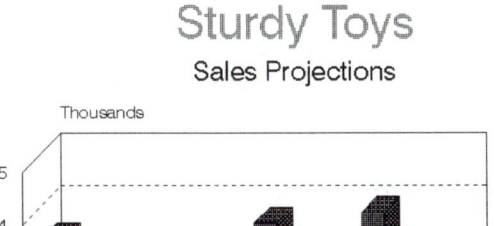

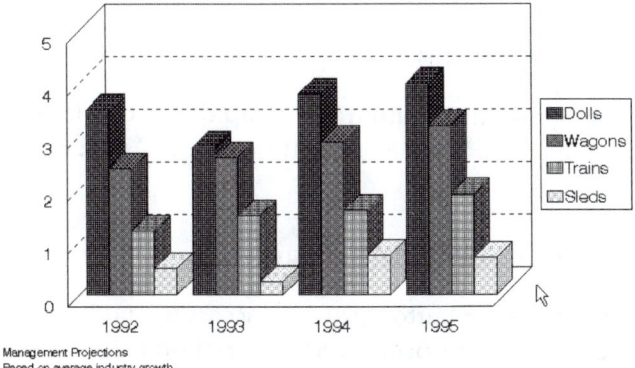

If you save the presentation after making these changes, they will affect future printouts for this presentation. You can make some of these same changes using the Print option from the File menu, but your changes only affect the current print job. Let's look at a few of the Setup options to expand your print capabilities.

Output Options

When you choose Setup from the File menu, the dialog box shown in Figure 4-11 displays. There are four output options that also appear on the Print dialog box. The difference is that when selected here, they can be saved with the presentation and kept in future printouts. The options and their effects are as follows:

Print background fill	This option allows you to change the default to eliminating background fill.
Print text black	This option is checked as a default since it allows you to read even text in light colors after printing.
Reverse black & white	This option prints white as black and black as white when selected.
Convert fills	When selected this option eliminates fill patterns, converting them to white. It is useful for draft printing.

Changing Margins

The margin settings within the Setup dialog box let you specify settings for all four margins. The default settings are 1/2 inch on all four sides.

Setting Up Your Print Device

The Setup device button provides access to another whole dialog box of options specific to your print device. To elaborate, the scaling factor used by

Chapter 4: *Learning XY Chart Basics with Bar Charts* 115

Figure 4-11. *The dialog box for File Setup*

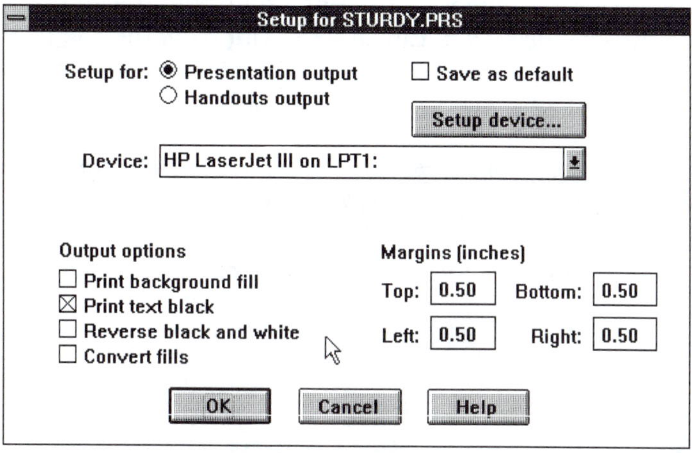

Harvard Graphics for the Y axis affects the appearance of the entries in this table. You might need to change the scaling options if you want your actual values to display as entered. You can specify the amount of memory, cartridge selections, and the paper feed. Some of the specific selections for the Hewlett-Packard Lasers III, for example, and their options are as follows:

Paper Source	Upper tray, Manual, or Envelope
Orientation	Portrait or Landscape
Memory	The amount of printer's memory in MB
Cartridge	Up to 2 cartridges selected from many popular Hewlett-Packard cartridges
Graphics Resolution	75, 150, 300 dots per inch

The options available for your printer may vary somewhat based on its features. You can always check your printer manual if you are uncertain of the meaning of specific options.

Printing Your Data Charts

After customizing your presentation printout with the Setup command from the File menu, you can choose Print from the File menu to print your data. The actual print operation for data charts follows the same procedure that you learned for text charts in Chapter 3.

Tip: The bright colors of the default palette may look surprisingly different if your output device only supports black and white. You might want to change your presentation to a monochrome palette before previewing your final print. You can use the Slide menu's Color palette "Apply" command to make this change.

Different Types of Bar Graphs

Harvard Graphics allows you to define the type of bar graph that you want in several ways. Your first choice comes when you first request a chart. You can select from a vertical or horizontal orientation for your bars. Once you enter your data you can choose Chart options from the Chart menu to display the Chart Options dialog box shown in Figure 4-12 and select which of seven different chart styles you like the best. You can also define other selections that customize the appearance of the bars in your chart from this dialog box. The combination of styles and other enhancement selections provides a wide range of options that allow you to create graphs with enough visual variation to maintain your audience's interest. Experiment with your entries to create the most attractive graphs possible.

Bar Chart Styles

The seven bar chart styles offered by the Chart Options dialog box are cluster, overlap, stack, linked stack, 100%, linked 100%, and paired. Table 4-2 presents each chart type along with a description, and Figure 4-13 presents this information visually.

Chapter 4: *Learning XY Chart Basics with Bar Charts* 117

Figure 4-12.   *Dialog box for Chart Options*

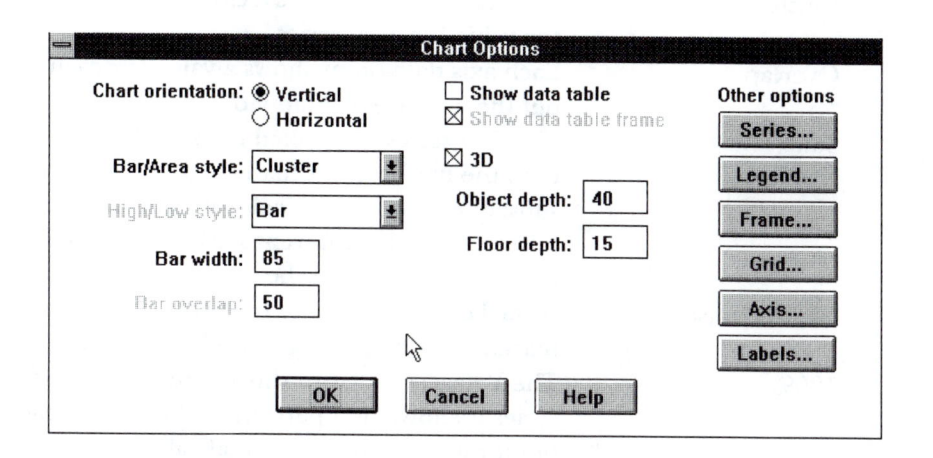

Figure 4-13.   *The different chart options*

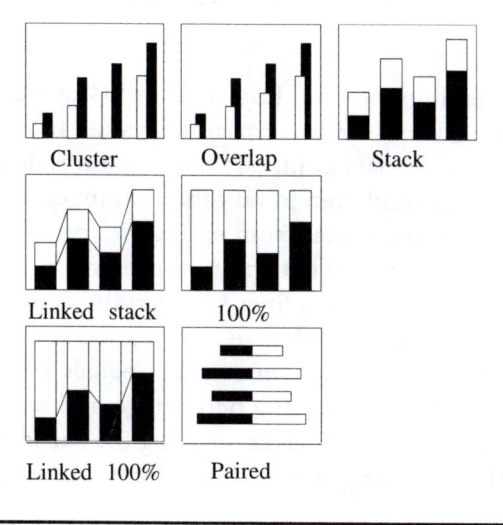

Table 4-2.   *Bar Styles*

Cluster	Each X-axis point shows a cluster of bars showing the value for each series.
Overlap	Each axis data point shows a value for each series but the bars are overlapped.
Stack	The first series is graphed for each X-axis point and then the bar height is made higher for each subsequent series with color or shading used to differentiate the different series. The total height of the bar represents the total for all series.
Linked stack	A stacked bar with lines between the data points marking the beginning of each new series.
100%	The Y axis is scaled to show percentages and each series is shown as a percent of the total at each data point rather than as an actual value.
Linked 100%	A linked bar style with lines from the data points on the bars.
Paired	A bar chart that uses two Y axes to show different data scales on the same chart.

The default graph style for a Harvard Graphics bar chart is a *cluster bar* chart, which groups the corresponding values from each series around each of the appropriate data points. The *overlap bar* style allows you to overlap the bars in the series and even to vary the amount of overlap that is used. A *stack bar* chart places the values from each series on top of each other. The total height of the bar at each data point represents the total of all values for that series. A *linked stack* shows lines between the data points in the same series, helping you monitor the change within a series. A *100%* bar style draws the bars so that the total height of each bar equals 100%, and the bar is divided so that each value represents a percentage of that total. A *linked 100%* chart is a 100% bar chart with lines connecting the bar sections, allowing you to see the variation between X-axis data points. A *paired bar* style is the most sophisticated bar option. It allows you to display data on a chart with two different sets of values for the Y axis. For example, you might show two different types of related data for branch offices. You can show sales data by office on the right and headcount numbers on the left. The sales data shown at the right can be measured on the Y2 axis, and the headcount numbers can be shown on the left on the Y1 axis.

Part of your decision process in selecting a style depends on the comparisons that you wish to make between different data values shown on the chart. When you want to make comparisons between the values in several series, a cluster or overlap style facilitates examining the relative height of each bar at a data point. On the other hand, if you are trying to determine the relative importance of the value of each series in comparison to the whole, a stack or 100% style would show this better.

Later you will get to try a few variations of bar styles, using the Sturdy Toys data. For now we want to examine a few of the other chart options that can affect the appearance of your chart.

Other Bar Chart Options

You can choose any number between 1 and 100 for the width of the bars in your chart. The narrowest bars possible have a width of 1 and a significant amount of space between adjacent bars. A bar width of 100 is the maximum allowed and creates adjacent bars that touch, allowing you to create a step bar (similar to a histogram) that shows each value as a bar with no spacing between the bars. The default setting is 85.

If you select Overlap for the bar style you can set bar overlap as any number from 1 to 100 with higher numbers providing the most overlap. The default setting is 50. This setting is only effective for 2-dimensional overlapped bars.

The default setting for horizontal and vertical bars is 3-dimensional. This means that the 3D option button is checked. If you have numerous data series, you might want to select 3D (remove the X) and show your bars as 2-dimensional.

The next few sections will allow you to try some different options for bar charts. You will need to enter new data to look at step bars and paired bars.

Creating an Overlap Bar Chart

Changing a bar chart to an overlap style is easy and can, along with the cluster bar chart, lend variety to your charts. Follow these steps to make the change to the Sturdy Toys chart that is still on your screen:

1. Choose Chart options from the Chart menu.
2. Select the arrow next to the Bar/Area style to activate the drop-down list box and then select Overlap.
3. Click on the 3D option to remove the X and show the chart as 2D.
4. Select OK and then press (F2) to view the graph, which is shown in Figure 4-14. Then press (ESC) to return to the Slide Editor.

The default for the amount of overlap on the bars is 50%. If you want to alter the amount of Overlap, you would need to choose Chart options from the Chart menu again and then type a different number for the bar overlap field, increasing or decreasing the overlap percentage. Just as before, you finalize your chart options selections by clicking OK.

Figure 4-14. Overlap bar chart

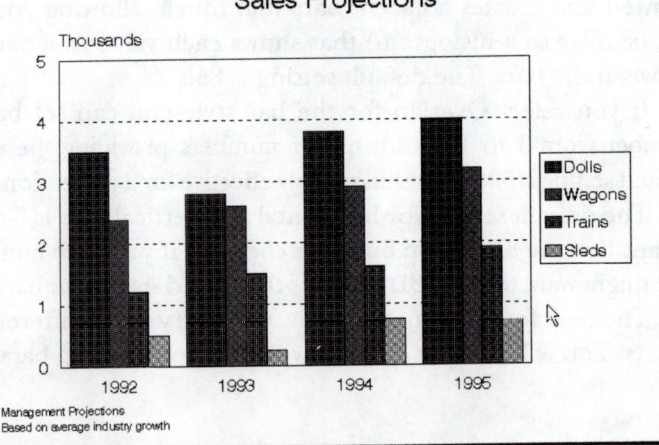

Creating a Stacked Bar Chart

A stacked bar style is effective when you want to know the total for all the series at each X data point. Each series represents total sales for a product. You can determine the total sales for all products by the total height of the stacked bar, because it is built by entering the value of each series one atop the other. This chart type is also effective for graphing data in several series that represent the headcount for several company divisions. The total height of the stacked bar represents the total company headcount.

To change the graph style to stacked bar, follow these steps:

1. Choose Chart options from the Chart menu.
2. Click the arrow next to Bar/Area style to activate the drop-down list box and then select Stack.
3. Select OK and then press (F2). Your chart will look like Figure 4-15.

Figure 4-15.   Stack bar chart

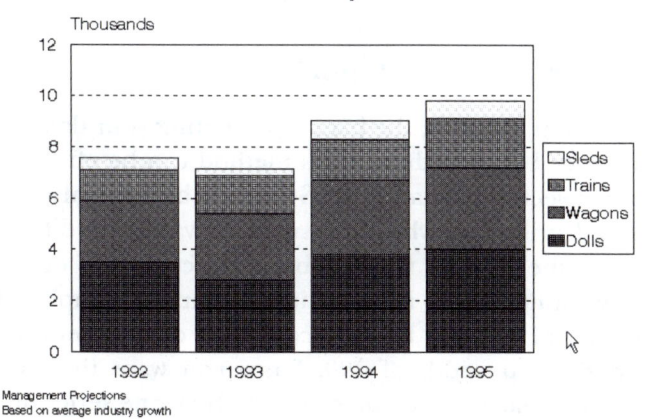

If you are working with a color monitor, you will see a bar for each X data point, with each component from the various series shown in a different color. If your display is monochrome, each component will display in a different pattern.

Creating a 100% Bar Chart

Although the stack graph shows the actual amount that each series contributes to the whole, it takes some calculations to even estimate the percentage contribution for each entry. If you would like to see the percentage contribution of each element, you can use a 100% bar style. The total height of the bar is considered to be 100%, and the amount of each series is measured with the Y scale serving as a percentage indicator.

To look at the Sturdy Toy data with a 100% bar style, follow these steps:

1. Choose Chart options form the Chart menu.
2. Click the arrow next to Bar/Area style to activate the drop-down list box and then select 100%.
3. Select OK and then press (F2). Your chart will look like Figure 4-16.

This chart provides an opportunity for you to see that the doll sales account for almost 50% of the total annual sales.

Creating a Step Bar Chart

With a step bar style, the bars representing your data values are created with no space between them. This method can be effective to show major changes between the data values. Step style bars can also be used to show a frequency distribution, which measures the values for different observations and groups the data by the number of occurrences of the same value (a frequency count). There is no option in Harvard Graphics for Windows to select a style of step bar but you can easily create them with a bar style of cluster and a bar width of 100. Since you want the bars to be directly comparable to each other, you can only show one series on the chart if you want it to look like a histogram.

Chapter 4: *Learning XY Chart Basics with Bar Charts*

Figure 4-16.   *100% bar chart*

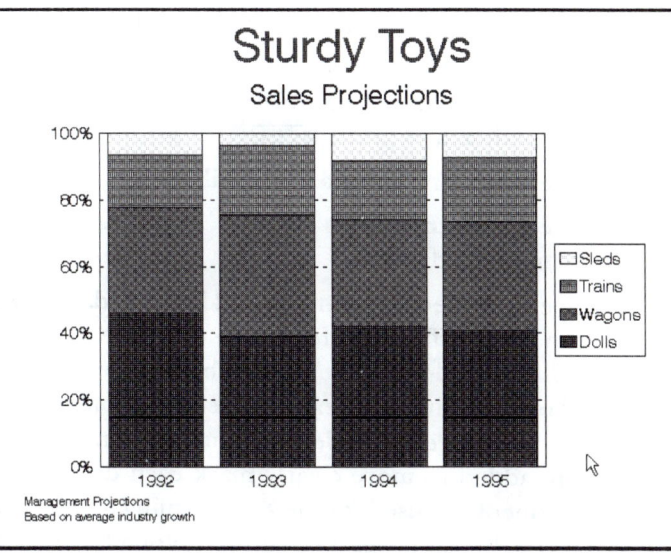

[Bar chart titled "Sturdy Toys — Sales Projections" showing 100% stacked bars for 1992, 1993, 1994, 1995 with categories Sleds, Trains, Wagons, Dolls. Footnote: "Management Projections / Based on average industry growth"]

If you want to show the variation in occurrences of production line failures in a given month, you can enter a series of values representing the failure rate each day. The one series shown will contain all the values for June, with a data point registered for each date. If you want to create a frequency distribution, you must organize the data differently. Each X data value must represent an observation or interval, like one to three failures. The number of days with one to three failures is measured along the Y axis, and the height of the bars shows the relative frequency of each interval on the X axis.

To create a chart to record the production failure that occurs on each date, follow these steps:

1. Select <u>A</u>dd slide.
2. Select "Vertical bar." Select OK.
3. Select X-Axis Labels, and then Month/Day from the Format list box.
4. Type **6/1** in the Start field and then press (TAB).
5. Type **6/30** in the End field and press (TAB).

6. Type **1** in the Increment field and then select OK.

   The Data Form is now on your screen with all of the X-axis labels completed for each day in June.

7. Press (↑) four times to move to the Title field, type **Refrigerator Production**, and press (ENTER).

8. Type **Mean Production Line Failures** and press (ENTER).

9. Type **Head foreman's records** and press (TAB) to complete the Footnote field.

10. Type a number between 1 and 12 for each date, pressing (ENTER) after each entry. (If you prefer to use the same numbers used in Figure 4-17, you can look at the bar heights to determine the actual entries.)

    To create the chart exactly as shown, some additional customization is required. The legend must be removed. Major tick marks were added to more clearly mark each date on the X axis and an increment was used for the X-axis scaling to prevent displaying every X-axis label and overlapping dates along the X axis.

11. Select OK and then choose Legend from the Chart menu. Then select "Show legend" to remove the X and prevent the legend display. Select OK.

12. Choose Axis from the Chart menu, click the arrow next to "X-Axis Major tick marks," and then select Out to add markers along the X axis for each date.

13. Click the Scaling button for the X axis to display a Scaling Options dialog box.

14. Select the Increment field, type **3**, and then select OK to return to the Axis Options dialog box.

    This changes the interval on the X axis to prevent crowding of the entries. If you do not make this change, the entries will overlay each other and the result will be a garbled appearance for the X-axis data point entries.

15. Select OK and then press (F2).

    Although your exact entries will determine the appearance of the chart, it will appear similar to the chart shown in Figure 4-17.

16. Press (ESC) to display the Slide Editor screen.

17. Press (CTRL)+(S) to save the presentation with the new slide.

Figure 4-17.   *Step bar chart*

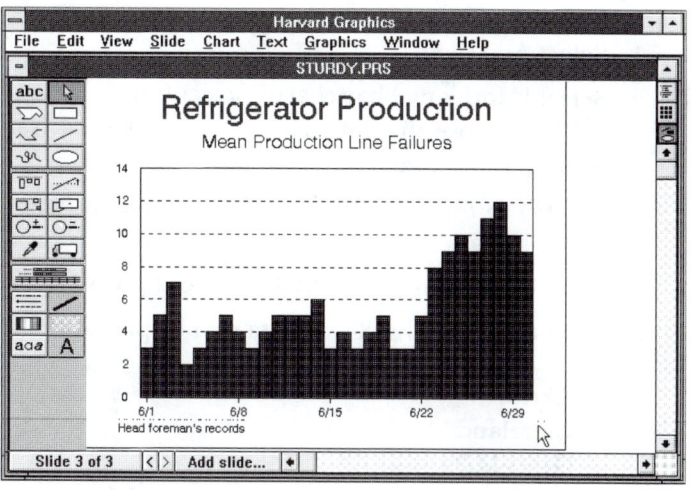

Creating a Paired Chart

A paired bar chart is actually two charts in one. You can use two different Y axes, allowing the combination of information that would not otherwise be possible due to different units of measure such as dollars and unit sales. It is also ideal for series with the same units of measure but disparate values. For example, the number of sales and headcount can both be measured in units, but the number of units for sales might be measured in thousands and the headcount for each branch might not exceed ten. If you were to try to show both quantities on the same chart, the Y-axis scaling would prevent the appearance of the headcount entries due to their small magnitude in comparison to sales. If two different Y axes are shown on the chart, both sets of data are visible.

There is no difference in data entry for a paired style chart and the other charts that you created. You will want to select a Horizontal bar chart, enter your data, and then assign the second series to the Y2 axis and change the Bar style to Paired.

For a step-by-step look at entering new data ideally suited for a paired style bar chart, follow these steps:

1. Select Add slide.
2. Select "Horizontal bar chart." Select OK.
   You will use the default X-axis data type of Names and will not need to select X-axis labels.
3. Use ↑ to move to the Title field and then type **Quick Sales** and press (ENTER).
4. Type **Headcount/Sales by Office** and press (ENTER) three times.
5. Type the following X-axis data points, pressing (ENTER) after each:

   Akron
   Cleveland
   Gates Mills
   Parma
   Zoar

6. Press (CTRL)+(HOME) followed by (TAB) to position on Series 1.
7. Type **Headcount** for the Series 1 legend and press (ENTER).
8. Type the following headcount entries for each city, pressing (ENTER) after each:

   Akron   10
   Cleveland   20
   Gates Mills   3
   Parma   5
   Zoar   12

9. Press (CTRL)+(HOME) followed by (TAB) twice to position on Series 2.
10. Type **Sales** for the Series 2 legend and press (ENTER).
11. Type the following sales figures for Series 2, pressing (ENTER) after each:

    550950
    925800
    625000

Chapter 4: *Learning XY Chart Basics with Bar Charts*

    300000

    212500

12. Select OK and then press (F2) to preview the chart as it will print. The headcount data is not readable since it is so small in comparison to the sales data. Obviously, some changes are needed for this chart.
13. Press (ESC) to return to the Slide Editor screen.
14. Choose Series form the Chart menu and then select Sales from the Edit list box.
15. Click Y2 (to add a second Y axis) for the Y axis and then select OK.
16. Choose Chart options from the Chart menu and then select Bar/Area style of Paired.
17. Remove the X from the 3D box if it is selected by clicking on it again and then select OK.
18. Press (F2) to view the chart again. Your chart will look like Figure 4-18.
19. Press (ESC) and then press (CTRL)+(S) to save the presentation along with the new chart.

Tip: *If the Y2-axis labels seem a bit crowded you can always choose Axis from the Chart menu and then select Y2 scaling and enter an increment of 400000 to reduce the labels on this axis.*

Other Bar Chart Enhancements

Now that you have seen some bar chart style options, you should take a look at some of the other enhancements you can make. There are four different options for filling the chart bars. In addition you can change the chart frame, gridlines, add a data table to the chart, change 3D options, and change the chart text.

Tip: *You can access all chart changes, such as Axis, Series, Legend, and so on, by choosing each item individually from the Chart menu; however, if you want to change several of these items at once, go directly to the Chart Options dialog box and click these items' buttons at the right side of the screen.*

Figure 4-18. *Paired bar chart*

Changing Fill Options

You can choose the fill color for a series by choosing <u>S</u>eries from the <u>C</u>hart menu and then selecting a new fill color swatch. You can also use more sophisticated fill options in the Graphics menu that allow you to select a hatchmark pattern or a bitmap image for a chart. You can use the Toolbox on the Slide Editor screen or your Graphics menu to make these changes. In all cases you must select the series whose bars you want to change first.

The Fill tool icon looks like this:

This initial icon represents solid fill colors but when you hold the mouse down while pointing to it, you will see three new icons to the right that offer hatch patterns, a gradient (or progression) from one color to another, and a bitmap picture fill. The choices Solid, Hatch, Gradient, and Bitmap appear when you choose Fill from the Graphics menu.

Solid Fill Colors

In Harvard Graphics, colors can be assigned to objects. These include the text on your chart as well as bar fill and outline colors. Darker colors can focus attention on a specific series in a graph. The combination of colors can also lend balance to a graph. Using a dark color for the data series with the lowest values and lighter colors for those with larger values can help to achieve this balance. Naturally, you can change the colors for aesthetic reasons or to use the same colors used in your company logo. You can change the values separately for each of the 16 series possible.

As a first step you will want to select the series that you want to affect. Then select the first Fill tool or choose Fill from the Graphics menu and then choose Solid. The Solid color dialog box shown in Figure 4-19 appears. Choose whether you want to change the Outline, Fill, or Text of an object. You can click a color in the palette or choose None if you are trying to create a transparent object.

Figure 4-19.   *Solid Color dialog box for filling*

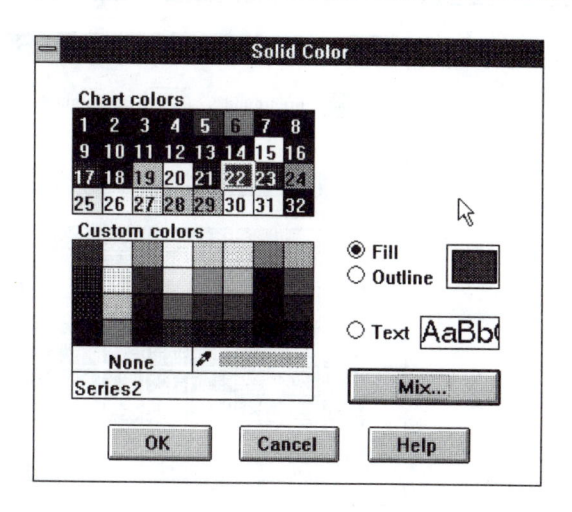

Hatch/Pattern Fill

Harvard Graphics for Windows supplies eight hatch patterns that can be used to distinguish series in a chart. Hatch patterns are lines that slant in different directions and work well when you are using a plotter to create your output. Pattern fills are available though the same dialog box and since these are actually bitmap pictures, more variation is possible with 56 options. These work fine onscreen and for graphic printers, but are not a good solution for a plotter. Figure 4-20 shows the Hatch/Pattern Fill dialog box that displays when you choose the second fill tool or choose Fill from the Graphics menu and then choose Hatch/Pattern. You can select colors for the foreground (patterns or hatches) or the background (colors behind the patterns or hatches) by clicking the appropriate box and then selecting a color before choosing the desired hatch or pattern fill. When you are finished you can choose OK to apply your selection to the selected series.

Gradient Fill

Gradient fills progress from one color to another gradually. Gradient fills will be used for the series you select and, in addition, will become the default

Figure 4-20. *Hatch/Pattern dialog box for filling*

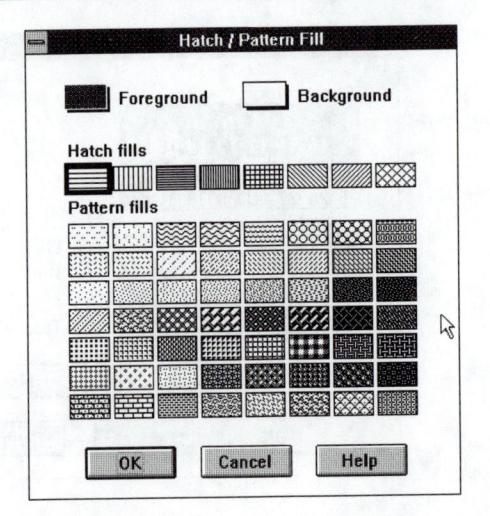

Chapter 4: Learning XY Chart Basics with Bar Charts

for any new presentations you create, unless you change it. You can select the third fill tool that will appear on your screen or choose Fill from the Graphics menu and then choose Gradient to display the dialog box shown in Figure 4-21.

In addition to selecting a start and end color, you can choose the angle at which the change will occur. Drag the needle on the wheel to 45 for diagonal shading, 90 for horizontal stripes, and 0 for vertical stripes.

Bitmap Fill

Bitmaps are pictures stored on the Windows Clipboard or in special file formats on disk. Harvard Graphics supports .PCX, .TIFF, .PCC, and .BMP bitmap files. The use of bitmaps is a more advanced feature since this involves the use of pictures stored in special files (and it is possible that you do not have any bitmap files on your disk nor the ability to create any). Bitmaps provide a unique look to bar charts when the bars are filled with images of what the chart represents.

Figure 4-22 shows the dialog box that displays when you select the fourth fill tool or choose Fill from the Graphics menu and then choose Bitmap. The

Figure 4-21.   *Gradient Options dialog box for filling*

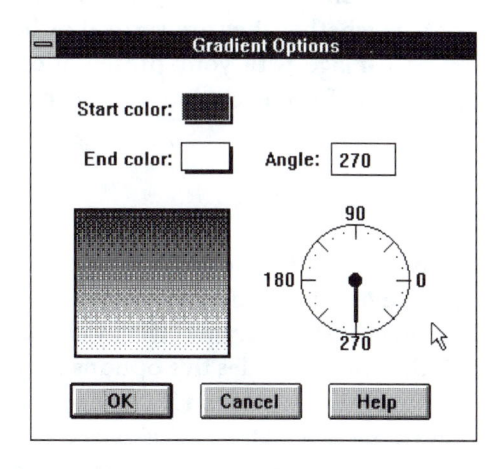

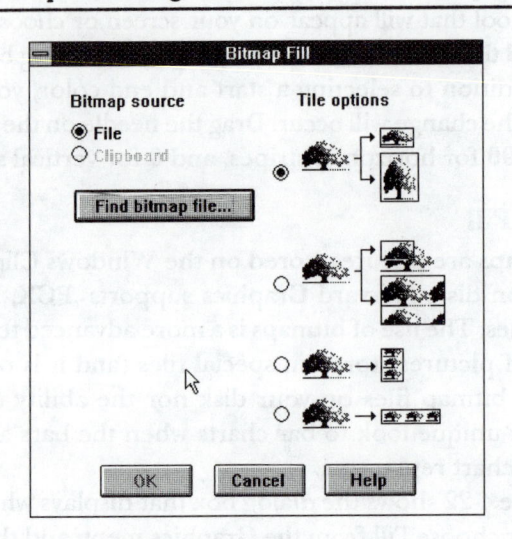

Figure 4-22.   Bitmap Fill dialog box

dialog box allows you to select any bitmap file on your disk although it initially looks in the directory where Harvard Graphics stores your presentation. There are several options in the dialog box for altering the bitmap image to fit the shape of bars whether they are vertical or horizontal. You can choose to save the bitmap image with your presentation or save space and have Harvard Graphics look for it each time you need it.

Changing the Chart Frame

The line drawn around the chart area where Harvard Graphics graphs the chart data is the *frame*. The default frame style is a full frame around the bar graph. You can change the frame style by choosing Frame from the Chart menu. Harvard Graphics provides five options for frame style: Full, XY, X, Y, and None. The Full option provides a frame line on all sides, and None creates a graph with no frame line. When XY is selected, the frame line is shown at the left and bottom of the graph. A selection of X or Y shows the graph with only a line at the bottom or the left side.

Complete these steps to change the frame style for slide 1 to XY:

1. Use the Arrow buttons at the bottom of the screen to move back to slide 1.
2. Choose Frame from the Chart menu and then click the arrow next to Frame Style to view the drop-down list box options.
3. Select XY and then select OK.
   You will notice other options in the dialog box that allow you to select a frame fill color or a frame outline color. The goal options in this box are discussed in Chapter 5, "Additional XY Data Chart Options."
4. Press (F2) to view the change and then press (ESC).

Changing Gridlines

You can choose to show gridlines or eliminate them. You can make your decision separately for each of the axes. If you decide you want to use them, you can even choose the style of line used to make the grid lines. To make a change to gridlines, choose Grid from the Chart menu. Check the boxes for the lines that you want to show and, if you like, use the drop-down Style list boxes for grids to select a line style and then choose OK. You can access this same feature from the Chart Options dialog box if you click the Grid button on the right side of the dialog box.

Changing 3D Options

In the remaining chapters on graphs, you will be introduced to more graph options that can add variety to your presentation. There is one more group of settings that is important to include here since this only affects 3D bar charts.

The 3D Object Depth and 3D Floor depth fields do not need to be altered unless you are unhappy with the output. These options are located on the Chart options dialog box accessed by choosing Chart options from the Chart menu. You can easily make a change to any of them.

Object depth for bar charts relates to the thickness as opposed to the width of bars. To change the actual depth of bars, you will type a new number in the Object depth box. You can use any number from 1 to 100 with larger numbers creating bars with greater depth perception. It is used in combination with Floor depth to give the appearance of deeper bars. The same depth object will appear deeper if you also increase the floor depth.

Floor depth is the depth from front to back of the floor on which the bars sit. You can choose any value from 1 to 100 with higher numbers creating a deeper floor on which the bars sit.

Changing Text

With Harvard Graphics you can create graphs without worrying about the text size or style. Although these characteristics of the text are determined by font selection, you can use the default settings until you want to make a change. Harvard Graphics follows the same rules for data charts that you saw with text charts in the last chapter. By default, Harvard Graphics uses a font called Swiss 721, and selects appropriate sizes for the various titles and other text entries on a graph. If you do not have a problem with the appearance of your graph, you can print it without change. On the other hand there are many options that can improve the appearance of your graphs.

The character style used is determined by two different factors. One is the default font selected. The other determining factor is the size of the text. You looked at several options for text charts as you selected text and chose a Geo Slab font in the last chapter, rather than the default. You also altered the point sizes of some of your text entries. Although your entire chart is no longer just text, there are a number of text entries (such as the title, subtitle, and footnote) that you can change if you want a customized chart appearance.

Changing the Default Font

Remember, just as with text charts, you can alter a font for the entire presentation or select a specific text object and change it. To alter the presentation font, you need to choose Change presentation fo<u>n</u>t from the <u>S</u>lide menu and then select a new font. To change the font for a specific text object, select it and then choose <u>F</u>ont from the <u>T</u>ext menu and pick another font.

Changing the Size of Entries

You may want to change the point size of titles or footnotes to achieve a more pleasing chart appearance. Or you may find that your chart looks crowded if you use the standard sizes for exceptionally long title entries. You may also want to reduce the size of X data names if they appear too close to the legend entries. Although you can change the location of legends, there is no option for altering their size.

As a brief reminder of changing the size of designated text, all you need to do is select the text and then choose Size from the Text menu. If you need something a little different than the seven sizes offered, choose All Attributes from the Text menu and then type any size you want from 4 to 512 points.

Changing the Location of Entries

You can reposition text entries. Some, such as legends, can be relocated just by choosing Legends from the Chart menu and clicking a new location. Others can be moved by aligning them differently. Of course you can also still select text as you did with text charts and drag the text to a new location.

Adding a Data Table

Although most of the time you want to replace numeric entries with a graph to convey your message, there are situations where you might want to provide the details for reference along with a chart. Harvard Graphics can add a table of the data values shown on the Data Form. Harvard Graphics places the data values beneath the chart in rows and columns.

You can show all the data series in the data table or just for a selected series. The default is to show all series (since each is set to display), but the data table option for the chart is initially turned off. If you set the data table option on, all series will display in the chart. You can then eliminate the ones that you do not want by choosing Series from the Chart menu, selecting the desired series, and indicating that you do not want the series included in any data table created. You will want to try out these features for the chart in slide 2 to see how they work.

1. Select slide 2.

2. Choose Chart options from the Chart menu.
3. Select "Show data table" (make sure the option box contains an X).

    This selection determines that a data table will be placed on the chart. The Series dialog box allows you to show series in the data table selectively.

4. Select the Series button to display the Series option box.

    You can select specific series in this box and then choose the option "Show series in data table" to change the default X, which marks each series for inclusion automatically.

5. Select OK to leave the Series dialog box and then select OK to complete the Chart Options box.

    The chart displays on the Slide Editor screen with the table at the bottom as shown in Figure 4-23.

You can always change the size of the data table text or move it slightly. You can also choose Labels from the Chart menu and then select Y1 axis format options such as currency, thousands separator, and scientific notation.

Figure 4-23. Data Table added to a chart

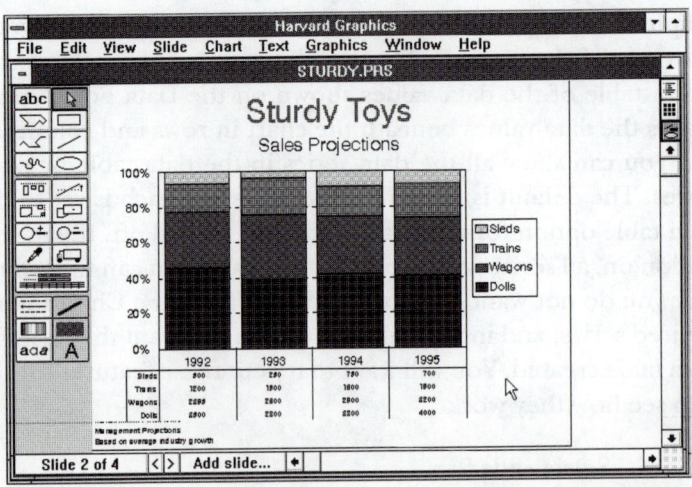

Chapter 4: *Learning XY Chart Basics with Bar Charts* 137

You can also use this dialog box to enter leading or trailing text with the entries to better label them if you have room in the table cells.

Checking Your Spelling

All of your hard work in selecting the most attractive graphics options are lost on your audience if the title and legends in your graphs contain spelling errors. These mistakes distract from the message your graph is supposed to convey and focus attention on the defective entries.

Use the techniques you learned in Chapter 3 to ensure error-free data charts. Remember all you need to do is choose Chec<u>k</u> spelling from the <u>E</u>dit menu to start spell checking.

5

Additional XY Data Chart Options

Now that you have mastered bar charts, you are ready to explore some of the other chart types that Harvard Graphics supports. This chapter covers additional XY chart types: line, area, and high/low/close, that can provide important variety to your presentation and maintain the interest of your audience. These chart types share many features with bar charts. You should, therefore, feel comfortable with creating and modifying these new chart types.

Line charts display each series of data as points and connect each point in a series with a line. You can use line charts to show trends, and lines are a much better choice than bar charts when you have a large volume of data. Using bars with many data values would create a very crowded chart, but a line chart of the same data creates an attractive chart that is easy to understand. There are several variations on line charts: a trend line, a curve line, or a *scatter chart*, which is a line comprised of unconnected markers for each point.

Area charts are like line charts, but with the area beneath the line filled with a solid color or a pattern. Area charts provide an effective way to show trends and volumes. They can also be combined with a line chart for a second data series. In a combination chart, revenues might be shown on the area chart and costs shown on a line chart imposed on top of the area chart.

High/low/close charts are used to display financial data, like stocks or bond prices, as well as error bars or other statistical data. These charts usually show the price range of a financial commodity along with the opening or closing prices.

Harvard Graphics supports formulas that you can use to compute values on the Data Form rather than entering each value. This feature is useful in making projections, forecasts, or other calculations where you want to estimate chart values.

Getting Started

Figure 5-1 shows a line chart that you can create with a few menu selections and then convert to an area chart once you enter the data. Follow these steps to enter the data and display the chart.

1. Choose Close from the File menu and decide whether any unsaved presentation files should be updated.
2. Choose New presentation from the File menu.
3. Select Line and click OK.
   The Data Form will appear, and you can immediately begin entering data since the default X-axis type of Name is acceptable.
4. Use (↑) to move to the Title field, type **Mel's Paperbacks** as the title, and press (ENTER) until the cursor is at the entry for the X-axis data point names.
5. Type **East** and press (ENTER).
6. Type **North** and press (ENTER).
7. Type **West** and press (ENTER).
8. Type **South** and press (ENTER).
9. Type **Central** and press (ENTER).
10. Press (CTRL)+(HOME) to move back to the top of X-axis labels column.

Chapter 5: *Additional XY Data Chart Options* 141

Figure 5-1. *Line chart to get you started*

Mel's Paperbacks

11. Press TAB to move to the first series, type **Books** for the legend, and press ENTER.
12. Type **60000** and press ENTER.
13. Type **70000** and press ENTER
14. Type **25000** and press ENTER.
15. Type **50000** and press ENTER.
16. Type **40000** and press ENTER.
17. Press CTRL+HOME to move to the top of the X-axis labels.
18. Press TAB twice to move to the second series, type **Records**, and press ENTER.
19. Type **45000** and press ENTER.
20. Type **40000** and press ENTER.
21. Type **90000** and press ENTER.
22. Type **65000** and press ENTER.
23. Type **80000** and press ENTER.

24. Select OK and then choose A*x*is from the *C*hart menu.
25. Move to the X-axis title field and type **Store Locations**.
26. Move the insertion point to the Y1-axis title field, type **Sales**, and then select OK.
27. Choose *L*egend from the *C*hart menu.
28. Click the text box for Legend Title and then type **Products:**, select the dot for Location that will place the legend at the middle far right and then select OK.
29. Press (F2) to create a chart like Figure 5-1.
    Harvard Graphics shows the lines in different colors or shades but does not use markers to indicate the individual data points as did the DOS releases of the product. You will learn how to add markers in the next section.
30. Press (ESC) to return to the Main Menu.
31. Choose Save *a*s from the *F*ile menu and then type **LINES** and press (ENTER).
32. Choose *P*rint from the *F*ile menu, change the print options if necessary, and then select OK to begin printing.

More Options for XY Charts

You may feel that you have seen all the possibilities for altering charts with the XY chart selections you have used, but there are more. Most of the chart options covered for bar charts in Chapter 4 also apply to line charts. Several options not discussed in Chapter 4 are covered in this chapter. These options allow you to hide series, add markers, draw lines that describe the trend of your data, label the data points, adjust the legend, create grid lines, set how the axes labels appear, change the axes settings—and change the line color, marker, and line style Harvard Graphics uses to display the data.

Entering the Data to Look at New Display Options

While a line chart can be created by simply selecting Add slide and selecting Line, Harvard Graphics has other options that you can use instead of Line. You will make many of these changes through the Series option in the Chart menu. From the dialog box that is presented you will be able to add markers for any of the series, change options that determine how to display a series, and what type of line-fitting technique to use. You can display any series as bars, lines, area, or points. Other options for this item allow you to choose the high, low, open, or close indications normally used to represent stock data. Line-fitting options provide different line types such as Trend, Exponential, Log Regression, and Average. To appreciate the difference between the options, you should enter the data for a new chart that tracks sales for six months. A chart like this might be used to evaluate employee performance or to determine the best months to increase advertising to promote sales.

To create this new line chart, follow these steps:

1. Select Add Slide, Line, and then OK.
2. Select X-axis labels and then Month for the X-axis label type.
3. Type **January** for the Start field, press (TAB), type **June** for the End field, and then select OK. Harvard Graphics generates the appropriate months as X-axis labels.
4. Move to the Title field, type **Mel's Paperbacks** for the chart title and press (ENTER).
5. Type **Sales Performance** for the subtitle and press (ENTER).
6. Move to the column for the first series, type **Anderson** for the legend, and press (ENTER).
7. Type **14000, 17000, 17500, 18000, 13000,** and **22000** in the first series column, pressing (ENTER) after each one.
8. Press (CTRL)+(HOME) to move to the top of the X-axis label column and then press (TAB) twice to move to the column for the second series.

9. Type **Johnston** and press (ENTER).
10. Type **13000, 14000, 15000, 14000, 11000,** and **16000** in the second series column, pressing (ENTER) after each one.
11. Press (CTRL)+(HOME) and then press (TAB) three times to move to the column for the third series.
12. Type **Saunders** and press (ENTER).
13. Type **16000, 18000, 18000, 19000, 15000,** and **25000** in the third series column, pressing (ENTER) after each one.
14. Press (CTRL)+(HOME) and then press (TAB) four times to move to the column for the fourth series.
15. Type **Williams** and press (ENTER).
16. Type **2000, 22000, 23000, 23500, 23500,** and **26000** in the fourth series column, pressing (ENTER) after each one. The completed Data Form will match Figure 5-2.
17. Select OK and then press (F2). The completed chart entries look like Figure 5-3.

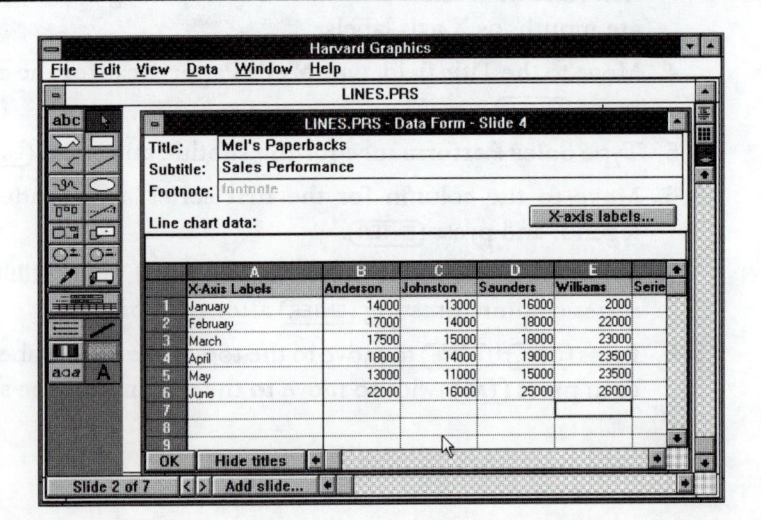

Figure 5-2. *Data for second line chart*

Chapter 5: *Additional XY Data Chart Options*

This line chart illustrates many of the default settings that Harvard Graphics uses for line charts. Now you will want to explore some of the changes you can make.

Changing the Line Thickness

Harvard Graphics established the thickness of each line in the chart. Since no markers are used for data points in the default settings, the thick lines that Harvard Graphics selected look fine, especially if you plan to make slides that will be viewed from a distance. This thicker default line size also makes it possible to distinguish between the series; when they are printed, they are thick enough to show a variation in the grey scale when printing on a black and white output device. Colors can be substituted later.

If you have additional data series or would like to use markers for each data point you may find the default setting for the lines too thick. You can use the Line tool in the Toolbox (shown momentarily) to make changes. You will need to select one of the series lines before invoking the tool. You can choose from any of several predefined sizes or enter your own size in points

Figure 5-3. Line chart created with data from Figure 5-2

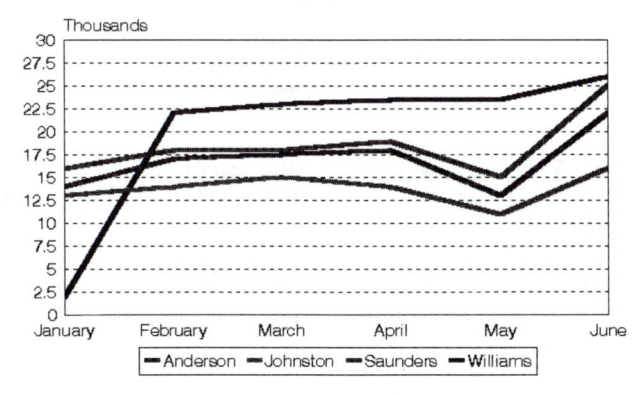

where 1 point is 1/72 of an inch. The predefined setting, Hairline, is the thinnest line possible and it is the only line thickness that will accept changes in the line style from a solid line to a multiple broken-line pattern.

Tip: Line colors that are close to the background color will disappear as a Hairline line. You may want to select the line and change its color with the Color tool (shown here expanded from the Fill tool from the Toolbox on the Slide Editor) before making it a Hairline line.

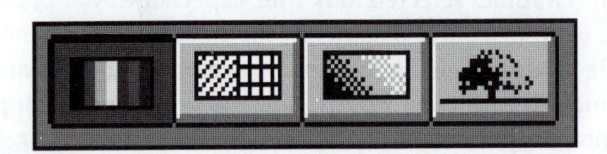

Let's take a look at changing the thickness of each line to Hairline before proceeding with other changes:

1. Press (ESC) to return to the Slide Editor screen and then select the line for the Anderson series by clicking it twice.

2. Choose the Line tool from the Toolbox by clicking the icon that looks like this:

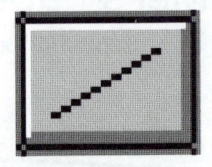

You can also choose Line attributes from the Graphics menu. A dialog box is displayed. Figure 5-4 shows the way this box looks after making your changes.

3. Here, Hairline is selected for line thickness, and OK is pressed. Pressing (F2) displays the chart. Press (ESC) after looking at the difference.

Chapter 5: *Additional XY Data Chart Options* 147

   The chart will display the first series shown with a much thinner line.

4. Repeat steps 1 through 3 for each of the remaining lines until all four lines are the same hairline thickness.

Using Markers for Data Points

You can mark each data point on the line with a distinctive marker for each series. This is important if you are planning to print your charts on a black and white output device since the legend will show each marker and make it easier to distinguish one series from another.

Harvard Graphics provides 13 marker options in addition to the default of None. You can choose from symbols such as a pound sign or filled square.

Figure 5-4.   *Line Attributes dialog box*

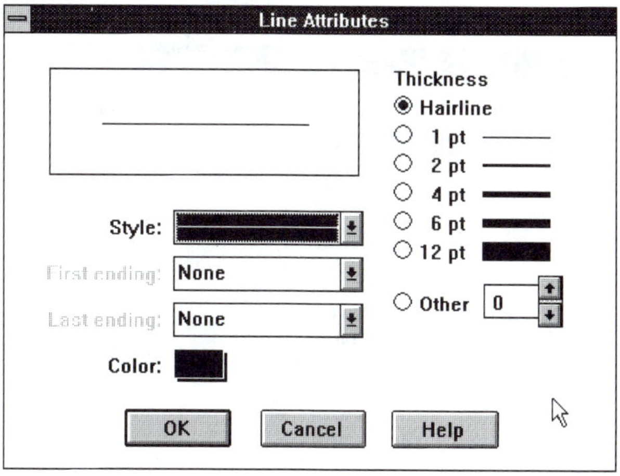

To make your selection you will choose Series from the Chart menu, select a series, and then select a marker style. Let's try it now for your four series:

1. Choose Series from the Chart menu.
   A dialog box like the one shown in Figure 5-5 is displayed.
2. Select the Anderson series and then click the arrow next to the Marker style to access the drop-down list box.
3. Select Sunburst.
4. Repeat steps 2 and 3 making the following selections for each of the series:

Johnston	Diamond
Saunders	Asterisk
Williams	Triangle

Figure 5-5. Series Options dialog box

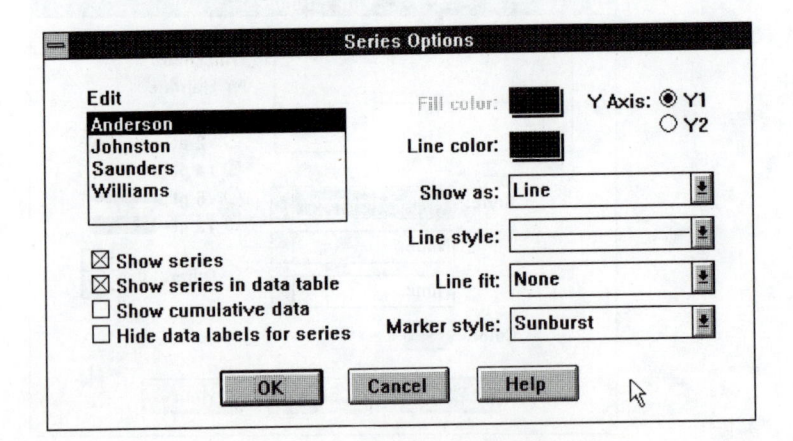

Chapter 5: *Additional XY Data Chart Options*

5. Select OK. Press F2 to view the chart, which looks like Figure 5-6. The data points for each of the series are marked with a unique marker and the legend has been updated to show these markers.

Changing the Line Style

Since you chose the Hairline thickness for your lines you have the option of selecting several different line styles. These styles use dots and dashes alone or in combination (in addition to the solid line, which is the default). These options are especially useful when you do not want markers to distinguish the different series.

To make a change to the line style for any series you would choose Series from the Chart menu, select a series, and then click the arrow next to Line Style. You can choose any of the styles shown in the drop-down list box.

Figure 5-6. Chart displayed with series markers

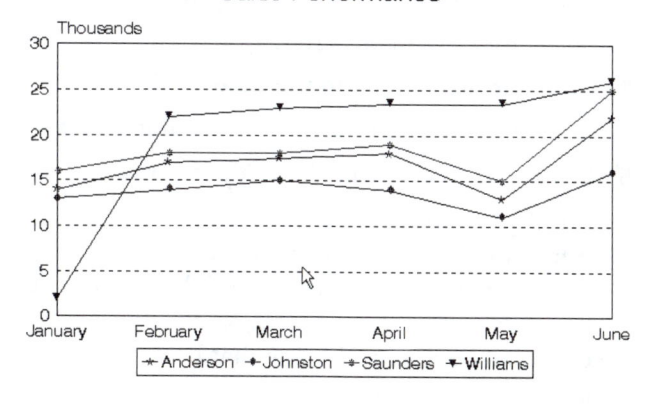

Tip: *If the Line Style option in your Series dialog box is dimmed, it means that you have a line thickness other than Hairline for the selected series. You will need to use the Line tool to change the thickness before you can select a style.*

Changing the Line Fit Option

The Line Fit option helps you control the display of your data. Harvard Graphics computes formulas from the actual data values and draws a line using its computed values to chart the line rather than the ones that you entered. If you normally perform regression analysis to smooth variations in your data, these options will be important to you. If you do not have a need for this type of sophisticated analysis, you can skip to the next section.

With the default Line Fit option of None, each point is plotted and a line is drawn connecting each point. The other six line-fitting options are Step, which simply uses both horizontal and vertical lines to connect the points in a stair-step fashion; Average, which averages the data values and plots them; Trend, which performs a linear regression; Exponential, which performs an exponential regression; Log, which performs a log regression; and Power, which performs a power regression. If you would like more information on regression techniques, you will find the topic in any basic statistics book at your local library. If you would like to look at your chart with a "trend" fit for each series follow these steps:

1. Press (ESC) and then select Series from the Chart menu.
2. Select the Anderson series.
3. Click the arrow next to the Line Fit field and then select Trend.
4. Repeat steps 2 and 3 for the remaining series.
5. Select OK to close the Series dialog box.
6. Press (F2) to preview the line chart as full screen size and show the trend for each data series. This chart looks like Figure 5-7.

    The trend chart displays a straight line that describes the trend of the data points (up, down, or steady). Mathematically, Harvard Graphics computes the line that best fits the data points, using the least-squares method.

Chapter 5: *Additional XY Data Chart Options* 151

7. Press ESC to return to the Slide Editor display.

Tip: *You can obtain more statistical information on each series in the chart. Choose Series statistics from the Chart menu and then select the series that you want statistics for to view data such as minimum value, maximum value, average, median, and standard deviation.*

Changing the Way Data Series Are Shown

Harvard Graphics allows you to select different styles for displaying your data even after designating that you wanted a line chart. You can change the display of a series to a bar, points, an area like a line with the area beneath the line filled with a color or pattern, or a curve. Unlike the other chart types, the point chart does not connect the values in a data series, nor does it draw any lines. Only the individual data points are displayed. It can be harder to see a trend, and if there are many data points, it can be difficult to distinguish

Figure 5-7. Trend chart displaying straight lines

Mel's Paperbacks
Sales Performance

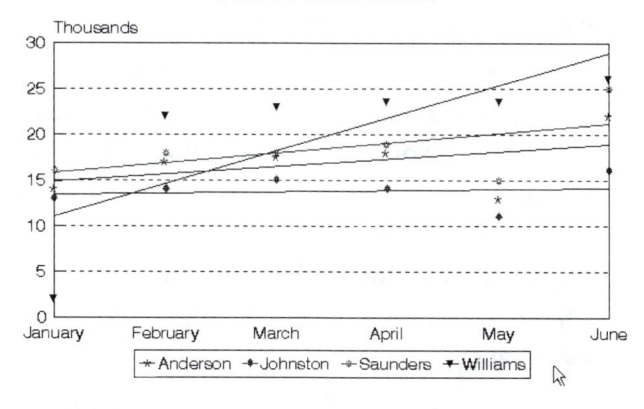

which data point belongs to each series. You can choose the way you want to show each series separately, allowing you to create a combination chart that displays each series in the most effective format.

Let's take a look at showing the current chart as points only.

1. Choose Series from the Chart menu.
2. Select Series 1, Anderson.
3. Click the arrow next to "Show as" and select Point.
4. Repeat steps 2 and 3 for the remaining series
5. Select OK and then press (F2) to display the chart.
6. Press (ESC) and then select Undo from the Edit menu to remove the changes.

Mixing Display Types

Changing the series options for one data series does not change them for another data series. This allows you to mix display types, selecting the options you want for each series. You can try mixing chart types using the data entered for slide 1.

1. Move to slide 1 by clicking the arrow at the bottom of your screen that allows you to move back one slide.
2. Select Series from the Chart menu and then select Series 1, Books.
3. Click the arrow next to the "Show as" field and select Bar.
4. Select Series 2, Records, and then click the arrow next to "Show as." Select Line if you have tried a setting other than Line.
5. Select OK and press (F2) to preview the chart, which will look like Figure 5-8.
6. Press (ESC) to return to the Slide Editor window.
7. Choose Undo from the Edit menu to return the chart to its former appearance.

While this example presents only one combination, your possible selections are almost endless. However, if you try combining more than two or

Chapter 5: *Additional XY Data Chart Options*

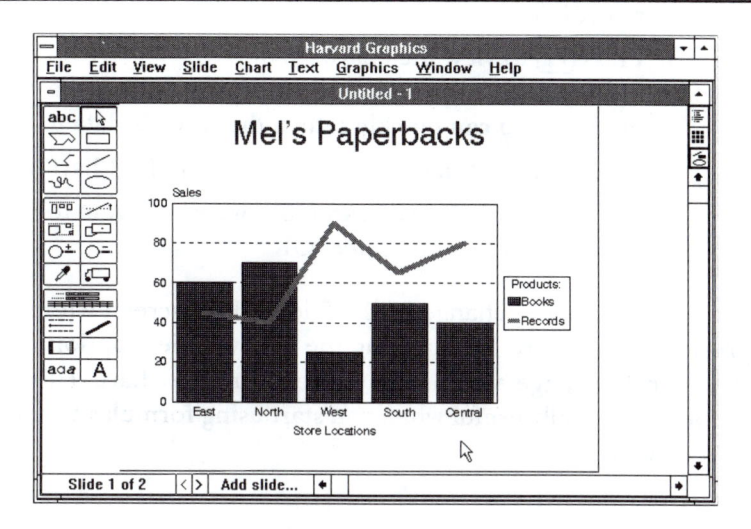

Figure 5-8.   Chart showing one series as a bar style and one as a line

three display types in a single chart, the result will look too busy for the reader to focus on the data.

Hiding Data Series

As you gain skills in working with charts, you may decide to use a chart in a different way. For example, if you are only interested in showing the proportion of books sold at each Mel's Paperbacks, you need not show the information for records. Harvard Graphics allows you to hide any series and select which data you want to present. You do not need to delete data from the Data Form to remove it from view. You can simply remove the X from the check box for Show series for any series that you do not want. To redisplay the series again later you need only to select the check box with the series selected again. To try this feature with slide 1, follow these steps:

1. Choose Series from the Chart menu (or press the (F8) speed key and choose Series).

2. Select Series 2, Records, and "Show series" to remove the X. Then select OK.

3. Press (F2) to view the chart.

    Only the data for books appears because the records data is hidden. You can quickly return the records data to the display.

4. Press (ESC) and then choose Series from the Chart menu.

5. Select Series 2, Records, and "Show series" again to place the X back in the check box and select OK.

You can see the change in the Slide Editor screen without a full-screen preview of the chart. By changing the "Show series" option for a series, you can quickly change which data appears in the chart. Hiding data series becomes especially useful when you start using formulas to add extra data to your charts.

Adding 3D Effects to Line Charts

Some of the options that you learned in Chapter 4 for bar charts do not work for line charts. The options for bar style, bar shape, bar width, and bar overlap do not affect line charts. The exception is if you create a line chart that uses the overlap bar style and 3D. The resulting line chart looks like a ribbon, as shown in Figure 5-9. Setting "Object depth" to a higher number increases the width of this ribbon. To create this chart using slide 1, follow these steps:

1. Select Chart options from the Chart menu.

2. Select Overlap for the Bar/Area style field.

3. Select 3D to place an X in the check box.

    You can change the fill color for a 3D line by selecting Series from the Chart menu or from the Chart Options dialog box. After selecting the series that you want to change you can select the color square next to "Fill color" and select from any of the colors displayed. You can also select a series and then choose Fill from the Graphics menu. You can select a solid color fill, a hatch pattern, a gradual shading, or a bitmap picture for filling.

Chapter 5: *Additional XY Data Chart Options*

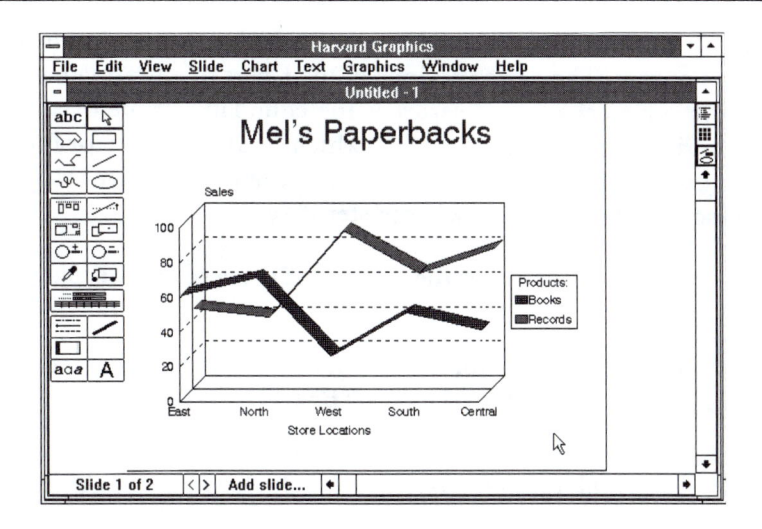

Figure 5-9.   *Line chart with overlap and 3D features*

4. Change "Object depth" to 60 from its default setting of 40 and then select OK.
5. Press [F2] to preview the chart.

In this type of chart, where each data series appears as a ribbon, you might want to label the data points, as described in "Adding Data Labels" later in this chapter. This will make it easy to determine the values of the data points that the ribbons connect.

6. Press [ESC] to return to the Slide Editor screen.
7. Return the lines to their original appearance by choosing Chart options from the Chart menu and then selecting Cluster for Bar/Area style, setting the object depth back to 40, and removing the X from the 3D check box.

Tip: It is important to change the object depth before turning off 3D; otherwise, the depth option will be faded and indistinguishable.

Creating a Cumulative Chart

On some charts you might be interested in the total value of all the data point entries. The Series options in the Chart menu provides an option that allows you to chart each series as the cumulative value of all data points in the series. For example, in slide 2, which charts the sales for four salespeople, you may want to chart the data to show their cumulative sales. To make this change to the chart, follow these steps:

1. Use the arrow at the bottom of the screen to display slide 2.
2. Choose Series from the Chart menu.
3. Select series 1 for Anderson and then select "Show cumulative data" to place an X in the check box.
4. Select series 2 for Johnston and then select "Show cumulative data."
5. Do the same for series 3 and 4, choosing "Show cumulative data" each time.
6. Select OK and then press (F2) to preview the chart. The chart looks like Figure 5-10. Each point in the chart is the salesperson's cumulative total sales up to that month.
7. Press (ESC) to return to the Slide Editor screen.

If you want to return the Cumulative item to the default, you need to choose Series from the Chart menu again. Select each series and then select the "Show cumulative data" check box to remove the X. You can display some series as cumulative and other series as their actual values.

Changing the Legend

You have been entering legend text since you first started entering data charts in Chapter 4. On several occasions you have been directed to make a quick change to the legend location. There are additional options that affect the appearance of the legend and its frame. You can even remove the legend from a chart.

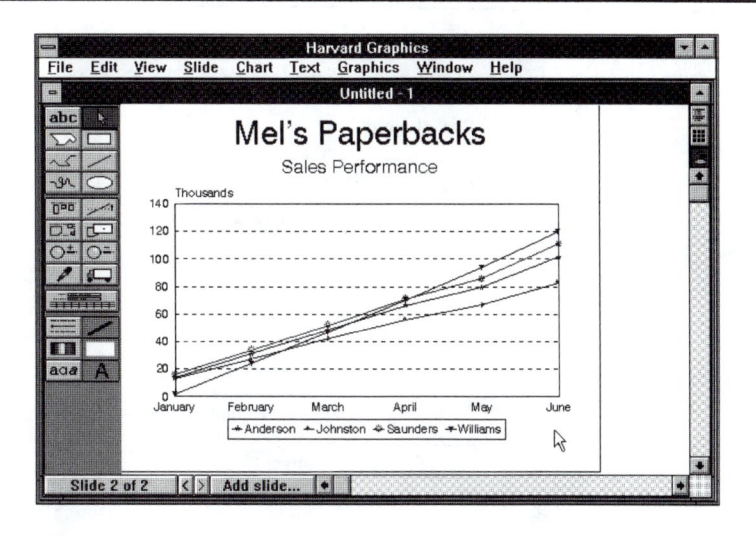

Figure 5-10.   *Line chart showing cumulative values*

Legend Location

By default, Harvard Graphics positions the legend at the bottom of a line chart, but you can select 24 positions through a combination of Placement and Location options from the Legend Options dialog box. You can also use the Selector Tool from the Toolbox in the Slide Editor to move the legend to a position other than the predefined location. To reposition the legend, follow these steps:

1. Select slide 1 by clicking the left arrow at the bottom of the screen.
2. Choose Legend from the Chart menu to display the dialog box shown in Figure 5-11.

    Notice the circular pattern of dots under Location. Each dot represents a potential location for the legend box. The Free dot is used by Harvard Graphics to note when you move the Legend by dragging it on the Slide Editor screen.
3. Select the dot for the bottom-left position from the circle of dots under Location.

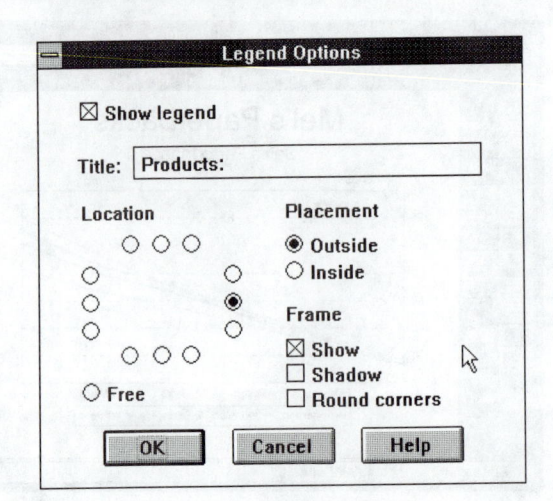

Figure 5-11.   Legend Options dialog box

```
┌─ Legend Options ──────────────────────┐
│                                       │
│  ☒ Show legend                        │
│                                       │
│  Title: │ Products:              │    │
│                                       │
│  Location           Placement         │
│      ○ ○ ○           ● Outside        │
│     ○      ○         ○ Inside         │
│     ○      ●        Frame             │
│     ○      ○         ☒ Show           │
│      ○ ○ ○           ☐ Shadow         │
│                      ☐ Round corners  │
│  ○ Free                               │
│                                       │
│   [  OK  ]   [ Cancel ]   [  Help  ]  │
└───────────────────────────────────────┘
```

4. Select OK and then press (F2) to preview your chart.
5. Press (ESC) to return to the Slide Editor screen.

Legend Placement

By default Harvard Graphics puts the legend outside of the box containing the chart data. You have the option of putting the legend within the chart. To move the legend currently located on the *outside* bottom-left to the *inside* bottom-left corner of the chart, follow these steps:

1. Choose Legend from the Chart menu.
2. Select the Inside radio button under Placement.
3. Select OK.
4. Press (F2) to preview the chart, which looks like Figure 5-12.

When you place the legend inside the chart data area, it is important to have the location set to where it will not interfere with the data. In the chart in Figure 5-12, you would not want the legend

Chapter 5: *Additional XY Data Chart Options* 159

to have a center-left or center-right position, since it would obscure data.

5. Press (ESC) and then choose Legend from the Chart menu.
6. Select the Show check box to remove the X.
7. Select OK to view the chart on the Slide Editor screen without the legend.

    When the legend is outside, Harvard Graphics adjusts the remaining chart elements to use the area left vacant by the legend. Any legend settings are ignored while the legend does not appear.

8. Choose Legend from the Chart menu and select Show to put the X back in the legend check box.

Legend Frame Style

A legend is an important component of a chart—it is the key that unlocks the meaning of the chart when several sets of data are presented. When you

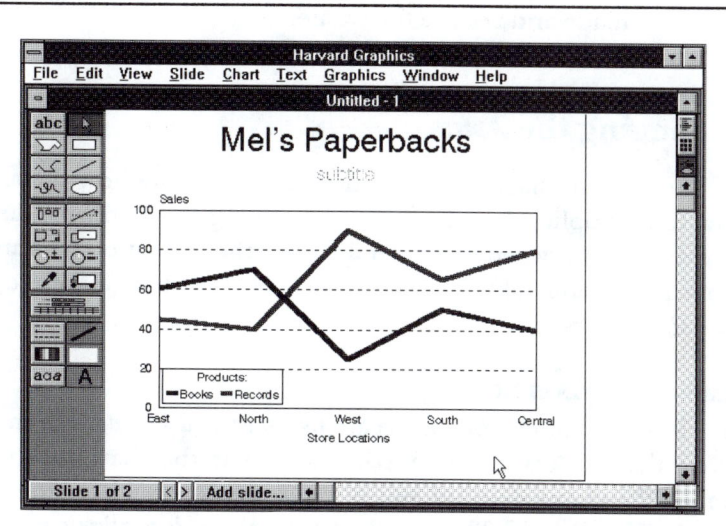

Figure 5-12.   *Chart with legend inside chart data area*

place the legend inside the chart data area, it can be difficult to see, or you may want to distinguish the legend from the chart data. The default setting that places a frame around the legend is often appropriate.

You can change the frame to display with a shadow effect as well as rounded corners. These changes are also made through the Legend Options dialog box.

To eliminate the frame around the legend of the chart in Figure 5-12, follow these steps:

1. Choose Legend from the Chart menu.
2. Select the check box Show under Frame to remove the X and then select OK.

The legend still displays inside the chart but without a frame. The Frame Style options are the same when the legend is outside the chart data area. When the legend has a frame, the entire portion of the chart within the frame area is hidden. When a legend does not have a frame, the chart information behind is overwritten only by the legend text.

3. Select Undo from the Edit menu to eliminate the change you just made and restore the frame.

Changing the Axes

So far, you have let Harvard Graphics decide how the axes are scaled. Harvard Graphics has chosen the beginning and ending values on the axes, the distance between values on the axes, the format of the numbers, and the appearance and value of tick marks. You can change these options and set the scale yourself.

Changing Axis Scaling

Most of the charts you create use *standard scaling*—the interval between every tick mark is the same. For example, in the chart in Figure 5-13, which shows the cumulative amount of sales, the interval between each tick mark on the Y axis is 20,000. Another option is a *logarithmic scale*, in which the increment between each major tick mark on a scale increases by a power of

Chapter 5: *Additional XY Data Chart Options* 161

10. The chart in Figure 5-14 shows the same data as Figure 5-13 but uses a logarithmic scale; therefore, the interval between the first tick mark and the second tick mark is 9000. The interval between the second tick mark and the third tick mark is 90,000, or 9000 multiplied by 10. Logarithmic scaling is often used to chart exponentially growing numbers.

To change the axes scaling, choose Axis from the Chart menu. Select Scaling under the axis that you want to change. Harvard Graphics only makes the scale type settings such as minimum and maximum for the X axis available if the values of the X axis are numbers. Select Linear for standard scaling or Log for logarithmic scaling. If you select Linear, the interval between each tick mark is equal. If you select Log, Harvard Graphics adds minor tick marks (they do not have numbers next to them) to divide the interval into ten sections. Since the scale is nonlinear, the tick marks are not evenly spaced. Another possible axis change is to reset the Scale Factor. You can display all the numbers as being divided by another number. For example, you can display numbers divided by 1000 (as they have been in the example Sales charts) by entering a Scale Factor of 1000.

Figure 5-13.   *Chart using standard scaling*

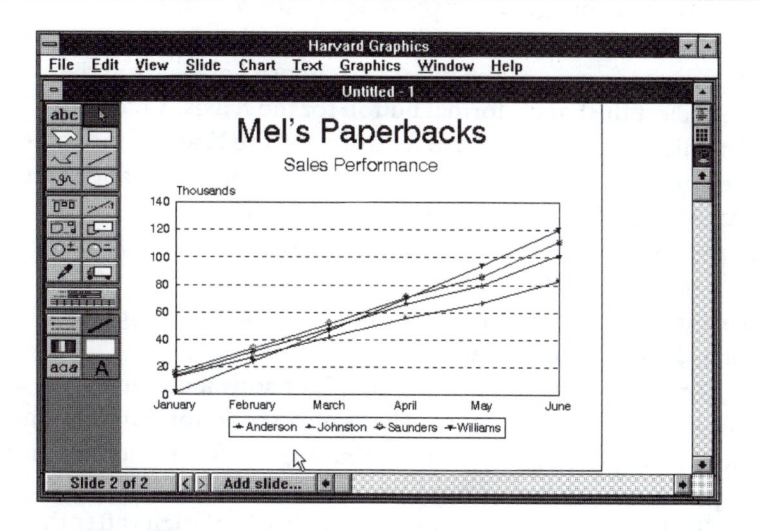

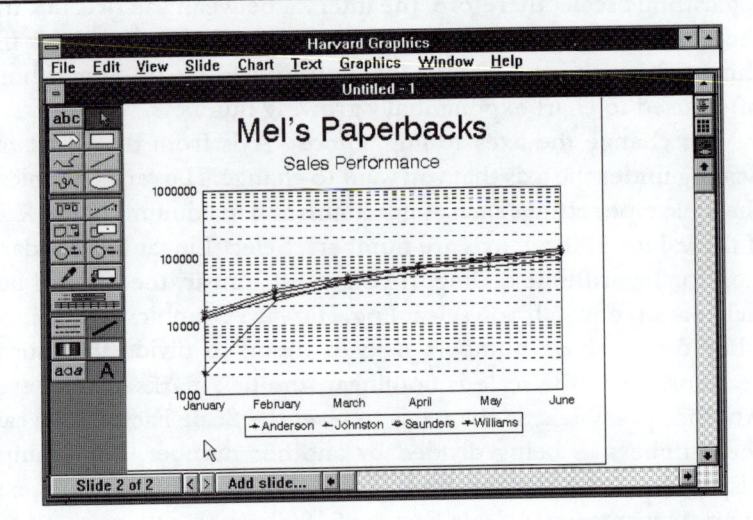

Figure 5-14.   *Chart using logarithmic scaling for the Y axis*

Changing the Format

You can change the appearance of the values in a chart by changing the axis format to currency ($), scientific notation, or to other styles as well. To change the format of the numbers, choose Labels from the Chart menu and then select the Labels format button for the X axis, Y1 axis, or Y2 axis. Harvard Graphics only uses the format setting for the X axis if the values of the X axis are numbers. Changing the format of a Y axis also changes the format of the data series values assigned to the Y axis. For example, if you set the format of the Y1 axis to have three digits displayed after the decimal point, all of the data series assigned to the Y1 axis will display labels with three digits after the decimal point. Changing the format of the number does not change the actual values, only the appearance of values.

To set an axis so Harvard Graphics adds a comma after the thousands, check to be certain that the Thousands separator contains an X. To display the numbers using scientific notation, set Scientific Notation to Yes. To display the numbers with a $ in front of them, select Currency.

To have all values with the same number of digits after the decimal point, type the number of digits you want in the Decimal Places text box. To place

Chapter 5: *Additional XY Data Chart Options* 163

text before or after the values, use the Leading and Trailing text boxes. The text you enter in these boxes either precedes or follows each label. You can use this feature (employing techniques learned in Chapter 3, "Creating Text Charts") to precede an entry with a foreign currency symbol or to add a measurement such as feet, acres, or lbs following the text. Both leading and trailing entries have a limit of 12 characters. You can also combine the label settings. For example, to use commas and add a pounds sterling sign (£) before the values, set Thousands Separator to Yes, select Leading Text, and press ALT+0163 with the numbers entered from the numeric keypad.

Changing Tick Marks

Tick marks are the markers used on the X and Y axes to indicate intervals of the scale. Major tick marks show the major divisions of the scale corresponding to the scale labels. Minor ticks marks are shown between the major tick marks to divide the scale evenly. By default there are no tick marks on the chart. Tick mark settings that you establish for the Y1 axis will also affect the Y2 axis. To eliminate the cumulative display of sales data and then change the major tick mark option for the chart on slide 2, follow these steps:

1. Choose Series from the Chart menu.
2. Select the first series, Anderson, and then select "Show cumulative data" to remove the X. Repeat this step for the remaining series.
3. Select OK and then choose Axis from the Chart menu.
4. Click the arrow next to Major tick marks for the Y1 axis and then select In, Out, Cross, or None.
   The In option starts the tick marks on the axis and causes them to point toward the inside of the chart. Out starts the tick marks on the axis and causes them to point away from the chart. The Cross option combines the tick marks created with In and Out to make a tick mark that crosses the axis. None removes all tick marks. All of these options work well with line charts. With bar charts, you may want to avoid In for X-axis tick marks, since you will overlap the bars.
5. Select OK to display the chart on the Slide Editor screen. Choose Undo from the Edit menu to remove the changes.

Changing Scaling for an Axis

Harvard Graphics makes certain assumptions about an axis, such as the beginning value, the ending value, and the increment between each tick mark. To change these values for slide 2, follow these steps:

1. Choose Axis from the Chart menu.
2. Select the Scaling button for the Y1 axis.
3. Move to the Minimum field and type **10000**, the lowest value the axis will start with, and press (TAB).
4. Type **30000** for the Maximum field and press (TAB).
5. Type **2500** in the Increment field, the value of the increment between each tick mark.
6. Select OK twice to end the Scaling dialog box and the Axis dialog box. Press (F2) to view the chart in Figure 5-15.
7. Press (ESC) to return to the Slide Editor screen.

Figure 5-15.   *Chart with new Y-axis scaling values*

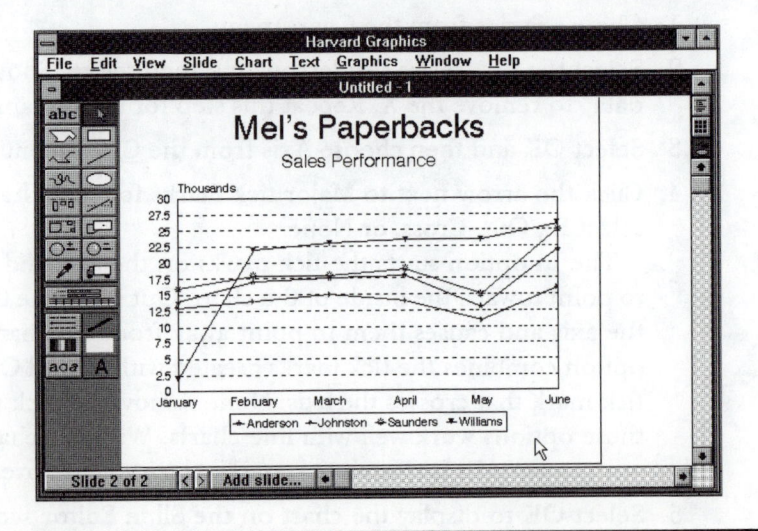

Chapter 5: *Additional XY Data Chart Options*

If you do not enter a minimum, maximum, and/or increment value, Harvard Graphics retains any previous entries as the default value. As mentioned before, Harvard Graphics only makes the minimum and maximum fields for the X axis accessible if the values of the X axis are numbers. You can still specify an *increment* for other types as X-axis labels since it will cause Harvard Graphics to eliminate some of the labels from the chart.

You can also use the Increment field to reduce congestion along an axis when it has many values with lengthy labels. For example, you can change the labels in the slide 2 chart so that the chart only displays the names of every other month. By decreasing the number of X-axis labels, you are increasing the space available for the remaining ones. To change the labels, follow these steps:

1. Choose Axis from the Chart menu.
2. Select the Scaling button under the X axis.
3. Move to the Increment field and type 2.
4. Select OK twice to exit both dialog boxes and display the Slide Editor screen.
   Only January, March, and May appear in the X axis. Harvard Graphics also has other options, such as displaying the labels vertically.
5. Choose Axis from the Chart menu and select Scaling under the X axis, remove the 2 in the Increment field, and select OK in both dialog boxes.
   Deleting a typed option returns the option to the default. You could also use Undo from the Edit menu to reverse the change.

Adjusting Grid Lines

Harvard Graphics can eliminate the horizontal dashed lines in the line chart or add vertical dashed lines to make it easy to see where data intersects both the X axis and the Y axis. These lines are called *grid lines*. Grid lines start from the X or Y axis and continue horizontally or vertically to the other side. The default is to display horizontal grid lines for a line chart. You can eliminate or change the appearance of grid lines.

To change the grid lines, choose Grid from the Chart menu. The check boxes "Show X grid," "Show Y1 grid," and "Show Y2 grid" should contain an X if you want grid lines, and the boxes should be empty if you do not. Use the arrows next to the Style box for each axis to select a different line pattern for the grid. Options include dotted grid lines, solid grid lines, dashed grid lines, and a few combination patterns (in addition to None). The grid lines start at each major tick mark on the selected axis. If you are using two Y axes, be careful not to add grid lines to both Y axes or your chart will look too busy.

Adding Data Labels

When you create a line chart, you can use grid lines to help the viewer estimate the value of each data point in the chart. Another option is to display the values next to each data point. To add data labels to the line chart, follow these steps:

1. Use the arrow at the bottom of the screen to select slide 1.
2. Choose Labels from the Chart menu.
3. Select "Show data labels" to add an X to the check box.
4. Select the radio button for "Above data points." (Other placement options are "On data points" and "Below data points.")
5. Select the radio button for Horizontal. Other placement options are Vertical up and Vertical down.
6. Select OK.
7. Press (F2) to display the chart shown in Figure 5-16.
8. Press (ESC) to display the Slide Editor screen.

Another option is to selectively display the labels. To display only the labels for the Books series of data, you would choose Series from the Chart menu, select the Records series, and then select "Hide data labels" for a series.

Chapter 5: *Additional XY Data Chart Options* 167

Showing a Goal Range

Harvard Graphics allows you to show a range of goals, or hypothetical data, on charts. This is especially useful for sales data and other information where you want to compare actual results to a quota or a projection. The goal that you establish will appear as a shaded area behind the series.

To set a goal range for a chart you need to choose Frame from the Chart menu. Next, type a number in the "Range minimum" and "Range maximum" text boxes. You may want to choose the color of the highlighting by selecting the color box next to "Goal range color." When you select OK you will see the goal range along with your data on the Slide Editor screen. If you feel that it detracts from your chart, you can choose Undo from the Edit menu to eliminate it.

Figure 5-16.   Chart displaying labels for data points

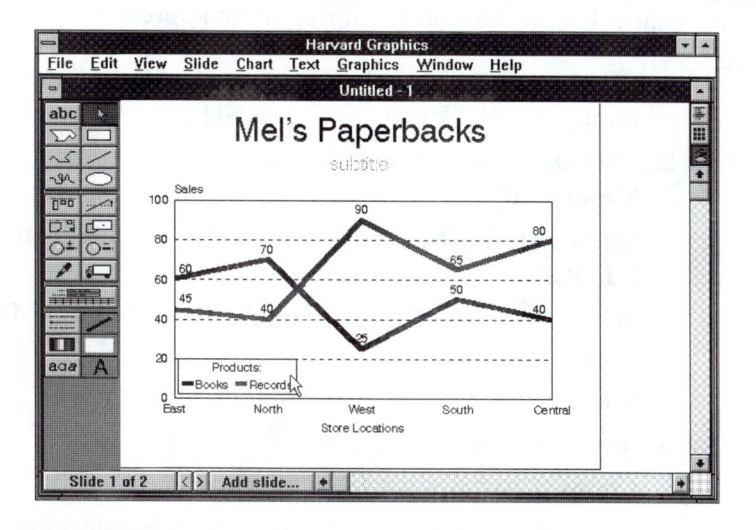

Area Charts

In some ways area charts are a combination of bar and line charts. Like line charts, area charts draw lines to each of the data points in a series. However, area charts fill in the area below the line with a color or pattern, which is more like a bar chart. Also, the area chart uses some of the bar chart styles and enhancements. Since the area filled with one series would otherwise obscure the other series, often the series in an area chart are stacked.

Creating an Area Chart

Creating an area chart requires the same steps that you perform with line and bar charts. To quickly create an area chart using the data from slide 1, copy the current slide with the Slide viewer and then change the chart type. You will want to eliminate the data labels that were previously added before copying the chart. (For a new chart you would select Add slide and choose Area chart.) Follow these steps for a shortcut approach:

1. Choose La*b*els from the *C*hart menu. Select Show data labels to remove the X. Harvard Graphics will remove the labels. Select OK.
2. Click the icon for the Slide Sorter or choose Slide *S*orter from the View menu.
3. Select slide 1. Choose *C*opy from the *E*dit menu and then choose Edit *P*aste.
4. Select the Slide *E*ditor icon or choose Slide Editor from the *V*iew menu.
5. Choose *C*hange chart type from the *C*hart menu.
6. Select Area and then select OK.
7. Choose Chart *o*ptions from the *C*hart menu.
8. Select Stack from Bar/Area style. (Stacking will eliminate the overlap that currently exists.)

Chapter 5: *Additional XY Data Chart Options* 169

9. Select OK and then press (F2) to preview the chart in Figure 5-17.

   Since Bar/Area style in the Chart Options dialog box was set at stacked, the first series is on the bottom of the graph. The second series is added on top of the first series. This continues for each of the series. Each series uses a different pattern and color, which you can change. You would select Series from the Chart menu, select the series, and choose a color by clicking the Color box next to Fill color. To change the pattern you must select the series from the Slide Editor screen and then choose the Fill tool or Fill from the Graphics menu to pick a new pattern.

10. Press (ESC) to return to the Slide Editor screen.

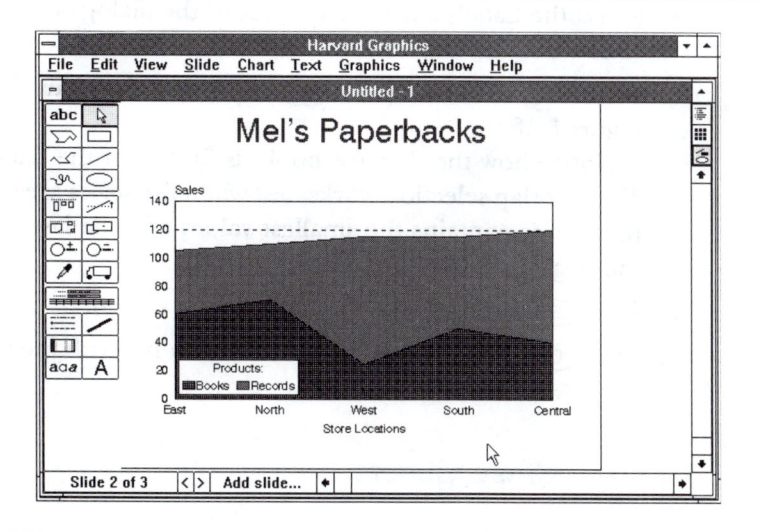

Figure 5-17.   *Area chart with stacked style*

Adding a 3D Effect

Most of the options used with line, trend, curve, point, and bar charts also operate with area charts, but the only Bar/Area Styles that pertain to area charts are Stack, Overlap, and 100%. Follow these steps to change the chart to display data labels again and select the Overlap and 3D options.

1. Select Chart options from the Chart menu.

Remember: *This is the best place to start since you can access so many options from the buttons in the Chart Options dialog box.*

2. Select 3D to place an X in the box.
3. Select Overlap for the Bar/Area style.
    Selecting Overlap places the second series behind the first and so forth for all of the series. With the current series, Overlap will always obscure part of the data. Adding data labels will make this even more obvious.
4. Select the Labels button at the side of the dialog box and then select "Show data labels."
5. Select OK twice and press (F2) to preview the chart that appears in Figure 5-18.
    Notice how the data for books is on top of the data for records. The Overlap selection works best when the series are ordered so the first series contains the smallest values and the last series contains the largest values.
6. Press (ESC) to return to the Slide Editor screen.
7. Press (CTRL)+(S) to save the presentation file with the new slide.

High/Low/Close Charts

When you are tracking the prices of financial commodities, you usually want to know more than the current price. Frequently traded stocks will vary

Chapter 5: *Additional XY Data Chart Options*

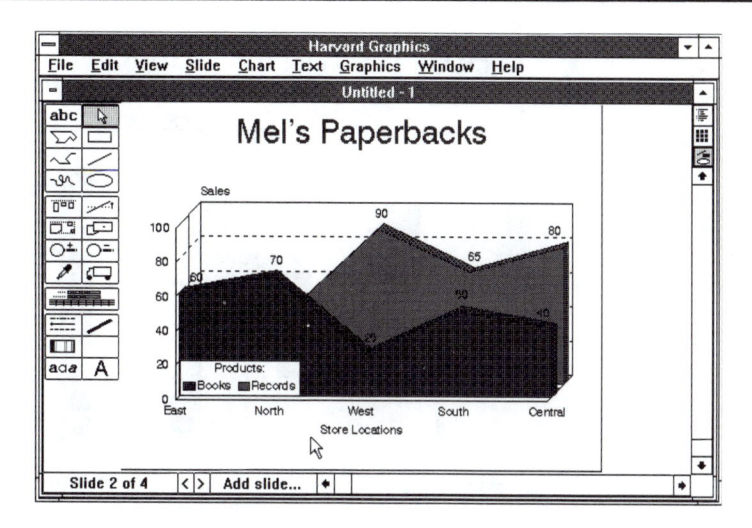

Figure 5-18.   *Area chart with overlap style and 3D enhancement*

in price. Often financial reports include the opening, closing, high, and low prices of a stock. Looking at only the raw data makes it difficult to analyze a trend. A high/low/close chart, like the one shown in Figure 5-19, creates a picture of the variations of a financial commodity. Harvard Graphics uses the first four data series to chart the high, low, closing, and opening prices. Any additional series may be charted as a bar, line, trend, curve, or points. A line or box is drawn between the high and low values, and tick marks in the line or bar indicate opening or closing prices. Opening prices have tick marks starting from the line or bar and going to the left. Closing prices have tick marks going from the line or bar to the right.

While high/low/close charts were developed for charting financial commodity prices, you can use this chart to chart other types of data, such as survey responses where the Open series represents the average value of the survey's responses and the Close series represents the median value of the survey's responses.

Figure 5-19. High/low/close chart

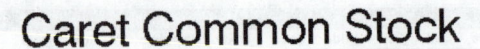

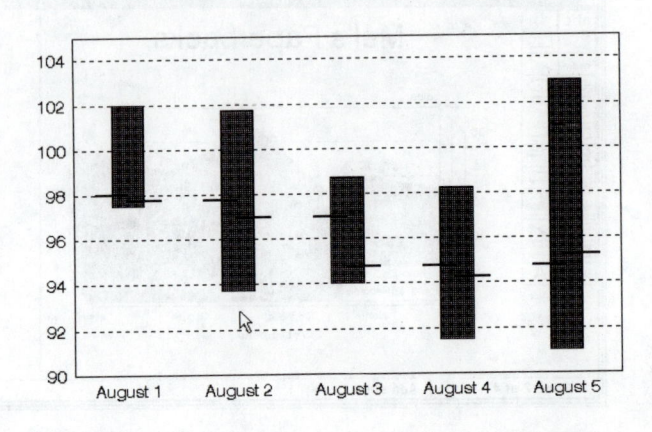

Creating a High/Low/Close Chart

High/low/close charts use different data than you have entered for your line and area charts. To create a high/low/close chart, follow these steps:

1. Move to slide 3 using the arrow at the bottom of the screen. Select Add slide.
2. Select High/Low/Close.
3. Select OK and then select X-axis labels.
4. Select Month Day as the X-axis label type.
5. Move to the Start field, type **August 1,** and press (TAB) to use August 1 as the starting date.
6. Type **August 5** as the ending date and press (TAB).
7. Type **1** as the Increment field entry and then select OK. (The High/Low/Close Chart Data screen already has the first four series labeled High, Low, Close, and Open.)

Chapter 5: *Additional XY Data Chart Options* 173

8. Move to the Title field and then type **Caret Common Stock** for the chart title and press (ENTER).
9. Use (ENTER), (TAB), and (↓) to move to the August 1 High value.
10. Type **102, 101.75, 98.75, 98.25,** and **103** in the High series column, pressing (ENTER) after each one.
11. Press (CTRL)+(HOME), press (TAB) twice, and press (↓) to move to the Low series column.
12. Type **97.5, 93.75, 94, 91.5,** and **91** in the Low series column, pressing (ENTER) after each one.
13. Press (CTRL)+(HOME), press (TAB) three times, and press (↓) to move to the Close series column.
14. Type **97.75, 97, 94.75, 94.25,** and **95.25** in the Close series column, pressing (ENTER) after each one.
15. Press (CTRL)+(HOME), press (TAB) four times, and press (↓) to move to the Open series column.
16. Type **98, 97.75, 97, 94.75,** and **94.75** in the Open series column, pressing (ENTER) after each one. The XY Chart screen should look like Figure 5-20.
17. Select OK and then press (F2) to display the chart, which looks like Figure 5-21.
18. Press (ESC) to return to the Slide Editor screen.

This chart illustrates many of the default settings that Harvard Graphics uses for high/low/close charts. By customizing the options, you can change how the data is displayed. You can also include more series in this chart to show how actively the stock was sold.

One of the problems with a high/low/close chart is that the Y axis starts at zero. Since the low values are usually greater than zero, starting the chart from zero pushes the display of the data to the top part of the chart. The variation of the data is more visible if you narrow the Y-axis range.

You can see the difference by following these steps, which set the Y-axis range from 90 to 105:

1. Choose A̲xis from the C̲hart menu.

Figure 5-20.   *Data Form for a high/low/close chart*

Figure 5-21.   *High/low/close chart created with data from Figure 5-20*

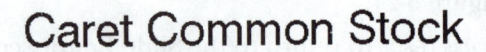

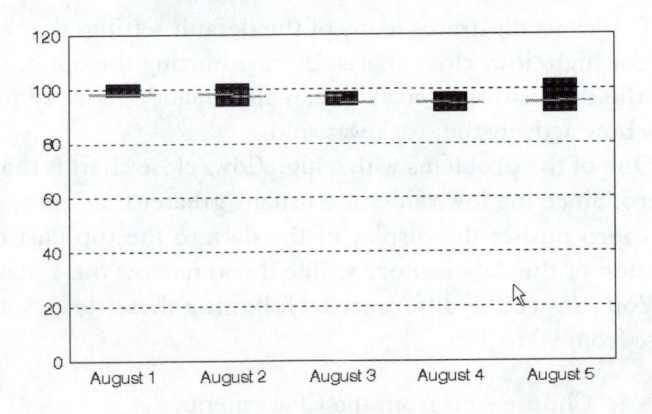

Chapter 5: *Additional XY Data Chart Options*   175

2. Select Scaling for the Y1 axis.
3. Move to the "Minimum axis value" field, type **90**, and press (TAB) to start the axis at 90.
4. Type **105** and press (TAB) to end the axis at 105.
5. Select OK twice and then press (F2) to display the chart, which should look much like the chart you saw in Figure 5-19. Changing the Y-axis range makes the day-to-day variation more visible.
6. Press (ESC).

High/Low/Close Chart Options

Although most of the options for high/low/close charts are the same as for other types of charts, some options have different defaults for high/low/close charts. For instance, the default is to not show a legend on this type of chart. There are also some style options that affect only this type of chart. For a close look at additional options, make the following changes to the high/low/close chart you have just created:

1. Choose Legend from the Chart menu.
2. Select "Show legend."
3. Select "Rounded corners" and Shadow.
4. Select the dot for the right center to set the location.
5. Select OK.
    You will want to change the style of the chart next. The High/Low style item controls how the range between the high value and the low value is connected. The default, Bar, creates a rectangular bar as you saw in Figure 5-19. You can try the other options to see how the chart differs.
6. Choose Chart options from the Chart menu.
7. Select Area for the High/Low style and then select OK.
8. Press (F2) to display the chart, which looks like Figure 5-22.

When the High/Low style is set to Area, Harvard Graphics fills the area between the high and low values. To see another option:

9. Press ESC to display the Slide Editor screen again.
10. Choose Chart options from the Chart menu again.
11. Select Error Bar from the High/Low style options.
12. Select OK and then press F2 to display a chart like the one shown in Figure 5-23.

    When the High/Low style is set to Error Bar, the chart draws a line from the high value to the low value and adds horizontal tick marks at both ends of the line for the opening and closing values.
13. Press ESC.

Other style options such as Bar Width and Bar Overlap affect only the fifth through sixteenth series.

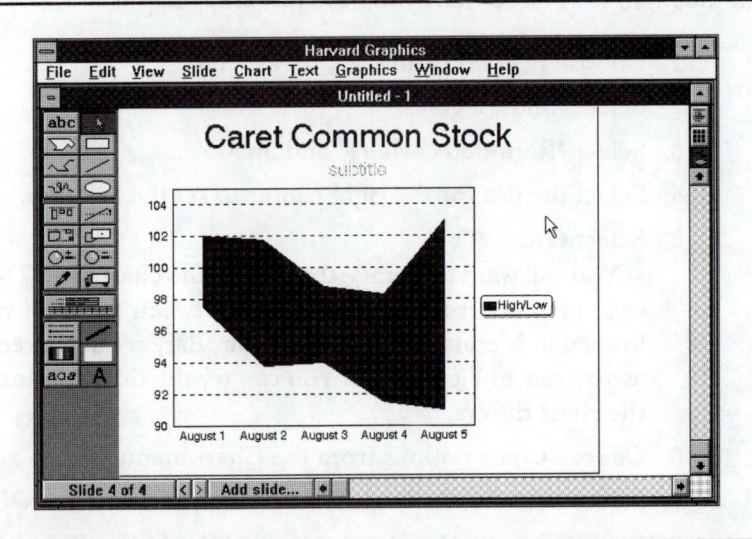

Figure 5-22. *High/low/close chart with Area style and Y-axis scale changed*

Chapter 5: *Additional XY Data Chart Options*   177

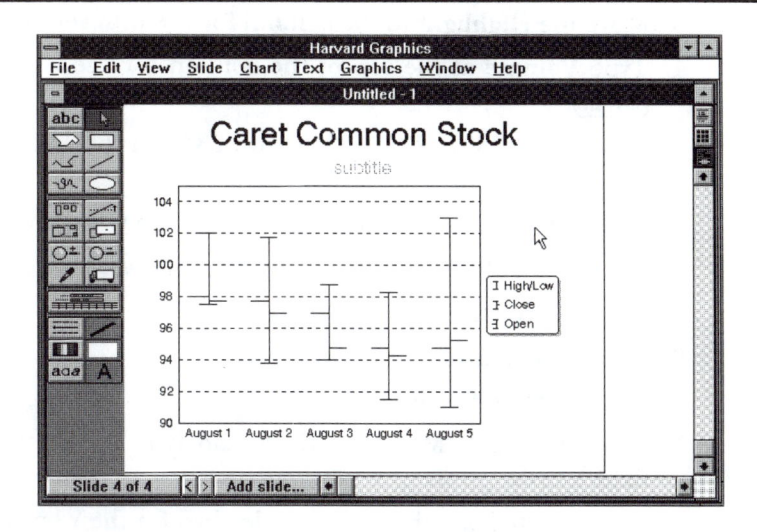

Figure 5-23.   *High/low/close chart with High/Low style set to Error*

Including Other Chart Types

The charts you create in a high/low/close chart can include other types of information besides the high, low, closing, and opening prices. For example, you may want to include a line chart that charts how the industry did on average so you can determine if the particular stock is performing better than average. You may also want to add bar charts that indicate how much stock was traded. When you add different types of data, you may want to assign the other types of data to the second Y axis. When you combine different types of data, you may also want to change the Y axis so the price data does not unintentionally overlay the fifth through eighth series of data. Try the following steps to add a fifth series that contains volume information displaying as a bar chart:

1. Choose Chart options from the Chart menu, set the High/Low style back to Bar, and then select OK.

2. Choose Edit data from the Chart menu.
3. Move the Highlight to the column for the fifth series.
4. Type **Volume** at the top of the column for the legend and press (ENTER).
5. Type **2250**, **2301**, **2288**, **2303**, and **2321** in the Volume (Series 5) column, pressing (ENTER) after each.
6. Select OK and then choose Series from the Chart menu.
7. Select the Volume series just created, "Show as," and Bar.
8. Select Y2 for the axis and then select OK..
9. Choose Axis from the Chart menu.
10. Select Scaling for the Y1 axis.
11. Type **70** in the "Minimum field" and type **105** in the "Maximum field."
12. Select OK to leave the Scaling dialog box for the Y1 axis. Then select Scaling for the Y2 axis.
13. Type **2200** in the box for the "Minimum field" and type **2500** in the box for the "Maximum field." Select OK twice to return to the Axis dialog box and then the Slide Editor.
14. Choose Grid from the Chart menu.
15. Select the check box labeled "Show Y2 grid" so that the X disppears.
16. Select OK. (Adjusting the lower limit of the Y1 axis makes room for the bars at the bottom of the chart.) Press (F2) to display the chart, which looks like Figure 5-24.
17. Press (ESC) to return to the Slide Editor.
18. Press (CTRL)+(S) to save the presentation again.

Chapter 5: *Additional XY Data Chart Options* 179

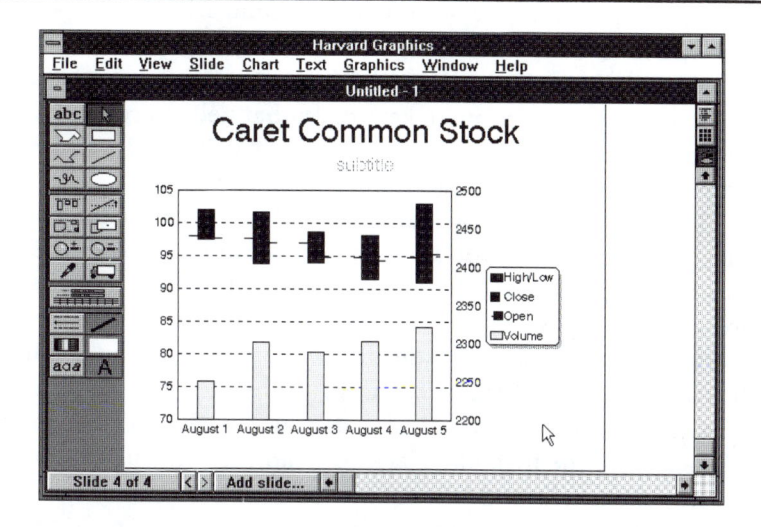

Figure 5-24. *High/low/close chart using additional series*

Using Calculations

If you used earlier releases of Harvard Graphics you found that—although there was an option to handle calculations—it was necessary to apply one formula to an entire series to generate a second series. Harvard Graphics for Windows is different since its Data Forms have the ability to support calculations in much the same way as does a spreadsheet package such as Excel, 1-2-3 for Windows, or Quattro Pro.

Calculations in Harvard Graphics are entered as formulas. Formulas can contain cell references (such as B1) or cell ranges (such as B1:E1). For instance, =SUM(B1:E1) sums the values in the range B1 through E1. A cell reference uses the current value in the cell, and a cell range uses the values of all cells in the range. Formulas can contain arithmetic operators, such as + and − (as in =B2−C3), which subtracts the current value in C3 from the current value in B2. Formulas can contain decimal values, such as 1.5 as in +B1−1.5. Formulas can also contain keywords that tell Harvard Graphics how to perform a computation for you, as in =AVG(B1:E1), which tells Harvard Graphics to average the values in cells B1 though E1.

To enter a calculation, display the Data Form for the bar, line, area, or high/low/close chart you want to use. Move to the cell where you want to put the computed data. Next, type an equal sign (=) and then the formula, pressing (ENTER) when you are finished. Any entry already in the cell is overwritten. The formula still displays on the edit line, but the cell itself displays the result of the calculation.

Once the values are calculated, you can change the values in any cell referenced by the formula. Harvard Graphics recalculates with the latest cell entries. Blank cells and text entries have the same value as cells that contain a zero. You can get a message indicating a "divide by zero error" if you try to use calculations employing division and fail to complete your entries.

Arithmetic Formulas

Arithmetic formulas use addition, subtraction, multiplication, division, exponentiation, and percent to compute a value using data in the Data Form. Harvard Graphics uses the plus (+) for addition, the minus or hyphen (−) for subtraction, the asterisk (*) for multiplication, the slash (/) for division, and the caret (^) for exponentiation or raising a number to a power. Harvard Graphics uses a priority sequence in evaluating expressions from left to right. The order of operation is: expressions in parentheses, exponentiation, multiplication and division, addition and subtraction. You will not get the same result from entering =4+5*2 as you would with =(4+5)*2. The first formula evaluates as 14 and the second as 18 since the addition is performed first in the second example due to the parentheses. Remember you can use parentheses to change the order of evaluation.

You can copy and move formulas just as you can other cell entries. You can use Edit Cut or Edit Copy depending on whether you want to move or copy data and then use Edit Paste to put the entry in a new location. You can

Chapter 5: *Additional XY Data Chart Options*

also use the Data Fill menu's down and right commands to automatically take the first formula in the selected cell range and duplicate it in all the other cells in the range. The formula is automatically adjusted to provide the same relative directions as it did in the first cell. In other words, if the formula was taking the cell to the right of the formula and multiplying it by 1.5, it will still take the cell to the right and multiply it by 1.5. Harvard Graphics copies the relative distance and direction needed to perform your calculation, not the actual cell address in the formula.

You will create a new slide to show the projections for sales and cost of goods sold for the ABC company. In creating this slide, only two values will be entered in the Data Form. The remaining values are all the result of formulas that you enter in a cell and copy down with the Data Fill down feature. Follow these steps to create the new model:

1. Move to slide 4 and select the Add slide button.
2. Select "Vertical bar," select "Chart Gallery," and pick the third option in the bottom row, which will automatically display a data table at the bottom of your chart. Then select OK.
3. Move to the title field, type **ABC Company,** and press (ENTER).
4. Type **Sales/Cost of goods sold,** press (CTRL)+(ENTER), type **1992 - 1996 Projections,** and press (ENTER) twice.
5. Type **1992** and press (ENTER). (You can also use the X-axis labels button and generate a series of years rather than type them in.)
6. Complete the entries for the remaining years 1993 through 1996 in A2 through A5.
7. Press (CTRL)+(HOME), press (TAB), type **Sales** for the legend, and press (ENTER).
8. Type **200000** and press (ENTER).

    The remaining years' sales will be projected, assuming a 15% growth rate. This means that sales for each year will be the same as last year's sales plus an additional 15%.

9. Type **=B1+B1*.15** with the highlight still in B2 and press (ENTER).
10. Select the cells B2 through B5.

    Your Data Form will look like Figure 5-25. In order to place the formula in the remaining cells, you will use the Fill down command

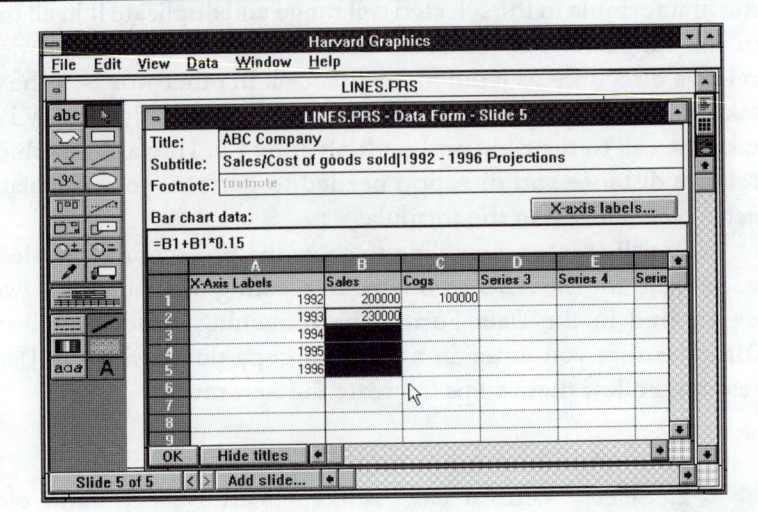

Figure 5-25.   Using Data Fill down to copy a formula

on the <u>D</u>ata menu. To use this command it is necessary to first select the cell containing the formula as well as the adjacent cells beneath it where you will also use the formula. In situations where you need to copy formulas to the right you can use the Fill <u>r</u>ight option.

11. Choose Fill do<u>w</u>n from the <u>D</u>ata menu.
12. Press (CTRL)+(HOME) and then press (TAB) twice.
13. Type **Cogs** as an abbreviation for Cost of goods sold and press (ENTER).
14. Type **100000** for the 1992 value and press (ENTER).
15. Type **=B2∗.45** and press (ENTER).
16. Select the cells C2 though C5 and then choose Fill Do<u>w</u>n from the <u>D</u>ata menu.

    Your Data Form looks like Figure 5-26. You will notice that Harvard Graphics adds a 0 in front of the decimal fraction so it reads as 0.45 and displays the results with varying decimal places.

17. Click OK to display the chart.

Chapter 5: *Additional XY Data Chart Options*

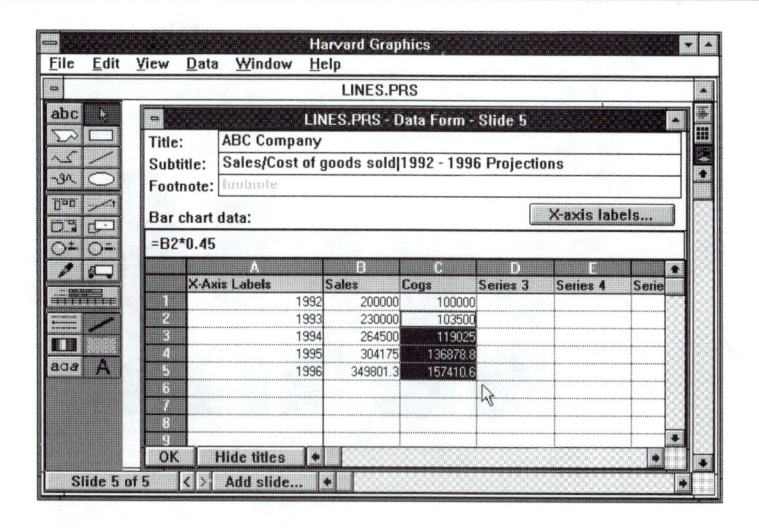

Figure 5-26. Completed Data Form with formulas

18. Now, you will make a few changes to improve the appearance of the chart. Select the Subtitle text and then choose Size from the Text menu and select 18 to make the subtitle text a little smaller.

19. Choose Labels from the Chart menu and then select Y1-axis label format. Select Currency and type a 0 in the Decimals field.

20. Select OK twice and then press F2 to display the chart shown in Figure 5-27.

Tip: If you are already a pro with spreadsheet entries you will be pleased to know that Harvard Graphics supports the $ character as part of a cell reference. This character stops Harvard Graphics from adjusting the cell reference as it is copied to new locations just as it does when used in spreadsheet formulas.

Using Keywords in Formulas

Harvard Graphics also provides many keywords that you can use in formulas. Table 5-1 shows the complete list of keywords supported. These

Figure 5-27.   Chart created with formulas

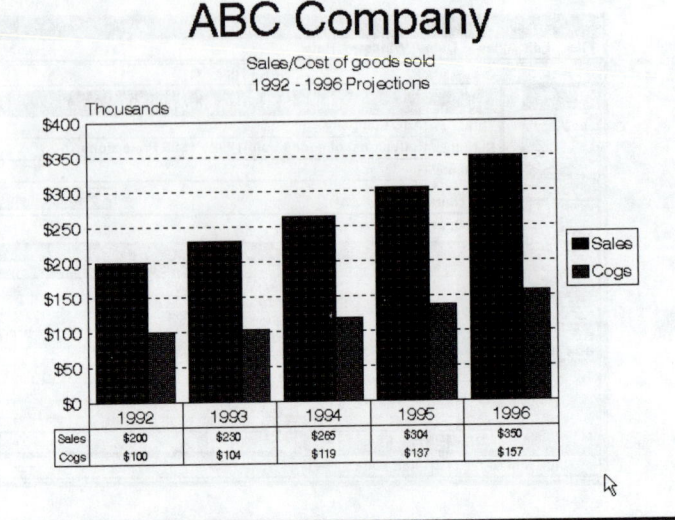

keywords are like the @functions in spreadsheet programs. This means that you do not need to know the statistical, mathematical, or trigonometric formula in order to perform a computation with it. All you need to do is spell the keyword correctly and follow the correct syntax when you provide other information such as data. Since these keywords minimize typing, they save time and minimize errors.

To calculate a series using a function, move to the cell needing the formula and type the equal sign =. Then type the keyword (for example, SUM). Next, you will need to supply an open parenthesis, arguments the function uses, and a closed parenthesis. Most function arguments are cell references (such as B2), cell ranges (such as B2:E4) specifying the first and last cell in a contiguous range of cells separated by a colon (:), or a value.

Table 5-1.   Formula Keywords

Keyword	Format Results
ABS(value)	Converts the value of the number to a positive number.
ACOS(value)	Returns the angle whose cosine is the value provided as the argument.
ASIN(value)	Returns the angle whose sine is the value provided as the argument.
ATAN(value)	Returns the angle represented by the tangent of value.
AVERAGE(cell range)	Averages the values in the cell range.
COS(angle)	Calculates the cosine of the angle.
COUNT(cell range)	Counts the number of nonblank cells in the range.
EXP(power)	Raises e (2.7182818) to a power.
INTEGER(value)	Returns the integer of the value.
LN(value)	Returns the natural logarithm of the value.
LOG(value)	Returns the common logarithm of the value.
@MAVG(cell,preceding, following)	Calculates a moving average of the values in the cell range. "Preceding" and "following" are used to select the number of cells before and after the cell.
MAXIMUM(cell range)	Returns the maximum value in the range.
MINIMUM(cell range)	Returns the minimum value in the range.
MOD(numerator, denominator)	Calculates remainder when the numerator is divided by the denominator.
@SIN(angle)	Calculates the sine of the angle.
SQRT(value)	Calculates the square root of value.
STDEV(cell range)	Calculates the standard deviation of the population specified by the cell range.
SUM(cell range)	Totals all the values in the cell range.
TAN(angle)	Calculates the tangent of the angle.
VARIANCE(cell range)	Computes the variance of the values specified by the population in the cell range.

To look at the use of a keyword, compute a series representing the average sales for the sales personnel in slide 3. Follow these steps:

1. Click the arrow at the bottom of the screen until slide 3 is displayed. Select Edit data from the Chart menu.

2. Move to the column heading for column F, type **Average**, and press (ENTER).

   Although Average is shown in the table of keywords as AVERAGE, it also has a short form, AVG, which saves a few keystrokes. You will use the abbreviated version when entering your formula in the next step. Other keywords with abbreviations are INT for INTEGER, MAX for MAXIMUM, MIN for MINIMUM, STD for STDEV, and VAR for VARIANCE. You can also use upper- or lowercase letters for any keyword entry.

3. Type **=AVG(B1:E1)** in F1 and press (ENTER).

Figure 5-28.   Using a keyword in a formula

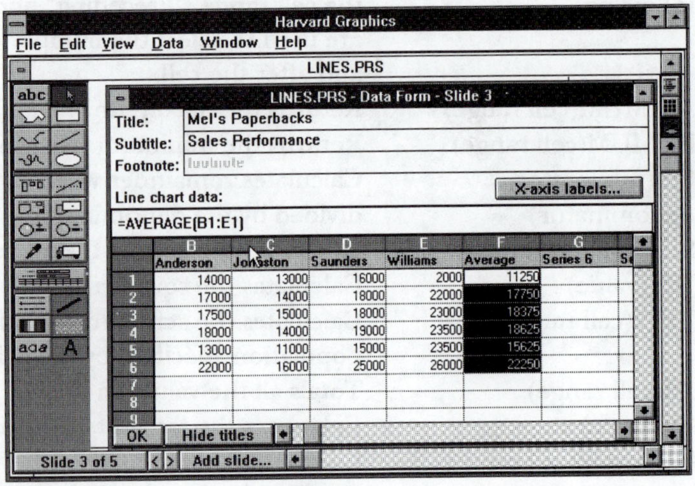

4. Select F1 through F6 and then choose Fill down from the Data menu.

   The formula is copied to the cells in the other rows and adjusted to average the sales for all personnel for that month. Figure 5-28 shows the formula.

   You can view this chart showing the detail for individuals and the average in Figure 5-29.

Figure 5-29. *Chart with details for individuals and average*

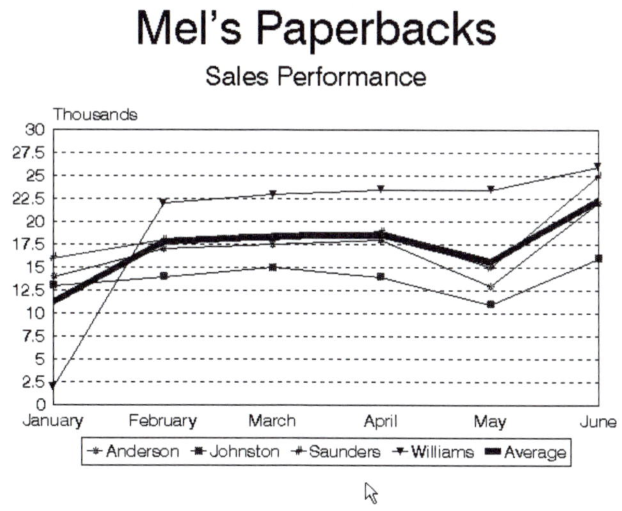
Mel's Paperbacks
Sales Performance
Thousands
30
27.5
25
22.5
20
17.5
15
12.5
10
7.5
5
2.5
0
January
February
March
April
May
June
Anderson
Johnston
Saunders
Williams
Average

6

Creating Pie Charts

Pie charts offer a different perspective than the other graph types and are ideal for showing the components of a whole, whether you are examining budget dollars, sales units, or headcount. They are particularly useful in presentations because your audience can identify important issues at a glance. As the chart name implies, a pie chart looks like a pie: The circle represents the whole, and each slice is sized according to the relative size of the data it represents in relation to the whole. Harvard Graphics provides many options for displaying data in a pie chart or in its close relative, a column chart. Added enhancements for pie and column charts include linking, 3D, multiple pies or columns, and cutting slices from the pie.

Getting Started

By now you are almost a pro at creating analytical charts, having made XY charts, but you need to add one final chart type to your list of options—the pie chart. Since pie charts do not use X and Y axes, they look very different from the other chart types. Pie charts are the ideal solution when you need to show data as part of a whole such as budget expenses or regional sales. Despite the differences, you will find that creating a pie chart is simple; you learned many of the basic steps when you created bar and line charts.

Figure 6-1 shows a pie chart on the Slide Editor window. Some of the tools used later in the chapter have been labeled for easy reference. To create this chart, follow these steps:

1. Choose Close from the File menu and determine whether you want to save any open presentations.

    Leaving unneeded presentations open will negatively impact performance and serve no useful purpose. Also, if you have not saved these presentations you are risking potential loss of some of your changes if the system should crash before you remember to close them.

2. Choose New presentation from the File menu.
3. Select Pie and then select OK.

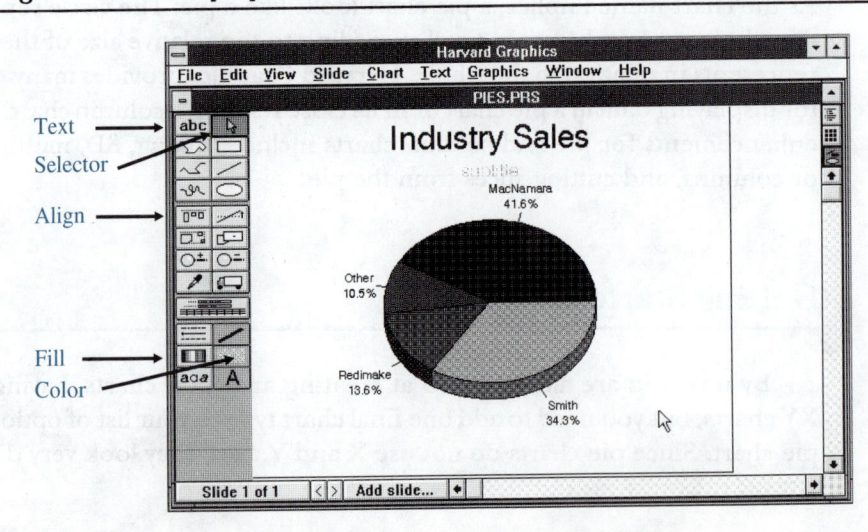

Figure 6-1.   Sample pie chart

Chapter 6: *Creating Pie Charts* 191

The Data Form for a pie chart appears. Although the top of the form is the same, the lower part differs due to the differences between XY charts and pie charts. Unlike the XY charts, pie charts do not have an X data type. Harvard Graphics assumes that the data in a pie consists of a series of labels and a series of values and provides for two columns of entries for each pie chart. The screen for entering the chart (Figure 6-2) shows the form for entering the data for the first nine slices of a pie with the data you will enter in cells A1:B4. You can enlarge the window or scroll down to enter data for 15 more slices since each pie can contain up to 24 slices.

4. Use (↑) to move to the Title field and then type **Industry Sales** in the Chart Title field and press (ENTER).

Tip: *There is no field for a pie label as in the DOS versions. You will be able to use the Text tool in the Slide Editor later to add pie titles and other text.*

5. Press (ENTER) twice to skip Subtitle and Footnote and move to the Pie1 Labels cell.

Figure 6-2. *Pie chart Data Form*

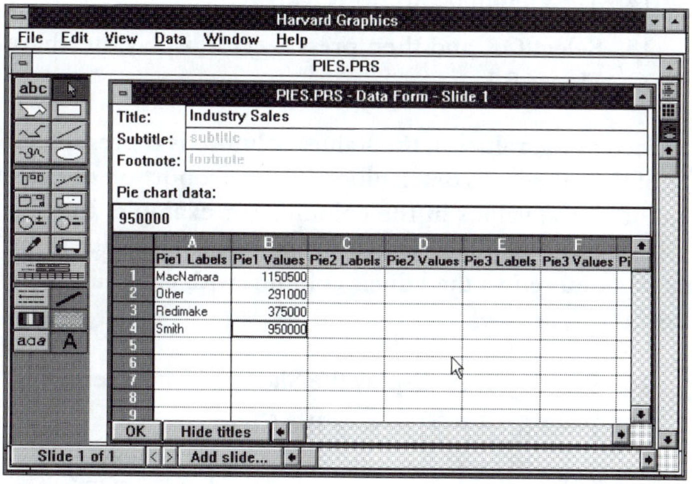

The table in the remaining portion of the screen is where you enter the data that will appear in the pie chart. The first column represents the pie slice label with each row representing a new slice up to a maximum of 24 slices. The second column is for the data representing the size of each slice in relation to the whole pie. Label and value columns alternate across the form for as many as six pie charts.

6. Type **MacNamara** for the first entry in the Pie1 Labels column and press (ENTER).
7. Type **Other** and press (ENTER).
   When a pie chart contains slices that are very small, you may not be able to distinguish them easily. It is a good idea to group them into a single category, usually called Other.
8. Type **Redimake** and press (ENTER).
9. Type **Smith** and press (ENTER).
10. Press (CTRL)+(HOME) so the highlight moves to the top of the column and press (TAB) to move to the Pie1 Values column.
11. Press (↓) and then type **1150500** and press (ENTER).
12. Type **291000** and press (ENTER).
13. Type **375000** and press (ENTER).
14. Type **950000** and press (ENTER).
15. Select OK and then press (F2) to display the chart shown earlier in Figure 6-1.

Each of the values in the Values columns is represented by a pie slice. The size of the pie slice is determined by the proportion of the slice's value to the total of all the values in the column. For example, the first slice represents 1150500 of 2766500, or 41.59%. Next to each pie slice is the descriptive label that you entered in the Labels columns with each slice's percent of the total below the slice label.

16. Press (ESC) to display the Slide Editor screen.
17. Press (CTRL)+(S) to save the Chart.
18. Type **PIES** for the filename and press (ENTER).

Chapter 6: *Creating Pie Charts*

19. Choose Print from the File menu, make any changes you need, and then select OK to print the presentation.

    If you want to change any print settings, do so at this point. For example, you may want to change whether the chart is printed in draft, high, or medium quality.

You are now ready to try the features Harvard Graphics provides to enhance the pie chart's appearance.

Tip: *You seldom want to use the theoretical limits for pie charts. Pies with 24 slices will be difficult to interpret and almost impossible to label since each slice will look like a sliver. Likewise, six pies on one chart will make each pie chart quite small and limit it to only a few slices.*

Setting the Slice's Appearance

You can control the appearance of the pie charts by selecting colors and fill patterns for individual slices. Or, you can cut slices from the pie to make them stand out. You can select bold patterns or bright colors to emphasize a particular slice. These options are not available as chart customization options from the Chart menu. As toolbox features, they are summoned from the Slide Editor screen using the mouse.

With the other graph types, you were able to exercise some control over the way each series of data was displayed from the Series option in the Chart menu. Pie slices are not series, but individual values, so you will control their appearance from the Slide Editor screen after selecting the slice of the pie that you want to change.

Selecting Colors

You can use solid colors for pie slices, although you will lose the ability to differentiate slices if your output is black and white. The first step in making this change is to select the pie slice that you want to alter. You will need to double-click on the first slice you want to change. If you only click once, Harvard Graphics selects the whole chart (as you can see by the handles around the entire pie chart). The second click places a single handle in the center of the pie slice and an outline around the entire chart. As long as this outline is around the chart, you can select another slice by clicking the next slice.

Once a slice is selected you can use the Color or Fill option in the toolbox to change it. To use the Color tool, click the color tool and then select the desired color from the dialog box displayed. The Color tool is shown in the earlier screen, Figure 6-1. Initially slice 4 of the pie was color 24, 15 was selected from the dialog box, and OK was selected to make this slice color 15. You can see the change to a lighter color. Follow these steps to make the change yourself:

1. Double-click the slice for Smith on the Slide Editor screen. A handle appears in the center of the slice and a box outlines the entire chart.
2. Select the Color tool.
3. Select Color 15 in the Chart Colors in the top table and then select OK.

    The color immediately changes to a solid color without a pattern. You can undo the change by selecting Undo from the Edit menu if you prefer the earlier appearance.

The Fill feature will allow you to change the color of a slice while retaining patterns within the slice.

Selecting Fill

To set the pattern of a pie slice, the slice must be selected. If this is the first slice you are changing, double-click the slice. If there is an outline around the chart and a different slice already selected you will only need to click the desired slice. You can use the Fill tool or choose Fill from the Graphics menu to make the change. These options could have also changed the color of the slice you just worked with to a solid pattern. It is the second option in the Fill bar that alters patterns. If you are using the menu you can simply choose Hatch/Pattern from the Fill menu. You can then choose from the Fill options discussed in Chapter 3, "Creating Text Charts," for bar chart changes. Selecting a different pattern or different background and foreground colors are all possibilities. To change the foreground or background color, all you need to do is select the existing color swatches to see a full dialog box of color options.

Cutting Pie Slices

One method of emphasizing a pie slice is to pull it away from the center of the pie. This is called cutting a pie slice. You must select the pie slice and then move to the handle in the center of the slice until the mouse pointer becomes a four-sided arrow. You can then drag the slice away from the center to cut it from the pie. Putting the cut slice back into the pie requires the same steps except the dragging is toward the center rather than away from it.

Try cutting the Smith pie slice from your pie chart by following these steps:

1. Move the mouse pointer to the Smith pie slice and double-click the mouse.
2. Move the mouse pointer toward the center of the Smith slice until it displays as a four-sided arrow.
3. Drag the slice away from the pie and then release the mouse button.
   Notice in Figure 6-3 how the slice for Smith is separated from the other slices and still contains the handle in the center. Clicking a blank area on the slide will remove the handle.

Displaying Multiple Pies

You can add a second pie to a pie chart and use it to break down a pie slice in the first pie. For example, you can add a second pie to the Industry Sales pie chart that breaks down the composition of Other or represents next year's sales. When you add a second pie, you can select options to make it proportional to the first and to link pie slices. The appearance of the second pie is controlled by the same options that control the first pie chart. You can add up to six pies to a chart.

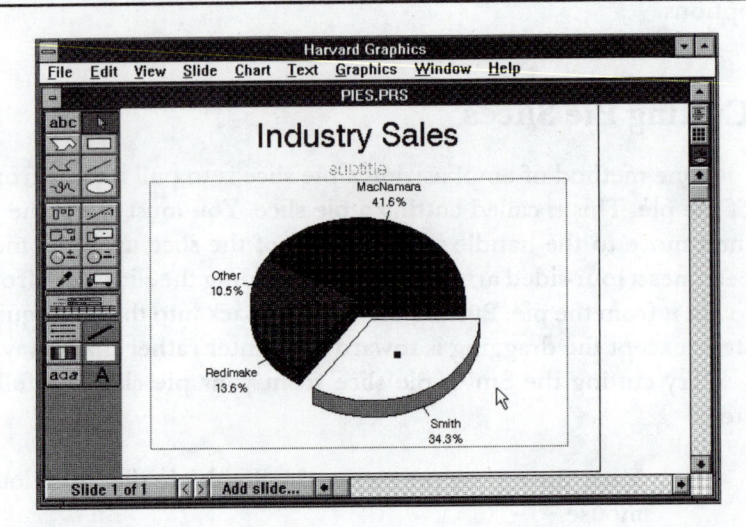

Figure 6-3. **Pie chart with an exploded slice**

Adding a Second Pie

To add a second pie, you only have to enter the data that you want to appear in the pie. You will also be introduced to some new features in this exercise to enable you to reorganize the data for one pie chart without affecting the others. In addition, you will add text labels to the pies and align them for a neat appearance. To add a second pie to the Industry Sales pie chart, follow these steps.

1. Select Edit data from the Chart menu.

    This displays the Data Form. Harvard Graphics uses this same form to enter the data that will appear in the second pie chart. The title, subtitle, and footnote at the top of the form will still be used since they appear at the top of the slide, not at the top of the first pie chart. If you want titles above the pie charts you will need to enter them with the Text tool in the Slide Editor.

2. Press (CTRL)+(HOME), press (TAB) twice, and then press (↓).
3. Type **Mardin** in row one of the Label column and press (ENTER).

Chapter 6: *Creating Pie Charts*

4. Type **Young & Sons** and press (ENTER).
5. Type **Taylor**.
6. Press (CTRL)+(HOME), press (TAB) three times, and then press (↓) to position for entering values for the Mardin slice.
7. Type **70000** and press (ENTER).
8. Type **71000** and press (ENTER).
9. Type **90000** and press (ENTER).

Let's change the order of the data in this example, making the entries alphabetical. To move Taylor before Young & Sons:

10. Move the highlight to C2 and then select C2:D2 with the mouse.
11. Choose Cu̲t from the E̲dit menu.
12. Move the highlight to C4 and then choose P̲aste from the E̲dit menu.
    The entries are in alphabetical order but there are blanks in C2:D2. Although you will actually want to add this blank row back in a minute you will delete this space for practice—in the event you need to duplicate this action on your own Data Form later. To eliminate the blank cells in columns C and D, you will move the entries in C3:D4 up one row.
13. Select C3:D4 and then choose Cu̲t from the E̲dit menu.
14. Move the highlight to C2 and then choose P̲aste from the E̲dit menu.
    Since the order of the data determines the order of the pie slice in a pie chart, another change you may want to make is to insert data points. You cannot insert an entire row without changing the data for pie chart 1 so you will need to move the data for pie chart 2 down to allow a blank row at an appropriate place to add data that comes before Taylor. This opens back up the space you removed earlier for a new entry.
15. Move the highlight to C2 and select C2..D3. Choose Cu̲t from the E̲dit menu, move the highlight to C3, and then choose P̲aste from the E̲dit menu. This action leaves space to add entries for Stattler.
16. Move to C2, type **Stattler**, and press (TAB).
17. Type **60000** and press (ENTER).

18. Select OK. Double-click the Smith slice and then drag this slice back to the center of the chart to eliminate the cut effect.
19. Press (F2) to display the slide with the two charts as shown in Figure 6-4.
    Once you have entered data in the Pie Chart 2 screen, Harvard Graphics includes the second pie in the pie chart. You can customize the second pie in the same way you did the first pie. You can change the appearance of slices in one pie without affecting the other pies.

To hide the second pie:

20. Press (ESC) to return to the Slide Editor screen.
21. Choose Series from the Chart menu.
22. Select Pie 1 in the Edit list box.
23. Select Show pie to remove the X from the check box and then select OK. Pie chart 2 displays without pie chart 1.
24. Choose Series from the Chart menu again, select Pie 1, select Show pie, and then select OK to show the chart with both pies again.

Figure 6-4. Two pies on a slide

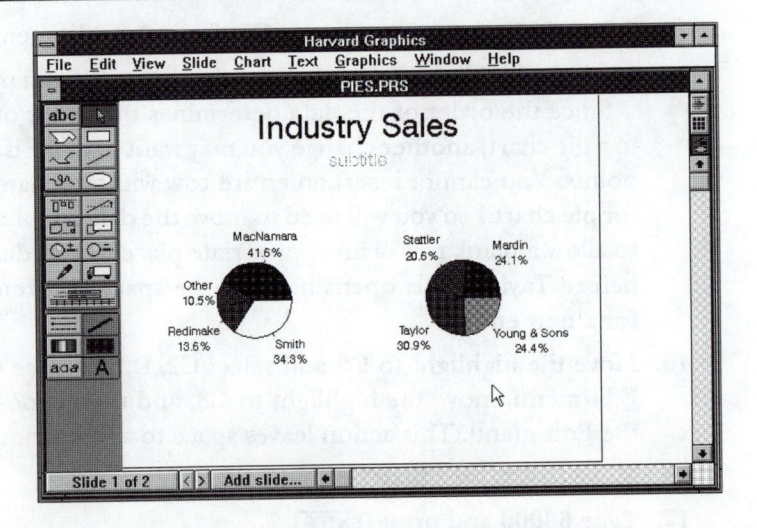

Adding Pie Chart Labels

Once you have multiple pie charts on a slide you may want to add a label for each pie. These labels are added with the Text Annotator tool in the Slide Editor, we will refer to this tool at the Text tool. You can use this tool to place text in any location on a slide. If you use it to add text at the bottom of several different pies, you may find it difficult to align the text perfectly. You do not need to be too concerned since you can use the Align tool to make it perfect.

Follow these steps to add labels at the bottom of the pie charts:

1. Choose Size from the Text menu and then select 18 to choose an appropriate size for the labels.

2. Select the Text tool.

3. Move to the bottom of Pie 1 at a location where you want to begin a label for the pie. Click the mouse and then drag across to create the box that will contain the label for this pie.

4. Type **1992 Sales** and then move the mouse pointer below the Pie 2 chart.

5. Click the mouse and then drag the mouse to make a box for this label and then type **Breakdown of Other**.

6. Click the Selector tool and then select both labels by using the Shift key in combination with the mouse.

    You will need to hold down the (SHIFT) key as you drag the mouse to create a box containing box text entries.

7. Select the Align tool and then select the second option in column two from the alignment options shown in the dialog box like Figure 6-5. Select OK.

    The text aligns along one line as shown in Figure 6-6. You can eliminate the box around both pie titles by selecting the Selector tool and clicking a blank area of the chart.

Tip: *You can add titles for multiple charts, but if you later decide to hide some of the pie charts, the titles do not automatically go away. You will have to delete the unneeded text. You can always restore it again after viewing the single pie, as long as there are not more than four actions in Harvard Graphics' Undo stack.*

Figure 6-5.   *Align dialog box*

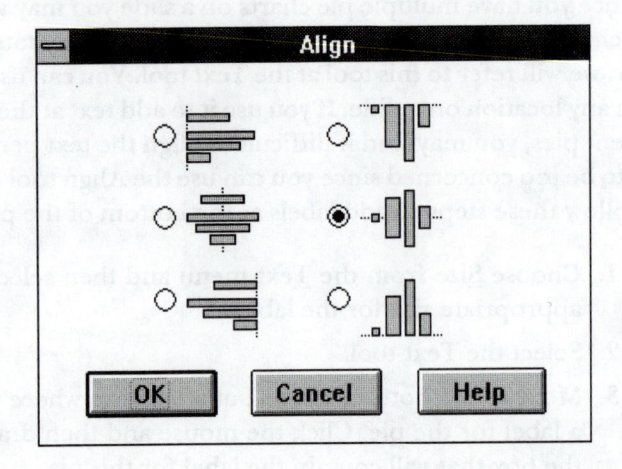

Figure 6-6.   *Pies labels aligned*

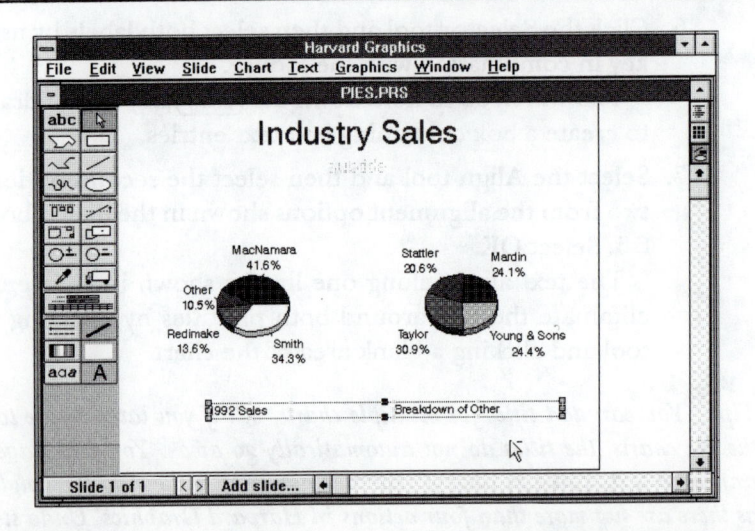

Creating Another Multiple Pie Chart Slide

Sometimes you want to create several pie charts that have the same labels. You might be showing the breakdown of product sales by region or year. There is no need to enter the labels multiple times as you will see in this next example. Follow these steps to create a new slide:

1. Select Add Slide, select Pie, and then select OK.
2. Move to the Title field, type **Product Breakdown**, and then press (ENTER).
3. Type **By Sales Dollars** and press (ENTER).
4. Move to A1 and type **Wagons** and press (ENTER).
5. Type **Bikes** and press (ENTER).
6. Type **Sleds** and press (ENTER).
7. Type **Dolls** and press (ENTER).
8. Press (CTRL)+(HOME), press (TAB), and then press (↓). Type the following values in B1..B4, pressing (ENTER) after each:

   B1:   235980
   B2:   345987
   B3:   125098
   B4:   298709

9. Press (CTRL)+(HOME) and then press (TAB) followed by (↓) to move to cell D1.

   There is no need to type labels for the second pie since they will be the same as for the first pie, allowing you to leave column C blank.

10. Type the following values in D1:D4 for the Pie2 Values:

    D1:   200000
    D2:   500000
    D3:   100000
    D4:   525000

11. Select OK and then choose Chart options from the Chart menu.

12. Select Share pie labels to place an X in the check box and then select OK.
13. Select the Text tools and then click where you want to begin typing text for the Pie 1 chart. Type **1992 Sales**.
14. Click where you want to enter the label for the Pie 2 chart. Type **1993 Sales** and then select the Selector tool and use Shift and the mouse to drag a box around both labels.
15. Select the Align tool, select the second option in column 2, and then select OK.
16. Select the Selector tool and click a blank area of the chart to remove the box around the labels.
17. Press (F2) to display the chart as shown in Figure 6-7.
    As you can see, Harvard Graphics shows both pies.
18. Press (ESC) to return to the Slide Editor screen.

Options for Multiple Pies

You can use two additional customizing options when you create a chart that contains more than one pie: you can size the pies based on the total of the values in the pies, and you can link one pie to another. Linking the pies creates a visual connection between a slice in one pie and the next pie.

Proportionally Sized Pies

You can size multiple pies to make them proportional to the values in the pies. This feature allows you to use the overall size of the pies to indicate a proportional increase or decrease. For example, the sales for 1993 may be 29% more than the sales for the previous year. You can graphically show this on the chart by making the second pie 29% larger than the first pie. Harvard Graphics will compute the percent increase or decrease for you when you select Proportional Pies and automatically apply this to the sizing of the two charts.

Figure 6-7. *Two pie charts*

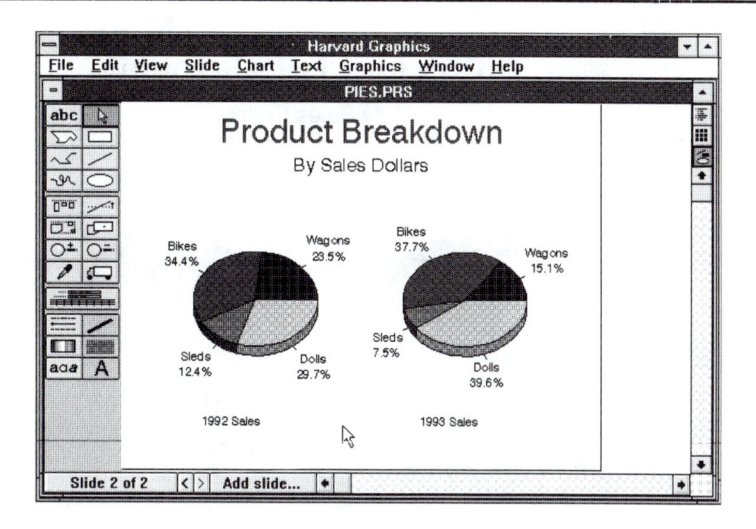

To try this feature using the data in slide 2 follow these steps:

1. Choose Chart options from the Chart menu.
2. Select "Make pies proportional" and then select OK.
3. Press (F2) to preview the chart that appears in Figure 6-8.

The first pie is smaller than the second. This provides a quick graphical illustration of the increase of sales in the industry. When you use this option, the totals of the two pies should not be so different that the smaller pie becomes too small to read or so similar they are almost identical in size.

4. Press (ESC) to return to the Slide Editor screen.
5. Press (CTRL)+(S) to save the presentation again.

Linking Pies

In the pie charts shown in Figure 6-6, the label under the second pie is the only explanation of its meaning. Many readers looking quickly at the chart

Figure 6-8.   Proportional pie display

Product Breakdown
By Sales Dollars

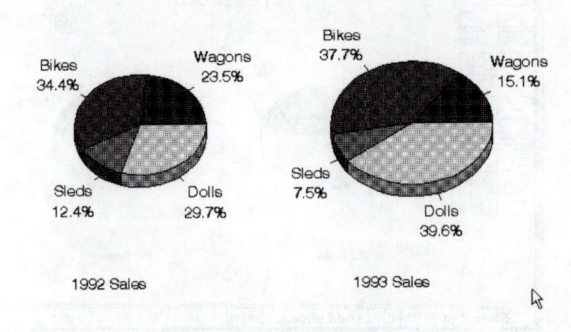

1992 Sales — Bikes 34.4%, Wagons 23.5%, Dolls 29.7%, Sleds 12.4%

1993 Sales — Bikes 37.7%, Wagons 15.1%, Dolls 39.6%, Sleds 7.5%

would not see that the second pie provides a more detailed breakdown of the category Other in the first pie. To improve this chart, you can add graphic lines to the pies to connect the Other slice from the first pie to the second pie. This is referred to as linking the two pie charts. You will need to specify which piece of chart 1 is linked to the second pie chart.

Try linking pie charts by following these steps:

1. Use the Arrow at the bottom of the screen to make slide 1 active.
2. Choose Chart options from the Chart menu.
3. Select "Link pies" and then select Slice 2 from the list since this is the slice that corresponds to Other.

    Harvard Graphics places slice 1 at the 3 o'clock position and travels in a counter-clockwise direction as it adds other slices to the chart.

4. Select OK.

    The chart now has lines connecting the first pie's Other slice to the second pie. This provides a graphical illustration of the title for

Chapter 6: *Creating Pie Charts* 205

the second pie chart. Harvard Graphics will rotate the first pie if the linked slice is not next to the other pie. You can link a slice of the first pie to the second pie, but not a slice of the second pie to the first pie. In this example, pie 1 is rotated to make the Other slice adjacent to pie 2 to allow for the linking lines. The lines linking the slice to pie 2 obscure part of the label for this slice. You can change the label position or try the charts as 2D to see if that eliminates the problem.

5. Choose Chart options from the Chart menu again.
6. Select 3D to turn 3D off and then select OK.
7. Press (F2) to preview the chart as shown in Figure 6-9.

   The 2D display takes care of the label problem that occurred initially.
8. Press (ESC) to return to the Slide Editor screen.

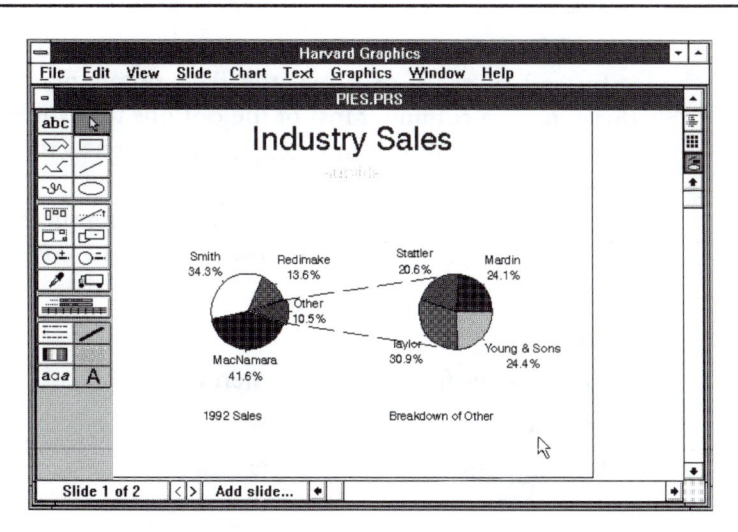

Figure 6-9.   *Linking two pies*

Enhancing the Pie's Appearance

Let's look at additional options for enhancing the appearance of a pie chart using the pie charts you have completed. Displaying pies as columns, sorting the order of the pie slices, adjusting the pie size and starting angle, changing the size of slice pointers, changing the slice labeling, and changing the depth and tilt of a 3D pie are some of the changes you can make.

Displaying Pies as Columns

Another pie chart option allows you to display pie data in a column, with the column divided into components. Figure 6-10 shows the chart from Figure 6-9 with the second pie displayed as a column instead of a pie. You can make this chart by following these steps:

1. Choose Series from the Chart menu.
2. Select Pie 2 from the Edit list box.
3. Select Column for Pie style.
4. Select OK.
5. Press (F2) to display the chart.

    Instead of slices of a pie, the data points are represented by divisions of a column. Most of the options that you can use for pie slices also apply to column components, such as three-dimensional effect.

    Although you will learn more about labeling slices later you need to make a quick change right now to make the column chart more readable.

6. Press (ESC).
7. Choose Labels from the Chart menu.
8. Select Pie2 from the Edit list box.
9. Select Adjacent below "Show percents."

Chapter 6: *Creating Pie Charts* 207

Figure 6-10.   Displaying one pie as a column chart

Industry Sales

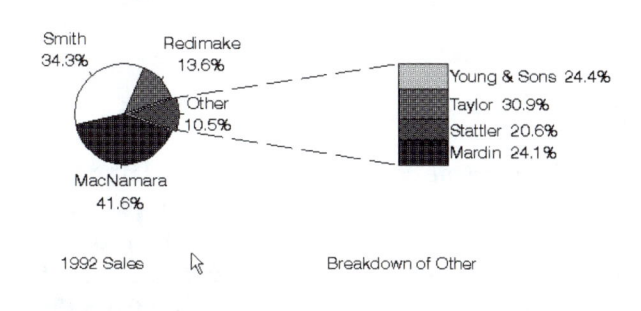

```
Smith        Redimake
34.3%         13.6%
                                    Young & Sons 24.4%
               Other                Taylor  30.9%
               10.5%                Stattler  20.6%
                                    Mardin  24.1%
MacNamara
41.6%

    1992 Sales                  Breakdown of Other
```

10. Select OK to display the slide as shown in Figure 6-10.

    The labels for the column sections present a better appearance now that the percentages are shown next to the labels rather than below them.

Sorting Pie Slices

You can control the order in which data for a pie chart is displayed on the chart by using the "Sort slices" option in the Series dialog box. For example, on slide 1 you entered the data for the four categories in pie 2 in alphabetical order. Another possible option is to order them according to size.

To sort the slices in the pie 2 (shown as a column in Figure 6-10) by size, follow these steps:

1. Choose Series from the Chart menu.

2. Select Pie 2 in the Edit list box.
3. Select "Sort slices" and then select OK.
4. Press (F2) to preview the pie chart.

    The sections of the column are now arranged from largest to smallest. For columns, the largest component is on the bottom. For pies, the slices are arranged in counterclockwise order.
5. Press (ESC) to return to the Slide Editor screen.

Changing the Pie's Starting Angle

In all of the pie charts you have created, the pies always start at one point and work counterclockwise. This may not present the image you want. You may want a particular slice to appear at the top. You can rotate the pie slices within the pie area by changing its *starting angle,* which is the angle at which the first pie slice starts. The pie continues from this angle around the circle in a counterclockwise direction. Initially, pies have a zero starting angle, which starts them at the 3 o'clock position in the circle.

You will enter data for one last pie chart slide and then try changing the starting angle to see the effect of this option by following these steps:

1. Move to slide 2 with the arrow at the bottom of the screen or select Add slide.
2. Select Pie and then select OK.
3. Move to the Title field and type **ABC Company** and then press (ENTER).
4. Type **1992 Budget Expenses** and press (ENTER) three times.
5. Type **Salaries** and press (ENTER).
6. Type **Travel** and press (ENTER).
7. Type **Rent** and press (ENTER).
8. Type **Utilities** and press (ENTER).
9. Type **Phone** and press (ENTER).
10. Press (CTRL)+(HOME), press (TAB) and then press (↓). Type the following numbers in B1:B5:

Chapter 6: *Creating Pie Charts*

        B1:   1250000
        B2:   500000
        B3:   415000
        B4:   250000
        B5:   300000

11. Select OK to display the Slide Editor screen with the chart.
    Notice how the Salaries slice is at the 3 o'clock position.

12. Choose Series from the Chart menu.

13. Use the mouse to drag the indicator on the dial shown in Figure 6-11 to 240 or type **240** in the "Starting angle" text box.

    The starting angle is a value between 0 and 360. As the starting angle increases, the starting position of the first slice moves counterclockwise. Once you enter a rough estimate, you can fine-tune the value of the "Starting angle option."

14. Select OK and then press (F2) to preview the chart in Figure 6-12.

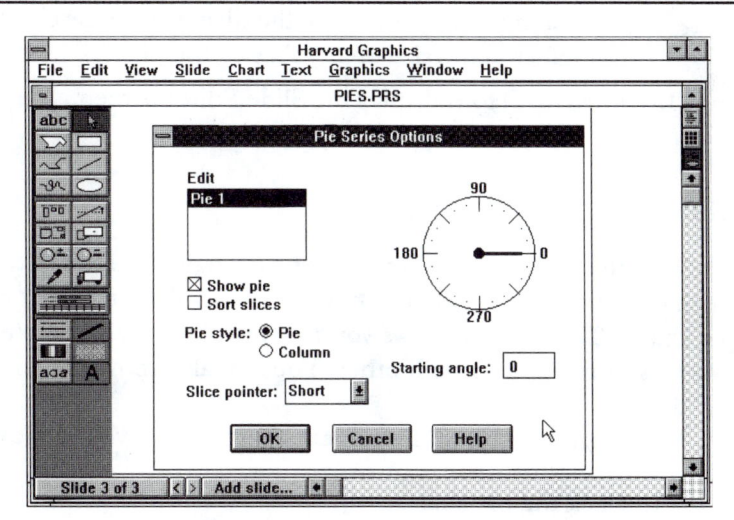

Figure 6-11.   *Pie Series Options dialog box*

Figure 6-12.   *Sorted pie slices*

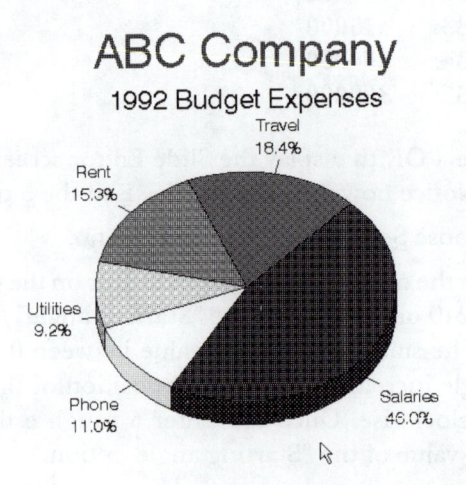

ABC Company
1992 Budget Expenses

- Travel 18.4%
- Rent 15.3%
- Utilities 9.2%
- Phone 11.0%
- Salaries 46.0%

You have moved Salaries to the right side of the pie. By changing the angle that Harvard Graphics starts drawing the pie slices, you are changing the position of the slices within the circle, but you have not affected the size of any slice of the pie.

15. Press ESC to redisplay the Slide Editor screen.

Changing the Pie Size

With the Proportional Pies field you changed the sizes of two pies to make them proportional. Another option is to manually set the size of one or more pie charts. This option allows you to control the size of a pie or the size of two pies in relation to each other. You can also move the pie to a different location.

To change the size of the current chart and move it, follow these steps:

1. Click the pie chart.
   Handles will appear around the chart.

Chapter 6: *Creating Pie Charts* 211

2. Grab the handle at the lower-right corner and drag down on it slightly.

   The chart becomes larger when you release the mouse. You can pull or push on any of the four corner handles to make the chart image larger or smaller.

3. Click the chart if the handles are no longer around it.
4. Move the mouse pointer to the center so a four-sided arrow appears.
5. Drag the chart slightly to the right.
6. Choose Undo from the Edit menu to move the chart back to its original location. Choose Undo from the Edit menu again to return the chart to its original size.

Tip: You may want to manually set the pie sizes if the pie size differential is too great to use the Proportional Pies field.

Setting the Size of Slice Pointers

Slice pointers are the lines that radiate from the pie chart and connect to the slice labels. You can change their size to Short, Medium, Long, or None to help prevent label overlap. The length of slice pointers are set for an entire pie, although you can use different lengths for different pie charts on the same slide. To change the length of the pointers for a pie you would choose Series from the Chart menu. You would select the pie chart you wanted to change from the Edit list box. Next you would click the arrow next to the Slice Pointer and select the length of the pointer that you want to use.

Changing Options for 3D Charts

Two pie attributes Tilt and Depth allow you to change the appearance of a 3D chart. As Tilt is increased, it is as if the top edge of the chart is raised allowing you to see more of the top surface and less of the side edge of the chart. The default setting for the pie chart shown in Figure 6-12 is 75. You can assign any value from 0 to 75 with higher numbers offering more tilt. Figure 6-13 shows a decreased tilt over the earlier figure with the tilt changed

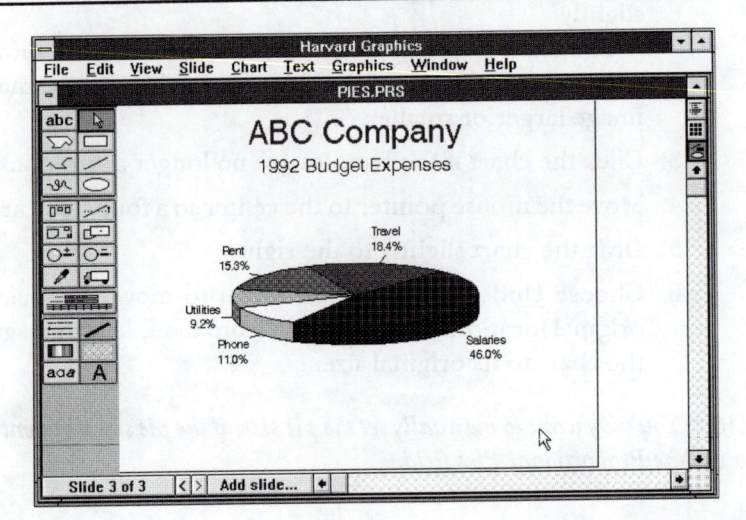

Figure 6-13. *Changing the tilt of a 3D pie chart*

to 25. This change was made by choosing Chart options from the Chart menu, changing Tilt to 25, and then selecting OK.

The depth option makes 3D more prominent since it makes the chart appear thicker. The default setting for the chart in Figure 6-12 is 15 with any number from 1 to 100 acceptable. High numbers offer added depth. Figure 6-14 shows the same figure with the depth increased to 40. This change was made by choosing Chart options from the Chart menu, changing depth to 40, and selecting OK.

Legends for Pie Charts

Since your pie charts have labels on each slice (the default setting), no legend is shown. You can add legends to pie charts. You will have the same options for placement and frames that you used with XY charts. If you decide to remove labels from slices in the sections that follow, you should consider adding legends to your pie chart. To work with legends on a pie chart, choose Legend from the Chart menu. You will need to select the "Show legend"

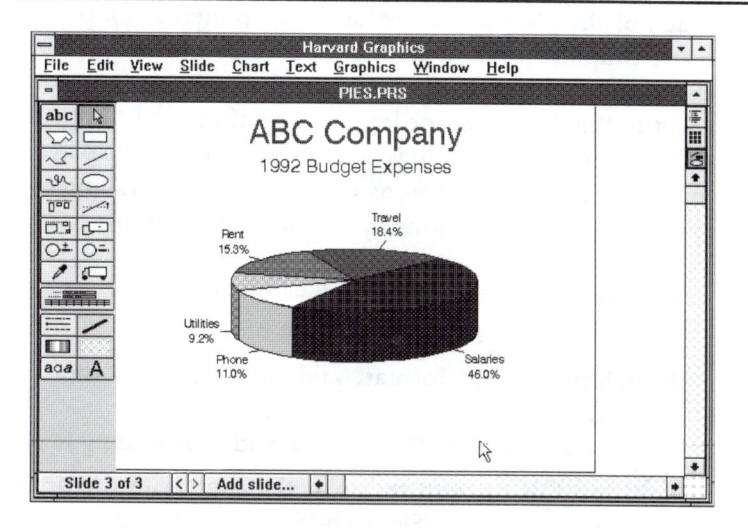

Figure 6-14.   *Changing the depth of a 3D pie chart*

option to add an X to the check box. The dialog box that displays allows you to change the location and frame as well. When you are finished making changes, you can select OK to return to the Slide Editor screen.

Selecting Label Display

The Labels dialog box provides options that determine if pie slice labels appear and their appearance. After choosing Labels from the Chart menu, the "Show slice labels" check box in the dialog box determines whether or not labels (entered in the pie chart labels column of the Data Form) display. You can also choose whether to show actual data values and/or percents along with the labels by selecting the appropriate check boxes on the dialog box. You can also choose where to place this extra information in relation to the slice labels. If you do not show values or percents the placement options are dimmed. All of these changes are made by choosing Labels from the Chart menu.

Using Percents

Each of the pie slices or column components is a portion of the total. Harvard Graphics' default settings add these percentages beneath the slice labels on your charts. You can place these percents inside the pie slices, adjacent to the slice labels or leave them off the chart entirely. You can also change the format of labels if you elect to keep them displayed. You can alter the number of decimal places as well as leading or trailing text.

Try some of these options by following these steps:

1. Choose La<u>b</u>els from the <u>C</u>hart menu.
2. Select Inside for the "Location of percents."
3. Select "Percent format" and then type **0** in the "Decimal places" field.
   Notice how the % symbol is added as trailing text.
4. Select OK twice to redisplay the chart with the percents inside the slices as shown in Figure 6-15.

Changing the Value's Appearance

In the pie charts you have created, the values entered in the Values columns of the pie Data Forms did not appear since this is the default setting. You can decide if the values should appear, where, and their format, using the options in the Labels dialog box that you just used. Values use the same settings that were described previously for Percents.

"Show values" determines if the values will appear. If you have an X in "Show values," you can select from Below, which places the values underneath the labels; Adjacent, which places the values to the right of the labels; and Inside, which places the values inside the pie slices. If you select Inside, make sure that the color or pattern does not obscure the labels.

Three check boxes allow you to choose whether or not to display extra symbols with the value. Currency selects whether Harvard Graphics displays

Chapter 6: *Creating Pie Charts* 215

Figure 6-15. *Percents inside slices*

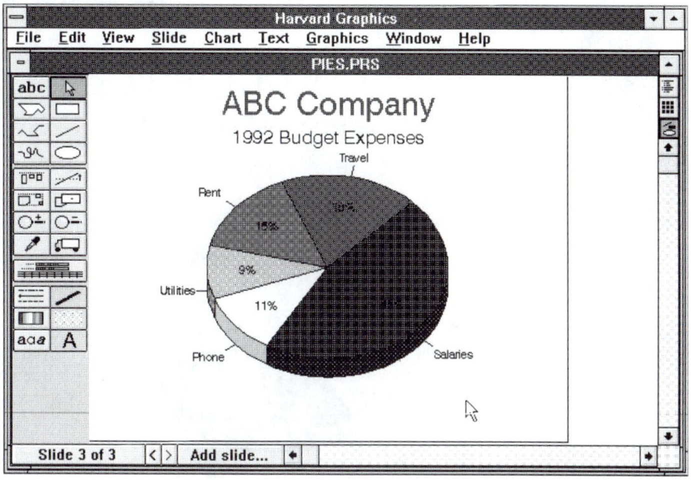

$ before values (or the currently selected currency symbol in the Windows Control Panel). "Thousands separator" determines whether the decimal separator defined in the Windows Control Panel is added to your entries. Scientific notation displays the values in scientific notation. The "Decimal places" text box allows you to show as many as nine decimal places. It is initially blank. The last two options, Trailing text and Leading text let you enter text that appears to the left or right of each value.

Try some of these options on the current slide by following these steps:

1. Choose Labels from the Chart menu.
2. Select "Show values" to add an X.
3. Select Location and then select Below.

Figure 6-16.   *Values displayed below labels with thousand separator and currency symbol*

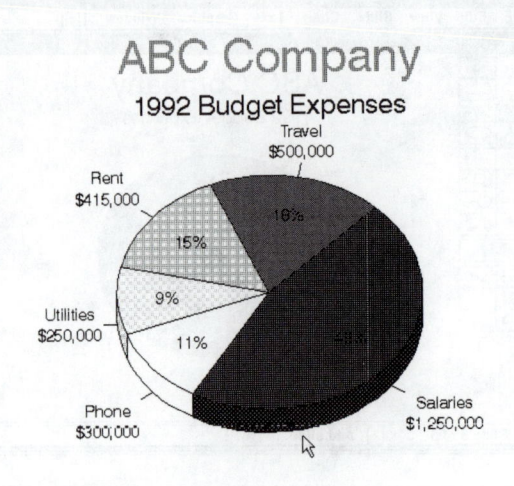

ABC Company
1992 Budget Expenses

Travel
$500,000

Rent
$415,000

15%

16%

9%

Utilities
$250,000

11%

Phone
$300,000

Salaries
$1,250,000

4. Select Value Format, "Thousands separator," and Currency to place an X in these boxes.

5. Select OK twice and then press (F2) to display the chart, which looks like Figure 6-16.

6. Press (ESC) and then press (CTRL)+(S) to save the presentation file again.

7

Creating Organization Charts

Organization charts are used to show the hierarchical structure representing a company, division, region, or department. Typically, organization charts are composed of a series of boxes in a pyramid shape, with the names and positions of managers in the organizational unit written in each box. Typing an organization chart has always been a nightmare for a typist trying to size the boxes properly in order to fit all the names inside the boxes and still place them symmetrically on a page. Harvard Graphics eliminates this problem because it automatically sizes all the boxes on a chart for you, making sure that all the boxes on the same level are the same size. Boxes at a lower level are also never made larger than the boxes at a higher level. A size is automatically chosen for the text in boxes to fit the longest name within the box size. Not only are these boxes quick to create initially, but they also are a breeze to revise; making modifications, deletions, and additions requires only a few seconds.

Harvard Graphics allows you to enter names, titles, and comments as you create organization charts. You can have as many as ten levels of entries, and you can control the appearance of these charts in a number of ways. You can make entries from the Outliner or the Data Form provided by the Slide Editor. An icon will mark each level in the chart, and a special icon is used for staff positions that have a different relationship to the hierarchical structure presented.

If you are creative, you may find that the organization chart format can be used for other things. For instance, you might use this format to show the stores within a region of the country, your family tree, or the organization of a software package. Figure 7-1 shows an organization chart used to diagram an accounting system that is composed of a series of program modules. The module name, description, and programmer's name are entered in fields normally used for employee names and job titles. After working only a few minutes, you have a graphical representation of the relationships within the programming modules and can tell at a glance who to contact if you experience a failure in any program module.

Figure 7-1.   *Stevens Accounting System modules*

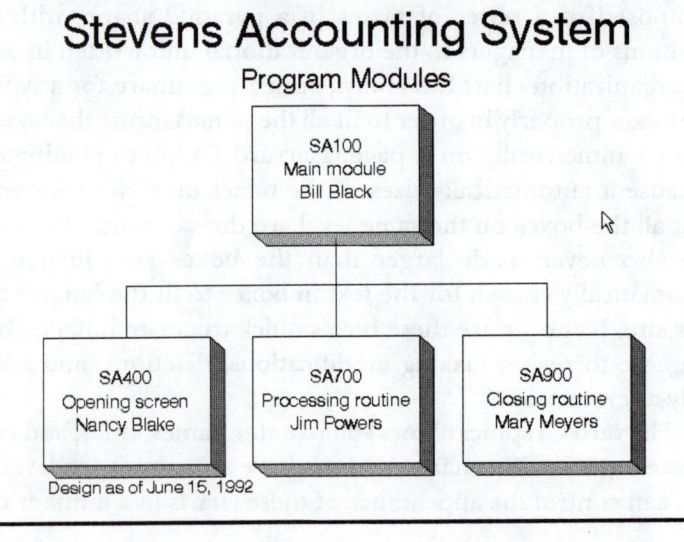

Stevens Accounting System
Program Modules

SA100
Main module
Bill Black

SA400
Opening screen
Nancy Blake

SA700
Processing routine
Jim Powers

SA900
Closing routine
Mary Meyers

Design as of June 15, 1992

Chapter 7: *Creating Organization Charts*

Getting Started

Creating an organization chart is easy with Harvard Graphics. You can focus on structure since Harvard Graphics makes it easy to enter text and create boxes. The chart in this exercise will be created from the Slide Editor as the first slide in a new presentation. It will duplicate the chart shown in **Figure 7-1** to provide an overview of Stevens Accounting System. Follow these steps:

1. Choose <u>N</u>ew presentation from the <u>F</u>ile menu after closing any presentations that you were previously working on. (These instructions assume that you still have the default view for new presentations set to Slide Editor.)
2. Select the Organization chart radio button and then select the OK command button.
   The Data Form for an untitled organization chart appears on your screen as shown in Figure 7-2. Harvard Graphics is ready for you to complete the entry for the top box on the form.
3. Press (↑) three times to move to the area for a title entry that will name the slide.
4. Type **Stevens Accounting System** over the faded title entry and press (ENTER).
5. Type **Program Modules** for the subtitle and press (ENTER).
6. Type **Design as of June 15, 1992** and press (ENTER).
7. Type **SA100** in the Name field for the top level and press (ENTER).
8. Type **Main module** for the Job Title field to provide a description for the module and press (CTRL)+(ENTER). ((CTRL)+(ENTER) forces the entry to the next line but not the next box.)
9. Type **Bill Black** for the programmer's name and press (ENTER). (Harvard Graphics automatically indents for the next level.)
10. Type **SA400** and press (ENTER) to specify the first module on the next level.

Figure 7-2. *Organization chart Data Form*

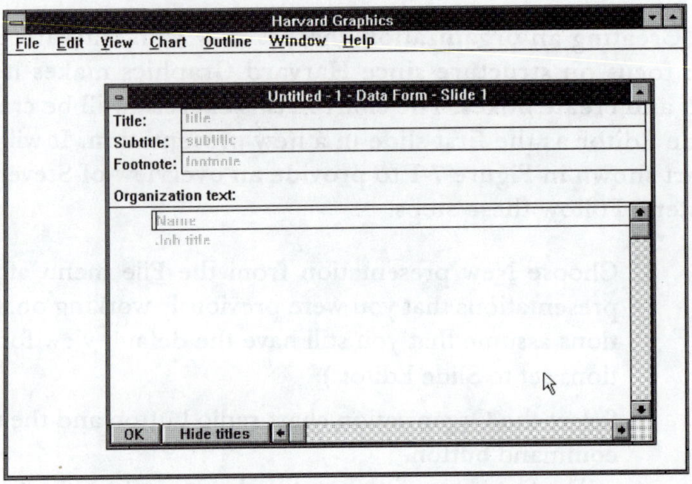
Harvard Graphics
File Edit View Chart Outline Window Help
Untitled - 1 - Data Form - Slide 1
Title:
title
Subtitle:
subtitle
Footnote:
footnote
Organization text:
Name
Job title
OK
Hide titles

11. Type **Opening screen**, press (CTRL)+(ENTER) and then type **Nancy Blake** and press (ENTER). Harvard Graphics assumes that each level entry is on the same level as the previous entry.
12. Type **SA700** and press (ENTER). Type **Processing routine** and press (CTRL)+(ENTER). Type **Jim Powers** and press (ENTER).
13. Type **SA900** and press (ENTER). Type **Closing routine** and press (CTRL)+(ENTER). Type **Mary Meyers**. Then select OK.
14. Press (F2) to view the chart as it would print. You will notice that level 2 is shown without boxes. Later, you will learn to change this default setting.
15. Press (ESC) to return to the Slide Editor. Choose Save as from the File menu. Type **STEVENS** and press (ENTER). Choose Close from the File menu.

The presentation that you just saved consists of a single slide. Later you can retrieve it and change the appearance of the last level of entries if you wish.

Chapter 7: *Creating Organization Charts*

Tip: *Harvard Graphics uses your entry for the name and title to determine the size of the boxes. Consider abbreviations if your entries are long—or the text will be too small to read.*

Adding an Organization Chart to a Slide

In Chapter 2, "Outlining a Presentation," you may have created the presentation for Mesopotamia Metals. A slide was entered in this presentation to mark the place for an organization chart to be added later. If you did not create this presentation, you can always create a new one at this time and add the organization chart as the first slide. Follow these steps to add the organization chart to the MESPO presentation:

1. Choose Open from the File menu and then select MESPO from the list box.
    If you did not create this presentation in Chapter 2, choose New presentation from the File menu instead and then select OK.
2. Select the Outliner icon or choose Outliner from the View menu.
3. Move to the title for slide 4 if you created the presentation in Chapter 2 as shown in Figure 7-3.
4. Type Mesopotamia Metals for the title and delete any extra characters from the previous title entry. (You can use the mouse to drag across the extra characters to select them and then press the (DEL) key.)
5. Choose Add chart to slide from the Chart menu and select Organization.
6. Choose Show subtitle and footnote from the Outline menu.
7. Press (↓) and then type **Organization Chart** for the subtitle and press (ENTER).
8. Type **June 15, 1992** for the footnote and press (ENTER).
9. Type **Jane Steel** for the first name field and press (ENTER).
10. Type **President** and press (ENTER). Your next entry will automatically be placed one level beneath the top entry.

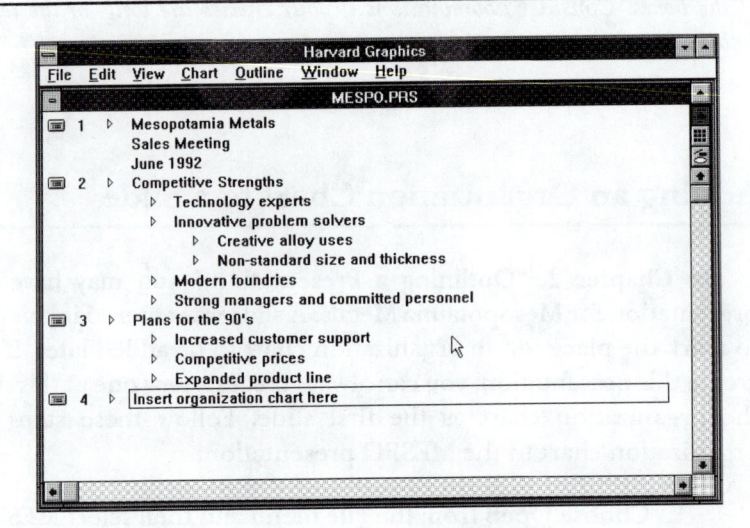

Figure 7-3.   *Slide 4 is current selection in the Outliner*

11. Type **Tom Iron** and press (ENTER). Type **Foundry Manager** and press (ENTER).
12. Type **Hilda Copper** and press (ENTER). Type **Office Manager** and press (ENTER).
13. Type **Jim Brass** and press (ENTER). Type **Purchasing Manager**.
14. Choose Save as from the File menu, type **ORG** (for "Organization"), and press (ENTER).
15. Press (F2) to display the chart.

    Your chart will look like Figure 7-4. The box at the top includes the name on one line and the title on the second line. Since the second level is also the last level, the names are not shown horizontally. This is the default style for the last level of an organization chart.
16. Press (ESC) to return to the Outliner display.

Now that you have mastered the basic skills for creating an organization chart, you can continue to build on your skills by adding more levels and changing the appearance of your entries.

Figure 7-4. *Organization chart with one level*

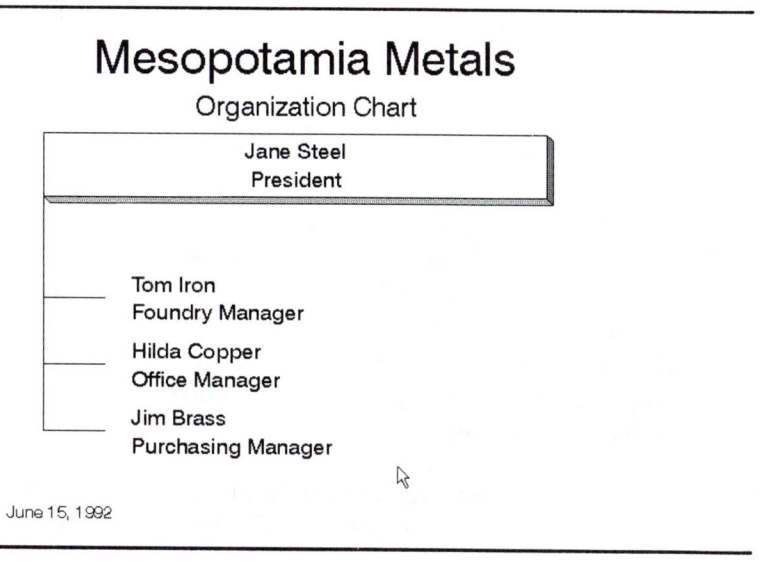

Mesopotamia Metals
Organization Chart

Jane Steel
President

Tom Iron
Foundry Manager

Hilda Copper
Office Manager

Jim Brass
Purchasing Manager

June 15, 1992

17. Choose Print from the File menu and then select Setup device.
18. Select the Landscape radio button under Orientation and then select the OK command button.
    The orientation for the entire printout is changed to landscape. Harvard Graphics does not allow you to set the orientation for individual slides unless they are the only slide printed.
19. Select OK from the Print dialog box to start printing.

Additions to the Organization Chart

Although you have mastered the basic procedure, you will need to make a few additions to the basic chart. In most companies there are more than two levels in the organization hierarchy, and you need to learn how to add those levels. Also, since Harvard Graphics allows you to add staff positions to a chart, you can try this feature by adding a staff position reporting directly to the president.

Adding More Levels

Since you can have as many as ten levels in a Harvard Graphics organization chart, you are nowhere near the limit. You can add subordinates beneath any of the individuals that report to Jane Steel by inserting a new entry beneath any of them and using the (TAB) key to indent the entry one level. If you indent too far you can use (SHIFT)+(TAB) to move a subordinate entry to the left. You will want to highlight the subordinate for which you want to add employee entries and press (ENTER). Follow these steps to add subordinates for each of Jane Steel's managers:

1. Move the highlight to **Foundry Manager** to add an entry beneath Tom Iron and press (ENTER). Initially the new entry is on the same level with Tom Iron.

2. Press the (TAB) key to indent the entry one level, type **Paula Tin**, and press (ENTER) twice.

   This leaves the title blank and moves to the next entry. It assumes that the new entry is on the same level as the previous one and adds another subordinate for Tom Iron.

3. Type **George Silver** and press (ENTER) twice.

4. Type **Mary Gold**.

5. Move the highlight to **Office Manager** under Hilda Copper and press (ENTER) and then press (TAB). This creates an entry for Hilda's first subordinate.

6. Type **Steve Chrome** and press (ENTER) twice.

7. Type **Larry Lead**.

8. Move the highlight to the entry for Purchasing Manager under Jim Brass and press (ENTER) and then (TAB).

9. Type **Molly Molybdenum** and press (ENTER) twice.

10. Type **Nancy Nickel** and press (ENTER) twice.

Chapter 7: *Creating Organization Charts*

11. Type **Zelda Zinc** and then press (F2) to display a chart that looks like Figure 7-5.
    Notice that the chart no longer shows Tom Iron, Hilda Copper, and Jim Brass vertically. With the vertical display reserved for the lowest level, the chart takes on a new appearance.
12. Press (ESC) and then choose Print from the File menu.
13. Select Slides from the dialog box, select Range to print the current slide, and then select OK.
14. Choose Save as from the File menu, type **ORG2**, and then select OK to save a copy of the presentation as ORG2.

If you decide to add additional levels you will use the same procedures just described to add levels to the chart.

Figure 7-5. Another level added to the organization chart

Mesopotamia Metals
Organization Chart

- Jane Steel, President
  - Tom Iron, Foundry Manager
    - Paula Tin
    - George Silver
    - Mary Gold
  - Hilda Copper, Office Manager
    - Steve Chrome
    - Larry Lead
  - Jim Brass, Purchasing Manager
    - Molly Molybdenum
    - Nancy Nickel
    - Zelda Zinc

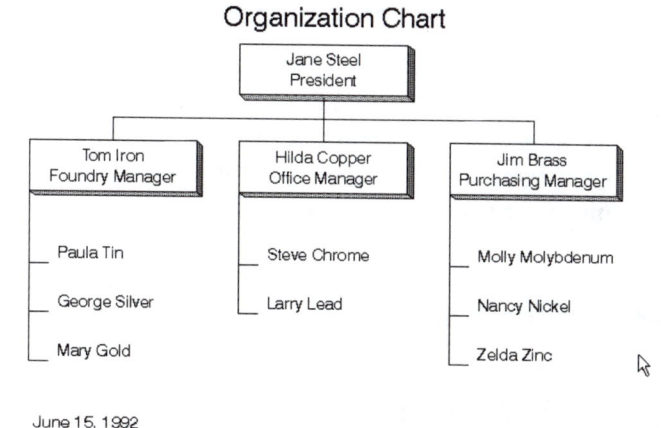

June 15, 1992

Adding a Staff Position

It is easy to add a staff position at any location in the organization chart. A staff position reports like other subordinates but cannot have lower levels of subordinates reporting to it. You can add two staff positions for each manager in your chart. An attempt to add more than two staff positions for a manager is ignored. Follow these steps to add an administrative assistant for the president:

1. Move the highlight to Jane Steel by pressing ↑.
2. Choose O_rganization charts from the C_hart menu.
3. Choose A_dd staff position from the O_rganization charts menu. Notice that the icon added is different than the other icons.
4. Type **Lucy Lithium** in the name field and then press ENTER.
5. Type **Administrative Assist.** Then press F2 to view the addition as shown in Figure 7-6.
6. Press CTRL+S or choose S_ave from the F_ile menu to update the saved version of the chart.

Organization Chart Changes

There are numerous options for changing the chart appearance. You can change the style of the text used for entries, the presentation of information in the last level, the placement of names and other information in the box—you can even create another chart as a subset of the organization chart if you want to focus on one area in particular.

Changing the Boxes

The default box appearance in Harvard Graphics has a 3D shadow effect. You can change the box appearance to a plain box, one with rounded edges, an octagonal shape, or present the information without a box. You can make these changes from the Slide Editor by pressing F8 or by selecting C_hart and

Figure 7-6.   *Staff position added*

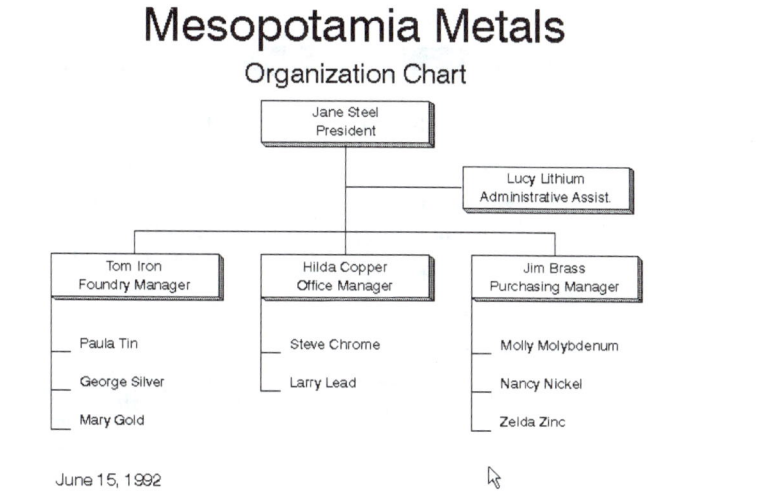

Mesopotamia Metals
Organization Chart

[Organization chart showing:
- Jane Steel, President
  - Lucy Lithium, Administrative Assist. (staff)
  - Tom Iron, Foundry Manager
    - Paula Tin
    - George Silver
    - Mary Gold
  - Hilda Copper, Office Manager
    - Steve Chrome
    - Larry Lead
  - Jim Brass, Purchasing Manager
    - Molly Molybdenum
    - Nancy Nickel
    - Zelda Zinc]

June 15, 1992

then Chart options. Follow these steps to add first a rounded and then a plain effect to the boxes for the current chart:

1. Click the icon for the Slide Editor or choose Slide Editor from the View menu.
2. Press (F8) to display the Organization Chart Options dialog box shown in Figure 7-7.
3. Select Rounded under Box style by clicking the option. You can also use the (TAB) key to highlight the desired selection, use the (SPACEBAR) to check its radio button, and then click OK.
4. Press (F2) to display a chart like the one shown in Figure 7-8.
5. Press (ESC) to return to the Slide Editor display.
6. Press (F8) to access chart options again and this time select Plain under Box styles.
7. Select OK to redisplay your chart.

Figure 7-7.   *Organization Chart Options dialog box*

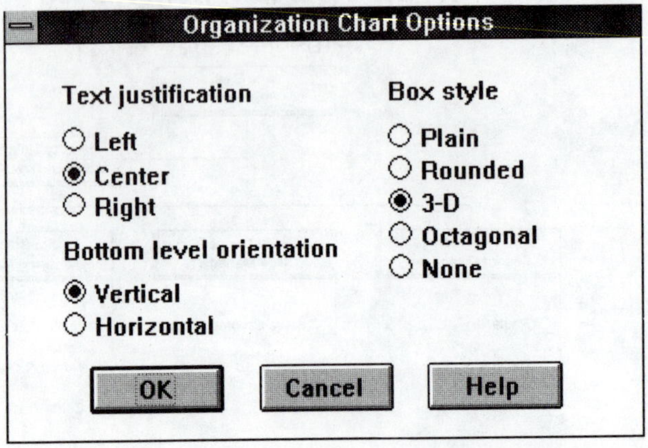

Organization Chart Options

Text justification
○ Left
● Center
○ Right

Box style
○ Plain
○ Rounded
● 3-D
○ Octagonal
○ None

Bottom level orientation
● Vertical
○ Horizontal

[OK]   [Cancel]   [Help]

Figure 7-8.   *Rounded boxes in the organization chart*

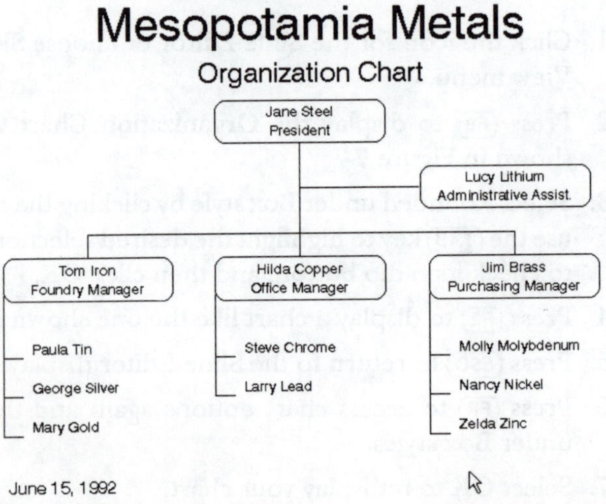

Mesopotamia Metals
Organization Chart

Jane Steel
President

Lucy Lithium
Administrative Assist.

Tom Iron
Foundry Manager

Hilda Copper
Office Manager

Jim Brass
Purchasing Manager

Paula Tin
George Silver
Mary Gold

Steve Chrome
Larry Lead

Molly Molybdenum
Nancy Nickel
Zelda Zinc

June 15, 1992

Chapter 7: *Creating Organization Charts* 229

Last Level Options

The last level in the hierarchy has displayed vertically on each organization chart you have created, because the default Arrangement setting for the last level is Vertical. You can change this setting to Horizontal and display the last level of entries as boxes. This may be appropriate for the current chart since there are not too many entries in the last level. But if each of the last-level entries contained five or six names, vertical placement would be the only option. As with the box styles, this change can be made only through the Slide Editor.

To display the last level of the current chart horizontally, follow these steps:

1. Press (F8) to display the Organization Chart Options dialog box.
2. Select Horizontal under Bottom Level Orientation and then select OK.
3. Press (F2) to display the chart shown in Figure 7-9. Although you cannot read the box text on the screen, you can see the arrangement of boxes.
   Since the Box style is set to Plain, even the new boxes do not have shadows. Also, the new boxes do not display titles since title entries were never added to the last level.
4. Press (ESC) to return to the Slide Editor screen.
5. Choose Chart options from the Chart menu and then select Vertical to reset the Bottom Level Orientation to its initial setting.
6. Select 3D for the Box Style.
7. Select OK.

Tip: Keep the last-level display as vertical unless you have only a few entries.

Changing the Text Style

Harvard Graphics has a number of options that affect the style of the text used in the organization chart. Some of these options can only be used with the title, subtitle, and footnote while others apply to information in the boxes

Figure 7-9.   Last level displayed as a box

Mesopotamia Metals
Organization Chart

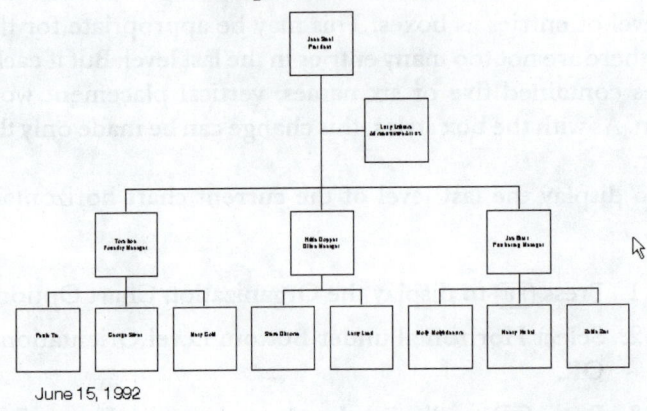

June 15, 1992

on the chart. You can make changes that affect the current slide, the current presentation, or all new entries that you type.

Changing Fonts

You can change the style of character or font used for an entire presentation, a section of selected text, an entire slide, or for any new entries that you make. To change the font or character style for the entire presentation, select Slide and then select Change presentation fo<u>n</u>t. To change the current slide select as much of the text as you want to affect, and then select Text and Font. In both situations you will need to select from among the available font choices presented. If you choose Text Font for the selected text, the default font will be changed for the next text that you enter.

The organization charts displayed earlier in the chapter were all created with the default Swiss font. To change the display for the entire chart you will want to select the entire slide and then use Text Font as follows:

1. Choose Select <u>a</u>ll from the <u>E</u>dit menu.

2. Choose Font from the Text menu.
3. Select Monospace.
4. Press F2 to display the slide with the new font as shown in Figure 7-10.
5. Press ESC to return to the Slide Editor. You can click any location on the slide to remove the selection marks.

Changing Size and Placement

You can place and size the title, subtitle, and footnotes in organization charts. You can change the placement of the name, title, and comments within a box, but not the size of this text since Harvard Graphics sizes the text automatically (based on your longest entry and the number of boxes in a level).

To change the size of title, subtitle, or footnote text, select the text that you want to affect. Select Text and then select Size and choose the desired font size. You can alter the alignment of this text by changing its justification. Again you should select the text that you want to affect and then choose Justify from the Text menu. You can change the justification to Left, Right, Center, or Full. Full justification adds extra spaces between words to spread the text across the full space available.

To change the alignment of text in boxes you must be in the Slide Editor. Press F8 to activate the options. Choose the desired alignment from the Organization Chart Options Dialog box in the section labeled "Text justification" and then select OK. The chart is redrawn with the new text justification.

Changing Your View of an Organization Chart

There are several options that allow you to alter the view of an organization chart. You can hide subordinates for a manager or hide job titles and comments. The change is not permanent and your entries can be displayed again.

You can also create a series of slides from one slide using the slide summary feature. This feature allows you to take a closer look at different sections of the organization chart.

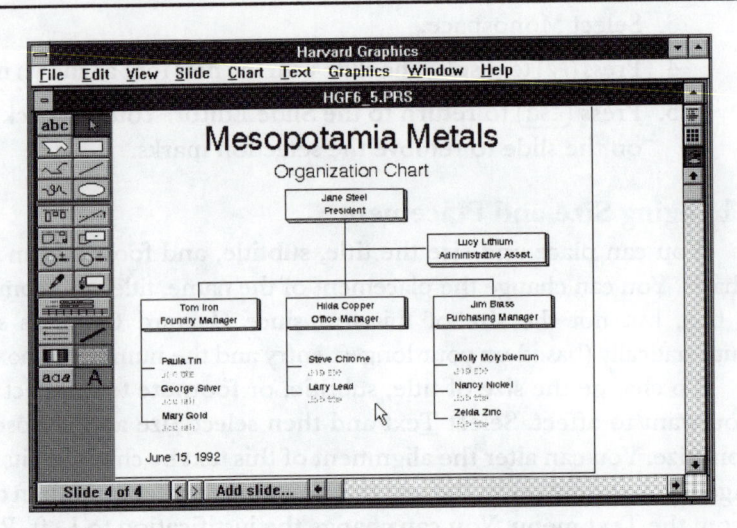

Figure 7-10.   *New font selected*

Collapsing and Expanding Your View

The Outliner provides a quick way to summarize and expand your display. If you are not in the Outliner you will need to click its icon to change the view. You can hide a manager's subordinates by double-clicking the manager's icon. The icon will be filled in, indicating that there is more detail within this section. A second double-click redisplays the subordinates.

To hide job titles and comments entered within the same field, select the name for which you want to hide job titles. Choose O<u>r</u>ganization charts from the <u>C</u>hart menu and then choose <u>H</u>ide job title from the O<u>r</u>ganization charts menu. Job titles for all levels below the selected entry are no longer displayed. To redisplay the job titles, select the names for which you want to redisplay the job titles and then choose O<u>r</u>ganization charts from the <u>C</u>hart menu. Choose <u>S</u>how job title from the O<u>r</u>ganization Charts menu that is presented.

Creating a Slide Summary

If you are discussing an organization chart as part of your presentation you might want to focus separately on each section of the chart. Harvard Graphics makes it easy to create a series of charts that begin with a summary of the levels that report to the top and then each level beneath the top level on a separate slide. You can create this summary and recombine it at any time. The following steps show you how to create the summary from the Outliner, look at it with the Slide Sorter, and combine it back to a single chart after returning to the Outliner:

1. Select the icon for the Outliner.
2. Move the highlight to the title of the organization chart.
3. Choose Make slide summary from the Outline menu.
   Notice that additional slides are created for each level reporting to the top. Currently these slides do not have titles although you can add them if you wish.
4. Choose Slide Sorter from the View menu.
   You can look at an overview of each slide as shown in Figure 7-11. Notice how the series of organization chart slides has a line that runs between them indicating that they were created as a summary.
5. Choose Outliner from the View menu.
6. Choose Remove slide summary from the Outline menu with the highlight on the title for the first organization chart slide.
   The summary charts are combined back into one chart.

Responding to a Reorganization

If you are the person who has responsibility for creating an organization chart quickly, this package will make your chore a breeze. It is possible to add subordinates or change the names of people or responsibilities with little time invested.

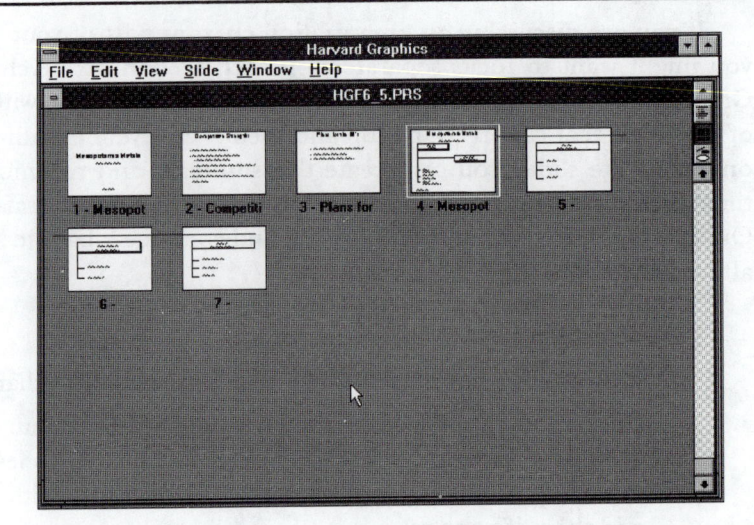

Figure 7-11. Slide summary can provide an overview

Changing Entries

You can change the Name, Title, or Comment by typing new entries. Alter a few of the name entries with these steps:

1. Choose Close from the File menu and confirm that you do not want to save the changes by selecting No.

    If you did not set the default view for an existing presentation to Outliner, you will need to click the Outliner icon after opening ORG2 in the next step.

2. Choose Open from the File menu and then select ORG2 to open a copy of the file without your recent changes.

    If your default view when you open files is something other than the Outliner you will need to click the Outliner icon at this time.

3. Move the highlight to Tom Iron, select Tom, and then press the DEL key.

    Instead of deleting the text first, you can actually start typing since Windows is designed to replace the selection within the entry.

Chapter 7: *Creating Organization Charts*

4. Type **Ian** and then press ⬇ to move to Hilda Copper.
5. Select the text Hilda and then press the (DEL) key to delete it.
6. Type **Carla** and then move to Jim Brass.
7. Select Jim, press (DEL), and then type **Ben**.
   Changes can be made to titles, comments, and names in the same manner.

Adding an Entry

You can add an entry at any level in an organization chart except as a replacement for the first entry. The procedure will require a minor adjustment depending on whether subordinates already exist and whether you want to make the addition at the same level as the current entry or beneath it. To add an entry beneath the current level as a subordinate, move to the job title for the current entry and press (ENTER). If there are no subordinates the entry created is at the same level as the current entry. If there are subordinates, a new subordinate entry is added at the top of the list. If you would prefer the subordinate entry at a different location in the subordinate list, you can either place it at the top and move it—or add it after the position you want to precede it.

To add a new subordinate for Jane Steel that follows Ian Iron follow these steps:

1. Move to the job title for Ian Iron, Foundry Manager, and press (ENTER). The new level is currently a subordinate of Ian Iron.
2. Press (SHIFT)+(TAB) to make this entry the same level as Ian Iron and move it after Ian's last subordinate.
3. Type **Martha Magnesium** and press (ENTER).
4. Type **Marketing Director**.

Changing the Location of an Entry

You can alter the location of any of the entries on your organization chart. You can change the level of the entry, change its order in a subordinate list, or move an entry to a different list. The easiest way to relocate an entry is to drag its icon to a new location. If you want Paula Tin to be the last subordinate entry under Ian Iron rather than the first, move the mouse pointer to the highlight for this entry and then drag it to the new location. A pointing hand will appear as you drag to indicate placement on the screen. Also, an arrow with a line attached will indicate where it will be placed when you release the mouse button. Try this now by performing these steps:

1. Move the mouse pointer to the icon for Paula Tin.
2. Drag this icon down until the pointer hand and line are located right below Mary Gold and then release the mouse button. (Paula Tin is moved to the new location and the appearance of the slide will reflect this change.)

Deleting a Subordinate

You can delete an entry at any level by selecting it and then pressing the (DEL) key. If the entry has subordinates, the subordinates will also be deleted. Delete the subordinate entry for George Silver who reports to Ian Iron with these steps:

Tip: *Remember that you can Choose Undo from the Edit menu if you accidentally delete too much and need to restore the data.*

1. Move the mouse pointer to the left of the icon for George Silver.
2. Drag down and across to create a rectangle that includes the icon. Press (DEL) to delete George Silver.
3. Press (F2) to display a chart like the one in Figure 7-12.
4. Press (ESC).
5. Choose Save as from the File menu, type **ORG5**, and then select OK.
6. Choose Close from the File menu.

Chapter 7: *Creating Organization Charts* 237

Figure 7-12.   *Subordinate deleted*

Mesopotamia Metals
Organization Chart

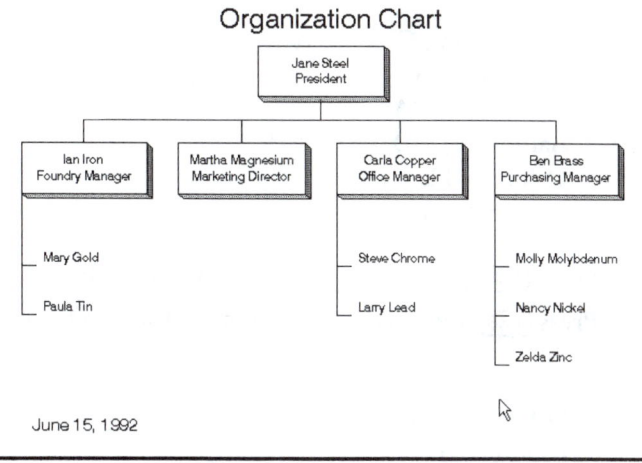

```
                      Jane Steel
                      President
    ┌────────────┬──────────┴──────┬────────────┐
  Ian Iron   Martha Magnesium  Carla Copper   Ben Brass
  Foundry    Marketing Director Office Manager Purchasing Manager
  Manager

  Mary Gold                    Steve Chrome   Molly Molybdenum

  Paula Tin                    Larry Lead     Nancy Nickel

                                              Zelda Zinc
```

June 15, 1992

Converting a Bullet Chart to an Organization Chart

Occasionally you may create a bullet chart and, due to the number of items, find that the format is ineffective in conveying your message. The hierarchical nature of organization charts may allow you to show more information on a single page. To create a slide for a new presentation as a bullet and then convert it to an organization chart follow these steps:

1. Select Pre<u>f</u>erences from the <u>F</u>ile menu and then change the drop-down list box option for "Default view for new presentation" and "Default view for open presentation" to Slide Editor.

2. Choose <u>N</u>ew presentation from the <u>F</u>ile menu, select Bullet, and then select OK.

3. Type **Eastern Region** and press ENTER.
4. Press TAB and then type each of the following, pressing ENTER after each:

   New Haven, CT
   Charlotte, NC
   Columbus, GA
   Baltimore, MD
   Orlando, FL
   Reading, PA

5. Press SHIFT+TAB and then type **Central Region**.
6. Press TAB and then type each of the following, pressing ENTER after each:

   St Louis, MO
   Chicago, IL
   Des Moines, IA
   Dallas, TX

7. Press SHIFT+TAB and then type **Western Region**.
8. Press TAB and then type each of the following, pressing ENTER after each except the last entry:

   Phoenix, AZ
   Las Vegas, NV
   St George, UT
   San Diego, CA

9. Select OK and press F2 to view the chart. You will not be able to see all your entries on one bullet chart.
10. Press ESC and then choose Change chart type from the Chart menu. Choose Organization to change the chart type to an organization chart.

Chapter 7: *Creating Organization Charts*

Figure 7-13. **Bullet chart entries converted to an organization chart**

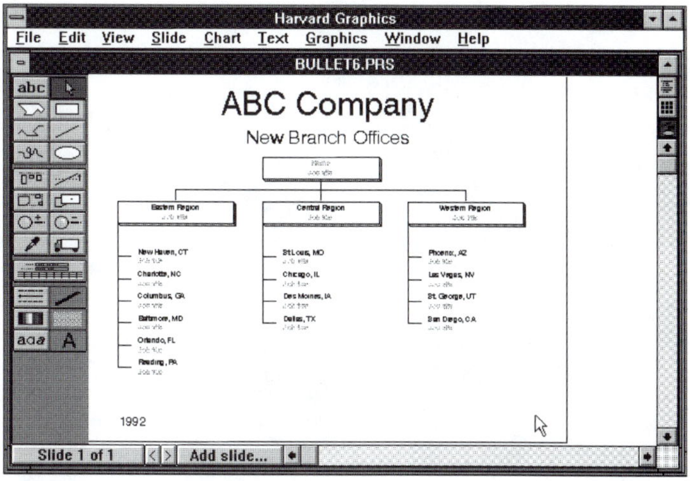

11. Press (F2) to display a preview of your chart.

    Your chart will look like Figure 7-13. Later you can add an entry for the top box, but your chart fits nicely on one page.

8

Using Drawing, Symbols, and Other Enhancements

Besides creating slides from entries on Data Forms, you can also use the Slide Editor features to create or enhance a slide. The Slide Editor features in Harvard Graphics for Windows allow you to add geometric shapes, arrows, and lines to slides. Pictures, known as *symbols,* and text can also be added. The geometric shapes and text that you add with the Slide Editor are called *objects.*

Whether you are working with a blank slide (called a *drawing* slide) in the Slide Editor or annotating a slide containing a chart, your mouse makes your task easier. The mouse lets you quickly point to the object in a chart, specify where you want to position an object, or select a tool from the toolbox at the left edge of the screen. Harvard Graphics can also use other input devices for drawing including drawing tablets.

Although you will continue to use menu selections as you work in the Slide Editor, many of the options will require the use of the toolbox. Table 8-1 shows each toolbox tool with its screen icon and the name with which it is referred to in text.

Table 8-1. **Icons Available from the Slide Editor Screen**

Icon	Description
abc	Text tool
	Polygon tool
	Polyline tool
	Freehand tool
	Align tool
	Group tool
	Zoom-in tool
	Eye dropper tool
	Line attributes tool
	Fill tool
aba	Text attributes tool
	Selector tool
	Rectangle tool

Chapter 8: *Using Drawing, Symbols, and Other Enhancements*

Table 8-1. **Icons Available from the Slide Editor Screen** (continued)

Icon	Description
	Line tool
	Ellipses tool
	Rotate tool
	Move to front tool
	Zoom-out tool
	Symbol tool
	Data form tool
	Line sample
	Color sample
	Text sample

Since slides created in the Harvard Graphics Slide Editor have more flexibility in positioning objects, you may find that the objects in your charts vary slightly from the ones shown in the figures in this chapter. Also, as you create charts you will find that objects appear in color, even though the figures illustrating these examples are in black and white with patterns where different colors appear.

Getting Started

You have already learned how you can create charts to show data and text. Although the chart you create in this exercise contains some text, it is not added as a title or footnote. Instead, the text is added through the Slide Editor so it can be placed anywhere on the chart. Follow these steps to add a symbol and text through the Slide Editor options:

1. If you currently have an open presentation you can choose Close from the File menu and choose New presentation from the File menu.
2. Select Drawing and then select OK.

Harvard Graphics displays the Slide Editor screen with a blank slide. Drawing slides allow you to place whatever elements you want on a slide without a predefined structure. You have already used a few of the tools in the toolbox and many of the menu options. In this chapter you will learn more about the Graphics menu options and the toolbox offerings. Figure 8-1 shows the Slide Editor screen with the different sections of the screen labeled. In this screen the current position is indicated by a *pointer*. This initially looks like an arrow but it will change depending on the action you are taking. The only thing on the screen is faded text marking the position where a slide title will display if you add one.

To make selections, point to an icon and press the left mouse button. You can select any of the tools in the toolbox by clicking the tool or using a menu option.

3. Select the Symbol tool or choose Symbol Library from the File menu to open the Symbol Library.
4. Select HUMANS4.SYW from the File list box and then select OK.
    You will experience a delay while Harvard Graphics expands the symbols and brings them into memory. You will see a thumbnail sketch of the first symbol and can scroll through the options. You can also choose List names from the Symbol Library's View menu to view the symbols as names. When you choose this approach you

Chapter 8: *Using Drawing, Symbols, and Other Enhancements* 245

Figure 8-1. *The Slide Editor*

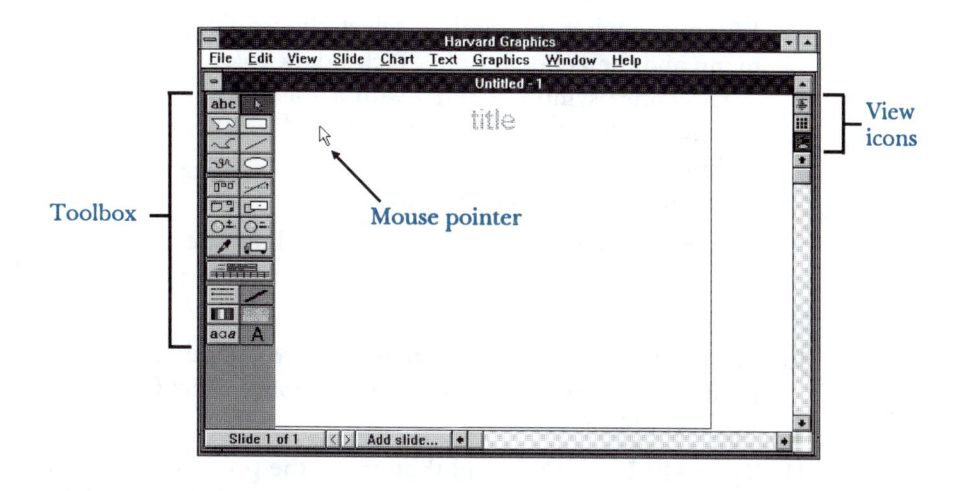

can see a number of names without scrolling. The picture associated with the selected name is displayed in the window.

5. Move the mouse pointer to the group silhouette symbol labeled Crowd and select it. A box will appear around this symbol.

6. Choose Copy from the Edit menu on the Library Symbol menu and then double-click the Control menu box in the upper-left corner of the Symbol Library to close it.

   If you plan to use more of the symbols from this file shortly you can simply click on your Slide Editor screen to temporarily leave the symbols and return to them later without reexpanding the symbol file.

Tip: The speed key for Copy is (CTRL)+(INS).

7. Choose Paste from the Edit menu to add the symbol to the center of the blank slide. Make the symbol a little smaller by pushing inward on the bottom right handle and then move the pointer to the center

of the symbol and drag it to the right and down slightly to place it in the center again after resizing.

8. Without moving the symbol, select choose **F**ill from the **G**raphics menu and then choose **S**olid. Pick a dark color and then select OK.

    The entire symbol is filled with a solid dark color. You can tell exactly which color is currently selected for fills, text, and lines by looking at the sample icons. These are the last three icons on the right side of the toolbox palette.

9. Choose **S**ize from the **T**ext menu and then select a size of 36. To add text to this drawing, select the Text tool (labeled "abc") by pointing and pressing the left mouse button.

10. Move the pointer to about an inch above the middle of the Crowd symbol and press the left button to display a box for entering text in a text object.

11. Type **ALLBEN, INC.** and then move the pointer to about an inch below the middle of the Crowd symbol and click the left mouse button.

12. Type **Benefits for all employees** and then click a blank area of the chart.

    It is unlikely that the three objects are centered properly on your chart but you can easily improve the appearance.

13. Click the text at the top and then drag the handles at the right until the handles just surround the text.

14. Repeat step 12 for the text at the bottom.

15. Using the (SHIFT) key select text at both the top and bottom as well as the symbol.

16. Select the alignment tool and then choose the second option in column 1 and select OK. Both text entries are entered along with the symbol to create an image that looks something like Figure 8-2.

17. Choose Save **a**s from the File menu, type **DRAWINGS**, and press (ENTER).

A chart like this can be the perfect lead-in to a presentation, and with the available symbol files you can create it in only a few minutes.

Chapter 8: *Using Drawing, Symbols, and Other Enhancements* 247

Figure 8-2.   Slide Editor with completed drawing

Adding Text and Objects in the Slide Editor

There is a wide variety of tasks you can perform with the toolbox in the Slide Editor. Objects like symbols, text, and geometric shapes can be added to dramatically alter the appearance of existing charts or create brand new transition charts that do not classify as either text or analytical charts.

You can add objects to any chart when you finalize the entries on its Data Form and display it in the Slide Editor screen. You can create a drawing slide when you want to start with a blank screen and draw all objects that appear on the chart as you did in the "Getting Started" section. When you are working with a chart in the Outliner or Slide Sorter views all you need to do is change the view to the Slide Editor to immediately begin adding objects to the current chart.

When you edit an existing slide in the Slide Editor screen, you can think of the resulting slide as a combination of layers. The chart layer is created and edited using the Data Forms. The drawing layers are created and edited through the Slide Editor screen. You can change some characteristics of the chart layer in the Slide Editor such as line attributes, text size, and fill for bars, yet some aspects of the chart layer are inaccessible (such as the size of the bars and the labels used for the X-axis data points) without returning to the Data Form to make changes.

To create a chart that contains only objects added from the Slide Editor screen, select Add slide and then select Drawing and OK, as in the example in "Getting Started." You then use tools to create everything that appears in the chart. You could use this method to create a company logo for a slideshow, or you might use it in place of a text chart if you wanted free-form placement of your chart data.

Adding Objects

Once you are in the Slide Editor screen, the first thing you will want to do is to add an object. An object can be a line, shape, symbol, or text. To add any of these objects, select one of the drawing tools (the first eight icons shown in Figure 8-1). You select one of these icons by pointing to it and clicking the left button.

Once you select a tool it will continue to remain active. If you would prefer to return to the Selector tool each time you create an object you will need to change "Tool lock" in the Graphics menu. When a check mark appears, a lock is in effect for the current tool; when there is no check mark, the Selector tool is reactivated after you add each new object.

Attribute options in effect for lines and text affect the appearance of objects that you add. These settings may be the default settings or changes that you have made through changes in Text and Graphics menus. You have already looked at some of these features in earlier chapters, but you will have an opportunity to explore additional options in the next section.

Remember if you make mistakes while adding objects you can always use the Edit Undo feature. You can use a shortcut key sequence of [ALT]+[BACKSPACE] for Undo. Redo (to restore what you undid) is available from the Edit menu. These keys will work as long as you have not saved the presentation file, switched views, or returned to the Data Form for editing. Harvard Graphics can undo four different changes if you keep selecting it.

Chapter 8: *Using Drawing, Symbols, and Other Enhancements*

After you select the type of object to add and the attributes this object will have, you are ready to position the object on the drawing area. For each of the listed object types, you need to take the following actions:

Text   Select the Text tool. Move the pointer to where you want the text to begin and click the left mouse button. You can also select a box that the text will occupy. With the mouse, move to the first corner, and drag the mouse to the opposite corner. Type the text you want to appear and then click another area of the screen to finalize you entry.

Polygon   Select either the polygon or rounded polygon tool after clicking the polygon tool. Point to the first polygon point and press the left mouse button. Move the cross-hair (that will appear onscreen) to the next point and click the left mouse button again. Continue with this approach until you are ready to add the last point with a double-click of the left mouse button. You can maintain 45-, 90-, or 135-degree angles for lines by pressing the (SHIFT) key as you take these actions.

Rectangle   Select the rectangle tool. Move the pointer to where you want one corner, and click the left mouse button. Next, position the pointer to the diagonally opposite corner and click the left mouse button. Harvard Graphics uses the horizontal and vertical positions of the two points you have selected to determine the lines of the box. If you want your rectangle to be a square, press the (SHIFT) key as you are taking these actions.

Polyline   You can create a polyline or polycurve with this tool. Both have two or more line segments. After clicking the polyline tool, select it or the polycurve tool that will appear next to it. Point to the first polygon point, press the left mouse button. Move the cross-hair to the next point and click the left mouse button again. Continue with this approach until you are ready to add the last point with a double-click of the left mouse button. You can maintain 45-, 90-, or 135-degree angles for lines by pressing the (SHIFT) key as you take these actions. Harvard Graphics does not create a joining line between the first and last point as it does with a polygon.

Line   Select the Line tool. Move the cross-hair to the beginning point and press the left mouse button. Then move the cross-hair to the next point of the line and press the left mouse button dragging to where you want to end the line before releasing the mouse button. Continue pointing and dragging until you have drawn all of the connected lines you want. Use the (SHIFT) key to keep the lines at a regular angles, such as 45, 90, or 135 degrees.

Freehand   This is the tool to use when you need irregular lines and closed shapes. Think of this tool as a pencil that you can use to draw on the slide. Select the freehand tool. Move the cross-hair to the point where you want to start drawing and hold down the left button while you drag the mouse along where you want the freehand line drawn. When the starting and ending point are close together, Harvard Graphics will create a closed shape for you. This is the tool that you would use with a graphics tablet to trace a drawing.

Ellipses   Select the Ellipses tool. Point to one edge of the ellipses and, while pressing the left mouse button, drag the cross-hair to the diagonally opposite corner before releasing the mouse button. Harvard Graphics draws the largest circle or ellipse that can fit inside the box formed by the two corners. If you want a circle, press the (SHIFT) key while performing these actions.

After you create one of these objects, you can repeat the same steps to add more of the same type of objects. You can copy an object by selecting it, which places handles around it, and then using the Edit Copy and Edit Paste selections to duplicate it. You will need to select each object to copy as well as the location for the copied object. If "Tool lock" is checked, this means that you will need to click the Selector tool.

Creating a Chart and Adding Annotations with Draw

Although the Slide Editor features can be used alone, as in the "Getting Started" example, they can also be used to add enhancements to existing charts. You can create a bar chart and add annotations by following these steps:

1. Select Add slide, select Horizontal bar, and then select OK.
2. Move to the Title field, type **Acme Industries** for the chart title, and press (ENTER) three times.

Chapter 8: *Using Drawing, Symbols, and Other Enhancements* 251

3. Type **Books** and press ENTER for the first entry in the X Axis Name column.
4. Type **Magazines** and press ENTER.
5. Type **Periodicals** and press ENTER.
6. Type **Kitchen Paper Products** and press ENTER.
7. Press CTRL+HOME, TAB, and ↓ to move to the column for the Series 1 data.
8. Type **50500** and press ENTER.
9. Type **95000** and press ENTER.
10. Type **75000** and press ENTER.
11. Type **35000** and press ENTER. Then select OK.
    At this point the chart could use some enhancements. Besides the enhancements available in the Options menu, you can also add enhancements by *annotating* the chart, which means adding objects. For example, you can use the annotation features to add arrows to the bars of the chart.
12. Choose Chart options from the Chart menu and then select 3D to remove the X selecting this option.
13. Select Legend and then select "Show legend" to remove the X from this check box. Select OK twice.
14. Click a bar to select all the bars in the slide. Select the Fill tool and then select its first icon. Select a color that closely matches the background and then select OK.
15. Select a blank area of the chart and then select the Line tool. Select 12 points, select the arrow for the "Last ending field" pull-down list box, select the "Small arrow option," and then select OK.
16. Select the Line tool.
17. Move the cross-hair to the center of the left edge of the top bar. Hold down the SHIFT key to ensure a straight line and drag to the right edge of this bar.
18. Repeat step 17 for the remaining bars to add an arrow to each.
    Your chart will look something like Figure 8-3. Since the arrows you added are separate objects, it is important that you decide what

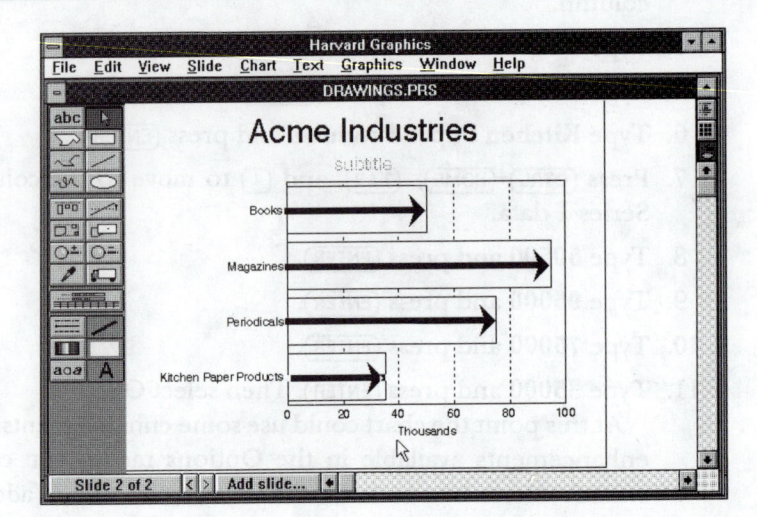

Figure 8-3.   Chart with arrows added using tools

type of chart you want before adding them. To see how disastrous a change in chart type can be for the appearance make the change that follows.

19. Choose Chart options from the Chart menu and then select 3D to change the appearance of the bars. Your screen will contain misplaced bars and look like Figure 8-4.
20. Choose Undo from the Edit menu to remove the 3D option that was just added.
21. Choose Save from the File menu.

Adding More Objects

You are not limited to one Draw feature. You can use many of the features to add symbols, text, and other enhancements to a chart. Try adding some objects to your chart by following these directions:

Chapter 8: *Using Drawing, Symbols, and Other Enhancements* 253

1. Choose Size from the Text menu and change the size to 18.

During any one session, Harvard Graphics retains the attribute settings. Some settings, like line width, are shared by multiple object types such as circles, rectangles, and polylines.

2. Choose Ruler/grid from the Graphics menu and then select "Show ruler" and "Show grid" to display a ruler grid on the screen. Then select OK.
3. Choose Line attributes from the Graphics menu and select a 1 point line size. Select OK.
    This completes the preliminary steps to set up the attributes that you want to work with.
4. Select the Text tool and then move the pointer to the far-left side of the screen a level slightly higher than the "M" in Magazines.
5. Click the mouse and then type **Sun Days** and press (ENTER).

Figure 8-4.   *Changing the chart appearance after adding objects*

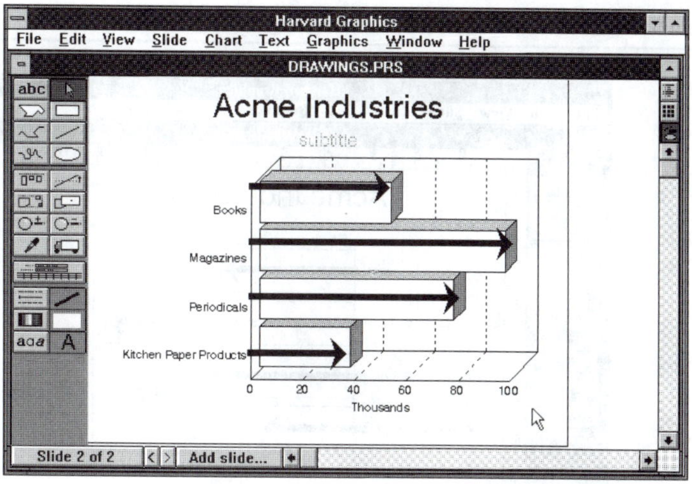

6. Type **News Express** and press ENTER.
7. Type **Gracious Living**.
8. Click the Selector tool.
9. Choose Justify from the Text menu and then select Center.
10. Select the Rectangle tool. Choose Fill from the Graphics menu and then choose Solid. Select None to eliminate fill from the rectangle you are about to create. Select OK.
11. Move the cross-hair above and slightly to the left of the text and then drag down and to the right to draw a box around your entries.
12. Click the selection tool and then click a blank area of the screen. Your chart should look something like Figure 8-5.
13. Choose Ruler/grid from the Graphics menu and then select "Show ruler" and "Show grid" to remove the ruler grid from the screen.

If you prefer to leave these markings on the screen to help you with object placement, you can—but the remaining figures will not show them.

Figure 8-5. Ruler and grid displaying with new objects

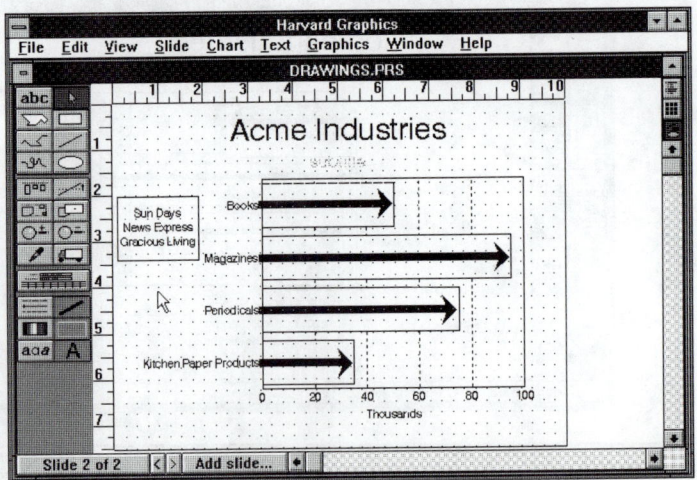

Chapter 8: *Using Drawing, Symbols, and Other Enhancements*

Modifying Objects

As you create a chart, you may want to change certain aspects of the chart's appearance, such as the position of objects, the size, or the color. Harvard Graphics allows you to change any of the attributes for the selected object using either tools or menu selections for the changes. Before you can change an object, you must select it with the Selection tool. The changes that you make are immediately visible in the drawing area of the Slide Editor.

Selecting Objects

You have already had some experience with selecting objects. To select one object, point to it and press the left mouse. Regardless of the object you select, the procedure is always the same. You can select one or more objects. Once objects are selected, you can continue to modify, copy, and delete them. Even after you have finished adding an object, it stays selected until you deselect it by choosing another object. Selected objects are indicated by *handles,* which are the eight small boxes that indicate the object's boundary.

When you click a symbol added as an entire unit, this symbol may be composed of many objects. Clicking other parts of the symbol will allow you to make a change in color or position of just one object within a symbol.

You can work with several objects at once. To select multiple objects, hold down (SHIFT) as you select an object—so the chosen object is included *with* the selected objects rather than *replacing* the previous selection. Another way to select several objects is to drag a selection box around them. This is done by positioning the Selector tool and dragging it to the diagonally opposite corner, which will form a box. Now you can change the attributes of all the selected objects at the same time. You can create a group from several selected objects, which maintains the multiple selections when applying new attributes.

Grouping Objects

Although selecting multiple objects provides a quick way to change an attribute such as color, if you then select another object and make a change you will need to use the (SHIFT) click approach to work with the original group of objects again. The group feature allows you to combine objects permanently and allows you to move the objects at any time and maintain their same relative position. To create a group, first select all the objects you want in the group, and next choose Group from the Graphics menu. To ungroup the objects choose Ungroup from the Graphics menu. You can select an entire group by clicking an object in the group.

Grouping and ungrouping are also useful with symbols. A symbol is a collection of objects that are treated as a distinct unit, or a group. You can group your own collection of objects to treat them as a unit or symbol. You can also ungroup a group and ungroup a symbol so you can work with the individual parts of the group.

To ungroup a group of objects or a symbol, select the group and then select the Ungroup tool from the Editing tools.

TIP: *In addition to grouping and ungrouping objects using the Group tool, you can also use the* (CTRL)+(G) *and* (CTRL)+(U) *speed keys*

Moving Objects

When you use the Slide Editor's drawing features, you probably will not design the slide perfectly when you add the objects. You may want to reposition the objects to improve appearance. For example, if your chart has many objects, you may want to position them so the chart does not appear crowded. You may also need to reposition objects that point to chart data that changes.

Try moving one of the individuals that you put on slide 1 with the crowd symbol.

1. Use the arrow at the bottom of the screen to redisplay slide 1.
2. Select the Selection tool.
3. Select the crowd symbol by clicking a location on the symbol to place handles around the entire symbol.
4. Select the individual at the far left by clicking this part of the symbol. The handles move to indicate that only this symbol is selected.

Chapter 8: *Using Drawing, Symbols, and Other Enhancements* 257

5. Move to the center of this symbol to have the four-sided arrow appear and then drag this individual away from the crowd. Your chart might look something like Figure 8-6 when you are through.

6. Choose Undo from the Edit menu to restore your initial display.

You might want to try another change that includes an example of grouping objects. In slide 2, the magazine titles and the box around them can be moved together (or otherwise changed) at any time if you group the two objects.

1. Use the arrow at the bottom of the screen to move to slide 2.
2. Drag a selection box around the box and the magazine titles by moving slightly above and to the left of the upper-left corner of the box and then drag down below the lower-right corner of the box.
3. Choose Group from the Graphics menu.

Figure 8-6. Selecting and moving an object that is part of the symbol

4. Move the mouse pointer to the center of the selection box and then drag the box and text to center the titles vertically with "Magazines."

   You can actually point to any part of the object except one of the handles and drag it downwards so the three magazine titles are vertically centered with "Magazines."

   Notice how as you move objects the pointer changes to a four-sided arrow. Just as when you add lines, you can hold down the (SHIFT) key so the selected objects are moved in 45- and 90-degree increments. As you move and size objects, Harvard Graphics draws an outline of the object to indicate where the object will be moved and its size.

5. Click a blank area of the chart. Your display will look something like Figure 8-7.

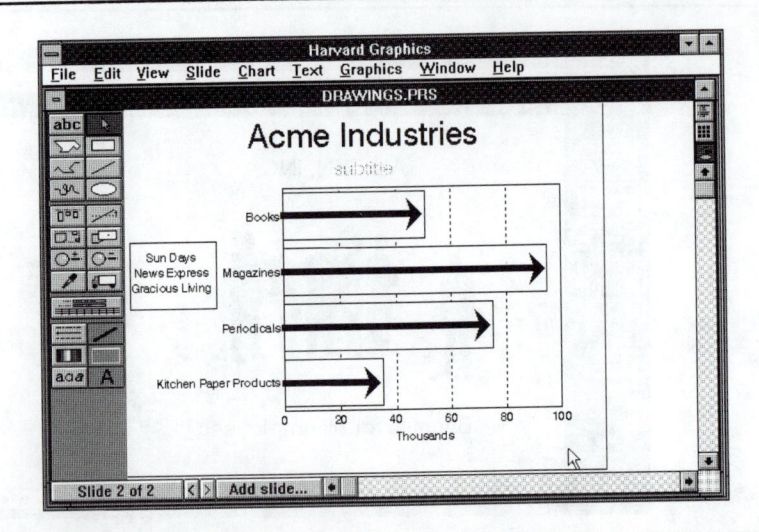

Figure 8-7.   *Objects moved together to new location*

Sizing Objects

Another change you will want to make to an object is to resize it. For example, you may want to reduce the box and text that you added to the bar chart. Later, when you learn to add symbols, you may want to resize them if you are not satisfied with the original size. When you size an object, you can also change its height-to-width ratio. For example, if you change the height-to-width ratio of a polygon, you can make the resulting object appear elongated or contracted. You can change an object's size and force the height-to-width ratio to remain the same.

Now, try changing the size of the boxed text object that you added to the ACME chart by following these directions:

1. Point to the lower-right handle of the selected group.
2. Drag this handle vertically and horizontally, causing the dotted lines representing the proposed size to overlay part of your chart data for an exaggerated size. Your chart might look something like Figure 8-8.
   When you release the mouse the two objects in the group are redrawn at the new size. Windows and hardware fonts are converted to Bitstream fonts when resized.
3. Choose Undo from the Edit menu to resize the objects.
4. Choose Ungroup from the Graphics menu.

If you press (SHIFT) as you change the size of an object, the height-to-width ratio remains the same. That means that as you make an object taller, it also becomes wider so it does not look stretched out.

Changing Object Attributes

When you add objects, you can set how each object appears by making the selections' attribute changes before adding the object. This way the color, line width, and other settings affect the object as it is added. You can also change an object's attributes after adding the object to a chart. First, select the object or objects you wish to change. Once the objects are selected, choose

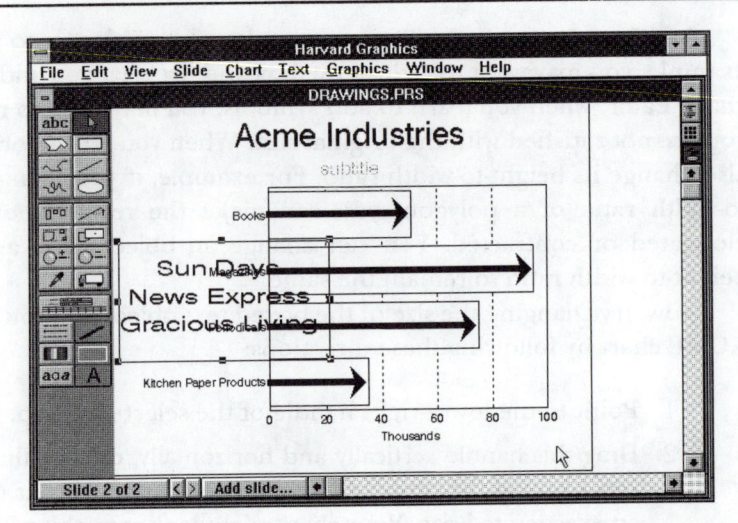

Figure 8-8. *Exaggerated sizing for the group*

menu selections or tools that can make the changes you want. If multiple objects are selected, all will be changed unless the objects are of different types. For example, a change in font will affect all selected text but leave rectangles and ellipses that are part of the selection unchanged.

You can try changing some of the attributes of the objects you have added to your chart by following these steps:

1. Move to slide 1 using the arrow at the bottom of the screen.
2. Use SHIFT and click the left mouse button to select the text at the top and bottom of the slide.
3. Choose Font from the Text menu and then select a different font from the list presented.
4. Select OK to see the text presented with a different font.
5. Choose Undo from the Edit menu.

Selecting Color and Fills

Besides changing attributes such as shape, line width, and text size, you can also select colors for the objects you create or the symbols you paste on the slide. You can use any of the colors from a color palette as well as other custom colors. You can also use patterns, gradients, and bitmap images in combination with color to make your objects distinctive.

Colors are selected by selecting from the Solid Color dialog box, which appears as a rainbow of color swatches. Selecting the Fill tool and then selecting the first icon displays the Color Options dialog box, which appears in Figure 8-9. From this dialog box, you can select the color used for an object. You can also choose Fill from the Graphics menu and then choose Solid to display the same dialog box.

Figure 8-9.   Solid Color dialog box

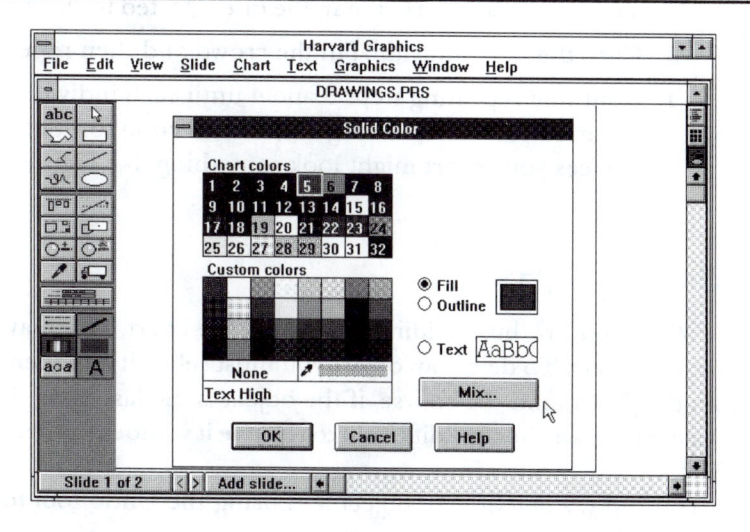

After you finalize your color selection by choosing OK, the color change affects the object that was selected at the time you chose the Fill tool. The change will also affect new objects that you add.

While this chapter only introduces the basic features of setting chart colors here, Harvard Graphics includes additional options for chart coloring including gradients to fade from one color to another and bitmaps to provide enhanced patterns. You can make color selections for some of these other options as well. When you choose Hatch/Pattern or Gradient from the Fill tool you will also have the option to make color selections. In the Hatch/Pattern dialog box you can select either Foreground or Background to change the color of both or either one of the options. In Gradient you can choose a Start color and an End color.

Try color change now by making each individual in the crowd symbol a different color with these steps:

1. Click the crowd symbol and then click the individual at the far right to display handles around this one individual.

2. Choose Fill from the Graphics menu and then choose Solid. Select a color that is different than the one selected initially and select OK.

3. Click the next individual in the crowd and then repeat step 2.

4. Continue repeating steps 3 and 4 until each individual displays in a different color. Depending on your selection for font and your color choices your chart might look something like Figure 8-10.

Deleting Objects

While you are busy adding objects to the chart, you may also want to remove objects. To delete an object you must select it and then choose Clear from the Edit menu. Of course, if the object is the last thing that you added to a slide you can choose Edit Undo to remove it without the need for selecting it first.

You can try deleting an object and using the Undo tool to restore it by following these directions:

Chapter 8: *Using Drawing, Symbols, and Other Enhancements* 263

1. With one of the individuals in slide 1 still selected, choose Cl*e*ar from the *E*dit menu to see it disappear.
2. Choose *U*ndo from the *E*dit menu.

Harvard Graphics restores the object, and the undeleted object has the original position and attributes it had when you deleted it.

3. Press (CTRL)+(S) to save the presentation, replacing the older copy on disk.

Copying Objects

For some slides, you will be creating multiple copies of the same object. For example, the top and bottom of the chart in Figure 8-11 contain similar information. Rather than recreating each part separately, you can create the

Figure 8-10.   *Colors changed for individual objects*

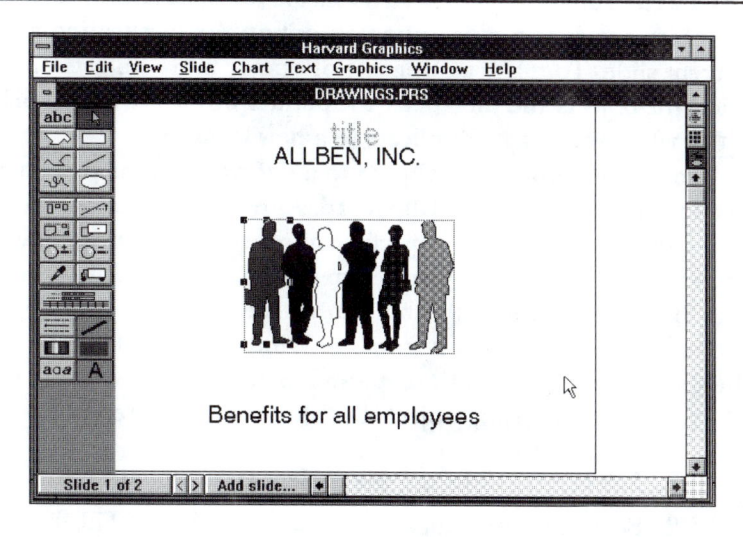

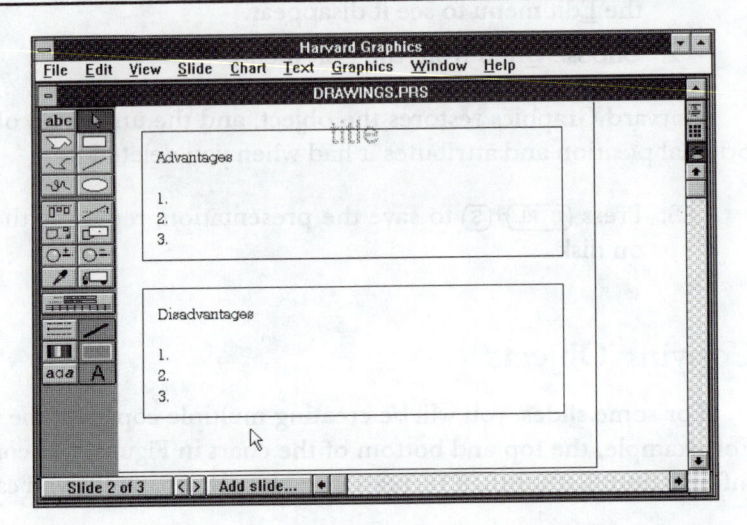

Figure 8-11.   Duplicated objects with modifications

box and text on the top, make a duplicate for the bottom, and edit it. Harvard Graphics provides a quick one-step option for duplicating an object in the current slide. To make a duplicate of one or more objects on the *same* slide, select the objects and then place the pointer inside the selection box and press CTRL while you drag a duplicate to a new location.

To copy one or more objects to a *different* slide or presentation you will need to use the Windows Clipboard. Although this is also easy it requires a little more work. To copy objects to another slide or presentation, select the objects, and then choose Copy from the Edit menu. Move to a different slide with the arrow keys at the bottom of the slide or move to another open presentation by choosing it from the Window menu. Position the pointer on the slide where you want the copy and then choose Paste from the Edit menu.

You can try copying objects by following these steps:

1. Select Add slide and then select Drawing and OK.
2. Select the Rectangle tool and then choose Fill from the Graphics menu. Choose Solid, select None, and then select OK.

Chapter 8: *Using Drawing, Symbols, and Other Enhancements*

3. Move the cross-hair to where you want the first box to start and drag across and down to create the rectangle.
4. Select the Text tool, choose Size from the Text menu, and then select 24 pt.
5. Move the cross-hair to the upper corner of the inside of the box and click it. Type **Advantages** and press (ENTER) twice.
6. Type **1.** and press (ENTER).
7. Type **2.** and press (ENTER).
8. Type **3.** and then click the Selector tool.
9. Use (SHIFT) while clicking the mouse to select both the text and box.
10. Move to the center of the selected group and then press (CTRL) and drag down to an area below the top box to create a duplicate.

    Harvard Graphics duplicates the box and text. Once you have the second copy, you can make further modifications to each copy. After you copy an object or a group of objects, the new copy is the currently selected object.
11. Select the Text tool.
12. Click the text in the box and change it to read Disadvantages and then click the Selector tool.
13. Press (CTRL)+(S) to save the presentation again.

Adding Symbols

For some of your charts you may be content with using the objects you add using the Drawing tools. On the other hand, you may want to add pictures of computers, people, and flowchart symbols to enhance the visual impact of your chart. While you can create these symbols by drawing them, you do not have to. Harvard Graphics provides 500 symbols available in symbol files that you can add to your charts. These symbols are shown in Appendix C, "Symbols Files." In addition, you can use symbols from prior releases of Harvard Graphics and from Harvard Graphics accessory programs, such as Business Symbols or Military Symbols.

You can add another symbol to the first slide by following these steps:

1. Use the arrow at the bottom of the screen to move to slide 1.
2. Select the Symbol tool.

    If you closed the Symbol Library earlier with the suggested double-click you will need to reopen Humans4 to get the symbol that you need. If you left this file open, you will be able to skip to step 4 and select the symbol. If you plan to reuse the same file many times, leave it open and just activate the Slide Editor by clicking it. When you want the Symbol Library again you can press CTRL+ESC to activate Windows Task List and select it.

    Harvard Graphics displays a list of symbol files in the symbol directory. Symbol files have an .SYW extension. If the symbol files you want are stored in a different directory, change the directory.

3. Select Humans4 from the File List. You can either double-click the symbol file that you want, or click it once and then select OK at the bottom of the dialog box.
4. Select the Family symbol with the parents and two children.
5. Choose Copy from the Edit menu at the top of the Symbol Library window.
6. Choose Paste from the Edit menu at the top of the Slide Editor in Harvard Graphics.

    The family symbol is pasted over the crowd. You do not need to worry—the overlay of an additional symbol did not damage the original symbol.

7. Select the text "Benefits for all employees" and then choose Clear from the Edit menu.
8. Move the family down in front of the crowd.
9. Select the Text tool.
10. Choose Size from the Text menu and then select 24.
11. Move the cross-hair between Allben and the crowd image, click the mouse, and then type **Security for your family**.

Chapter 8: *Using Drawing, Symbols, and Other Enhancements* 267

12. Click the Selector tool and then drag the right handle for this text to the left to contain only the text.
13. Use (SHIFT) while clicking to select all four objects, or choose Select all from the Edit menu.
14. Select the Align tool, select the second option in column 1 to center all the objects on the slide, and then select OK. Your screen will look like Figure 8-12.
15. Press (CTRL)+(S) to save the presentation.

Since a symbol is an object to Harvard Graphics, you can modify the symbol or parts of a symbol with the same steps you have already performed. For example, you can change the color of an object as small as the father's tie.

Other Changes

There are many other options for changing your slides with Slide Editor features. You will want to take a look at ways to rotate and flip objects once

Figure 8-12.   *Another symbol added*

you have added them to the screen. You will also want to look at a few of the special effects that Harvard Graphics offers. These options can take a simple object and make it the focal point of a slide as you add a frame or sweep effect to the object. A close-up look at objects is available with the zoom feature.

Rotating and Flipping Objects

Harvard Graphics has two ways you can change an object's orientation. You can either flip an object or you can rotate it. For example, you may want to use the symbol of a hand pointing, but you want the hand pointing to the right instead of the left. To visualize the difference, imagine putting your finger on the middle of an object. If you rotate the object, you spin the object clockwise or counterclockwise, with your finger always remaining on the center point. If you flip the object, imagine a vertical and horizontal line crossing the point where you have your finger. You can flip the object around either line—as long as the center point remains in place. Figure 8-13 shows a handle extending from the hand to allow you to drag the handle around in

Figure 8-13.   *Rotating an object*

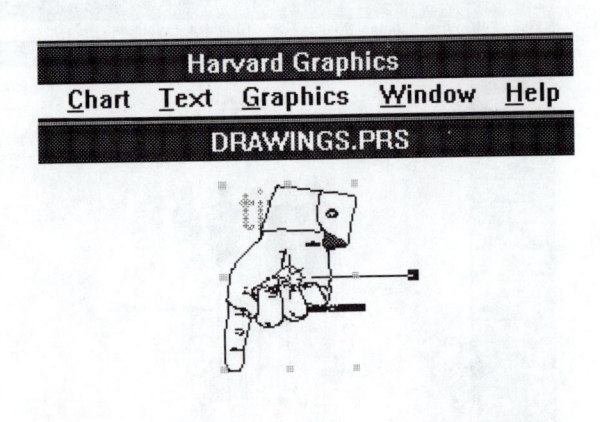

Chapter 8: *Using Drawing, Symbols, and Other Enhancements* 269

a circle. The object will receive the same number of degrees of rotation as the handle that you drag. When used with the (SHIFT) key, the hand will move in 45-degree increments. Figure 8-14 shows how you can flip an object either vertically or horizontally. These changes are made through menu selections rather than by using a handle.

You can try rotating and flipping an object by following these directions.

1. Select Add slide, Drawing, and OK.
2. Select the Text tool.
3. Choose Size from the Text menu and then select a size of 24 points.
4. Move the cross-hair to the center of the drawing area and press the left mouse button to display a Text box.
5. Type **Your Message Here** and then select the Selector tool and drag the handles at the right inward to enclose only the text.

Figure 8-14.   *How Harvard Graphics flips objects*

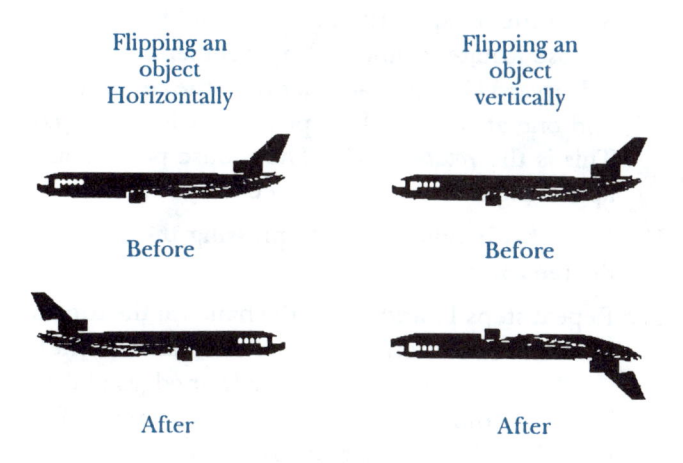

Flipping an object Horizontally

Before

After

Flipping an object vertically

Before

After

Tip: *If you are not happy with the position of the text you can always choose Center on slide from the Graphics menu to achieve an exact center placement for any selected object.*

6. Select the Symbol tool and then select PRESENT3.SYM from the File list in the Symbol Library window.
7. Select the pointing hand symbol.
8. Choose Copy from the Edit menu at the top of the Symbol Library window.
9. Double-click the Control menu box in the upper-left corner of the Symbol Library to close this application and then choose Paste from the Edit menu in the Slide Editor window.
10. Point to the hand and select it.
11. Drag the hand to the right side of the chart if you have selected another area of the screen.
12. Drag the upper-left handle of the hand symbol to shrink the hand's size.
13. While pressing the (CTRL) key drag a copy of the hand away and place it on the left side of the screen.
14. Repeat step 13 twice, placing the copies at the top and bottom of the screen.
15. Select the hand on the right side and then select the Rotate tool or choose Rotate from the Graphics menu.

    Harvard Graphics adds a dot to the center of each selected object and one at the 3 o'clock position, with a line connecting the two. This is the *rotate handle.* The mouse pointer assumes a new look, appearing as a + sign inside a circle.
16. Drag this handle up while pressing the (SHIFT) key to obtain a 90-degree rotation.
17. Repeat steps 15 and 16 for the hands at the top and left, altering the amount of rotation to make all the hands point toward the center.

    All four hands are now at the four edges of the screen and should look something like Figure 8-15. Two hands still need to be flipped to achieve the desired appearance. The hand at the bottom must be flipped horizontally and the hand at the left needs to be flipped vertically.

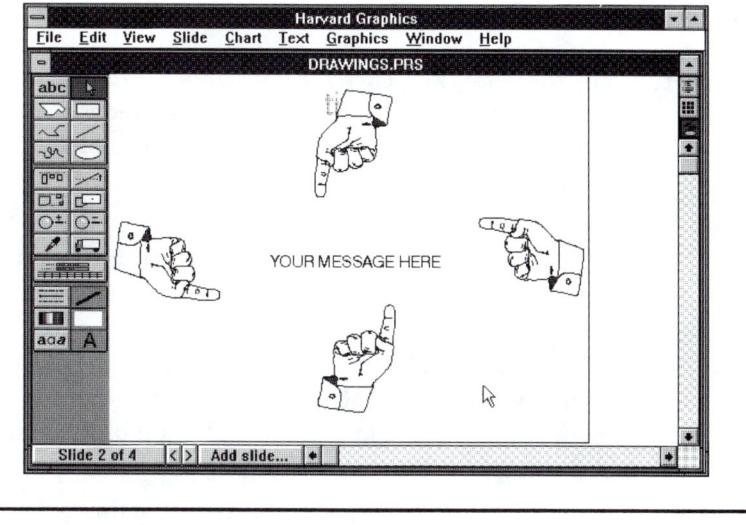

Figure 8-15.   *Objects duplicated and rotated*

18. Select the hand at the bottom, choose Flip from the Graphics menu, and choose Horizontal.
19. Select the hand on the left, choose Flip from the Graphics menu, and then choose Vertical.

    Unless you were very precise in your positioning, you will want to align the hands and the text with the steps in the next section before you consider your slide finished.

Aligning Objects

You have several methods available to align objects. You can move them into position and visually confirm that the objects are aligned. Another option available is letting Harvard Graphics align the objects for you. You can use the alignment features to quickly reposition objects. While alignment is usually thought of for numbers and text, you can use the alignment feature with other types of objects as well. To align objects, you must select the objects and then select the Align tool.

You can try some of these alignment options by horizontally centering the hands pointing up and down and vertically centering the hands pointing left and right. To align the objects, follow these steps:

1. Using the (SHIFT) key, click the left hand, the text, and the right hand. Then select the Align tool and choose the second option in column 1 to align the three objects around a horizontal line running across the center of the screen.

2. Using the (SHIFT) key, click the hand at the top, the text in the center, and the hand at the bottom. Select the Align tool and choose the second option in column 2 to align the objects with a vertical line running through the center of the screen.

    Your chart should look like Figure 8-16 as you finish this step. Clicking a blank area of the slide will remove the selection box. Remember the title that you see at the top of the picture is actually faded text and will not appear if you preview or print the slide.

3. Press (CTRL)+(S) to save the presentation again.

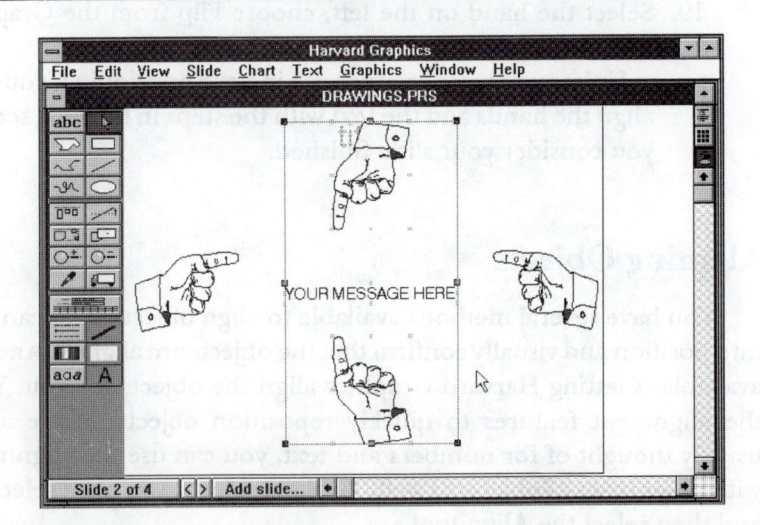

Figure 8-16.   *The drawing after objects are flipped and aligned*

Looking Closer at a Drawing

When you are creating a drawing, you may want to look at the drawing more closely. Rather than looking at the computer screen from an inch away, you can expand, or *zoom*, a portion of the drawing to fill the drawing area. This lets you look at objects closely. Once you zoom the drawing size, you will want to change the drawing area you are viewing. You can use the horizontal and vertical scroll bars to alter the portion of the slide that you are viewing.

You can try zooming by following these steps:

1. Select the hand pointing to the right. Select the Zoom-in tool, which looks like a magnifying glass with a + sign.

    The magnifying glass with a – is the Zoom-out tool. You can also choose Zoom from the View menu. Options are "Zoom in," "Zoom out," "Fit in window" to resume the slide's original size, and "Actual size" to display objects in the size they will print.

2. Select the button on this magnified image.

    It is easier to precisely select a small area of a symbol if you want to make a change in the fill. You could change the color of the button now if you wanted. You can also zoom in larger by choosing the Zoom-in tool again. Your screen should look something like the one in Figure 8-17.

3. Use the scroll bars to view a different area of the slide at the same magnification.

4. Select the Zoom-out tool or choose Zoom from the View menu and then choose Zoom out.

Adding Special Effects

Harvard Graphics has some interesting special effects that are easy to add to any selected objects. You can add a frame around any objects or group of objects. You can use this feature to add a frame around an entire chart or box in some text. You can also add a drop shadow to any object, selecting its color and making it transparent or opaque. A sweep effect provides the most

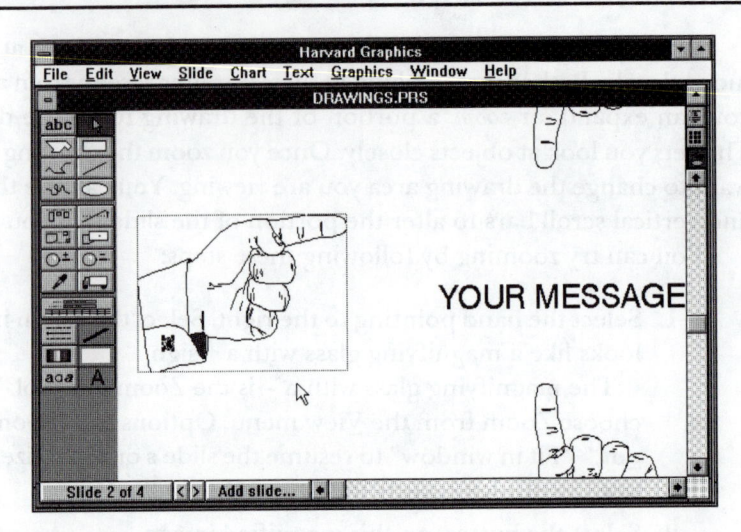

Figure 8-17. *Zooming in on objects*

depth to an object and allows you to create some interesting visual effects as you make a spiral with the object by rotating copies of the object.

Figure 8-18 provides an example of all three effects. A frame like the one shown in this figure can be added around any object or group of objects. To add a frame follow these steps:

1. Select the object.
2. Choose Special effects from the Graphics menu.
3. Click the arrow next to Effect and select Frame. Change the color, transparency/opaqueness level, size, or click 3D to add an X to the check box for a three-dimensional frame like the one in the example.
4. Select OK.

A drop shadow effect can be added to text as well as geometric figures in any color you choose. To add a drop shadow to a selected object follow these steps:

1. Select the object.

Chapter 8: *Using Drawing, Symbols, and Other Enhancements*   275

Figure 8-18.   Adding special effects

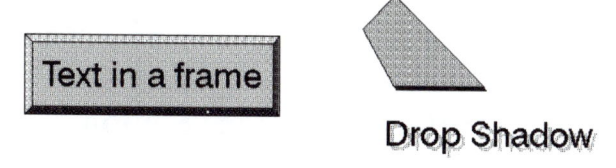

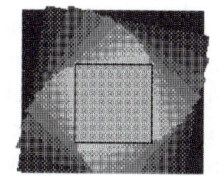

2. Choose Special effects from the Graphics menu.
3. Click the arrow next to Effect and select Drop shadow. Change the color or transparency/opaqueness level.
4. Select OK.

The sweep effect replicates the selected object. You can change the size, direction of the sweep, and even the rotation of the replications for creative effects. Follow these steps to create a sweep effect:

1. Select the object.
2. Choose Special effects from the Graphics menu.
3. Click the arrow next to Effect and select Sweep. Change the color for the first replica or the color for the last replica with Color and End color. Change the size of the replicas, the direction of the sweep, or the number of replicas. You can also drag the handle on the dial to provide a degree of rotation. The radio buttons for Rotate allow you to choose whether this rotation is to the left or right.

In the lower part of Figure 8-18, both a text character and a square were replicated.

4. Select OK.

Creating Multiple Charts with Symbols

If you worked with Release 3.0 of Harvard Graphics, you needed to save your charts as a symbol in order to add multiple charts to a slide. This is not true with Harvard Graphics for Windows. Although you can still save slides as a symbol and use them as you would any other symbol, this approach is not required. In fact, this would not be the recommended approach since you cannot edit a Data Form for a symbol. You can simply choose Add chart to slide from the Chart menu to overlay the current chart with another one. You can then grab the handles on the new chart to shrink it so that both charts will display on the slide at the same time. You can make any chart active by clicking it and then choosing to edit its data.

9

Enhancing Your Presentations

In earlier releases of Harvard Graphics it was necessary to organize individual slides into a presentation. With Harvard Graphics for Windows you have seen that presentations are the focus of your efforts from the start. Your first slide is placed in a presentation file and slides are always saved as part of a presentation. There are further enhancements that you can make to the presentations that you have created. You can display the presentation slides on your screen as a ScreenShow. ScreenShow capabilities provide many transition effects to create professional presentations. You can also use HyperShow options to extend the basics even further and allow you to create an interactive presentation. In addition to the basic printing options for presentations, you can ship them to a slide service or use a special output device, such as a film recorder, to create 35mm slides. Another option for enhancing presentations is the use of presentation styles. You will learn about presentation styles in the next chapter.

In this chapter you will have an opportunity to enhance a presentation created in an earlier chapter. If you did not create this presentation, you can use any presentation file on your disk to try the options presented. You will also have an opportunity to look at reorganizing your presentations and outputting them in other formats.

Getting Started

In this exercise you will enhance a presentation created earlier. Follow these steps to display a ScreenShow:

1. Choose Open from the File menu, select PIES or any other presentation, and then select OK.
2. Choose ScreenShow from the File menu and then choose From beginning.

Tip: *You can also press* (CTRL)+(F2) *rather than activating the File menu.*

3. Press (ENTER) to move to the next slide or click the right mouse button.
4. Press the left arrow to move back to the previous slide and then press (ENTER) again when you are ready to advance.
    Table 9-1 shows all the special keys that you can use to move from slide to slide in a presentation.
5. Continue pressing (ENTER) after viewing each slide until you have viewed the last slide and are looking at the Slide Editor window.
6. Select Close from the File menu to close PIES.

Editing an Existing Presentation

After you preview a presentation, you may decide that you need to add some additional charts. You can do this from the Slide Editor by selecting Add slide from any slide. You can select the type of chart that you want on the slide and then proceed to enter the data. You may also want to eliminate some unneeded slides or reorder the slides after seeing the effect of the

Table 9-1. Default Key Assignments

Key	Slide displayed
BACKSPACE	Backs up one slide to the one previously displayed
BREAK	Ends the ScreenShow
END	Displays the last slide
ESC	Ends the ScreenShow
HOME	Displays the first slide
←	Displays the slide that precedes the current slide sequentially
→	Displays the slide that follows the current slide sequentially
Left mouse button	Displays the previous slide
Right mouse button	Displays the next slide

presentation. Although you can delete a slide from any view, the Slide Sorter is the best view to use when you want to change the order of your slides.

Reordering Slides

You can change the order of the slides in a presentation. To change the location of a slide, the Slide Sorter provides the easiest approach although you can use the Outliner to accomplish the same task if you prefer. If you work in the Slide Sorter you can simply drag slides to their new location. Assuming that the Slide Editor is the default view when you open a presentation, follow these steps:

1. Choose Open from the File menu, select LINES from the File List, and then select OK.

2. Click the Slide Sorter icon or choose Slide Sorter from the View menu.

280   *Harvard Graphics for Windows Made Easy*

3. With the highlight around slide 1, drag to the right after slide 2.

As you drag, an icon will appear to indicate the proposed location for the current slide, as you can see in Figure 9-1. When you release the mouse button, the slide is moved to its new location as shown in Figure 9-2.

You can continue moving your slide around just as you would slides on a light table. The miniature images of the slides make it easy to tell which slide you are working with. If you need to see an expanded view of the slide you can double-click the slide or click the Slide Editor icon.

Deleting Screens from a Presentation

If you have a slide in the presentation that you no longer need, you can easily delete it. If you do not want certain screens to appear in a ScreenShow,

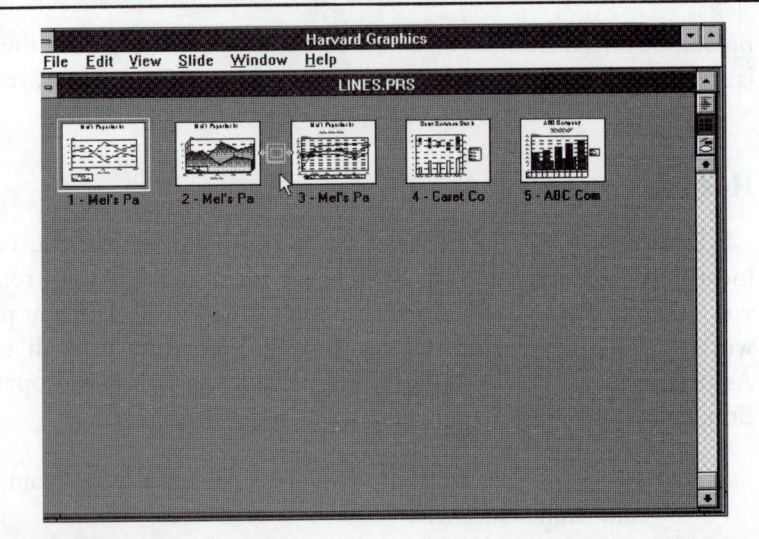

Figure 9-1.   Moving a slide in the Slide Sorter

Chapter 9: *Enhancing Your Presentations* 281

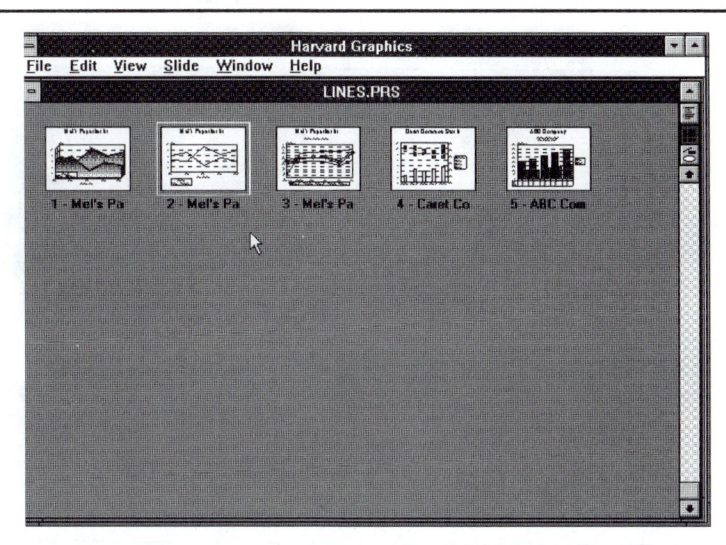

Figure 9-2.   *Slide in new location*

there is no need to delete them, just move them to the beginning of the presentation and then start the ScreenShow at the current slide rather than the beginning by choosing "From the current slide" on the ScreenShow menu. Use these steps to delete slide 3 from the presentation:

1. Click slide 3 to select it.
2. Choose Clear from the Edit menu.
    Slide 3 is deleted and cannot be put back with Edit Paste since Clear does not copy it to the Windows Clipboard. Your screen will look something like Figure 9-3 if you started with five slides since one is now deleted.
3. Choose Undo from the Edit menu.
    The deleted slide is restored.

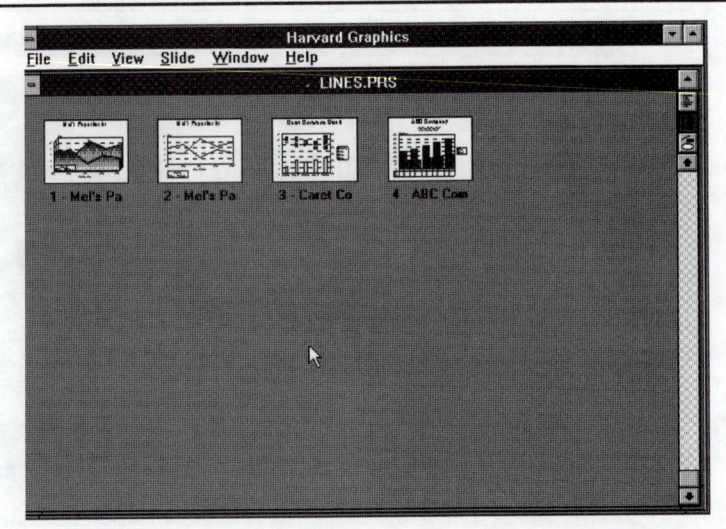

Figure 9-3.   Presentation after deleting slide

Adding ScreenShow Effects

You have already seen how you can display a presentation as a Screen-Show from start to finish, but you did not use any of the special effects. Using these special transition effects adds a professional quality to your onscreen presentations. The ability to control the time each chart displays will allow you to relax and focus on your presentation. You can also use ScreenShow to define special effects either as a default or for each individual slide in the show. These effects control the manner and direction for displaying and erasing screens. After choosing ScreenShow from the File menu, you will need to choose Edit ScreenShow effects to alter the transition effects.

Setting Defaults for the ScreenShow

The dialog box for Edit ScreenShow Effects appears in Figure 9-4. To change the default effects for the entire presentation, you must select Default Transition Effect from the "Slide list" box.

Chapter 9: *Enhancing Your Presentations* 283

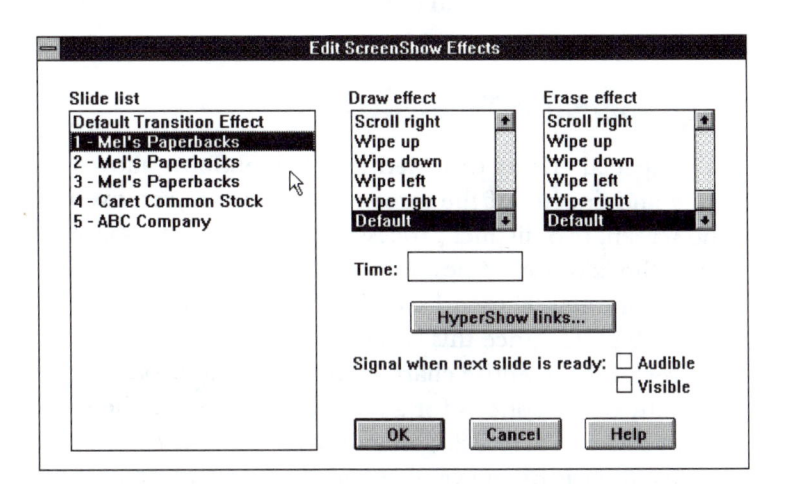

Figure 9-4. **Edit ScreenShow Effects dialog box**

There are four options that you can set the default for. The first option is the "Draw effect." This is the method that Harvard Graphics uses to place the image on the screen. The initial default setting is Replace. This setting causes Harvard Graphics to replace the entire screen image at one time.

The "Erase effect" is the method that is used to remove the current slide from the screen. The default setting is None, which means that the current slide is overwritten by the new entries rather than actually erased. The default display Time is blank. This causes Harvard Graphics to wait for you to click the right mouse button or click a key before proceeding. The last setting is the signal for indicating that the next slide is ready to be displayed. The default setting is to provide neither a visible nor audible indication. Any selections for specific slides will override the default settings. Other options for each of these settings are discussed in more detail in the next section.

Setting Options for Individual Charts

Any time you want to override the default settings, you can select an individual slide from the slide list and make entries in the dialog box to affect this slide's presentation. The same settings discussed here for individual slides are available as presentation defaults.

Using Special Effects

The special effects provided with ScreenShow allow you to control the drawing and erasing of the screen. As charts are removed from and placed on the screen, two distinct processes occur: the removal of existing information and the addition of new information.

As mentioned, Harvard Graphics' default setting for each slide's "Draw effect" is Replace, since this is the default setting for the presentation. This option replaces the entire chart at one time as it displays the new image all at once. Many other options for adding a new chart to the screen are available and are listed in Table 9-2. Some of these options create unique effects: Iris opens like the iris of an eye to reveal more and more of the new image, and Blinds creates the new image with a series of vertical or horizontal strips that expand in size to reveal more of the image until the entire chart is displayed.

Remember, the default setting established for "Erase effect" is None. Unless you supply a different presentation default or a different setting for an individual slide, the old chart is removed as the new one is added.

Experimentation will help you select attractive options that complement each other. The more interesting options require you to take into consideration the direction with which these special effects are supplied. For example, you may decide to choose "Iris in" to draw a new screen and "Iris out" to erase the old screen.

The draw and erase effects combine a direction along with a method of refreshing the screen information. The direction can be as important as the effect to the look of your presentation. Some special effects, for example Replace and Overlay, have no direction settings as part of the selection. Fade can be selected alone to gradually fade the entire slide or to fade down, which starts at the top and progress to the bottom. Iris is the only setting that uses In and Out. The remaining settings support Up, Down, Right, Left, Vertical, or Horizontal. Consider how the directions selected for Draw will combine with the Erase option that you select.

Table 9-2.   *ScreenShow Draw and Erase Effects*

Setting	Effect
Blinds up Blinds down Blinds right Blinds left	Uses horizontal or vertical strips to open or close a screen.
Close horizontal Close vertical	Opens or closes the screen in a horizontal or vertical line.
Fade Fade down	Gradually removes the slide image. You can choose to do the entire screen at once or from the top down.
Iris In Iris Out	Opens out from all directions or closes in from all directions.
Keep	Used for an erase effect to keep the current slide on the screen.
None	Used only for an erase effect. Does nothing, leaving the current slide to be overwritten.
Open horizontal Open vertical	Opens the screen in a horizontal or vertical line that gradually enlarges.
Overlay	Used only for the "Draw effect" to display charts element by element.
Rain up Rain down	Uses gradual drops of rain to draw or erase the screen.
Replace	Entire screen is replaced at once.

Table 9-2.   *ScreenShow Draw and Erase Effects* (continued)

Setting	Effect
Scroll up Scroll down Scroll left Scroll right	Scrolls the slide on or off the screen.
Wipe right Wipe left Wipe up Wipe down	Erases or displays horizontally or vertically.

Setting the Display Time

Once you have practiced your presentation a few times, you will probably know how long you need to display each chart. You can set the display time of each chart if you want to automate your presentation. If you are a bit nervous in front of an audience, this may be what you need because it eliminates your worries about manipulating a screen while trying to speak. Adding a display time is also a good idea when you are creating a presentation for a trade show or other display where passersby will stop to look at the screen. Automating the display allows you to reach more users, since they are not required to take an active role in changing the information presented.

If you want to set different times for all of your charts, use individual settings in the Time text box on the Edit ScreenShow Effects dialog box. As you make your selections, keep in mind that you should allow enough time for everyone viewing the presentation to read a text chart or comprehend the message in a graph. Since there is a great deal of variation in reading speeds, you should read the information slowly when you try to determine the appropriate time to use. Naturally, multiple charts and charts with a great deal of text require more time than a logo or simple graphics image.

You use the *mm:ss* format for entering display times. Entering **1:05** displays the chart for one minute, five seconds. If you enter a number by itself without a colon, seconds are assumed; for example, enter **5** to display the slide for five seconds. Enter **0** to display the slide for as short a time as possible. Leave the box blank to tell Harvard Graphics that you want a key press or right mouse click to indicate that it is time to advance to the next slide.

Signaling the Next Slide

As soon as Harvard Graphics displays the current slide, it begins processing the information for the next slide to get it ready for display. If you press a key before Harvard Graphics finishes preparing the next slide it will not erase the screen or attempt to redraw it until it is ready. If you want an indication that the next slide is ready, you can choose to hear an audible beep or a visible arrow indicating this. All you need to do is place an X in the check box for Audible or Visible.

Trying ScreenShow Effects

You have had a chance to read about all the options that can help you create a professional ScreenShow. Now it's time to try some of these with the slides in whichever presentation you used in the last exercise. Follow these steps to add your selections:

1. Choose ScreenS*h*ow from the *F*ile menu and then choose Edit ScreenShow effects.
2. Select the first slide in the list.
3. Use the scroll arrows on the Draw effect list box to display "Iris in" and then select it.
4. Use the scroll arrows on the "Erase effect" list box to display "Iris out" and then select it.
    The options for Erase are the same as Draw, except for Keep, which retains the current chart and draws the next chart on top of it and None, which leaves the current chart on the screen unless another chart displays overlaying it.
5. Select the Time text box and then type **10** for 10 seconds.

6. Select Audible to place an X in the check box.
7. Select slide 2 from the Slide list box.
8. Use the scroll arrows on the "Draw effect" list box to highlight "Wipe down" and then select it.
9. Use the scroll arrows on the Erase effect list box to select "Wipe up."
10. Select the Time text box and then type **20**.
11. Select Audible to remove the X placed there for the previous slide and then select Visible to place an X in the check box.
12. Continue selecting the remaining slides and trying different transition options as a test of how well you like them.
13. Select OK when you are finished defining all the transition effects.
14. Choose ScreenShow from the File menu and then choose From beginning to view the ScreenShow with all of the transition effects you have added.

You should hear a beep after slide 1 before Harvard Graphics automatically displays slide 2. After slide 2, a small arrow should appear on the screen before slide 3 is displayed. These signals are especially useful when you leave the time field blank and use a key press to advance to the next slide.

Using HyperShow Features to Control the Presentation Order

When you start a ScreenShow, it is designed to proceed from the starting point to the last slide sequentially. If you would like to tailor the presentation to the audience or have the flexibility to otherwise change the order in which slides are presented, you can use the HyperShow features. You can use key presses to indicate which slide you want to show next. You can have default assignments for keys that will apply when any slide is displayed or key presses that only take effect for a single slide. HyperShow features are accessed through the "HyperShow links" button on the Edit ScreenShow Effects dialog box. The Slide HyperShow Links dialog box is shown in Figure 9-5.

Figure 9-5.   Slide HyperShow Links dialog box

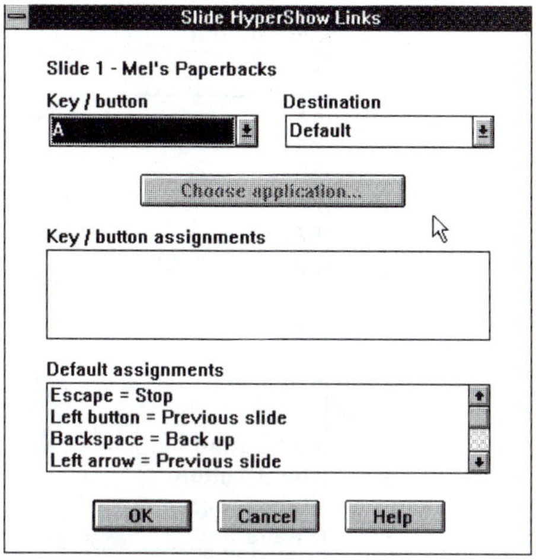

Defining the Key to Activate the Link

When a slide displays on your screen it remains until the time assigned in the Edit ScreenShow dialog box elapses or you press one of the keys in Table 9-1. You can assign keys to individual slides that allow you to press a key while the slide is displayed, which will display the slide that you have linked this key to in the "HyperShow Links" dialog box. This means that you can assign several function keys or letters to any slide to cause it to display any slide next—even if it is not the next slide in the presentation.

First select a slide before selecting the "HyperShow links" button in the Edit ScreenShow Effects dialog box. You can specify which key will be recognized when this slide is displayed by clicking the arrow next to the Key/button pull-down list box. You can scroll through a list of keys like the ones in Figure 9-6. You can see that letters, function keys, and other special keys such as Escape, Enter, and the mouse buttons are included in the list. If you assign a key from this list that is already assigned as a default key (shown earlier in Table 9-1), its default effect will be overridden for the current slide.

Figure 9-6.   Drop-down list box for Key/button

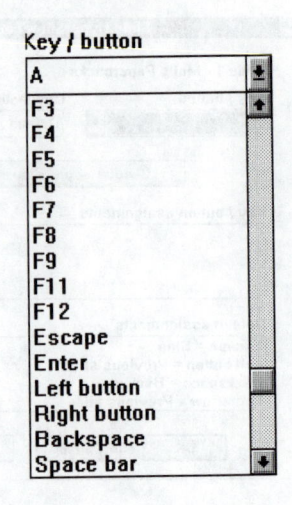

```
Key / button
A
F3
F4
F5
F6
F7
F8
F9
F11
F12
Escape
Enter
Left button
Right button
Backspace
Space bar
```

After selecting the key you want to assign, you will select the destination slide that this keypress will display.

Defining the Destination Slide

The destination slide is the slide that the keypress specified above will display. This slide can be specified as a specific slide number within a presentation or can be indicated by its relative position such as next, last, or first. To specify the slide for the key selected in the Key/button box, click the arrow next to the Destination drop-down list box and select a destination slide. Figure 9-7 shows some of the destinations that might display. A selection of Default will clear any setting for the key for the current slide only.

Chapter 9: *Enhancing Your Presentations* 291

Figure 9-7. Drop-down list box for Destination

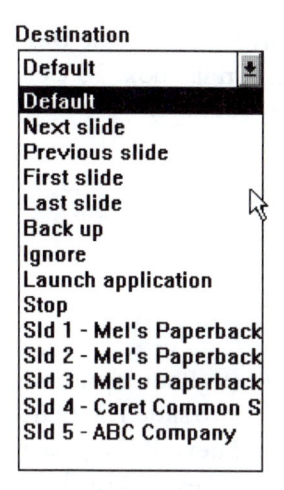

```
Destination
Default              ▼
┌─────────────────────┐
│ Default             │
│ Next slide          │
│ Previous slide      │
│ First slide         │
│ Last slide          │
│ Back up             │
│ Ignore              │
│ Launch application  │
│ Stop                │
│ Sld 1 - Mel's Paperback │
│ Sld 2 - Mel's Paperback │
│ Sld 3 - Mel's Paperback │
│ Sld 4 - Caret Common S  │
│ Sld 5 - ABC Company     │
└─────────────────────┘
```

Changing Default Key Assignments

You can change the settings for default keys. These are the assignments that are in effect for the entire presentation rather than a single slide. For example, you might want to define a keypress as ending a presentation regardless of the slide that is active when you press the key. This type of assignment would be done as a default assignment. To change the default key assignments follow these steps:

1. Choose ScreenS<u>h</u>ow from the <u>F</u>ile menu and then choose <u>E</u>dit ScreenShow effects.
2. Select "Default transition effect" from the Slide list.
3. Select "HyperShow links."

4. Click the arrow next to the Key field and select the key that you want to define.
5. Click the arrow next to the Destination field and select a slide from the drop-down list box. To clear an assignment for a key, choose a destination of None.
6. Click OK.

Trying HyperShow Links

You can try the HyperShow options for the former presentation. You will assign destination slides to slide 1. When A is pressed while slide 1 is displayed, slide 5 will be displayed next. If C is pressed, slide 4 will display next. If neither key is pressed, and no key with a default assignment is pressed, the next sequential slide will be displayed. Follow these steps to set up the links for A and C for slide 1:

1. Choose ScreenShow from the File menu and then choose Edit ScreenShow effects.
2. Select the first slide in the Slide list labeled with a 1.
3. Select "HyperShow links."
4. Click the arrow next to the Key field and select the letter A.
5. Click the arrow next to the Destination field and select slide 5 from the drop-down list box. In this example slide 5 contains data for the ABC Company.
6. Click the arrow next to the Key field and select the letter C.
7. Click the arrow next to the Destination field and select slide 4 from the drop-down list box. In this example slide 4 contains data for Caret Common Stock.

Your selections appear in the Key/button assignments list box shown here:

Chapter 9: *Enhancing Your Presentations* 293

> Key / button assignments
> **A = Sld 5 - ABC Company**
> C = Sld 4 - Caret Common Stock

8. Select OK twice to return to the Slide Editor.
9. Press (CTRL)+(F2) to begin to display the presentation.
10. Type A to display the ABC Company chart (slide 5).
11. Press (BACKSPACE) to redisplay slide 1.
12. Type C to display the Caret Common Stock.
13. Click the right mouse button twice to end the presentation.
14. Press (CTRL)+(S) to save the presentation again.

Creating a Menu of User Choices

When you create ScreenShows about several topics, you may want to let users select the topics they want to see. You accomplish this by creating a menu on a text chart that lists their options and uses the HyperShow feature to display the part of the show that they select.

Building the Special Screens

You will want to create a menu of user selections and a text chart to display after the selected screens have displayed. The menu chart shown in Figure 9-8 and the ending chart shown in Figure 9-9 use the text chart features you learned in Chapter 3, "Creating Text Charts." Follow these steps to build the two charts:

1. Move to the last slide in the presentation and select Add slide from the bottom of the screen. You will add both slides to the end of the presentation and then move the menu slide to the beginning.

Figure 9-8.   Menu slide

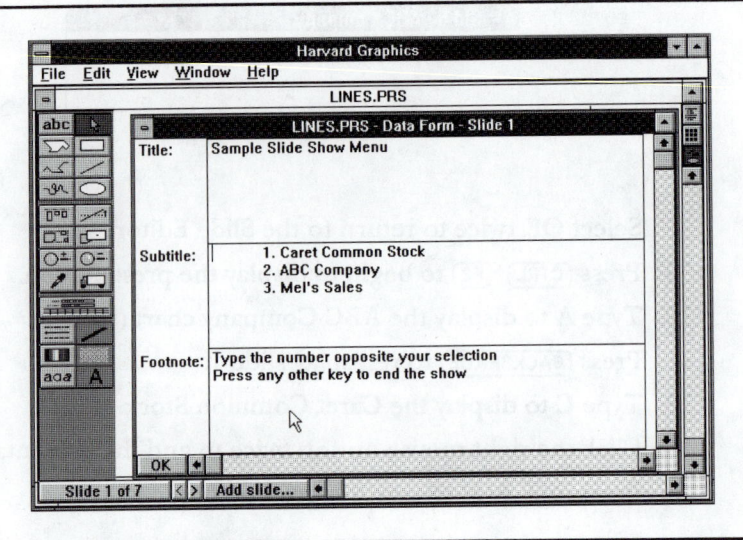

Figure 9-9.   The ending slide

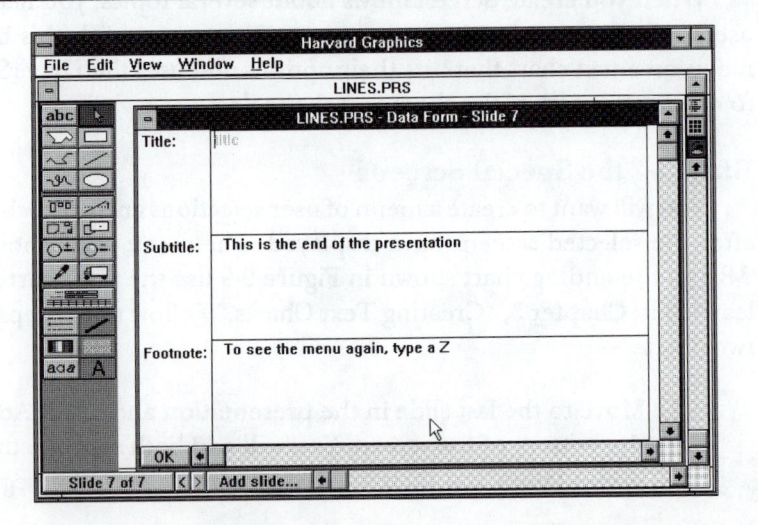

Chapter 9: *Enhancing Your Presentations* 295

2. Select Title and then select OK.
3. Using the text in Figure 9-8 as your guide, type **Sample Slide Show Menu** and press (TAB).
4. Press the (SPACEBAR) 12 times to push the menu entry further to the right, and then type **1. Caret Common Stock.**
5. Press (ENTER), press the (SPACEBAR) 12 times, and type **2. ABC Company.**
6. Press (ENTER), press the (SPACEBAR) 12 times and type **3. Mel's Sales.**
7. Press (TAB) and type **Type the number opposite your selection.**
8. Press (ENTER) and type **Press any other key to end the show.**
9. Select OK. Select the text at the top and then choose Size from the Text menu and select 48.
10. Select the text in the center for the menu choices and then choose Justify from the Text menu and choose Left. Choose Set anchor point from the Text menu and select the second option on line 2. Select OK.
11. Select Add slide.
12. Select Title and then select OK.
13. Using the text in Figure 9-9 as your guide, press (TAB), press the (SPACEBAR) two times, and then type **This is the end of the presentation.**
14. Press (TAB), press the (SPACEBAR) two times, and type **To see the menu again, type a Z.**
15. Select OK and then click the Slide Sorter icon. Drag the menu slide before the first slide.
16. Press (CTRL)+(S) to save the presentation.

Creating Menu Selections

Now that you have created the two new screens, you are ready to alter the ScreenShow to make user selections from these new screens. Then when either of these two screens are displayed, the user can influence the next action. Carry out the following steps to create new entry points into the current presentation:

1. Choose ScreenShow from the File menu.
2. Choose Edit Screenshow effects.
3. Select slide 1. and then select "HyperShow links."
4. Press CTRL+INSERT.
5. Click the arrow next to Key/button box and select 1. Click the Arrow next to Destination and select the slide for Caret Common Stock.
6. Click the arrow next to Key/button and select 2. Click the Arrow next to Destination and select the slide for ABC Company.
7. Click the arrow next to Key/button and select 3. Click the Arrow next to Destination and select the first slide for Mel's (slide 2 if yours are arranged the same way as the sample presentation).
8. Select OK to return to the Edit Screenshow Effects dialog box.
9. Select the last slide from the "Slide list" and then select "HyperShow links."
10. Click the arrow next to Key/button and then select Z. Click the Arrow next to Destination and select the first slide to make the menu display if users press a Z. Select OK twice.

From the first chart, you can type a number to select which chart you want to see. You can browse through the presentation to display all of the charts. When the last slide is displayed you can choose whether or not to start over by pressing a Z. The menu is not set up to offer all slide options, but you could extend it further with new entries and "HyperShow links."

11. Press CTRL+S to save the presentation and then click the Slide Editor icon.
12. Choose Close from the File menu.

Building a Chart in Stages

Because a completed chart can contain more information than your audience can absorb at one time, you can create a building effect by gradually

Chapter 9: Enhancing Your Presentations

adding more information to the chart. With a text chart this might mean adding one line at a time. With an analytical chart it might mean adding data series one at a time. In both cases the most efficient way to create the chart is to build the final product and save it. Next, make as many copies of this slide as there are steps in the building process. Delete the unneeded elements from each slide, stripping away one layer at a time. Set the Draw effect to Overlay and the Erase effect to to Keep. Follow these steps to build and display a bullet chart using these principles:

1. Choose **N**ew presentation from the **F**ile menu.
2. Select Bullet and then select OK.

In the following steps you will create the final chart and save it. Then you will use it to build other charts.

3. Press (↑) to move to the Title field, type **Keys To Successful Sales**, and press (ENTER) three times.
4. Type **Set goals** and press (ENTER) twice.
5. Type **Set time frames for achieving goals** and press (ENTER) twice.
6. Type **Determine cost you will incur to meet goals** and press (ENTER) twice.
7. Type **Establish a plan** and press (ENTER) twice.
8. Type **Monitor progress** and then select OK.
9. Click the Title, choose **S**ize from the **T**ext menu, and select 36.
10. Click one of the bullets, choose **S**ize from the **T**ext menu and then select 24. Choose Set Anchor point from the Text menu and select the first option on line 1. Select OK.
11. Press (F2) to display a chart that looks something like Figure 9-10.
12. Click the Slide Sorter icon and then choose **C**opy from the **E**dit menu.
13. Choose **P**aste from the **E**dit menu four times to create four copies of the slide.
14. Click slide 1 and then click the Slide Editor icon.
15. Choose Edit **d**ata from the **C**hart menu.

16. Select the last four bullets and then press (DEL).
17. Select OK, move to slide 2, and choose Edit data from the Chart menu. Select the last three bullets and press (DEL).
18. Select OK, move to slide 3, and choose Edit data from the Chart menu. Select the last two bullets and press (DEL).
19. Select OK, move to slide 4, and choose Edit data from the Chart menu. Select the last bullet and press (DEL).
20. Choose ScreenShow from the File menu and then choose Edit ScreenShow Effects. Select Default Transition Effect, select "HyperShow links," and then select Overlay for the "Draw effect" and Keep for the "Erase effect."
21. Select OK. Press (CTRL)+(F2) to view the ScreenShow, pressing a key when you are ready to move to each new slide.

Figure 9-10.   Completed bullet chart

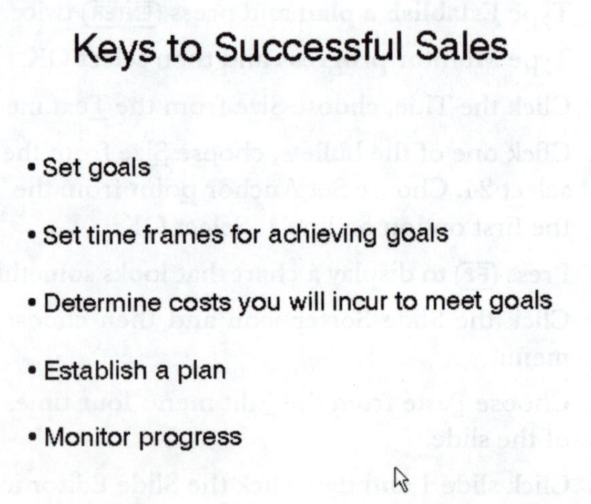

Keys to Successful Sales

- Set goals
- Set time frames for achieving goals
- Determine costs you will incur to meet goals
- Establish a plan
- Monitor progress

Outputting Presentations

In Chapter 4, "Learning XY Chart Basics with Bar Charts," you learned how to print all the slides in your presentation or to print just a few as a range. You also learned that a quick click of the Handouts radio button allows you to print a snapshot of several slides on a page for use as handouts.

There are several other output options that may be useful to you. These are outputting your slides to a plotter or film recorder or sending special files to a service that will create 35mm slides or other output media for you. There are some special considerations for these options, which will be covered in this chapter. Although not all the details are included here, the discussion will serve as a guideline for some of the things that you need to do.

Using Plotters and Film Recorders

When you first acquire a plotter or film recorder, you must set up the device in Windows. This step is required before you can use it for your Harvard Graphics Output. The setup procedure will install the drivers that tell Windows how to interface with the new device. Follow these steps to install a new device:

1. Double-click the Control Panel icon.
2. Double-click the Printers icon.
3. Select Add printer.
4. Select the device from the List of Printers box.
5. Insert the Windows drivers disk in drive A or B when instructed.
6. Select Configure to specify the port you are using to attach the device.
7. Select OK.
8. Select Active under Status.
9. Select OK.

You will need to refer to the Setup options discussed in Chapter 4 to ensure the best settings for your device. For instance, if you have a film recorder you will want to set "Print background fill" to capture all the detail (extra detail is merely confusing when you have a device such as a plotter that cannot handle it). You will select these specialized devices as your printer in Setup to route your presentation output to these devices.

Using the Autographix Service

If you originally installed all the files for Harvard Graphics, you will find an Autographix program available to you along with Harvard Graphics. This program allows you to transmit files in encapsulated postscript format to a service that can provide professional-looking output. This can be an ideal solution when you occasionally need a presentation in a 35mm format. If you were not able to install the full version of Harvard Graphics, you will need to go back and install selected files in order to make this program available.

Special File Format

To send a presentation to Autographix, you must have it in an encapsulated postscript format. In order to do this you must install a postscript printer in Windows. It does not matter that you do not actually have a printer device, but in order to get the .EPS file format, Harvard Graphics must think that it has a postscript printer available.

After installing the printer, you must configure it for Autographix using the Configure option from within the Control Panel of Windows. You can choose Autographix after requesting that a printer be added and insert your Harvard Graphics disk to make the required information available.

The Procedure for Using Autographix

Once Autographix is installed you can double-click its icon to start it. Your first step is to choose "Communications setup" and select options such as the baud rate and tone. You will want to select the COM port where your modem is attached, and you should also specify a destination and telephone number after selecting Add. These steps are only required the first time that you use the package.

Each time you want to transmit presentation files, you must print them out as .EPS files. This is done by selecting the postscript printer you installed earlier in the Device drop-down list box. You will want to select "Setup device," select Options, and check to be sure that the radio button for "Encapsulated PostScript File" is the option chosen under "Print to." After you click OK three times the slides will start to print.

With the slides written to disk as an EPS file, you can start the Autographix program. You can choose the name of your EPS file from the Filename list. You can select one or more files to send. You can also enter processing, billing, and delivery information with the order. When everything is all set up, you can choose Send from the File menu.

Tip: Using Compression will save significant time and space. To compress your files before sending them, choose Compression from the File menu and then choose "Use compression." You can expect a compression rate of 50% to 90%.

10

Using Templates, Backgrounds, and Styles

A background is the area behind the information you show on a slide. The default background that Harvard Graphics provides is blank and similar to creating your slide on a plain sheet of paper. You can use a background to add a border or logo. You can use the same background for an entire presentation to provide a consistent look.

Templates are chart definitions used to speed up the production of charts—especially the types you create frequently. Templates can also be the ideal solution for users who do not work with Harvard Graphics frequently, but want to be able to create a chart immediately after entering their data. If you build a template for these users, they can create their charts month after month without any additional help.

Styles affect your entire presentation and consist of templates for the different chart types along with backgrounds and palettes. You will learn how to create a presentation style after learning more about backgrounds and templates.

Getting Started

To create a background you need to have a slide in the Slide Editor. You can start with a slide of any type but you might as well start with a blank one. Think of the slides as being created on clear sheets of mylar that will allow any background you create to show through. In this section you will create a background for bullet charts. Later you will see that you can use this same background for other types of slides if you like. You will also learn how to edit your first background design to make further improvements. Follow these steps:

1. Choose Close from the File menu to close any open presentations. You can decide whether or not you need to save these presentations as you progress.

2. Choose New presentation from the File menu, select Bullet, and select OK.

3. Select OK to finalize the Data Form without entering data. You must be in the Slide Editor screen to access the menu option for creating a background.

4. Choose Background from the Slide menu and then choose Create. The Create Background dialog box appears.

5. Click the New Background text box and type **bckbllet**.

    Since you can use up to 30 characters, you do not have to abbreviate unless you want to. A list box displays existing backgrounds. You can select one of these and select "Copy from background" to s art from this rather than a blank screen.

    If you do not remember what your existing backgrounds look like, rather than choose the wrong one you can select the "Show background" check box on the right side of your dialog box to see a graphic image of your background.

6. Select OK. Harvard Graphics presents the Slide Editor with a blank screen. You can use the menu and toolbox tools to add graphics or make other changes.

7. Choose Line attributes from the Graphics menu.

Chapter 10: *Using Templates, Backgrounds, and Styles*

8. Select Hairline by clicking its radio button. Click the arrow next to Style and select the third dotted line option that will appear from the drop-down list box and then select OK.
9. Select the rectangle tool. Move the cross-hair to make it touch the upper edge of the slide and the left edge at the same time. Click the left mouse button and then move the cross-hair to make it touch the right and bottom edges of the slide at the same time and click it again.
    A large rectangle appears on the slide with a narrow border.
10. Choose Fill from the Graphics menu and then choose Gradient.

Tip: *You would use Set fill from the Background menu if you wanted the entire background covered with the selected fill. Using this option with the rectangle leaves an unfilled band at the outer edges of the window.*

11. Select "Start color," select 24, and then select OK.
    Your screen will look something like Figure 10-1. The rectangle is filled with a gradient pattern while the narrow band around the outside edges remains blank.
12. Click the "Back to slide" button at the bottom of the screen and then choose Edit data from the Chart menu.
13. Click the Title field and then type **Exponential Sales Growth**.
14. Press (ENTER) three times and then type **Sales have tripled each of the last three years**. Press (ENTER).
15. Type **Increases attributable to several factors** and press (ENTER).
16. Press (TAB), type **Customer loyalty**, and press (ENTER).
17. Type **Sound product** and press (ENTER).
18. Type **Production cost efficiencies** and press (ENTER).
19. Press (SHIFT)+(TAB) and then type **1993 projected to be record year**.
    Your Data Form entries should match Figure 10-2.
20. Click OK to display your slide on the Slide Editor screen with the Background that you created. Press (F2) to preview the chart as shown in Figure 10-3. Press (ESC).

Figure 10-1. Background with rectangle frame and gradient fill

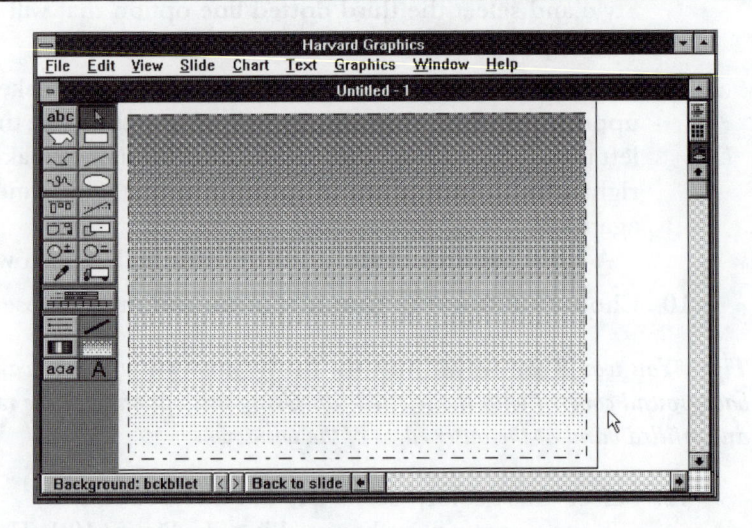

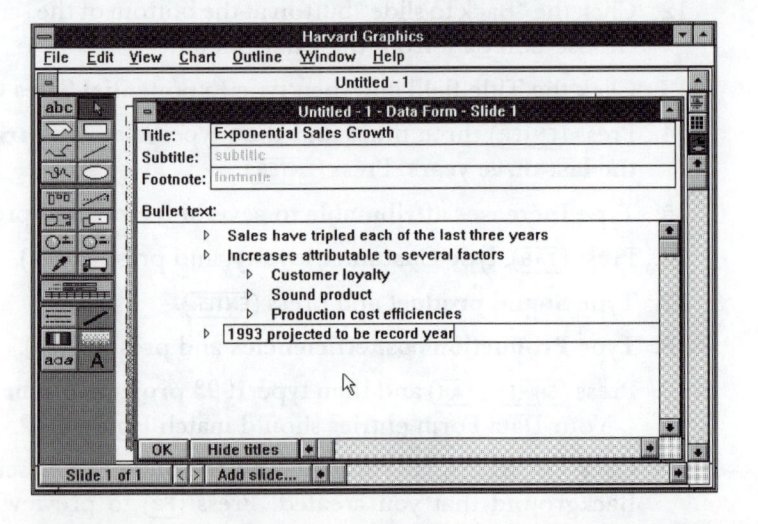

Figure 10-2. Data Form entries to try the background

Figure 10-3. *Chart using the background*

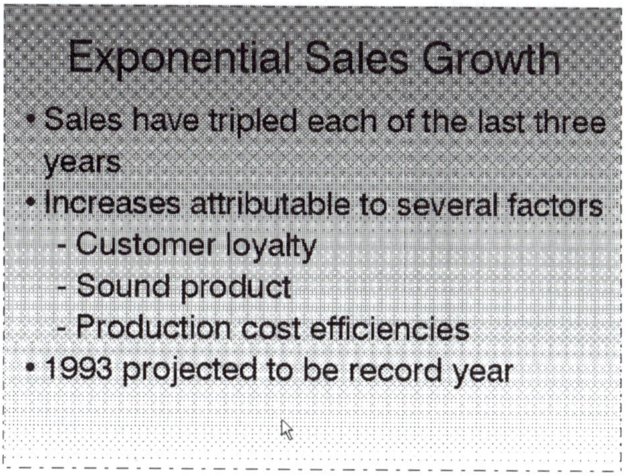

> **Exponential Sales Growth**
> - Sales have tripled each of the last three years
> - Increases attributable to several factors
>   - Customer loyalty
>   - Sound product
>   - Production cost efficiencies
> - 1993 projected to be record year

Working with Backgrounds

As you saw in "Getting Started" it is really quite easy to create a custom background for your slides. You can use one background for all types of slides or you can create different backgrounds for different slide types. There are many additional things that you can do with slides.

First, let's look at making a few changes to the background you created before moving on to templates and styles.

Editing a Background

Changes that you make to the slide with the slide data displaying on the Slide Editor screen will not affect the background. It is necessary to specify that you want to edit the background. You can then add new elements and make changes to existing entries just as you would on a slide.

Adding a Stamp

Harvard Graphics allows you to add the date, time, or slide number to a slide. This information is dynamic and will be updated at the time that the slide is displayed. This is important since clients and others observing your presentation will feel that it is new and created especially for the presentation date. If you add information like this it is automatically updated when the slide is displayed.

You must be creating a background or editing one to add a slide number, although you can add the other elements from the Slide Editor. You must also activate the Text tool and start a text box at the point where you want to add a *stamp* (which is a placeholder that inserts variable information). Follow these steps to add a date stamp to the lower-right corner of the slide:

1. Select the Text tool, move the cross-hair approximately one third of the way back from the right edge of the screen and far enough away from the bottom to allow for the entry of a line of text. Click this area to place a text box on the screen.

2. If you want fixed text to precede the stamp, type it here.

3. Choose Size from the Text menu and then choose 24.

4. Choose Add stamp from the Text menu. A menu appears to offer you choices of "Slide number," "Short date," "Long date," and Time.

5. Choose Long date.
   You can drag this text to a different location if it is not placed on the screen exactly where you want it. You are actually dragging a special code that will always display the current system date, not the date that is currently displayed.

6. Click a blank area on the screen to close the text box.

7. If you click "Back to slide" and press (F2), the chart displays with a date stamp in the bottom-right corner. Press (ESC) to return to the Slide Editor.

Changing Existing Elements

You may decide that you want to change existing elements on the chart rather than just adding new ones. As an example you might want a wider solid

Chapter 10: *Using Templates, Backgrounds, and Styles*

line around the edges, or you might want the gradient to start with the light color and progress to the darker color. Either change can be made by selecting the object on the background and then changing the desired attribute. Follow these steps to change the line attribute and gradient fill:

1. Choose Background from the Slide menu and then choose Edit.
2. Select the rectangle by clicking it. Handles appear around the edges of this box.
3. Choose Line attributes from the Graphics menu.
4. Select 6 points for the size, and the style automatically changes to a solid line. Select OK.
5. With the rectangle still selected, choose Fill from the Graphics menu and then choose Gradient. Select "Start color" and then select 15, or any other color number you like. Select "End color," select 24 and OK.
6. Select "Back to slide" and then press F2. Press ESC to return to Slide Editor.

Your slide will look something like Figure 10-4.

Backgrounds are an important building block for templates and presentations. When you have some free time you might want to prepare some unusual slide backgrounds that can hold the reader's attention without competing with a slide's message.

Applying an Existing Background

You can use the background you just created for as many slides as you want. You can even apply this background to an entire presentation. For now, let's see how to use it for another slide. Follow these steps to start another chart using this background:

1. Click the "Add slide" button at the bottom of the Slide Editor window.
2. Select Bullet and then select OK.

Figure 10-4. *Adding a date stamp and reversing the gradient fill*

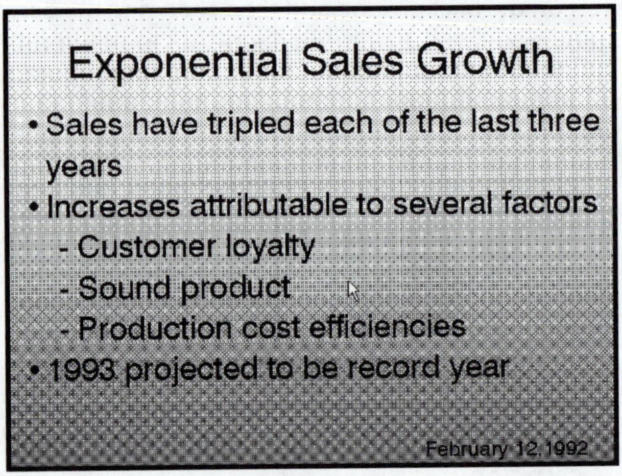

Exponential Sales Growth
- Sales have tripled each of the last three years
- Increases attributable to several factors
  - Customer loyalty
  - Sound product
  - Production cost efficiencies
- 1993 projected to be record year

February 12, 1992

3. Click the OK button on the Data Form to see the Slide Editor window.
4. Choose Background from the Slide menu and then choose Apply.

A dialog box like the one in Figure 10-5 appears.

5. Choose "bckbllet" from the Background list box.
6. Select "This slide" for the "Apply background to" field and then select OK.

Even though you have not entered data you can see how the background has already been added for you, as shown in Figure 10-6.

Creating Templates

You can think of templates as the dye or mold used to shape the appearance of a slide. Unlike backgrounds, templates are specific to a chart

Chapter 10: *Using Templates, Backgrounds, and Styles* 311

Figure 10-5. Apply Background dialog box

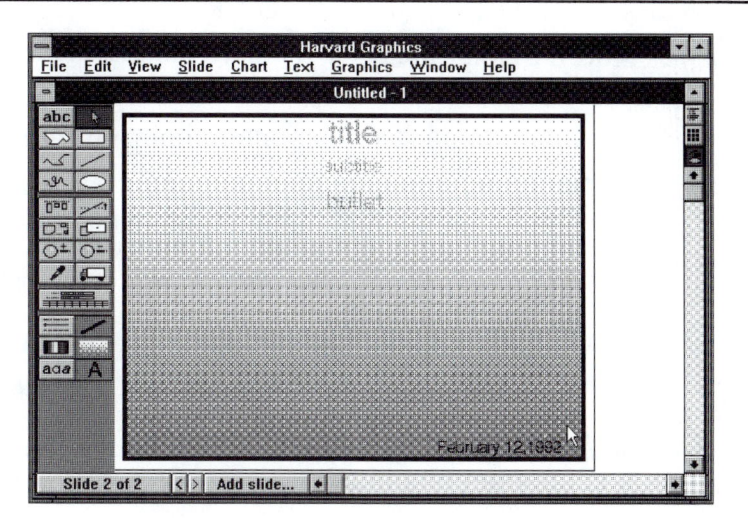

Figure 10-6. New bullet chart showing background applied before data is added

type since they control where the elements of a slide, such as the title, appear. Every slide you have created thus far has used a template but it has used the default template for the slide type you created. Harvard Graphics provides twelve of these default templates, one for each type of slide. When you create a new slide and choose a slide type, the appropriate default template is used.

Template options that you can set include establishing a slide background, selecting a color palette, altering text placement and sizing, changing text attributes and anchor points, setting a chart type, setting chart options, changing the location of a chart on the slide, adding symbols and other enhancements with the toolbox features. Almost anything that can be changed for a chart can be established as a default through the use of a template. Data links are an exception and cannot be saved with a template. When you examine presentation styles later in this chapter you will see that a set of slide templates are stored with each presentation. You can have as many sets of templates as you have presentations.

Follow these steps to create a template for title charts that uses the background you have already created:

1. Select "Add slide" from the bottom of the Slide Editor window. Select Title and then select OK. Select OK on the Data Form.

2. Choose Background from the Slide menu and then choose Apply. Select "bckbllet" and then select OK.

3. Move the mouse pointer to the faded subtitle, click it, and then drag it to the midpoint of the slide.

4. Click the title and then drag it until it is slightly above the 1/4 point on the slide.

5. Click the footnote and drag it until it is approximately 1/4 of the way from the bottom of the screen. Your chart should look like the one shown in Figure 10-7 but without trees at this point.

In the next section you will add a symbol to further enhance the template you are building. Notice that so far you have not done anything different than you would do in creating a slide with special features. This is always true for building templates—you will just need to tell Harvard Graphics to save your specifications as a template when you are through designing the template.

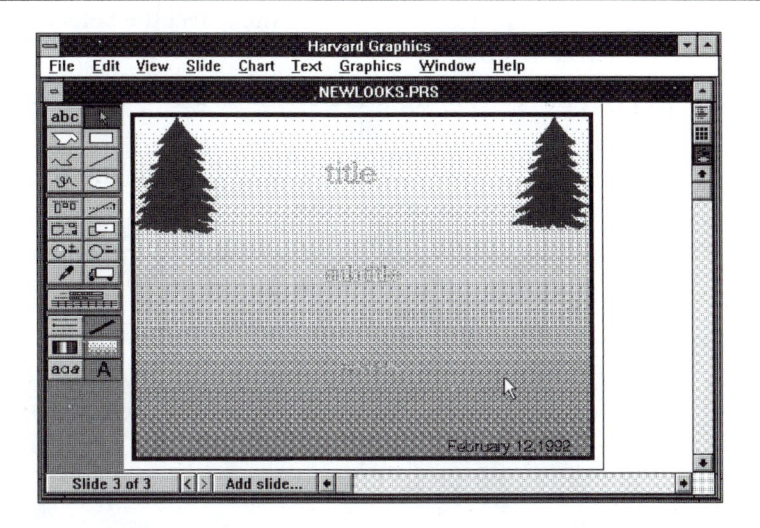

Chapter 10: *Using Templates, Backgrounds, and Styles*   313

Figure 10-7.   *Position of title, subtitle, and footnote changed and symbols added*

Adding Symbols

Although basic text and analytical charts are easy to create, drawing with the toolbox tools requires a little more practice for many users. If you want to add a symbol or drawing, like a company logo, to a series of charts, you may want to use a template so you only have to do it correctly one time. In the following steps you will add two trees to the template. When you finish, the template will contain placement instructions for the title, subtitle, and footnote, a background, and two fir tree symbols. Whenever you need a title chart in this presentation you can use this template to create the chart and simply type in the text.

Follow these steps to add the trees:

1. Select the Symbol tool.
2. Select ANIPLANT.SYW from the Files list and then select OK.
3. Select the Fir tree.
4. Choose Copy from the Edit menu at the top of the Symbols Library.

5. Close the Symbols Library by double-clicking its Control Menu box.
6. Choose Paste from the Edit menu. Select the Selection tool and click the tree symbol.
7. Push the bottom-right handle inward to shrink the tree symbol to approximately 1/2 its size.
8. Move the pointer to the center of the tree and then drag it to the upper-left corner of the slide.
9. Press (CTRL) while dragging this symbol to the upper-right corner to make a duplicate, as shown in Figure 10-7.
10. Choose Slide template from the Slide menu and then choose Create from slide.
11. Press (DEL) with the highlight in the "Slide template name" text box to remove the current entry and then type TREE_TITLE as shown in Figure 10-8. Select OK.

Figure 10-8.   *Create Template from Slide dialog box*

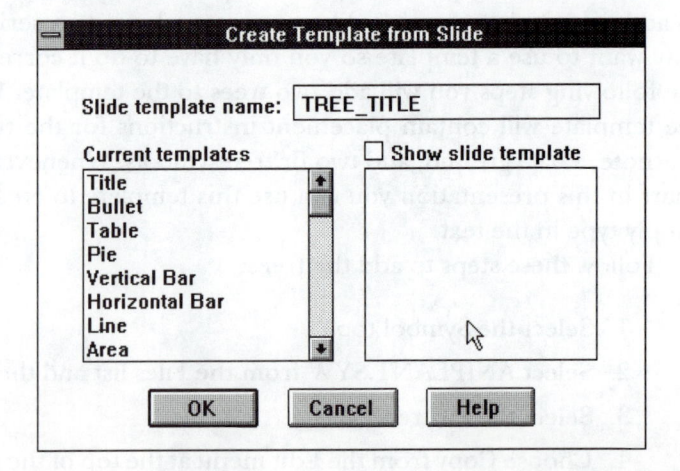

Applying a Template to a Chart

You can retrospectively apply template settings to an existing chart. This feature lets you restructure how a chart appears without having to reenter the chart data. This also means that you can make several previously created charts use the same settings. With your chart active in the Slide Editor, all you need to do is choose Slide template from the Slide menu and then choose Apply. Harvard Graphics displays the Apply Slide Template dialog box shown in Figure 10-9. After selecting the desired template select OK. You will see your chart on the Slide Editor screen with the template positioning, objects, and selections.

Using a Template When You Create a New Slide

Now that you have created a special template for the title charts you will want to use it throughout the current presentation. The availability of this

Figure 10-9.   Apply Slide Template dialog box

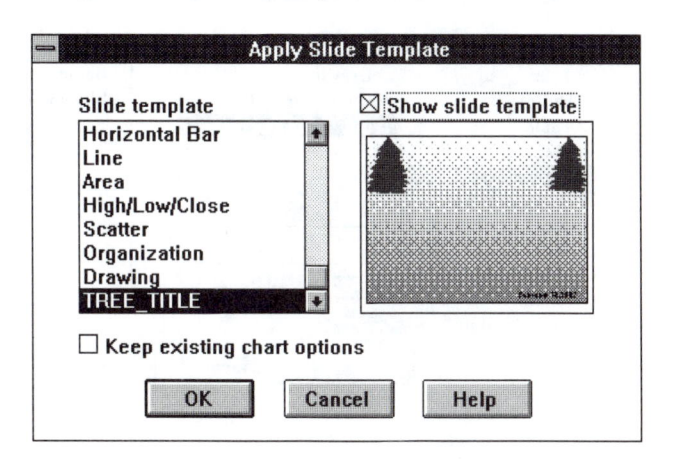

template will allow you to create a chart by entering a few lines of text. Follow these steps to add a new slide and choose a custom template for it:

1. Select Add slide at the bottom of the screen.
2. Select Custom Template from the Add Slide dialog box that looks like Figure 10-10.
    The list box will display all the custom templates that you have created. If you have many custom templates in a presentation, you can select "Show slide template" to place an X in its check box and display a small sample below it.
3. Select OK.
4. Move to the Title field, type **All Pines** and then press (TAB).
5. Type **Trees for Every Location** and press (TAB).
6. Type **Al & Betty Rogers** and then select OK.
    When you press (F2) to see the chart it should look like Figure 10-11.

Figure 10-10.   Add Slide dialog box showing "Custom template" option

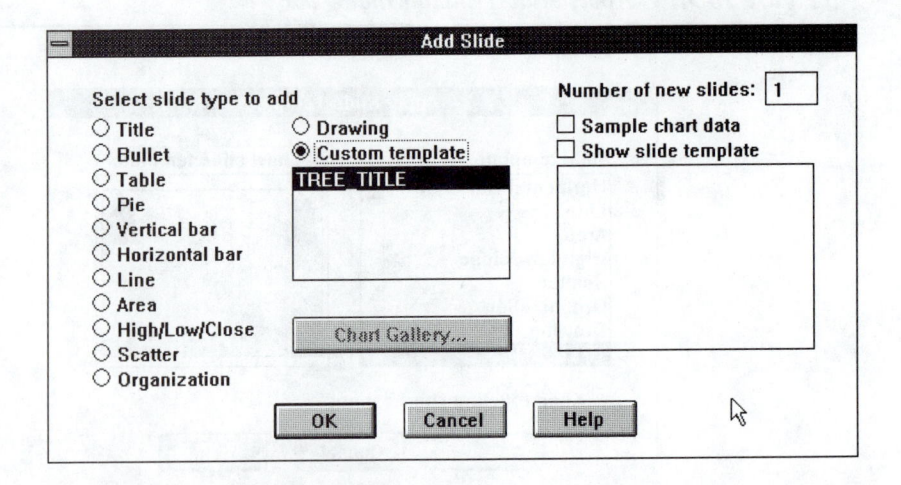

Chapter 10: *Using Templates, Backgrounds, and Styles* 317

Figure 10-11.   Slide created with the template

Changing the Default Templates

In addition to creating templates for individual projects, you can create standard templates that appear any time you create a specific chart type. You do not need to ask Harvard Graphics to get a template in order for the options stored in this special template to take effect. If you do not like the size or placement of characters or would prefer to use a different font on all graphs of a particular type, you can modify the way this chart type looks. If you always want vertical bar charts to be overlapped by 50 and use 3D effect, you can make the necessary changes and save them as a special template. Each new vertical bar chart will then be automatically established with an overlap of 50 and a 3D effect. The key to making changes to each of the chart types with a template is to use the default template names shown in Table 10-1 when saving the template.

Table 10-1.   Template Names to Create Default Templates

Default Template Name
Area
Bullet
Drawing
High/Low/Close
Horizontal Bar
Line
Organization
Pie
Scatter
Table
Title
Vertical Bar

Using Styles

A presentation style is a set of all the templates that you used in creating your presentation as well as any color palettes or backgrounds used. Each of the presentation styles that comes with Harvard Graphics has twelve standard slide templates. If you choose to create your own, you can add as many custom templates as you want up to the limit of 100 for any presentation. You can also have as many as 100 backgrounds within a presentation.

If you have created a presentation with custom templates and background, you will want to save the presentation style. Once you assign it a name it will be available to assign to new presentations.

Saving a Presentation Style

You might continue to work in the current presentation, building another custom template or two. When you are finished you may want to save all the work that you have done both as a presentation file with the standard File Save sequence but also as a presentation style that will allow you to have the same set of templates and backgrounds readily available for new presentations. To save a presentation style from the current presentation follow these steps:

Chapter 10: *Using Templates, Backgrounds, and Styles* 319

1. Choose Presentation style from the Slide menu.
2. Choose Save to display a dialog box like the one shown in Figure 10-12.
3. Click the Filename text box then type **allpine** or any other filename you want to use.
4. Select OK.
5. Choose Save from the File menu to save your presentation.
6. Choose Close from the File menu to close the presentation.

Applying a Presentation Style

If you want to try a different style for your presentation you can select from any of the 54 styles Harvard Graphics provides. Many of these styles provide creative backgrounds for your presentation with everything from redwood to leaves as possibilities. Harvard Graphics' style names that begin

Figure 10-12.   *Save Presentation Style dialog box*

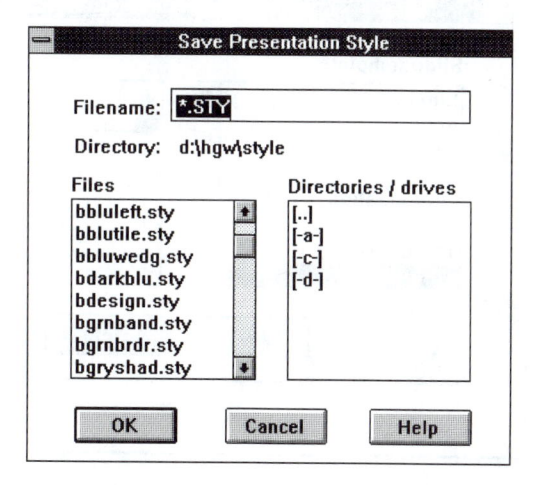

with a "B" use Bitstream fonts that can be printed on any output device, and those that begin with a "P" use Postscript fonts that require a postscript compatible output device. You can also select any style created earlier for one of your own presentations as long as you saved it. To apply a style to your current presentation you would follow these steps:

1. Choose <u>P</u>resentation style from the <u>S</u>lide menu.
2. Choose <u>A</u>pply.
3. Select the style name that you are interested in.
4. Select Preview if you want to see the style first.
    A dialog box similar to the one in Figure 10-13 appears to let you examine each template in the style.
5. Select OK twice to apply the style.

Figure 10-13.   Preview Presentation Style dialog box

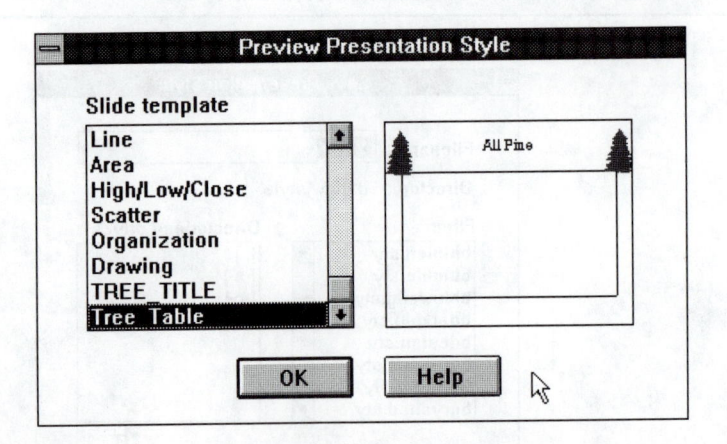

11

Importing and Exporting Data

In all the charts that you have created up to now you have entered the data in the Outliner or on a Data Form. Often you will have data stored in another format, such as WordPerfect or 1-2-3, and will not want to reenter it. If the program containing the text or numeric information needed for a chart is supported by Harvard Graphics, you can bring the data into memory to use with Harvard Graphics without retyping the data. This process is called importing the data.

The essence of the import process is converting data from another format into something that is usable to Harvard Graphics. Harvard Graphics supports importing from 1-2-3 and Excel as well as ASCII text created with any program. Later you will learn how to import some graphic image files as well. These include files with extensions such as .BMP, .CGM, .DRW, .PCX, .PCC, .TIF, and .WMF.

If the data that you need in a Harvard Graphics chart was created in another Windows applications such as Excel or 1-2-3 for Windows, you can link to this information. Linking goes one step further than importing since new information in the external source automatically updates your Harvard Graphics slide any time you change the source data. Harvard Graphics also updates the data when you open the presentation containing the link and tells Harvard Graphics that it is OK to update the linked data. You can also have Harvard Graphics update these links automatically when opening a presentation.

Another Harvard Graphics option allows you to export a slide as an image. When you export a slide you are interested in storing it in the format needed by another package, such as a desktop publishing program. Harvard Graphics can export a slide as a Windows Bitmap, TIFF Bitmap, and other popular graphics file formats including .CGM. .PCX, and .TIF. When you export a slide image, the data is not exported with it, only the image that you see on the screen when you press (F2) to preview the slide.

Using import and export features can dramatically reduce data entry time. Entering data more than once to use it with different programs is not only frustrating, it is error prone. You might make a mistake in one of your entries and end up with two sets of data that are not in agreement. When you are able to import and export between programs, these problems do not occur.

You will want to use the sections in this chapter selectively. Unlike other chapters where it was important to learn all the new skills, there is no sense trying to do an exercise to import 1-2-3 data if you do not have 1-2-3. You will want to at least glance over the entire chapter so you will know what features are covered when you need them later. Also, you should be aware that most word processors have the ability to create an ASCII file, although the procedure for creating the file is different for each word processor. The majority of software packages can write their output to disk as reports rather than to the printer. When these reports are written to disk they are stored in an ASCII format, making it possible to use the data with Harvard Graphics.

In this chapter you will have an opportunity to take a close-up look at importing data from 1-2-3 to Harvard Graphics. You will also see the steps needed to establish a DDE (Dynamic Data Exchange) link to other Windows applications data. You can learn how to export slides created in earlier chapters to graphics image files. Once exported to a file you can import these files to a word processing or desktop publishing package. Although you can perform the export examples without any other packages you will need data from 1-2-3 as well as some ASCII text to try the other examples.

Importing Lotus Data

Harvard Graphics can read data stored in Lotus release 1.*X* and 2.*X* worksheet files (that is, 1-2-3 Releases 1A, 2, 2.01, 2.2, and 2.3). If you are not familiar with 1-2-3, the program is what is called a spreadsheet or worksheet package. This type of package turns your computer into an electronic columnar pad that is ideal for entering formulas.

1-2-3 files are stored in .WKS and .WK1 file formats. You can create these files in Lotus or in other packages such as Quattro Pro that can write a Lotus data file format.

Tip: You can also import Excel worksheet data in .XLS format using the steps outlined in the next section.

This means that you can take budget figures or sales projections from 1-2-3, Quattro Pro, or Symphony and import the data into a Harvard Graphics Data Form. The data can be imported for bar, line, area, pie, scatter, table, and high/low/close charts. You can import as many as 32 columns and 1,024 rows. This can be the entire set of worksheet entries or a selected range of worksheet cells. You can even create a warm link to this worksheet data that will prompt you about getting updated data whenever you open the presentation with a slide built from this data.

Taking a Look at the 1-2-3 Data

You must understand the layout of the 1-2-3 worksheet before attempting to import any data. Actually it is a lot like the Data Form used for earlier XY charts except it is much larger. The 1-2-3 2.3 worksheet has 256 columns and 8,192 rows. The rows and columns are labeled the same as Harvard Graphics Data Forms with numbers used for rows and letters used for columns. If you are importing less than all of the spreadsheet entries, you must specify the range of cells that you want to import. This range is specified as a cell range, such as in A1..B10, to specify that you want all the cells from A1 through B10. It can also be specified as a range name such as Sales or Budget if you used the /Range Name command in Lotus to assign a name to the range of cells.

If you are uncertain of the assigned range names in your 1-2-3 worksheet, you can use the /Range Name Table command to create a list for you before trying to import the data.

Figure 11-1 shows some data entered on a 1-2-3 worksheet. The entries were created with labels, numbers, and formulas entered in worksheet cells. If you use 1-2-3 this worksheet creation process is familiar to you. The entries in F5..F7 are created with formulas rather than numbers since 1992 is not over at the time the worksheet is created and these figures are projected sales. When the formulas were entered in 1-2-3, as many as three decimal digits displayed in these cells. Whole numbers were displayed using 1-2-3's formatting features, which also added commas to the entries. When this data is imported into Harvard Graphics, the displayed data is what is imported. This allows you to control the decimal accuracy of the imported data through 1-2-3's format commands.

Figure 11-1.   *1-2-3 worksheet data*

A1: [W12]   READY

	A	B	C	D	E	F	G
1			Royston Company				
2			1988 - 1992 Sales				
3							
4		1988	1989	1990	1991	1992	
5	Tires	2,560	2,765	2,986	3,225	3,483	
6	Batteries	3,500	3,815	4,158	4,533	4,941	
7	Chains	4,000	3,500	3,000	2,100	1,000	

Chapter 11: *Importing and Exporting Data* 325

The worksheet file must be saved before you can import the data. The /File Save command in 1-2-3 creates the .WKS or .WK1 file depending on the version of 1-2-3 you are using.

Importing the Entire Worksheet

To import spreadsheet data you must have a Data Form for one of the supported chart types on your screen. This means that you must have an open presentation file that you have added a slide to. The position of the highlight on the Data Form is important since it marks the location where the top left cell in the imported data is added. Next, all you need to do is choose Import from the File menu. You can choose Import and then select a file format from the File Format drop-down list box. A list of files of the type specified are displayed for your selection. After picking the file you want, you select OK to have Harvard Graphics get all the file data and place it on the Data Form. Follow these steps to create the 1-2-3 file and import the data that you enter into Harvard Graphics:

1. With 1-2-3 release 1.*X* or 2.*X* loaded in memory, complete the data entry needed to duplicate the worksheet shown in Figure 11-1.
   Although the entries in F5..F7 were originally created with formulas, type the numbers you see on the screen to save time. The results will be the same with either type of entry.

2. Save the 1-2-3 file by typing **/fs** to select the File Save command. Type **ROYSTON** for the filename and press (ENTER).

3. Print a copy of the 1-2-3 worksheet for reference by turning your printer on and typing **/ppra1..f7** and pressing (ENTER) to invoke the Print Printer Range command and specify the print range. Press (ENTER) and then type **gpaq** to select Go Page Align Quit.

4. Exit from 1-2-3 by typing **/qy** to select Quit Yes.

5. Start Windows and Harvard Graphics and then choose New Presentation from the File menu.

6. Select Vertical Bar and then select OK.

7. Move the highlight to the X-Axis Labels entry above column A and then choose Import from the File menu.

8. Select a File format of Lotus from the drop-down list box and then select "Import all data."

9. Select the drive and directory containing your 1-2-3 file and then select the name ROYSTON from the File list box.

10. Select OK and the data is placed in a Data Form as shown (with corrected data for years 1990 and 1991) in Figure 11-2.

You will notice that importing all the data presents a problem with the worksheet title information from C1..C2. It is not recognized as a title (and stored at the top of the Data Form in the Title field) but is instead treated as any other entry. This presents a problem with Legend entries at the top of the columns and the proper assignment of data to series. Importing all data from a spreadsheet is practical in two situations. The first is when the spreadsheet only contains needed data such as series names, X-axis labels, and data values in a tabular form. The second requires a bit more work on your part

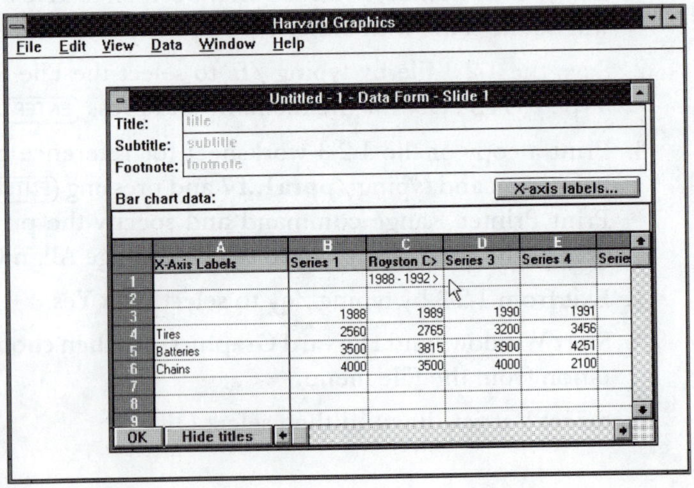

Figure 11-2.   Data Form after importing the entire worksheet

but would allow you to handle the Royston data. You would need to position the highlight lower on the Data Form and then delete unneeded rows after importing, entering the series names for legends yourself.

Importing a Selected Portion of the Worksheet

If you work with spreadsheet packages regularly you probably have some fairly large worksheets. You may want to show only a small portion of this data on a chart. Also, you might want to use selective importing when you have extraneous information such as with the Royston data presented earlier. To import some of the spreadsheet, you can specify the data you want with a range or a range name. A range is a contiguous group of cells that form a rectangle.

Just as when you imported the entire spreadsheet, when you import a range, the highlight position marks the location for the first entry on the Data Form. The procedure is almost identical to importing an entire worksheet. Follow these steps to import the 1992 data from the ROYSTON file to create a pie chart on a new slide:

1. Select "Add slide."
2. Select "Vertical bar" and then select OK.
3. Move the highlight to X-Axis Labels above column A and then choose Import from the File menu.
4. Select a File format of Lotus regardless of which version of 1-2-3 you used to create the worksheet and then choose Selective Import (.WKS or .WK1 format).

    If you are using 1-2-3 for Windows you will want to use a .DDE link as you would for Excel.
5. Select the drive and directory containing your 1-2-3 file and then select the name ROYSTON.WK1 from the Files list box.

    Your dialog box looks something like Figure 11-3. Your filename and directory settings will, of course, depend on the location of your data. You can also type the name of your file into the Filename text box.

Figure 11-3.   Import dialog box

[Import dialog box showing Filename: royston.wk1, Directory: d:\hgw\pres, Files list with royston.wk1, Directories/drives with [..], [-a-], [-c-], [-d-], radio buttons for Import all data and Selective import (selected), checkbox for Keep link to data source, File format: Lotus, and OK, Cancel, Help buttons]

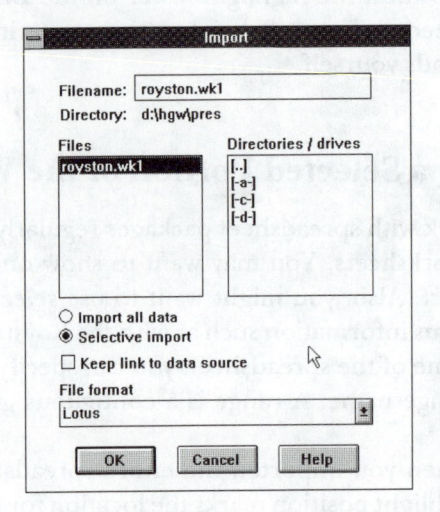

6. Select OK and Harvard Graphics presents an Import dialog box like the one in Figure 11-4.

7. Change the "From cell" item to A4 and then select OK.

8. Move to the Title field on the Data Form and type **Royston Company** and press (ENTER).

9. Type **1988-1992 Sales**. Your Data Form looks like Figure 11-5.

10. Select OK then press (F2) to display a chart like the one shown in Figure 11-6.

Tip: *You can import ranges from several different worksheet files by repositioning the highlight and repeating the procedure with a different worksheet file.*

Creating a Warm Link

Harvard Graphics allows you to add a link to a worksheet file when you import data the first time. Unlike a regular import where the data is never updated unless you import it again, a link can be refreshed each time you

Chapter 11: *Importing and Exporting Data* 329

Figure 11-4.   *Selective Import dialog box*

Figure 11-5.   *Data Form after selective importing*

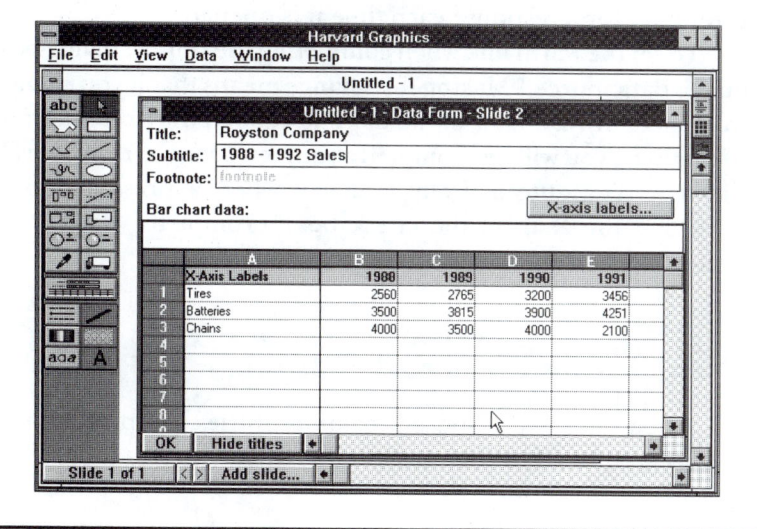

Figure 11-6. Royston bar chart

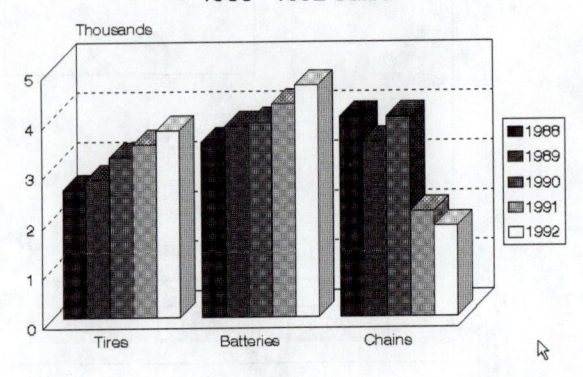

open the presentation containing the slide with the link. Depending on how you set File Preferences the link update can be automatic or you can be prompted for a response each time it is opened.

To set the warm link when completing the Import dialog box select "Keep link to data source." Making this change means that if you change the Royston worksheet in 1-2-3 later in the day and reopen the presentation with the link to this data, you will be prompted about retrieving a fresh copy. You can make the new data automatically available when a presentation is opened by removing the X from the check box "Prompt for data links" in the File Preferences dialog box.

Transposing Rows and Columns

When data is transposed, column entries are placed in rows and row entries are placed in columns. A table of entries that looks like this:

Chapter 11: *Importing and Exporting Data* 331

	1992	1993
Accidents	50	75
Tickets	300	500

changes to this after transposing:

	Accidents	Tickets
1992	50	300
1993	75	500

This allows you to change the way that the data is assigned to series and gives you an option for the appearance of the chart. To make this change as you import a selected range of data from a file, all you need to do is select the check box "Swap rows/columns."

Figure 11-7 shows the way the slide for the Royston data would look if you swapped rows and columns.

Figure 11-7. Bar chart created from transposed data

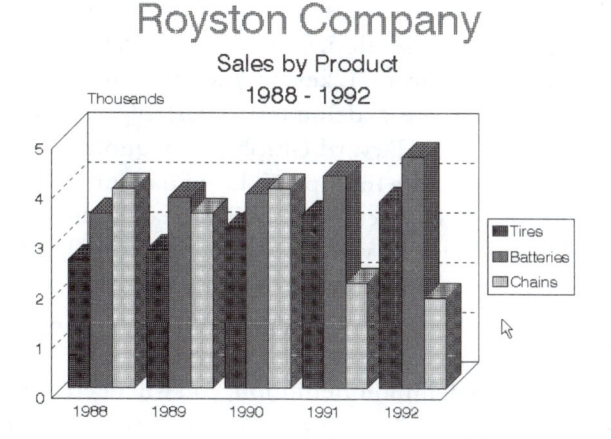

Importing ASCII Data

ASCII data has even broader applicability than 1-2-3 data since all database programs, many accounting programs, and other software can create a delimited ASCII file.

ASCII files contain text characters. The text is devoid of any codes that might instruct your printer how to print certain text. In essence ASCII data is plain text with everything else stripped away. The only difference between a standard ASCII file that you might create with your word processor and a delimited ASCII file is that the delimited file contains markers that separate different pieces of information on a line in the file. You might have a name address and phone number with a delimiter between each new piece of information. Although some word processors can also create delimited files, it is normally in a database setting where you might be using a delimited ASCII file (creating a mail merge, for instance).

Harvard Graphics can import standard ASCII files without delimiters into the Outliner. Delimited ASCII files can be imported into Data Forms. Importing into the Outliner is easy since all you need to do is choose Import from the File menu while in the Outliner. Lines with indentation become bullets of the previous line in the Outliner.

Delimited files are also easy to work with, but you will want a closer look at the method of delimitation. The delimiter used within ASCII files varies from program to program. Likewise, the procedure that you use with different programs to create a delimited ASCII file varies greatly. The default delimiter expected by Harvard Graphics is a quotation mark around strings and a comma to separate multiple fields of data on the same line. The length limit for a line is 256 characters including the delimiters. If your program uses a different delimiter you will have to define it to Harvard Graphics. Most spreadsheet programs allow you to print a worksheet to disk, creating an ASCII file. The delimiter in this situation is a space and must be defined to Harvard Graphics as a custom field separator.

To change the delimiter definition, you will need to first indicate that you want to import data and select a delimited ASCII format. You can then use the Delimiter dialog box to change either the string or field separator.

Figure 11-8 shows some delimited ASCII data on a Windows Write screen. If you look closely you will see the quotes around labels and comma delimi-

Chapter 11: *Importing and Exporting Data* 333

ters. The first line even has a delimiter added at the front to push the other data over to serve as series titles. Import data into the Data Form by carrying out the following steps:

1. The ASCII file has been created and saved to disk.
2. With the Harvard Graphics Data Form on the screen, select the cell where the first entry from the ASCII file will be placed.
3. Choose Import from the File menu.
4. Select either "Import all data" or "Selective import."
5. Select a "File format" of Delimited ASCII, and then select the file and location containing your data.
6. Change the definition of delimiter characters used if necessary.
7. Select OK.

    If you chose selective data you will need to complete another dialog box indicating the location of the selective data in the file. It is as if each line is a row and the information between delimiters is

Figure 11-8. Delimited ASCII data

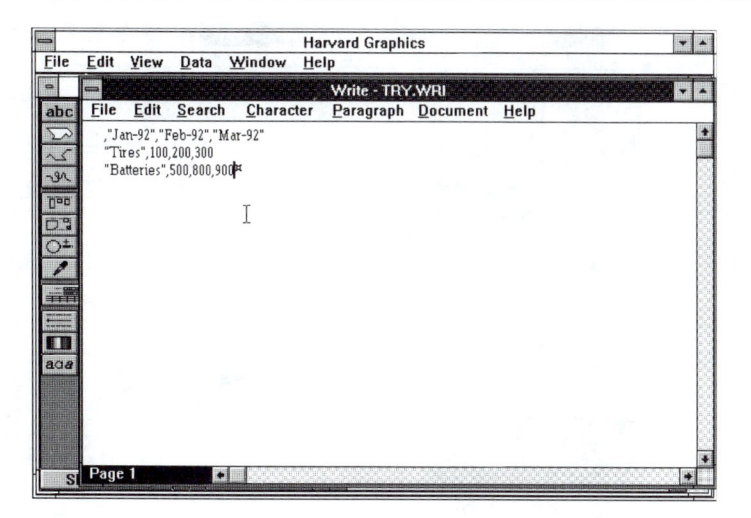

a column. Looking at the data in Figure 11-8, Jan-92 is in B1 and Batteries is in A3.

8. Select OK again if you are importing selective data. Your screen should look like Figure 11-9.

Creating a DDE Link

Dynamic Data Exchange (DDE) links are referred to as hot links. Data entered in one Windows application immediately causes a change in the application linked to this data. It is like having information that is "hot off the press." The very latest update is immediately available. Links are established to cells on the Data Form from applications such as Excel. Charts dynamically change before your eyes if you have the Windows for Harvard Graphics and the other application on your screen at the same time.

Figure 11-9.   Imported ASCII data

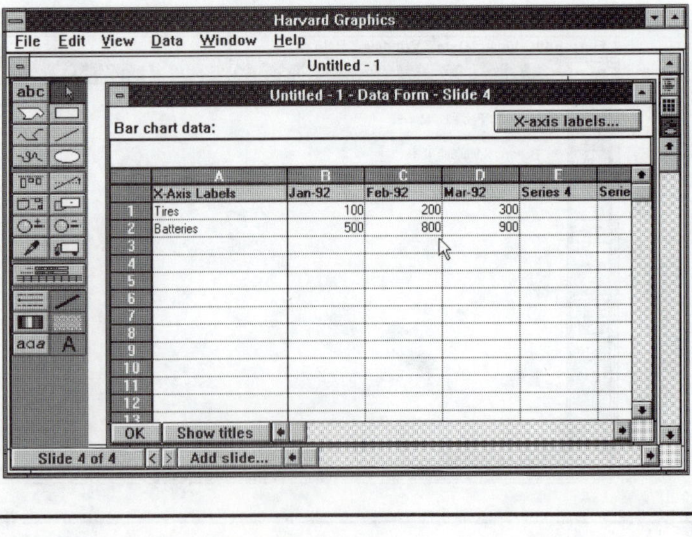

Chapter 11: *Importing and Exporting Data*

To establish a link, both Harvard Graphics and the source application for your information must be running. Within Harvard Graphics you should have the Data Form open where the link will be established. You should then switch to the application (CTRL + ESC to activate the Task List and select the desired application) containing the data you need and activate the saved file that contains the data. Select the data that you need within this application and then choose Copy from the Edit menu to place the information on the Windows Clipboard. Since there is a consistency between Windows applications, the command that copies data to the Windows Clipboard is Edit Copy in almost all applications. Switch to Harvard Graphics and select the upper-leftmost cell on the Data Form that will be linked to the source. Next, choose Paste from Harvard Graphics' Edit menu. The data appears in a different (blue) color if you have a color monitor.

Although you cannot edit this data within Harvard Graphics, you can change it in the source application. This change is immediately shown in Harvard Graphics.

The DDE link is represented in the Edit line of the Data Form as a *triplet*, which is a representation of a link. A triplet consists of the application name, the document name and its path, and the data location.

When you close a presentation with a DDE link, the link is inactivated. When you reopen the presentation you can choose whether or not to reestablish the link. You can also set Harvard Graphics to reestablish links automatically through the File Preferences dialog box. When you attempt to reestablish a link, an inactive application can be started for you. If Harvard Graphics cannot locate the file specified in the triplet, the link will not be reestablished.

Tip: *Removing a DDE link is easy. All you need to do is select the range of linked cells and then choose Cut from the Edit menu.*

Exporting Slide Images

If you are working in the Slide Editor or Slide Sorter you can export charts in graphics file formats. When you select Export from the File menu, your options under "File format" offer a variety of file types in addition to a chart format for Harvard Graphics 3. Table 11-1 shows each file type supported and the filename extension used.

You will want to work in the Slide Editor to export individual slides. If you want to export an entire presentation as image files you must be in the Slide Sorter.

The file types that Harvard Graphics supports when exporting can be grouped into vector and bitmap images. Computer Graphics Metafile (.CGM), Micrografx Drawing (.DRW), and Windows Metafiles (.WMF) are vector files composed of a number of individual objects. Most programs that work with these file types support ungrouping them and working with the individual file objects. The bitmap file types—Windows Bitmap (.BMP), PC Paintbrush Bitmap (.PCX), and TIFF Bitmap (.TIF)—all record a raster of dot patterns. These files do not have objects that can be manipulated individually. When you export these bitmap files you can complete a dialog box specifying the color format, the resolution in terms of dots per inch, and the size. Each of the three bitmap file formats provides a unique dialog box of options.

Exporting an Image for a Slide

If you want to incorporate a slide image directly into the report you are typing with WordPerfect or you plan to incorporate a slide image into your

Table 11-1.   *Export Graphics File Formats*

Format	Extension
ANSI Computer Graphics Metafile	.CGM
CGM Harvard Graphics	.CGM
CGM Lotus Freelance Plus	.CGM
PC Paintbrush Bitmap	.PCX
TIFF Bitmap	.TIF
Windows Bitmap	.BMP
Windows Metafile	.WMF

Chapter 11: *Importing and Exporting Data* 337

Pagemaker or Ventura layout, you will need to export a graphic image of the slide from the Slide Editor. The procedure is quite simple, although it is important to determine exactly what type file the package you are using supports before beginning. Since many packages support several of the file types offered, you might want to test several options to see which provides the best results.

The steps for exporting an image from one of your charts are:

1. Display the slide you want to export on your Slide Editor screen.
2. Choose Export from the File menu. A dialog box is displayed.
3. Select the File format by clicking the arrow next to it and then select the desired file format.
4. Specify the directory you want to use for storing the file by selecting from the Directories/drives list box.
5. Choose a filename if you are overwriting a file in this directory or type a new filename in the Filename text box. The appropriate extension for the file type you selected will be added.
6. Select OK.
7. If you chose one of the bitmap file formats, complete the dialog box presented, and select OK.

Exporting Image Files for a Presentation

Exporting a presentation is similar to exporting a slide except you must be in the Slide Sorter. Harvard Graphics will automatically create a graphics file for each slide using the first five characters of the filename that you supply and will append a series of sequential numbers after these five characters. If you enter SLIDES as the filename, the names become SLIDE001, SLIDE002, and so on, with the appropriate filename extension added after the filenames. If you need to export an entire presentation to graphics files follow these steps:

1. With your presentation active in the Slide Sorter window choose Export from the File menu.

2. Select the File format, specify a filename and directory, and then select OK.

   If you selected one of the bitmap formats you will need to complete another dialog box to describe the way in which the file should be saved.

3. Select OK again to indicate that you agree with exporting the entire presentation.

Exporting a Presentation Outline

You may have a presentation outline like the one in Figure 11-10 that you want to export to a word processor or desktop publisher for further enhancement, such as font changes. Rather than retype your entries you can have

Figure 11-10.   *Presentation outline*

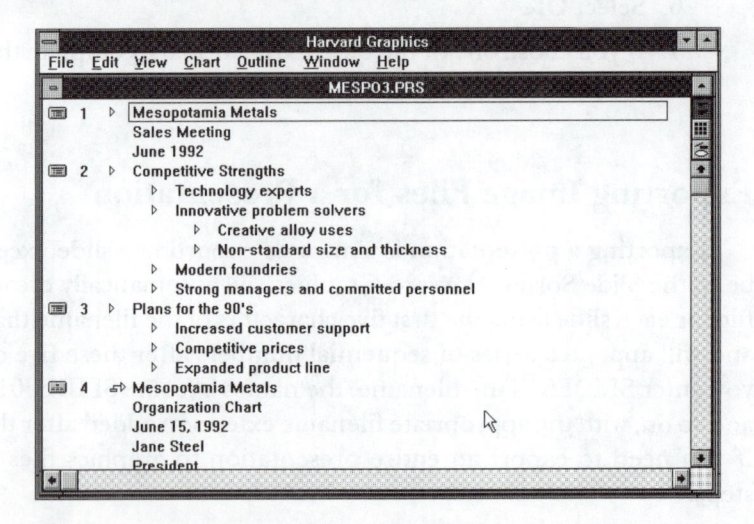

Chapter 11: *Importing and Exporting Data* 339

Harvard Graphics record each entry in an ASCII file. You can read this file into any word processing package and make further changes in format or content. You must be in the Outliner to export this file.

To export an ASCII file containing your outline follow these steps:

1. If you only want to export part of the presentation text, select the text to be exported. Otherwise, skip this step to export everything.
2. Choose Export from the File menu to display a dialog box that looks like the one in Figure 11-11.
3. Specify a filename and directory.
    It is not necessary to specify a file type since only ASCII exports are supported from the Outliner window.
4. Select OK.

Figure 11-11.   *Export dialog box*

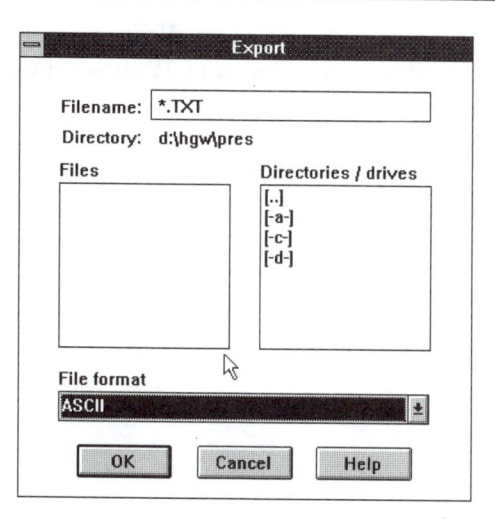

Figure 11-12.   *ASCII file created when exporting*

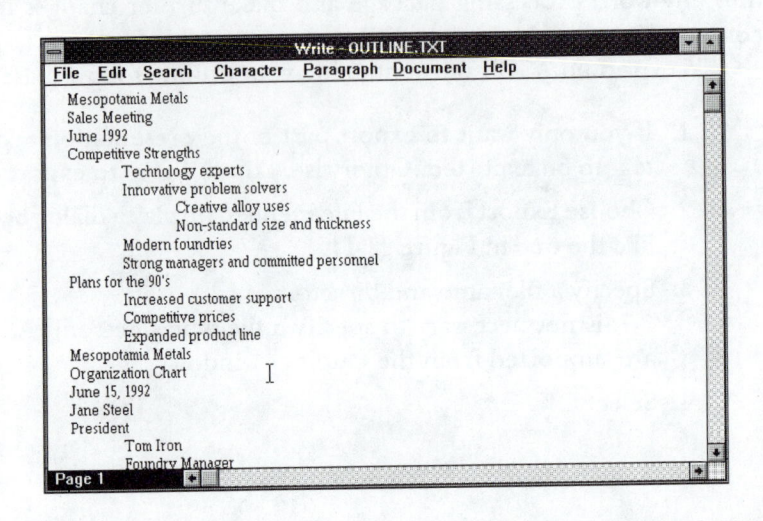

```
                          Write - OUTLINE.TXT
 File  Edit  Search  Character  Paragraph  Document  Help
    Mesopotamia Metals
    Sales Meeting
    June 1992
    Competitive Strengths
            Technology experts
            Innovative problem solvers
                    Creative alloy uses
                    Non-standard size and thickness
            Modern foundries
            Strong managers and committed personnel
    Plans for the 90's
            Increased customer support
            Competitive prices
            Expanded product line
    Mesopotamia Metals
    Organization Chart
    June 15, 1992
    Jane Steel
    President
            Tom Iron
            Foundry Manager
 Page 1
```

If you later retrieve the exported file into a word processor or text editor you will see all of your text. Figure 11-12 shows the data file created from the presentation that you viewed earlier.

12

Customizing Harvard Graphics

You can use Harvard Graphics and create many presentations without learning the techniques in this chapter. As long as you are happy with the results that you are getting you may not find a need to make further customizing changes to the package. If you get to the point where you feel like you want to more fully utilize the sophistication available to you, you will be ready to learn about creating custom color palettes, changing the full range of preference settings, and using the Windows recorder feature to create macros that can automate your tasks.

Color palettes are a set of colors that make up the color scheme for your slides. You can change the color palette to give your slides a new look.

Preference settings allow you to specify the location of files and other default settings. You can make these changes through the File Preferences option.

Macros are recorded keystrokes that can be played back at any time to perform a task. Although Harvard Graphics for Windows does not have its own set of macro features, it fully supports the Windows Recorder feature giving it macro capabilities.

Customizing with Color Palettes

The palette you choose for a presentation provides a set of colors to ensure that the elements in all slides blend together harmoniously. This palette is composed of two sets of colors, a set of chart colors and a set of custom colors. You can change the palette for individual slides to offer a new set of chart colors but once you assign a custom color to a slide element this element will remain that color even if you change the palette. Harvard Graphics for Windows provides 30 predefined color palettes. Table 12-1 provides a list of each color palette, its background color, and predominant colors.

Chart Colors

Chart colors are the 32 colors assigned to chart elements. They are each numbered and assigned to a specific chart element based on their number. As an example, chart color number 1 is always assigned to the title. Initially the title is displayed in color 1 from the default palette. If you apply another palette to the current slide or the presentation, the title will automatically change to display in color 1 for that palette unless you have assigned the Title object a custom color (since changing the palette does not affect custom colors).

Table 12-2 shows the chart color numbers and the elements that they are assigned to. Although you can change the color of any of the chart elements by selecting the element and then selecting another color, automatic assignment to a color number cannot be changed.

When you apply a different color palette to a chart you will automatically get a new set of color assignments for your chart elements, but each will blend with the new palette's color scheme. Your choice of a color palette should depend on the output device you have selected in combination with preferences. A few devices can support any palette and the choice will be determined by your preferences. These include a color printer, slide services, and film recorders. A few output devices can only legitimately support one color palette. These include monochrome printout, a monochrome ScreenShow, or a plotter. MONOW.PL should be selected for black and white printout, MONOB.PL should be used for a black and white ScreenShow, and PLOTTER.PL should be used for plotter output. If you are planning to create a

Table 12-1.   *Chart Palettes*

Palette	Background	Predominant Colors
DEFAULT.PL	White	Blacks, browns
MONOW.PL	White	Monochrome
MONOB.PL	Black	Monochrome
1BLU.PL	Dark blue	Blues
2BLU.PL	Dark blue	Blues, greens
3BLU.PL	Dark blue	Blues, grays
4BLU.PL	Dark blue	Blues, reds, grays
5BLU.PL	Dark blue	Reds, grays, yellows
6BLU.PL	Dark blue	Greens, blues
7GRY.PL	Gray	Reds, grays, oranges
8RED.PL	Red-black	Reds, greens
9CYN.PL	Cyan	Blues
10GRY.PL	Gray	Grays, yellows
11WHI.PL	White	Blacks, browns
12WHI.PL	Ivory	Blacks, browns, reds
13WHI.PL	White	Blacks, browns, blues
HR1BLU.PL	Dark blue	Blues
HR2BLU.PL	Dark blue	Blues
HR3BLU.PL	Dark blue	Blues, browns, grays
HR4BLU.PL	Dark blue	Blues, grays, oranges
HR5BLU.PL	Dark blue	Reds, oranges, grays
HR6BLU.PL	Dark blue	Greens, blues
HR7GRY.PL	Gray	Reds, grays, browns
HR8RED.PL	Red-black	Reds, greens, browns
HR9CYN.PL	Light blue	Blues, reds
HR10GRY.PL	Gray	Blues, reds
HR11WHI.PL	White	Blacks, browns, blues
HR12WHI.PL	Ivory	Blacks, browns, reds
HR13WHI.PL	White	Blacks, browns, blues
PLOTTER.PL	White	Blacks, blues, reds

ScreenShow and have a VGA monitor capable of supporting 16 colors, any of the palettes that begin with the numbers 1 through 13 are appropriate choices. If your VGA monitor supports 256 colors, select any palette beginning with HR1 through HR13.

Table 12-2. *Chart Element Colors*

Chart Color #	Chart Element
1	Title
2	Subtitle 1
3	Subtitle 2
4	Main chart text
5	Highlighted text
6	Dim Text
7	Footnote
8	X Label
9	Y1 Label
10	Y2 Label
11	X-axis Title
12	Y1-axis Title
13	Y2-axis Title
14	Chart and Legend Frame
15	Fill for Chart Frame
16	Bullet symbols
17	Dim Bullets
18	Lines drawn
19	3-D Legend Shadow
20	Legend fill
21	Series 1
22	Series 2
23	Series 3
24	Series 4
25	Series 5
26	Series 6
27	Y1 Goal
28	Y2 Goal
29	Default Fill
30	Solid Background Fill
31	Gradient Background Fill Color 2
32	Outlines for Bars, Pie Slices, etc.

To apply a different color palette to whatever slide is displaying on your screen follow these steps from the Slide Editor window:

1. Choose Color palette from the Slide menu and then choose Apply.
2. Select the palette you want from the Files list box or type the name in the Filename text box. Within the recommendations made in the above paragraph you can select any of the palettes.
3. Select "This slide" and then select OK to change the palette for the current slide. You would choose "Entire presentation" if you wanted to apply the palette to all your slides.

After applying the new palette, chart objects will assume the color that represents their number on the new palette. This is true for objects with standard chart number assignments as well as those to which you had assigned a new chart color. Objects with custom color assignments are unaffected.

Custom Colors

Custom colors allow you to assign a color to a chart element and know that it will not change regardless of the changes made to the palette. These color assignments are ideal for logos and other objects where color is part of the identification process.

Editing a Color Palette

You will want to edit the palette when you change one of the chart colors. Although you can change custom colors from other dialog boxes, the Edit option from the Slide menu's Color palette is the only option for changing the chart colors. Once you have changed the palette colors, you can use the Save option to save them under the same name or a new name.

To edit a color palette choose Color palette from the Slide menu and then choose Edit. A dialog box like the one shown in Figure 12-1 displays. You can select the chart or custom color that you want to change by clicking its color swatch. You can also choose the method for mixing color. Harvard Graphics supports the HSV and RGB methods of color mixing. HSV represents hue, saturation, and value. *Hue* is thought of as the shade of the color (red, yellow, blue, green, or violet). The *saturation* indicates the purity of the hue. *Value*

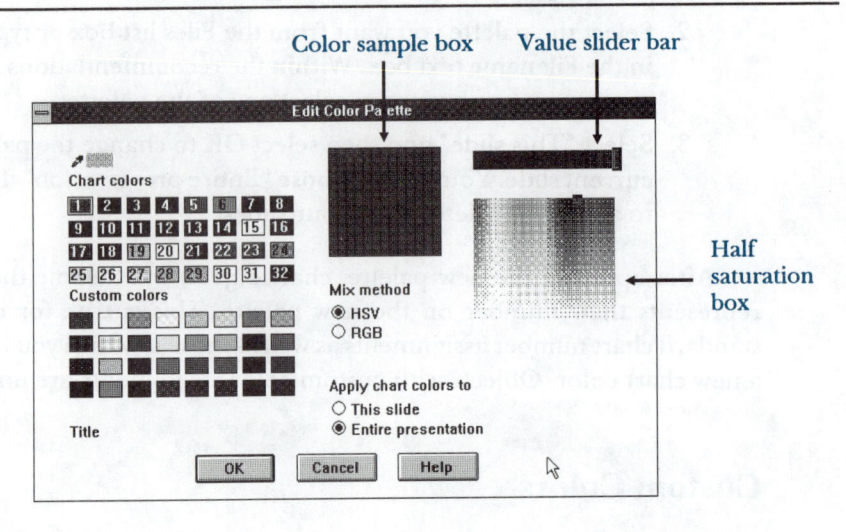

Figure 12-1. Edit Color Palette dialog box with HSV color mixing

indicates the lightness or darkness of the color. You will learn how to set each of these color attributes.

The Edit Color Palette dialog box has several important elements as shown in Figure 12-1. The first element is the *color sample box* that shows the selected custom color. As you begin to mix colors, the original color will remain in the upper-left corner of this box. You can click this area to return to the original colors. To change the hue and saturation of the color, drag the marker inside this box to mix the original color with other colors. To change the value or brightness, drag the marker or click the bar to make an adjustment. When you are finished you can click OK, choose Color palette from the Slide menu, and choose Save. You can select an existing filename or use another name.

RGB color mixing represents mixing red, yellow, and blue to make a color. Since this is not the default method you will need to click RGB if you want to mix colors and then drag the red, green, and blue slider bars that will appear. Figure 12-2 shows the dialog box for the RGB mix method. You can use any value from 0 to 99 for red, green, and blue. You can type your choice or drag the slider bar to select it.

Chapter 12: *Customizing Harvard Graphics* 347

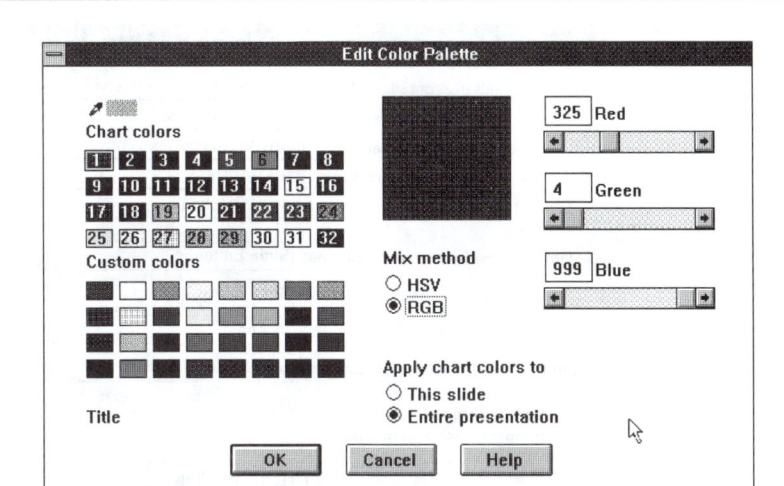

Figure 12-2. *Edit Color Palette dialog box with RGB color mixing*

Customizing Preference Settings

Harvard Graphics has default settings that let you get started without spending time defining what you want. You can change any or all of these settings as needed from the File Preferences option. Some of these defaults refer to the location of files whereas others offer other settings. The following list provides a brief overview of each of the options that you can change in the File Preferences dialog box shown in Figure 12-3.

These options are described below:

Default presentation style   You can enter the name and location of any of the 54 styles provided with Harvard Graphics or specify a name for a style that you created.

Main dictionary file   The default is WINUS.LEX. Although you may want to change the directory location there would be no need to change the name of the dictionary unless you have renamed it.

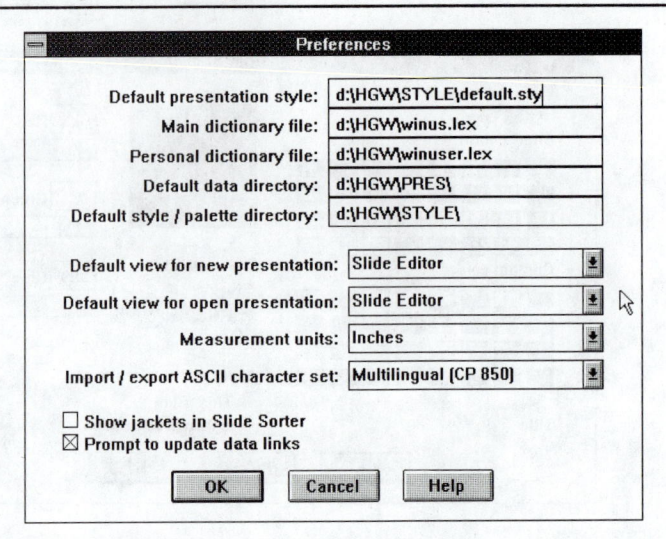

Figure 12-3. *Preferences dialog box*

```
                           Preferences
     Default presentation style:  d:\HGW\STYLE\default.sty
          Main dictionary file:   d:\HGW\winus.lex
        Personal dictionary file: d:\HGW\winuser.lex
         Default data directory:  d:\HGW\PRES\
    Default style / palette directory: d:\HGW\STYLE\

     Default view for new presentation:  Slide Editor
     Default view for open presentation: Slide Editor
              Measurement units:  Inches
     Import / export ASCII character set: Multilingual (CP 850)

     ☐ Show jackets in Slide Sorter
     ☒ Prompt to update data links
              [ OK ]   [ Cancel ]   [ Help ]
```

Personal dictionary file   This is the file where you keep your own personal dictionary entries for proper names and specialized terms.

Default data directory   You would change this entry if you prefer to keep your data files on another drive or in another directory.

Default style/palette directory   The location where Harvard Graphics looks for (as well as saves to) names of palettes and styles.

Default view for new presentation   You can choose from Slide Editor, Outliner, or Slide Sorter.

Default view for open presentation   You can choose from Slide Editor, Outliner, or Slide Sorter.

Measurement units   The default is inches although you can change to centimeters.

Chapter 12: *Customizing Harvard Graphics*

Import/export ASCII character set   This setting allows you to choose the code page that determines the ASCII character set assignments. It is likely that other applications may use different assignments for the upper range of numbers called the extended ASCII set. Windows ANSI is used by many Windows applications, but as shown in Figure 12-4, there are also a few other options for your use. The code page for each is shown.

Show jackets in Slide Sorter   The default is to not display Slide jackets, but you can change that setting by clicking this box to add an X.

Prompt to update data links   Harvard Graphics will prompt you about updating data links when you open a presentation that contains links as long as this box is checked. If it is not checked, links are updated automatically without prompting.

Figure 12-4.   *Options for the ASCII character set*

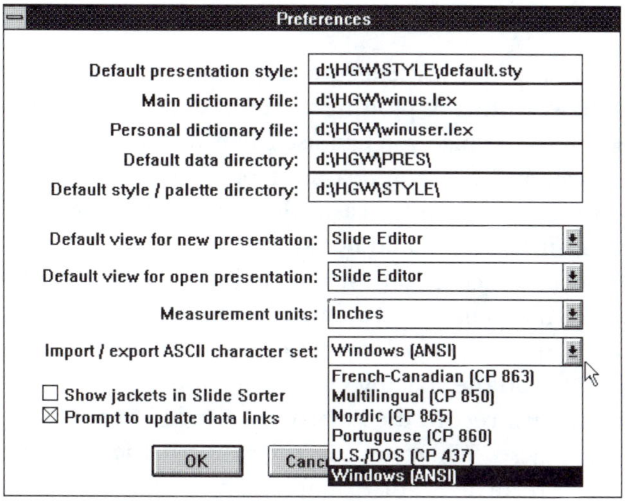

Customizing with Macros

Macros are stored sets of keystrokes that allow you to repeat a task without all the work. Once you store the keystrokes, only a keystroke or two is needed to repeat the entire task.

If you have worked with other packages like the popular word processors, spreadsheets, and databases, you may have encountered macro capabilities in these programs. Even some earlier versions of Harvard Graphics provided their own macro capability. The problem was that every package had its own set of rules for recording and playing back these keystrokes. You could not apply the skills you learned in one package to another and many users became frustrated with macro features. With Windows applications, you can learn how to use the Windows Recorder for recording and playing back macros regardless of which package you are in. Even if you have never tried macro features before, you will find that you can be successful from the start with the easy-to-follow exercises in this chapter. Adding macros is as simple as capturing and replaying keystrokes.

Recording a Macro

Any task that you execute repeatedly is a good candidate for a macro. Tasks like printing or plotting a copy of the current chart are excellent choices for a macro because you can use them with any chart. Tasks that change the style, size, and other appearance options are also excellent choices if you repeat them frequently. Tasks that you seldom perform do not make good macros, since they would not save you much time.

You can record almost any activity that you perform from a Harvard Graphics menu in a macro, including mouse actions. Depending how you set up the Windows Recorder you can also use Toolbox features that draw objects dependent on the starting cursor location.

You must record the keystrokes needed to complete the task in order to create a macro. When you execute a macro, the macro repeats the keystrokes you have recorded. For example, if you start recording a macro and then choose Text, Size, and 36, Harvard Graphics will record these selections. Therefore, if you execute this macro from one view, it may not work if you

Chapter 12: *Customizing Harvard Graphics* 351

try it with a different view on the screen since the second view may not offer the menu selections you recorded.

To record a macro you must first think about which presentation is open and which view you are in. Next, activate the Windows Recorder. This means that you must go back to the Program Manager window, open the Accessories window, and then open the Recorder.

You will have an opportunity to create a macro that can underline selected text. In the example, one of the slides from the DRAWINGS presentation created in Chapter 8 is used. You can use any slide that has several text objects for recording and then testing the macro. If you have another open presentation you may want to close it and open the one you plan to use. Follow these steps to record a macro that underlines selected text:

1. From the Slide Editor, select the text that you wish to underline.
    Figure 12-5 shows some selected text from slide 1 in the DRAWINGS presentation.

Figure 12-5.   Text selected before recording keystrokes

2. Press CTRL+ESC to display the Task List and then double-click the Program Manager.
3. Double-click the icon for the Accessories window. If this icon is obscured by other windows you can press CTRL+TAB to scroll through displays until you can double-click it.

    After opening the Accessories window, your screen will look something like Figure 12-6.
4. Double-click the Recorder icon.

    A recorder window displays. You can activate the menu with ALT + a letter as in Harvard Graphics. One letter in each menu (the mnemonic) is also underlined in Windows. After activating the Macro menu, your screen will look something like Figure 12-7.
5. Choose Record from the Macro menu. The Record Macro dialog box shown in Figure 12-8 appears. (Notice that the Windows dialog boxes—in addition to the menus—have underlined letters.) You can use ALT + the assigned letter as a quick approach to making a selection.

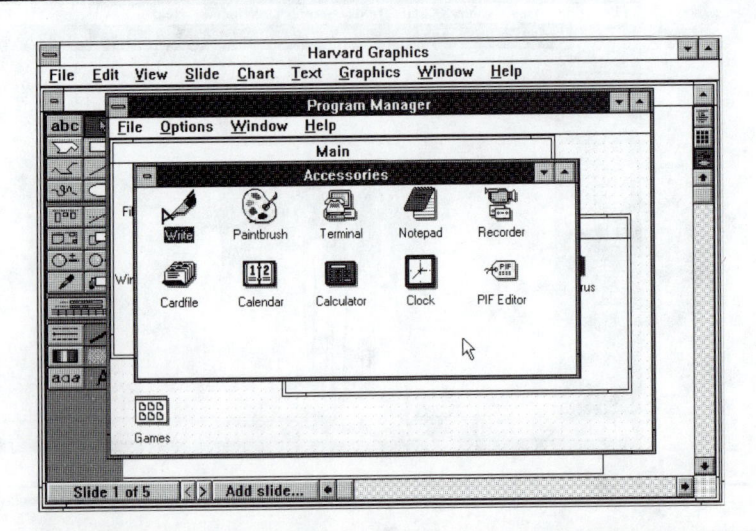

Figure 12-6.   Accessories window

Figure 12-7.   *Recorder window*

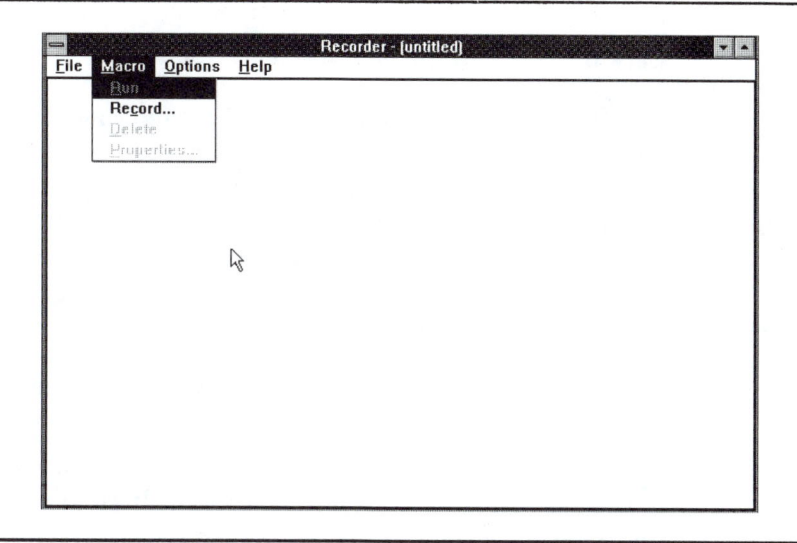

Figure 12-8.   *Record Macro dialog box*

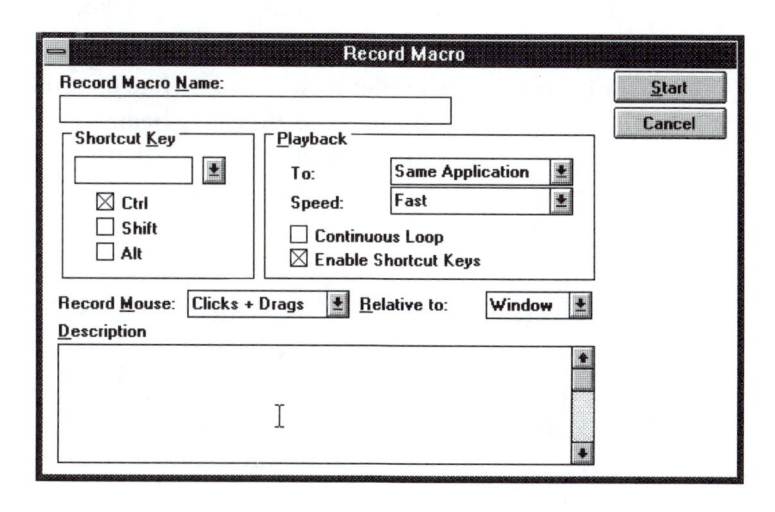

6. Click the Record Macro **N**ame box and type **Underline**. You can use up to 40 characters for a macro name.
7. Click the Shortcut **K**ey box and then type **u**.

Windows offers many options for shortcut keys allowing you to use (CTRL), (SHIFT), and (ALT) in combination with a key. In fact, you can assign more than one of these in combination with a letter. If you would prefer to use other keys you can click the arrow and choose options such as the function keys to use in combination with (CTRL), (ALT), and (SHIFT).

8. Click the check box for "Ctrl" to uncheck it and click the check box for "Alt" to add an X, thus selecting it.
   Your selections in the last two steps will cause your macro to be activated by (ALT)+(U) once the recording is complete.
9. Click the Description field and then type **Underline selected text**.
   The dialog box will look like Figure 12-9. In this example you did not need to change any of the other settings. These additional options are briefly described in Table 12-3.
10. Select Start to begin recording. The dialog box closes automatically.
11. Click the Harvard Graphics window if it is not active.
12. Choose St**y**le from the **T**ext menu and then choose **U**nderline.
    The selected text is underlined and your keystrokes have been stored.
13. Double-click the recorder icon and a box like the one in Figure 12-10 displays telling you that recording has been suspended. You can choose to save your keystrokes, throw them away, or continue recording.
14. Click **S**ave Macro. Select OK.
15. Press (CTRL)+(ESC) to display the Task List, select Recorder and then choose Save **A**s from the **F**ile menu and type **HG1**. You can save many different macros in one recorder file. Select OK.
16. Press (CTRL)+(ESC) and select Harvard Graphics. You are now ready to practice using this macro. You may want to add other macros to select the text attributes differently.

Chapter 12: *Customizing Harvard Graphics*　　355

Figure 12-9.　　*Completed Record Macro dialog box*

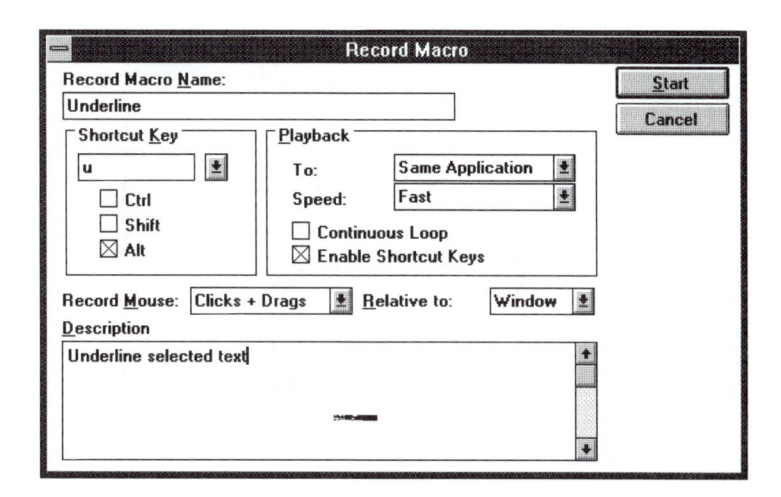

Table 12-3.　　*Other Macro Options*

Selection	Description
Record Mouse	You can choose to ignore mouse actions, record mouse clicks and drags, or to record all mouse actions even without clicks.
Relative to	You can choose to record relative to your current window or the entire screen.
Playback to	You can choose to playback to any application or the current application.
Speed	You can choose the recorded speed or a faster speed.
Continuous Loop	Macro would loop continuously if this was selected.
Enable Shortcut Keys	Lets you turn off shortcut keys if your application uses your assignments for other functions.

Figure 12-10. *Recorder window for suspended recording*

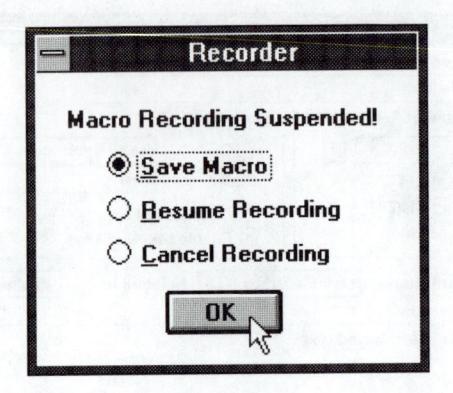

Executing a Macro

You can select a macro to run by using the Run Macro command on the Recorder menu. You can also use the shortcut keys if you have assigned them. You will want to try the shortcut keys for the macro you just created but you must check to be certain that you are in the Slide Editor before following these steps:

1. Select another text object such as the one shown in Figure 12-11.
2. Press (ALT)+(U).
   The selected text should be underlined as shown in Figure 12-12.

If you want to use this macro in other presentations you can. You can also use it in later Harvard Graphics sessions but you will need to open the HG1 file from the Recorder's File menu before it will work. If you want to delete a macro from a file you can use the Delete command in the Macro menu. If you try to use this macro in another application, the keystroke playback will be aborted and a message box like the one in Figure 12-13 will be displayed. In order to allow playback in other applications, you must select Playback to

Figure 12-11. *Selecting text to try macro*

Figure 12-12. *Text after executing macro*

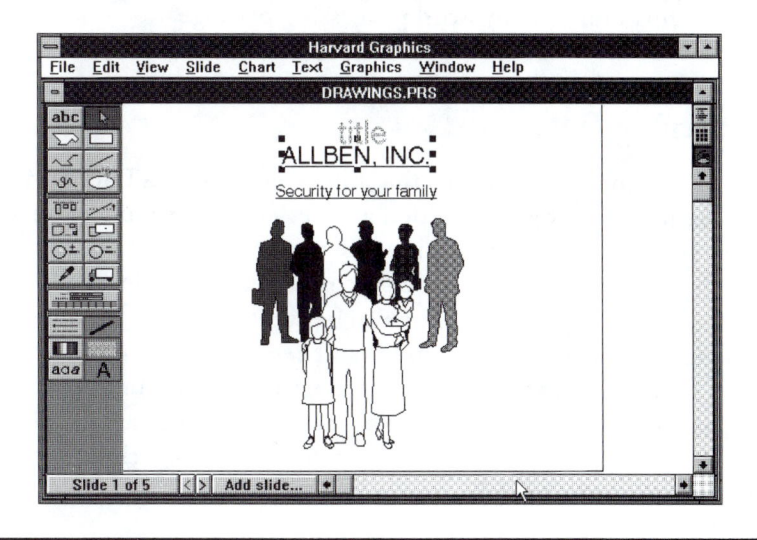

Figure 12-13.   Box that displays when macro playback is aborted

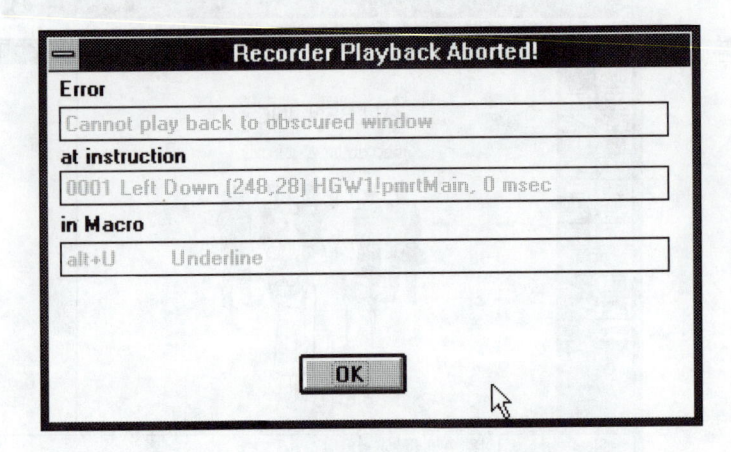

```
┌─────────────────────────────────────────────────┐
│  ─        Recorder Playback Aborted!            │
│  Error                                          │
│  ┌─────────────────────────────────────────┐    │
│  │ Cannot play back to obscured window     │    │
│  └─────────────────────────────────────────┘    │
│  at instruction                                 │
│  ┌─────────────────────────────────────────┐    │
│  │ 0001 Left Down (248,28) HGW1!pmrtMain, 0 msec│
│  └─────────────────────────────────────────┘    │
│  in Macro                                       │
│  ┌─────────────────────────────────────────┐    │
│  │ alt+U      Underline                    │    │
│  └─────────────────────────────────────────┘    │
│                                                 │
│                   ┌──────┐                      │
│                   │  OK  │                      │
│                   └──────┘          ▷           │
└─────────────────────────────────────────────────┘
```

Any Application and ensure that the keystrokes are compatible as they would be for text entry in any word processing package.

Entering Data

You can create a macro that fills in entries on a Data Form just as easily as the macro you just recorded and tested. You simply enter the fixed data that you want to add every time the macro is run.

You can use a macro's ability to enter data for title, subtitle, and footnote information. This information can be created in a macro once and then used any time a chart uses the same first three entries.

Be patient as you learn to use macros. You will undoubtedly make a few mistakes. Practice will make the process seem quite easy in a short time. Keep in mind the time they can save you and work at including this new skill in your own toolkit of skills.

A

Installing Harvard Graphics

This appendix describes the steps you will perform to install Harvard Graphics and the equipment you might use. This appendix also covers installing supplemental printer drivers to improve output appearance on some devices.

Installing Harvard Graphics

Installing Harvard Graphics is a simple process. Since Harvard Graphics has several hardware requirements, you should check that your computer meets those requirements. Once you know you have the correct equipment, you can begin installation. The steps you perform are the same whether you are using 3 1/2- or 5 1/4-inch disks.

Hardware Requirements

Harvard Graphics for Windows has a few requirements that your computer must meet in order to run the program. The following requirements must be met:

An 80286 (although higher is preferred), 80386, or 80486 IBM or IBM compatible computer.

DOS 3.1 or later and Windows 3.0 or later.

At least 2MB of memory (4MB recommended).

A Microsoft Windows compatible mouse.

A hard drive and at least one disk drive.

At least 7MB of available space on the hard disk (preferably 14MB so that you can install all the files).

An EGA, VGA, or SVGA monitor.

Any of the many supported graphics cards listed on the outside of the Harvard Graphics for Windows package.

Backing Up Your Disks

Your Harvard Graphics disks represent an investment. Since you want your investment protected, you should make a second copy of the disks so you can use them in place of your originals if they are damaged. Since making additional copies is an infringement of the copyright law, you only want to make a copy for backup, which is specifically allowed by the software license. The backup instructions will work for either 3 1/2-inch or 5 1/4-inch disks.

To back up these disks, follow these steps:

1. Format a blank 3 1/2-inch or high density 5 1/4-inch disk for each disk that you want to back up by inserting a disk in drive A, typing

Appendix A: *Installing Harvard Graphics*

FORMAT A:, and pressing (ENTER). You must format each disk separately. Type a **Y** and press (ENTER) after formatting a disk to format the next one.

2. Put the first Harvard Graphics disk in drive A and the newly formatted disk in drive B.
3. Type **COPY A:*.* B:** and press (ENTER). This copies all of the files on the disk in drive A to drive B.
4. Repeat steps 2 and 3 for the remaining disks.

If you do not have disk drives that are the same size, you must create a temporary subdirectory on your hard disk, copy the Harvard Graphics disks to the temporary subdirectory, and then copy the files in the temporary directory to formatted disks.

Once the backups are made, label the disks and place the original disks in a safe location.

Installing Harvard Graphics on Your Hard Disk

Once you have the backup copies made, you are ready to install Harvard Graphics on your hard disk. Follow these steps:

1. Boot your computer with DOS.
2. Put Disk 1 in drive A or drive B.
3. Start Windows.
4. Choose Run from the File menu.
5. Type **A:INSTALL** and click the OK command button to select it.
    INSTALL is a utility program created to copy the Harvard Graphics files to your hard disk. Since the files on the disks are in a compressed format and the INSTALL program uncompresses them, you must use the INSTALL program to copy the files to your hard disk. Harvard Graphics assumes that you would like to copy your files to C:\HGW but allows you to change the default if you want to.

6. Change the drive and directory if desired.

    You will be asked to decide whether to install the full package or only some of the files. You will need 14MB of available space for all files and 7MB for minimum files.

7. Choose Install all files, Install minimum file set, or Install selected files. Select OK.

8. Respond to the onscreen prompts for inserting disks until the "Add icon to a program group" dialog box appears. The default description displayed is Harvard Graphics.

9. Change the description if you would prefer to use another.

10. Select the program group for the icon and then click OK.

    If you selected a full installation of Harvard Graphics another dialog box may appear for the Autographix slide service program. You can repeat steps 9 and 10 for this box as well.

Using Supplemental Drivers

Windows 3.0 provides drivers for all the output devices you can use with Harvard Graphics. In other words, you can use any of your Windows output devices with Harvard Graphics. Because you will want to get maximum output, install drivers for all of your own devices as well as any devices you might require in the future. Harvard Graphics is shipped with replacement drivers for LaserJet series II and III, LaserGraphics film recorders, IBM Quickwriter, Canon LBS III, SCODL devices, and Postscript printers. If you have one of these devices and want to install the supplemental driver, follow these steps from the Windows Program Manager:

1. Open the Main program group and then double-click the Control Panel icon.

2. Double-click the icon for Printers.

3. Select Add Printer from the Printers dialog box.

4. Select Unlisted Printer from the List of Printers list box. Select Install.

Appendix A: *Installing Harvard Graphics*

5. Place your Harvard Graphics driver disk into drive A and then select [-a] in the Directories box in the "Add unlisted printer" dialog box.
6. Select the driver from the Drivers File list box.

    The driver filename will not exactly match the name of your printer but represents an abbreviation of the printer, Postscript, or SCODL interface.

    Although some program installations complete with only one file (a .DRV file) copied, if you choose a Postscript driver for Harvard Graphics, you will also need to install a second driver with a .WPD extension by selecting Configure from the Printers dialog box. You will need to choose Setup from the Printers Configure dialog box and then choose Add Printer and select the second file that you need.
7. Select OK until the Control Panel is closed.

B

Using Windows

You combine Windows with your DOS operating system to make working with programs easier. Windows features an easy-to-use interface that is more comfortable than the DOS prompt. Windows lets you run multiple applications simultaneously and share data between them. While you are in Windows, you can select which applications you are using and how the applications appear on your computer screen. If Harvard Graphics for Windows is your first Windows application, read this appendix to learn about some basic Windows features you will want to use with Harvard Graphics for Windows.

Windows is frequently used with a mouse. Using a mouse allows you to point to the objects on the screen you want to use. Some of the terms a mouse uses and their meanings are listed in Table B-1. Most of the time, you use the left button on the mouse. While using a mouse may be convenient for making selections, Windows has keyboard equivalents for making the same choices.

Table B-1.   *Mouse Terms*

Mouse Term	Meaning
Click	Point to the object and press the mouse button once
Double-click	Point to the object and quickly press the mouse button twice
Drag	Point to one location and hold down the mouse button as you move the mouse to another location

Starting Windows

Before you can use Windows, it must be installed. You install Windows by putting the first Windows disk into drive A. Next, type **A:**, press (ENTER), type **Setup**, and press (ENTER). At this point, the Windows installation program guides you with onscreen instructions. Once Windows is installed, you can start it by typing **WIN** and pressing (ENTER). Once Windows is started, a display like the one in Figure B-1 appears. A Windows screen has several components, which are labeled in Figure B-1 and described in Table B-2.

With Windows, each program or application you run is put in a separate window, an *application window*. Sometimes these application windows have windows of their own, called *document windows*. Document windows are miniature versions of the application window, with a title bar, minimize button, maximize or restore button, and control menu boxes. Some applications run in full-screen mode. *Full-screen mode* means that when the application is one you are currently using, it occupies the full screen and the other application windows do not appear on the screen. When you run a non-Windows application, it runs in full-screen mode.

Exiting Windows

When you finish using Windows and its applications, you will want to exit your open applications and Windows. This is important for two reasons: it

Appendix B: Using Windows

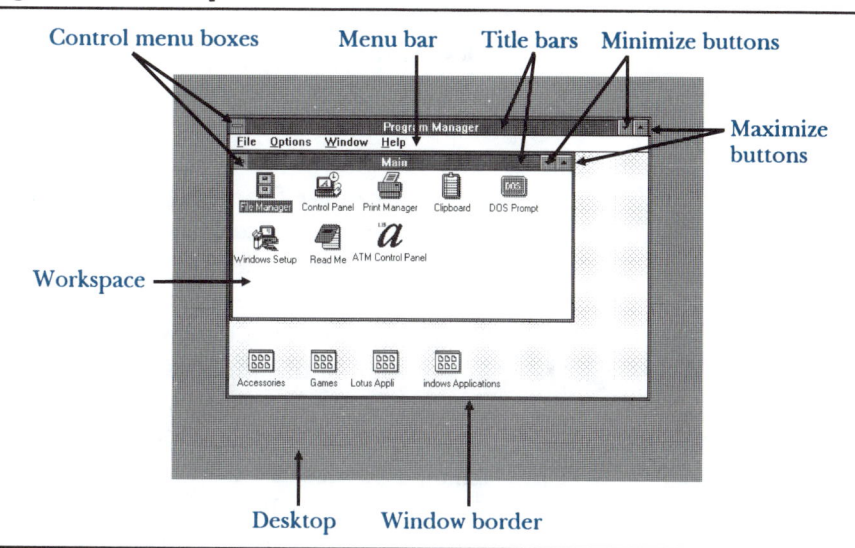

Figure B-1. Sample Windows screen

[Figure B-1: Sample Windows screen showing labeled components — Control menu boxes, Menu bar, Title bars, Minimize buttons, Maximize buttons, Workspace, Desktop, Window border — in the Program Manager window with Main group icons (File Manager, Control Panel, Print Manager, Clipboard, DOS Prompt, Windows Setup, Read Me, ATM Control Panel) and other group icons (Accessories, Games, Lotus Appli, indows Applications).]

ensures that you do not lose data that you intended to save, and it enables Windows to perform any necessary housecleaning. For example, some applications create temporary files that are deleted when you exit the application.

To leave Windows, first switch to the Program Manager window by pressing (CTRL)-(ESC), and then click Program Manager or press (↓) until Program Manager is highlighted and press (ENTER). Next, click the control menu box or press (ALT)-(SPACEBAR) to display the control menu, and select Close Windows by clicking it or pressing "C". You can also press (ALT)-(F4) from the Program Manager window. You must then select the OK command button by clicking it or pressing (ENTER) to confirm that you want to leave Windows. You should close and exit any applications you have running before you leave Windows.

The Windows Interface

Once you are in Windows, you can manipulate the windows you use and select which ones are open. Many of the Windows applications include menus

Table B-2. *Windows Screen Components*

Component	Description
Desktop	The area of the screen that is not covered by another application.
Control menu box	The box in the upper-left corner of a window that you can use for controlling the window.
Menu bar	The bar in an application window that contains menu selections. Selecting one presents a pull-down menu that offers additional choices.
Title bar	The top line of a window, which displays a description of the application it contains or the information a document window contains.
Window border	The edge of a window, which you can use to change the size of a window with a mouse.
Minimize button	The down arrow box in the upper-right corner that you can select to reduce the window to an icon (a small symbol).
Maximize button	The up arrow box in the upper-right corner that you can select to expand the window to fill the screen. (When selected, this icon changes to the Restore button with an up and down arrow.)
Workspace	The area below the menu bar (in an application window) or title bar (in a document window) area where you will work with the data.

that behave just like the menus you will learn to use in Harvard Graphics for Windows. You can customize where each window appears and its size.

The Program Manager

The Program Manager is part of Windows that lets you easily decide which programs you are using. Many of the programs that you use with Windows are in the Program Manager. When you installed Windows, you probably added many of the programs installed on your machine to the Program Manager. When you install a Windows application like Harvard Graphics for Windows, the installation program adds the application to the Program Manager.

The Program Manager divides the applications into group windows. These are document windows to the Program Manager application window. Many of the features you learn about using Windows also applies to the Program Manager application window and the group windows.

Two of the group windows are Main and Accessories. Main includes programs like the Control Panel, which selects how Windows looks and operates, and the Print Manager, which controls how Windows sends information to the printer. Accessories includes programs that make working with Windows easier, including the Notepad to read and write text files. You probably also have a group window called Non-Windows Applications, which includes DOS programs that were not designed for Windows. While certain operations are beyond the scope of this appendix, you can add and delete programs from group windows, add and delete group windows, and change the properties of programs.

Menus in Windows

Most application windows have a menu in a menu bar. For example, the Program Manager window in Figure B-1 has a menu bar that contains File, Options, Window, and Help. With a mouse, you can make selections by clicking the menu item you want. For example, to select File, click File. With a keyboard, you first need to activate the menu bar by pressing (ALT). Next, press the underlined letter for the menu item you want. For example, to select File from the menu, press (ALT) and then press F. Once you select an item from the menu bar, you usually see a pull-down menu. For example, the Program Manager's File pull-down menu looks like this:

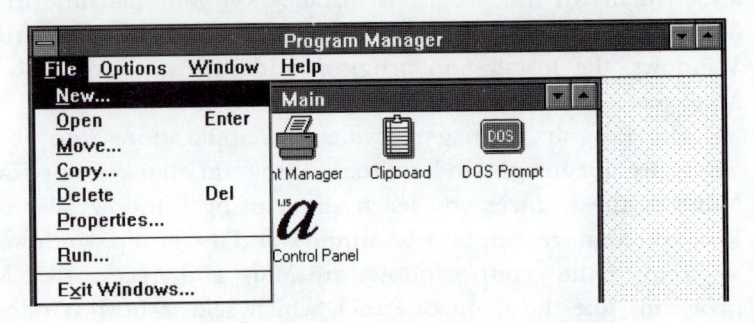

Like selecting an item on the menu bar, you can select an item in the pull-down menu by clicking the one you want or by pressing the underlined letter. After you make a selection, you may see a dialog box. Dialog boxes are used extensively in Harvard Graphics for Windows.

Opening Applications

To use an application in Windows, you must open an application window for the application from the Program Manager window. First, you must display the group window and make it active. With a mouse, double-click the window or icon. With the keyboard, press (ALT) to activate the menu bar, press "W" for Window, and press the number next to the group window you want to activate. With the group window active, you can double-click the application you want to run. You can also use the arrow keys to highlight the application to run and press (ENTER). The application starts and an application window is added to the screen. If it is a full-screen application, the application fills the screen, so you do not see Windows in the background. If your computer's resources are limited and you have other applications running at the same time, you may not be able to start an application until you close other ones.

Appendix B: *Using Windows* 371

When you finish with an application, you want to close the application window and exit the application. For non-Windows applications, you should use the application's own commands for exiting. For Windows applications, you can press (ALT)-(F4) when the application is the active window or select File Exit from the application's menu bar. You may also select Close from the application's control menu. Windows applications may display prompts about saving your data, which you need to respond to. Once an application is closed, the previous active window becomes the active window again.

Switching to a Window

To switch from running one application to running another one, you must select the application window or the full-screen application you want to be the active window. The *active window* is the window your keystrokes and mouse selections will affect. (If you make a selection outside of the application window with a mouse, you are selecting the other application rather than making a selection in that application). You can press (ALT)-(ESC) to switch to the next application in the Task List. To switch to any open application, press (CTRL)-(ESC) to display the Task List, like the one shown here:

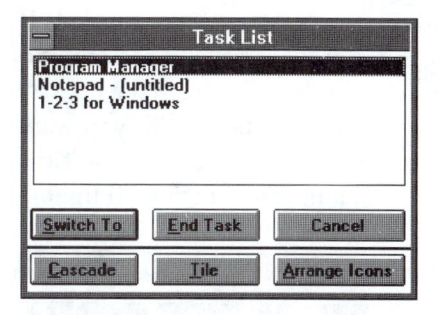

```
┌─────────── Task List ───────────┐
│ Program Manager                 │
│ Notepad - (untitled)            │
│ 1-2-3 for Windows               │
│                                 │
│                                 │
│  [Switch To] [End Task] [Cancel]│
│  [Cascade]   [Tile]    [Arrange Icons]│
└─────────────────────────────────┘
```

You can also display the Task List by double-clicking an empty desktop area (an area that is not filled with an application). You can also click an application's control menu box and select Switch To.

From the Task List, you can double-click the application you want or press the (↑) and (↓) keys to highlight the one you want and then press (ENTER). Another option for switching to an open application is to click the application, if it is visible on the screen. In the next section, you learn how to shrink an application window into an icon. When an application window appears as an icon, you can make it active by double-clicking it.

Another special key combination is (ALT)-(TAB). (ALT)-(TAB) switches you to the last application you were using. This means if you are using Harvard Graphics for Windows and a word processor, you can press (ALT)-(TAB) to keep switching between these two applications.

Positioning and Sizing Windows

Windows lets you put your application windows anywhere on the screen and make the windows any size you want. You can make these changes with a mouse or with the control menu. The control menu appears when you click the control menu box. To display this menu for an application window, press (ALT)-(SPACEBAR), and to display this menu for a document window, press (ALT)-(HYPHEN). Sometimes some of the control menu selections are dimmed or grayed to indicate they cannot be selected.

To move a window, select Move from the control menu, and then press the arrow keys to move the temporary outline of the window to a new location and press (ENTER). With a mouse, drag the title bar of the window to move the temporary outline where you want the window. If you are moving a document window, you cannot move it beyond the edges of the application window.

To size a window, select Size from the control menu. Next, press an arrow key to move the pointer to the border you want to change. Press the arrow keys to move that border to where you want it and press (ENTER). To change a window's size with a mouse, begin with the border when it looks like this:

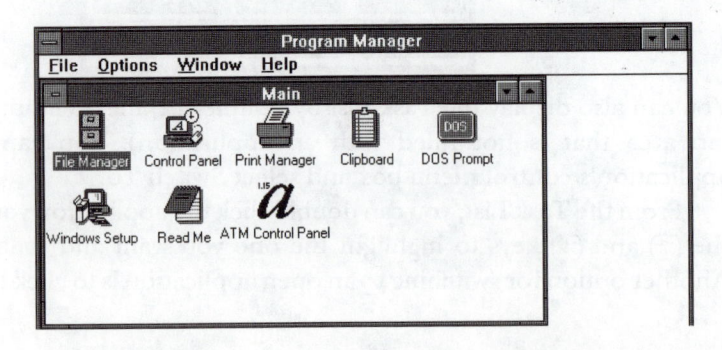

Appendix B: *Using Windows*

Drag the window's border to where you want it. Some document windows have size restrictions. Some other windows, like Window's Calculator, cannot change sizes. These windows have thin borders rather than the thicker borders of the windows you can resize.

Most windows have three window sizes you can select with the minimize button and the maximize or restore button, or with selections from the control menu. You can quickly enlarge a window so it fills the entire screen by clicking the maximize button or by selecting Ma*x*imize from the control menu, if the window has one. When you select a minimize button or select Mi*n*imize from the control menu, the window shrinks to an icon. An icon is a symbol that represents the application. Some applications, like Harvard Graphics for Windows, even let you turn document windows into icons. While a window is an icon, you can move the icon by dragging it to a new location or selecting *M*ove from the control menu for the icon, pressing the arrow keys to move the icon, and pressing (ENTER). After you minimize or maximize a window, you can return it to its previous size by selecting the restore button (the one that takes the place of the maximize button) or by selecting *R*estore from the control menu. An icon is also restored to its previous size when you double-click it.

Windows has two other quick options for positioning and sizing windows. One option is *tiling*, which divides the screen area between the non-minimized windows. Figure B-2 shows a screen that has the opened windows tiled. *Cascading*, on the other hand, makes each application window less than full size and stacks them so you can see only the title bar for each application except the top one. Figure B-3 shows a screen that has several windows cascaded. To tile or cascade windows, select the *T*ile or *C*ascade command button from the Task List by pressing (CTRL)-(ESC) and then either clicking the command button or pressing (ALT)-(T) or (ALT)-(C). Windows does not include minimized applications in the tiling or cascading, nor does it include DOS applications, which must be run in full-screen mode. Some applications let you tile or cascade the document windows within the application window. The Program Manager and Harvard Graphics for Windows are like this. For either application window, select the *W*indow pull-down menu and then select *T*ile or *C*ascade. (In some applications, you use different commands.)

Figure B-2. *Windows applications tiled*

Figure B-3. *Windows applications cascaded*

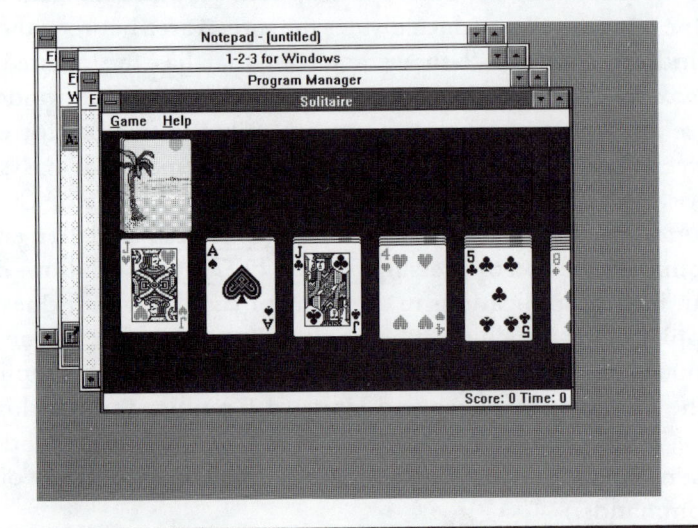

Appendix B: *Using Windows* 375

The Windows File Manager

The features of the File Manager you may want to use as you work with Harvard Graphics for Windows include listing files, deleting files, copying files, and preparing floppy disks for data storage. The File Manager provides a graphical way to look at the files you have stored on a disk. Since the File Manager uses different document windows to store diagrams of directories on a disk and the files contained in a directory, you can look at the directory structure of multiple drives and look at the files in multiple directories at once. This description of the File Manager applies to Windows 3.0.

To start the File Manager, make the Main group window in the Program Manager active and select File Manager from this group window. This displays a diagram of the directory structure of your disk, like this one:

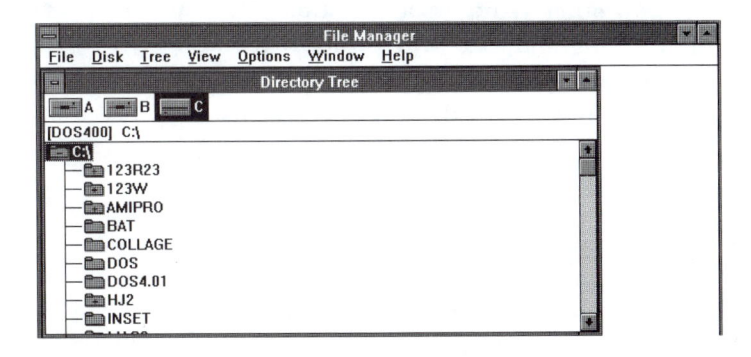

To change the disk displayed, click, at the top of the display, the drive you want or press (CTRL) and the letter of the drive you want, as in (CTRL)-(A). From the directory tree, you can move between the directories you want to display. When a directory contains subdirectories, a + appears in the file next to the directory name. For example, 123W contains a SHEETICO subdirectory, so the file next to 123W has a + in it. You can add the SHEETICO directory to the display by clicking 123W or by highlighting it and typing +. To display the files in a directory, double-click the directory or highlight it and press (ENTER). This displays another window, which contains a list of the files, like this:

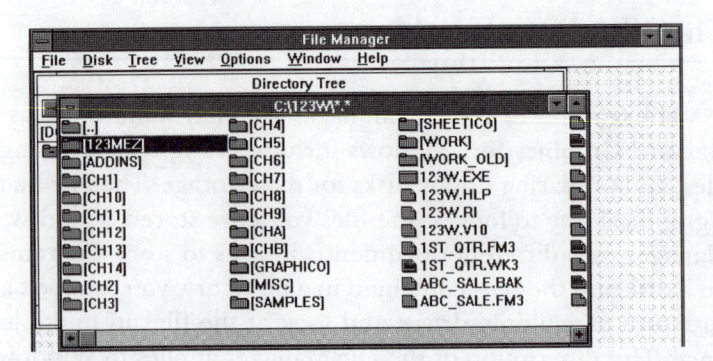

If you want to see the time and date the file was saved, its size, and its file attributes, click View and then File Details from the View pull-down menu, or press ALT+V+F. To return to the list of just the filenames, click View and then Name from the View pull-down menu or press ALT+V+N.

As with other Windows applications, you can switch between the document windows and size and position them. To leave the File Manager application window, press ALT+F4, click File and Exit, or press ALT+F+X. You need to select the OK button to confirm that you want to exit the File Manager.

Deleting Files

To delete a file, point to the file you want to delete in the list of files in a File Manager window and then press DEL or click File and Delete. From the Delete dialog box, click the Delete command button or press ENTER. Next, from the File Manager dialog box that confirms that you want to delete the file, select the Yes command button by clicking it or by pressing "Y" and pressing ENTER. This removes the file from the disk. (At this point, you can recover the file only if you have a file utility like Norton that can undelete files or if you are using DOS 5, which has an UNDELETE command.) You want to delete files you no longer want since they take up space on your disk that you may later want to use for storing other data.

Appendix B: *Using Windows*

Formatting a Disk

Before you can save data to a floppy disk, it must be formatted. Formatting a disk sets it to receive data and checks to see if the disk has any bad spots, which are noted and avoided. When you format a disk, you are preparing it to receive new data, so any data that was on it before is lost. To format a disk in the file manager, follow these steps:

1. Click Disk and Format Diskette or press (ALT)+(D)+(F).
2. Select the drive to format from the Format Diskette dialog box either by pressing the (↑) or (↓) key until the drive you want to format is shown or by clicking the down arrow icon and the drive letter containing the disk to format.
3. Click the OK command button or press (ENTER).
4. Click the Format command button, press "F", or press (ENTER) to confirm that you want to format the disk.
5. Click the High Capacity check box or press "H" if you want a 3 1/2-inch disk formatted as 1.44MB or a 5 1/4-inch disk formatted as 1.2MB (if the disk drive is capable of it).
6. Click Make System Disk or press "M" if you want to be able to start your system with the disk in drive A.
7. Click the OK command button or press (ENTER) to start formatting your disk.
8. Click Yes or press "Y" to format another disk. Click No or press "N" to finish formatting.

Copying a File

You can copy a file to make a duplicate of it in another location. You may want to use this command to copy a file to a disk to make a backup copy of an important worksheet. To copy a file, follow these steps:

1. Highlight the file you want to copy.

2. Click File Copy, press (F8), or press (ALT)+(F)+(C) to copy the file.

3. Type the location where you want the file copied.

You can just type the drive, as in **A:**, the drive and directory, as in **D:\HGW**, or even a new filename, as in **D:\HGW\PRES\MYPRES.PSS**. If you supply the filename, make sure you use the same file extension as previously, as shown here:

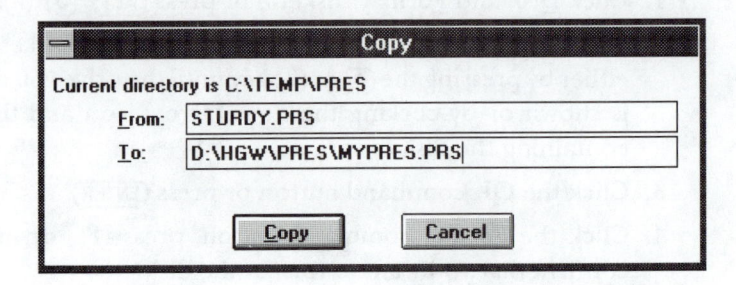

```
┌─────────────────── Copy ───────────────────┐
 Current directory is C:\TEMP\PRES
     From:  [STURDY.PRS                    ]
     To:    [D:\HGW\PRES\MYPRES.PRS        ]

              [  Copy  ]    [ Cancel ]
```

4. Click the Copy command button or press (ENTER) to copy the file.

The Windows Print Manager

Windows has a Print Manager that takes information you want to send to the printer from each of the applications and sends the information to the printer, one printout at a time. This prevents your worksheet data from appearing in the middle of your word processing documents. Windows waits until it has all the information to print before it prints any data. That is why when you print, you notice a delay between when an application starts printing and when the printer starts printing.

Most of the time, you do not need to look at the Print Manager when you print in Windows. The exception is if you try to print something and your printer is not connected, is not turned on, or runs out of paper. In these instances, Windows delays sending more information to the printer until you tell it to start sending information again. To do so, after correcting the problem, make the Main group window in the Program Manager active and

Appendix B: *Using Windows*

select Print Manager from this group window. This displays a list of the current print tasks, as shown here:

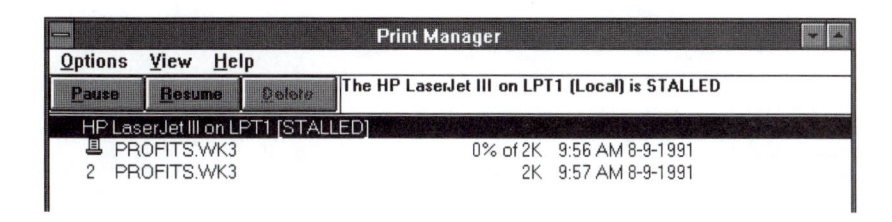

```
                           Print Manager
Options  View  Help
  Pause    Resume    Delete   The HP LaserJet III on LPT1 (Local) is STALLED
  HP LaserJet III on LPT1 [STALLED]
     PROFITS.WK3                       0% of 2K   9:56 AM 8-9-1991
  2  PROFITS.WK3                           2K    9:57 AM 8-9-1991
```

To tell Windows to send information to the printer again, click the Resume command button or press (ALT)-(R). Consult your windows documentation if you would like the Print Manager to cancel printing tasks and change the order of them.

C

Symbols Files

Harvard Graphics provides a number of symbols files that you can use to add interest to any chart. Each file contains a number of different symbols that you can select after choosing the file. This appendix provides a look at each of the symbols in these files to allow you to easily select the file you want.

The only difference between these symbols and the ones on your screen is that some of the symbol patterns printed here have been changed slightly to provide the necessary contrast for black and white. Chapter 8, "Using Drawing, Symbols, and Other Enhancements," includes more information on how you can add these symbols to your charts.

If you do not have symbols files on your disk, you may have selected a "minimal" installation to limit Harvard Graphics' space on your hard disk. Use install again and choose full installation or install only the symbols files you need.

382   *Harvard Graphics for Windows Made Easy*

ANIMALS.SYW

ANIPLANT.SYW

ARROWS2.SYW

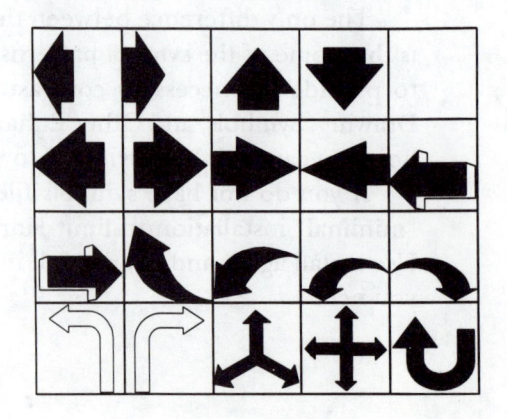

Appendix C: *Symbols Files* 383

BORDERS.SYW

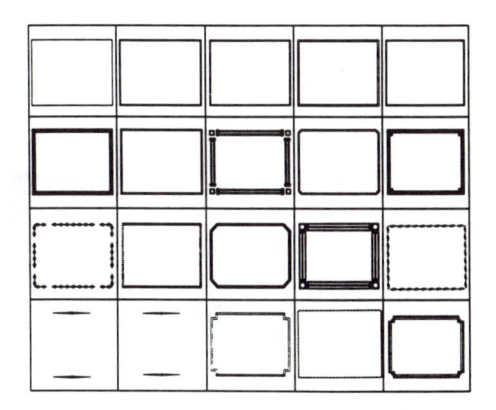

BUILD3.SYW

BUTTONS1.SYW

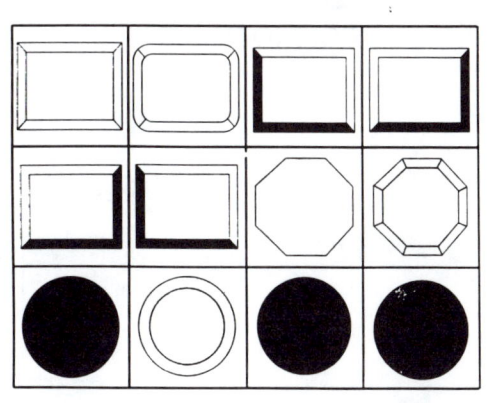

BUTTONS2.SYW

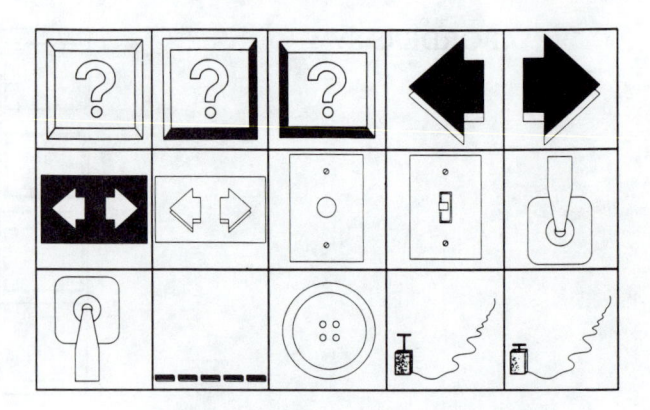

CALENDAR.SYW

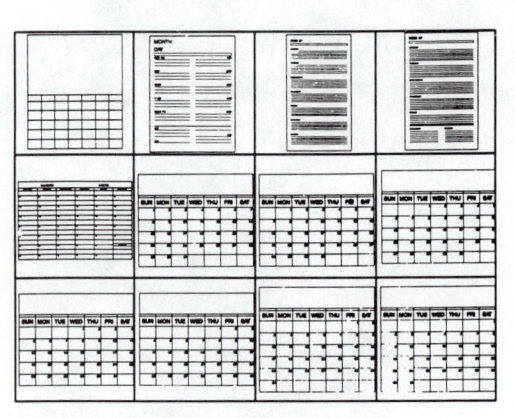

COMNOBJ1.SYW

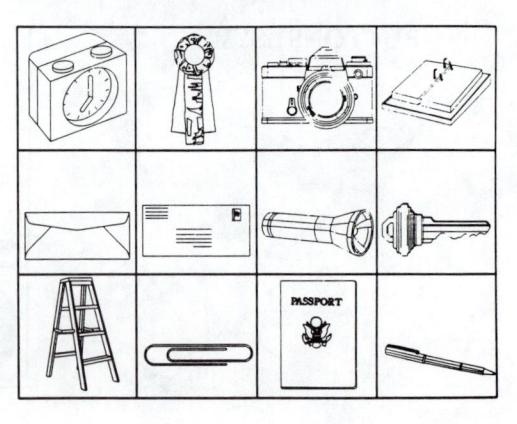

Appendix C: *Symbols Files* 385

COMNOBJ2.SYW

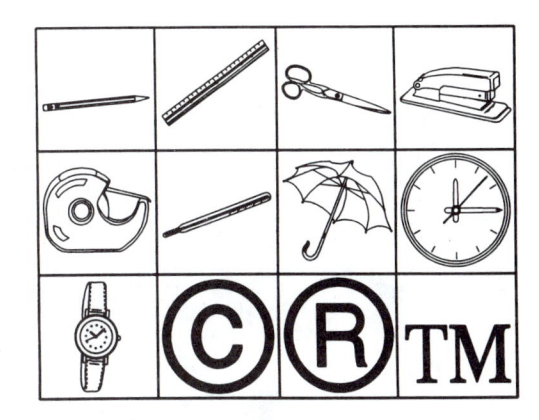

COMPUTR2.SYW

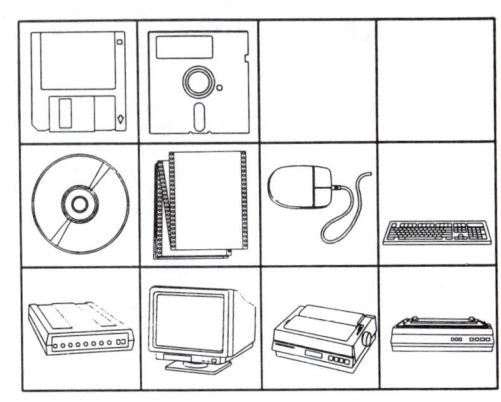

COMPUTR3.SYW

FLAGS1.SYW

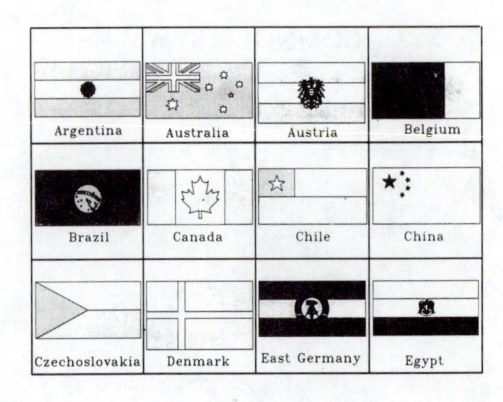

Argentina	Australia	Austria	Belgium
Brazil	Canada	Chile	China
Czechoslovakia	Denmark	East Germany	Egypt

FLAGS2.SYW

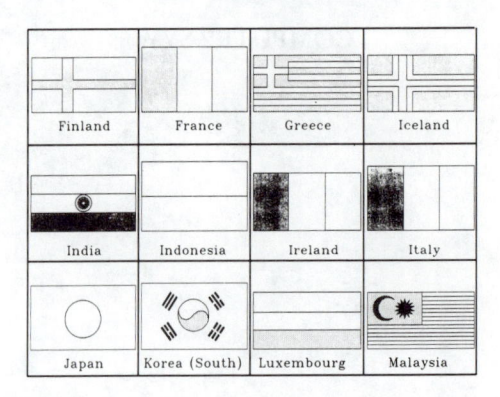

Finland	France	Greece	Iceland
India	Indonesia	Ireland	Italy
Japan	Korea (South)	Luxembourg	Malaysia

FLAGS3.SYW

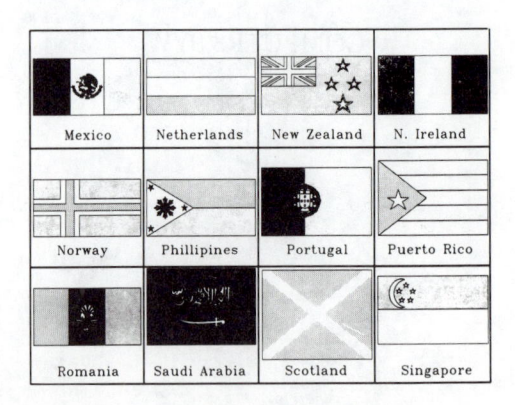

Mexico	Netherlands	New Zealand	N. Ireland
Norway	Phillipines	Portugal	Puerto Rico
Romania	Saudi Arabia	Scotland	Singapore

Appendix C: *Symbols Files*

FLAGS4.SYW

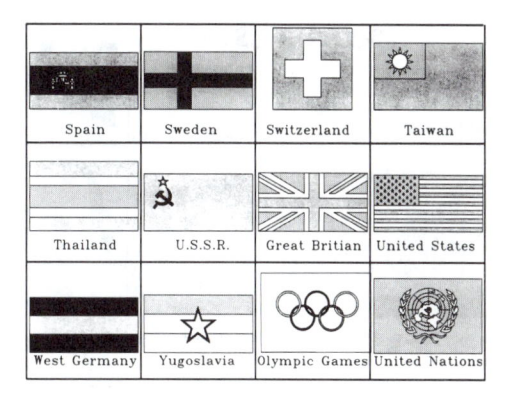

FLOWCHT.SYW

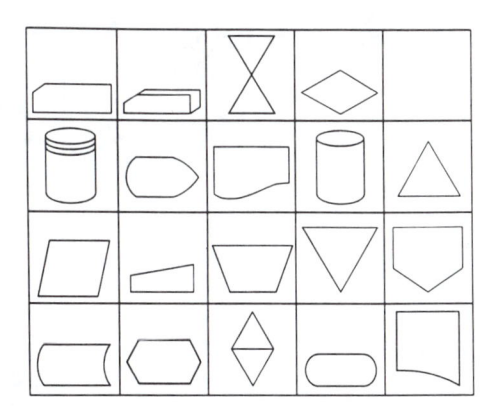

GREEKLC1.SYW

GREEKLC2.SYW

ν	ξ	ο	π	
ρ	σ	ς	τ	υ
φ	χ	ψ	ϕ	ω

GREEKUC1.SYW

Α	Β	Γ	Δ
Ε	Ζ	Η	Θ
Ι	Κ	Λ	Μ

GREEKUC2.SYW

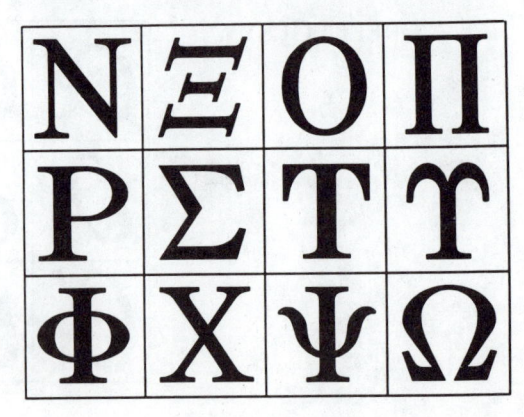

Ν	Ξ	Ο	Π
Ρ	Σ	Τ	Υ
Φ	Χ	Ψ	Ω

Appendix C: *Symbols Files*

HUMANS4.SYW

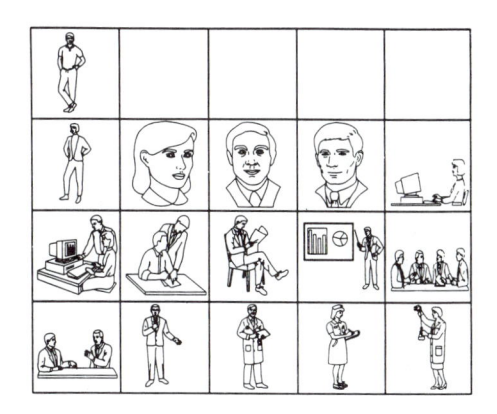

HUMANS5.SYW

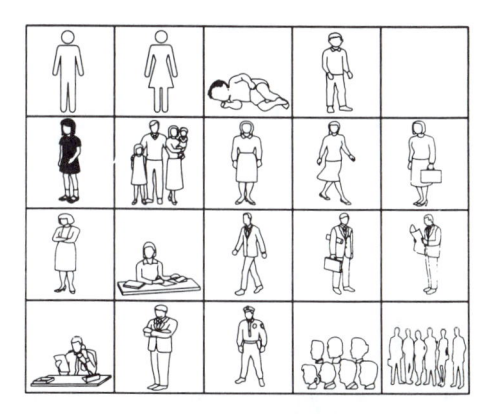

INDSTRY1.SYW

INDSTRY2.SYW

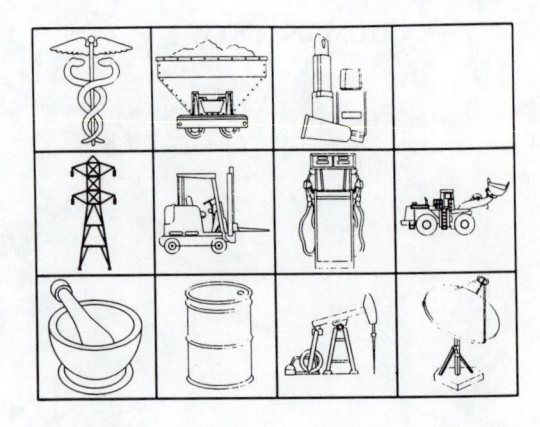

MAPS1.SYW

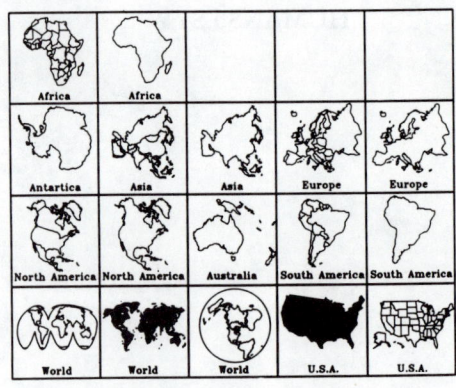

MAPS2.SYW

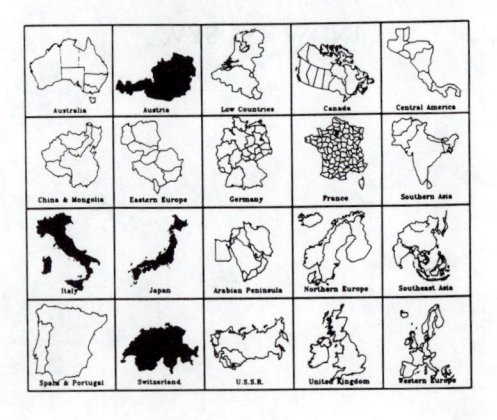

Appendix C: *Symbols Files*   391

MONEY.SYW

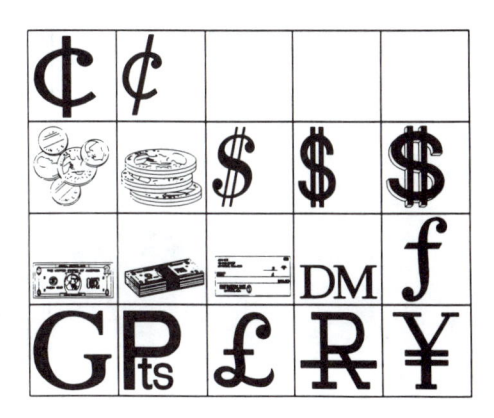

OFFICE4.SYW

PRESENT2.SYW

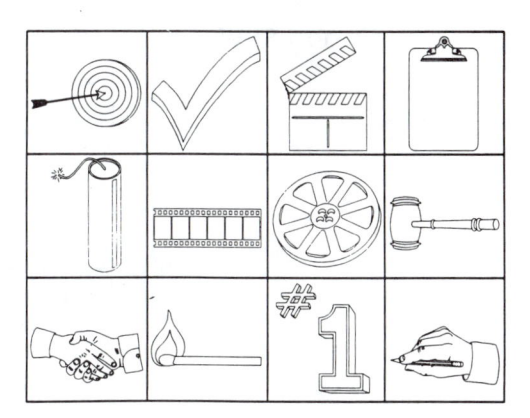

PRESENT3.SYW

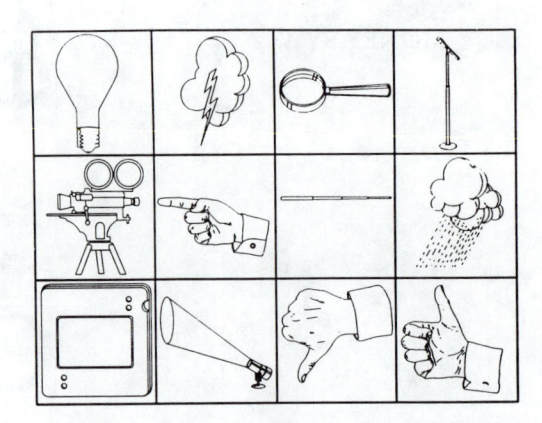

SIGNS.SYW

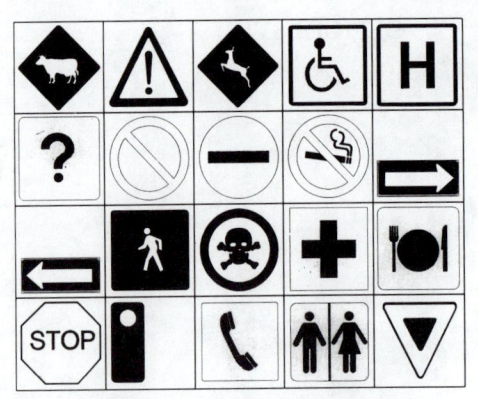

STARS1.SYW

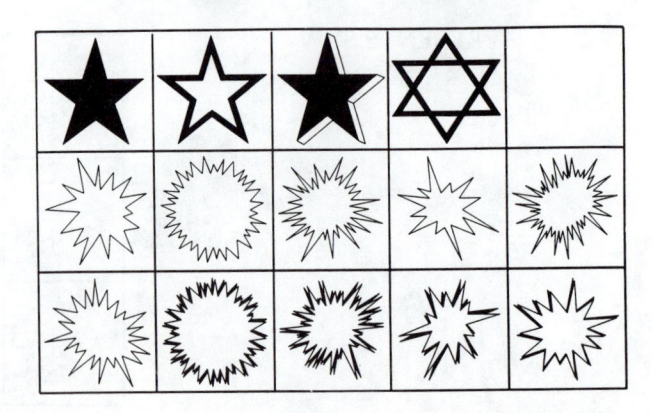

Appendix C: *Symbols Files*

393

TRANSPT1.SYW

TRANSPT2.SYW

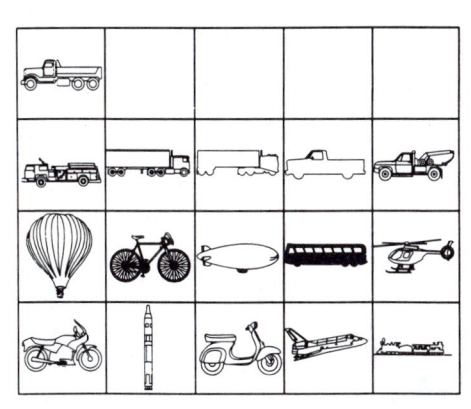

C

D

Harvard Graphics Speed Keys

This appendix provides *two* quick-reference tables of Harvard Graphics' speed keys. The first listing is organized alphabetically by the name of the key and the second by the name of the function each key performs.

Speed Keys

ALT+C	Chart menu
ALT+E	Edit menu
ALT+F	File menu
ALT+G	Graphics menu
ALT+H	Help menu
ALT+O	Outline menu
ALT+S	Slide menu
ALT+T	Text menu
ALT+V	View menu
ALT+W	Window menu
ALT+F2	Display ScreenShow from the current slide

ALT+F4	Exit
ALT+BACKSPACE	Undo an action
CTRL+A	Select all objects
CTRL+B	Bold
CTRL+E	Edit selected object
CTRL+G	Group
CTRL+H	Center object horizontally
CTRL+I	Italic
CTRL+N	New presentation
CTRL+O	Open presentation
CTRL+P	Print presentation
CTRL+S	Save presentation
CTRL+U	Ungroup objects
CTRL+F2	Display ScreenShow from the beginning
CTRL+ESC	Display Task List to switch to another application
CTRL+INS	Copy selected objects to the Clipboard
SHIFT+DEL	Cut selected objects, placing them on the Clipboard
SHIFT+INS	Paste Clipboard contents
SHIFT+TAB	Remove indent added with Tab
SHIFT+F4	Arrange windows in a tiled pattern
SHIFT+F5	Arrange windows in a cascade fashion

Functions Performed by Speed Keys

Editing Tasks

Center selected object horizontally	CTRL+H
Change Chart Options	F8
Copy selected objects to the Clipboard	CTRL+INS
Cut selected objects, placing them on the Clipboard	SHIFT+DEL
Edit selected object on the Slide Editor or cell on the Data Form	CTRL+E
Group selected objects	CTRL+G
Paste Clipboard contents to current location	SHIFT+INS
Remove indent added with Tab	SHIFT+TAB
Select all objects	CTRL+A
Select multiple text blocks	SHIFT+CLICK
Undo an action	ALT+BACKSPACE
Ungroup selected object into separate objects	CTRL+U

Appendix D: *Harvard Graphics Speed Keys*

Changing Text

Make selected text bold	CTRL+B
Make selected text italic	CTRL+I

File and Print Tasks

Create a new presentation	CTRL+N
Exit	ALT+F4
Open a presentation	CTRL+O
Preview print	F2
Print a presentation	CTRL+P
Save presentation	CTRL+S

Working in the Outliner

Indent entry	TAB
Unindent entry	SHIFT+TAB

Working with a ScreenShow

Display ScreenShow from the beginning	CTRL+F2
Display Task List to switch to another application	ALT+F2

Window Tasks

Arrange windows in a tiled pattern	SHIFT+F4
Arrange windows in a cascade fashion	SHIFT+F5

E

Harvard Graphics Movement Keys

The following keys are used throughout the different views of Harvard Graphics. Even within a single view, the key may work differently depending on your task. The keys are described in terms of their general capabilities except where the function is unique to a specific task.

(BACKSPACE)   If in Edit mode (press (CTRL)+(E) to get to this mode) will delete the previous character—otherwise deletes all characters on the edit line! Delete selected text, or line break, or a blank line above the current line if the cursor is at the beginning of the line.

(CTRL)+(→)   Move to the end of the current range, or the beginning of the next range in the same row, or right one word.

(CTRL)+(←)   Move to the beginning of the current range, or to the end of the previous range in the same row, or left one word.

CTRL+↑ Move to the beginning of the current range, or to the end of the previous range in the same column, or move the characters you type on the edit line to the current cell.

CTRL+↓ Move to the end of a contiguous range, or to the beginning of the next range in the same column, or move the characters you type on the edit line to the current cell.

CTRL+ENTER Add a new line to a cell, topic, or subtopic or—when entering text—split a line into two lines with a vertical bar (|) in between.

CTRL+HOME Move to cell A0 (or A1, if the first row is not currently displayed), or to the first character of the first line.

CTRL+END Move to the end of the last column, or to the last character of the last line.

CTRL+PGDN In a Table Chart Data Form move right one screen.

CTRL+PGUP In a Table Chart Data Form move left one screen.

DELETE Delete the next character, selected text, or bring one line up.

↓ Move down one row or one line. Move the characters you type on the edit line to the current cell. In a text box when the last line is reached, move to the next text box.

← Move left one character or column.

→ Move right one character or column.

↑ Move up one row or line, or move the characters you type on the edit line to the current cell. In a text box move up one line until the first line is reached and then move to the previous text box.

END Move to the last column in the current row of a Data Form, or to the last character of the current line.

Appendix E: *Harvard Graphics Movement Keys*

ENTER Move down one row or line, or add a new line or bullet, or move the characters you type on the edit line to the current cell.

HOME Move to the first cell in the current row in a Data Form, or to the first character of the current line.

PGDN In a Table Chart Data Form move down one page.

PGUP In a Table Chart Data Form move up one page.

SHIFT+**ENTER** Move up one row.

SHIFT+**←** Begin selecting text to the left of the cursor one character at a time.

SHIFT+**→** Begin selecting text to the right of the cursor one character at a time.

SHIFT+**TAB** Move left one column, or move a bullet or topic one level to the left, or move to the previous field.

TAB Move right one column, or move a bullet or topic one level to the right, or move to the next field, or move the character you type on the edit line to the current cell.

Index

A

Abbreviations, keyword, 186
Active window, 371-372
Add chart to slide option, 276
Add Slide option, 9, 53, 56, 293-295, 309, 312, 316
Advance slide, 283, 286-287
Align tool, 242, 267, 271-272
Alignment
    of justified text, 85
    of objects, 271-272
    of pie charts labels, 199-200
    of text in organization charts, 231
Analytical slides, 7-12
Anchor point, text, 295
Annotations to existing charts, 250-254
ANSI (American National Standards Institute) symbols, 67-69, 87, 349
Applications, 321-322, 366, 370-372
Area charts, 11, 139-140, 168-171
Area, High/Low style chart, 175-176
Arguments, function, 184
Arithmetic formulas and operators, 180-184
Arrow, four-sided, 195, 211
Arrow keys, 71, 279, 400

Arrow objects, adding, 251-253
ASCII data, 321-322
    character sets, 349
    exporting, 338-339
    importing, 332-334
Assignments
    color palette, 342-345
    key, 279, 291-292, 299-401
@functions (spreadsheet), 184
Attribute options, 248
Attribute settings (object), 253-255
Attributes, text and size, 135
Autographix program (slide service), 300-301, 362
Automatic slide dating, 308
Automatic text sizing (organization chart), 231
Automatic update of data links, 322, 328, 330, 334-335, 349
Average (cell range), 185-187
Average line fitting option, 150
Axis scaling, 160-162, 164-165

B

Back to slide button, 305, 308
Background, 16-17, 262, 303-311

Backup disks, 360-361
Bar charts, 91-96
    bar styles, 118-120
    enhancements for, 127-137
    from transposed data, 331
    horizontal, 125-128
    mixed line and, 152-153
    100%, 116-118, 122-123
    overlap, 116-118, 120
    paired, 125-128
    pie charts as, 206-207
    stacked, 116-118, 121-122
    step, 122-125
    3D, 252-253
    3D options for, 133-134
    types of, 116-127
    vertical, 325-326, 327-328
Bar/Area chart
    100%, 122-123
    Overlap, 120
    Paired, 127
    Stack, 121-122
Bar/Area styles, 24, 154-155
Bitmap files, supported, 83, 131, 321-322, 336-337
Bold text, 85
Border line, background, 305, 309
Border, window (Windows), 367-368, 372-373
Box style, 226-228
Boxed text object, 199-200, 259-260
Break key, 279
Bullet charts, 34
    conversion to organization charts, 237-239
    creating, 36-37, 65-68
    creating backgrounds for, 304-307
    from the gallery, 58-60
    importing ASCII files into, 332
    as a numbered list, 65-67
    set of overlay, 296-298
Bullet radio button, 58
Bullet Symbol dialog box, 87-88
Business Symbols, 265

C

Calculations, 179-187
Cancel command button, 20
Cell reference, 181-183, 323-324
Cell, table, 70-71, 324
Centering objects, 267, 270
Change presentation font, 83, 134, 230
Characters, ANSI, 67-69
Characters, for bullets, 87-88
Charts. *See individual chart types*
Chart galleries, 14-15, 56-59
Chart palette, changing, 81, 83

Chart series, 149
    line-fitting options, 143
    show cumulative data, 156-157
    show series, 153-154, 198
Closing
    the control menu box, 245
    a presentation, 40, 44
Cluster bar charts, 116-118
Code page, ASCII character set, 349
Collapse option (outline menu), 47-48, 232
Color Options dialog box, 261-262
Color palettes, 80-83, 116, 341-343
Color tool, 146
Coloring objects. *See* Fill tool
Column width marker, 71
Columns
    bar chart, 104-105
    1-2-3 worksheet data, 323-324
    pie chart, 206-207, 208
    table chart, 73
    transposing rows with, 330-331
Combination keys
    for ANSI symbols, 67-69
    for movement, 399-401
    Windows, 354
Command buttons, 24
Commas, 163, 332-333
Compression, file, 301
Control menu box (Windows), 245, 367-368
Converting
    bullet to organization chart, 237-239
    data for import or export, 321
Copy and Paste, 43-44, 264
Copying
    disk, 360-361
    existing backgrounds, 304, 309-311
    a file (in Windows), 377-378
    a file with Save as, 73
    a formula with Data Fill, 181-183, 187
    from the Symbol Library, 266, 270, 314
    objects, 250, 263-265
    to a different slide or presentation, 264
Cross-hair pointer, 249-250
Currency format, 162, 183, 214-216
Custom colors, 80-81, 83
Cut and Paste a row or column, 105-106

D

Data
    changes in graphics, 102-113
    delimiters, 332-334
    exchange (DDE), 322, 327, 334-335
    retaining original, 102-103
Data fill menu, 181-183
Data Form, 56, 219-220, 247-248

Index

bar chart, 93-96
bullet chart, 58-59
entering formulas in a, 181-183
highlight position on a, 325, 327-328
HLC chart, 174
importing data into a, 325-329, 333-335
pie chart, 191
symbol, 276
table chart, 68-73
Data Form tool, 243
Data links. *See* Links
Data point charts, 151-152
Data point line charts, 147-149, 166-167
Data series
 in a bar chart, 96-98
 as columns, 104
 data types, 108-113
 in HLC charts, 170-179
 line chart display options for, 151-152
 mixed chart types for additional, 177-179
 X-axis, 181
Database files, importing, 332-334
Date stamp, background, 308
Decimal numbers, 183
 chart labels format, 162-163
 in formulas, 180
 fractions as, 182
 from 1-2-3, 324
Default settings. *See* File Preferences
Deleting
 a bar chart legend, 95
 a bar chart row or column, 104-105
 blank cells, 197
 files, 376
 labels of hidden charts, 199
 objects, 262-263
 slides from a presentation, 280-282
 subordinate entries from an organization chart, 236-237
 table chart columns, 73
 text using the mouse, 221
 topics, 42-44
Dialog boxes, 23-24, 370
Dictionary, 61, 347-348
Directory
 default, 26-27, 348
 Harvard Graphics, 348, 361-362
 symbols, 266
Disks
 backup, 360-361
 changing, 375-376
 formatting, 360-361, 377
Display options for slides. *See* ScreenShow
Distribution diagram, 15-16
Dollar sign ($), 183, 215-216
DOS, 25, 360-361, 369, 373, 376
Dragging, 41-42, 255, 346, 366

Drawing slides, 241, 244-245, 250-254
Drawing tools, 242, 248-249
Drivers, output device, 361-363
Drop shadow for text or objects, 273-275
Duplicating an object, 264-265
Dynamic Data Exchange link (DDE), 322, 327, 334-335

E

Edit mode, 71
Editing
 backgrounds, 307-311
 bar chart titles, 98-100
 a color palette, 345-347
 data in a bar chart, 96-98
 data in graphs, 102-103
 existing presentations, 278-282
 existing slide in Slide Editor, 247-248
 speed keys for, 396
 text in a bar chart, 98-100
Ellipses, 24, 243, 250
Excel worksheet data, 323, 327, 334
Exit
 File Manager (Windows), 376
 Help, 24
 1-2-3, 325
 other applications, 371
 Windows, 366-367
Expanded display, 47
 organization chart, 232
 slide in Slide Sorter, 280
Exploded-slice pie charts, 196
Exporting, 17, 335-340, 349
Eyedropper tools, 81, 242

F

Fade slide image, 284-285
Faded text (on-screen), 244-245, 311, 312
File Manager (Windows), 375-378
File Preferences, 34-35, 50, 341
Fill options, 114-115, 128-132
Fill tool, 242, 251, 261-263
Film recorders, using, 299-300
Flipping objects, 33, 268-272. *See also* Rotating
Footnotes, 79-80, 99, 111, 135, 312
Foreign currency symbols, 163
Formatting disk, 360-361, 377
 for output devices, 278
Four-sided arrow, 195, 211, 258
Free-form chart, 55, 88-89
Freehand tool, 242, 250
Frequency distribution bar chart, 122-125
Full frame style (graph), 132-133
Full-screen mode, 366, 370, 373

Function (speed) keys, 396-397. *See also* Key assignments

G

Gallery options, viewing, 57
Go to button, 74-75
Graphics Group/Ungroup, 256
Graphics Line attributes, 253
Graphs. *See individual chart types*
Group tool, 242
Grouping objects, 255-256, 257-258, 336

H

Hairline lines, 146, 149-150, 305
Handles, 210-211, 246, 255, 268-270
Handouts radio button (Print), 39, 299
Hardware requirements, 360
Height, table row, 86-87
Height-to-width ratio. *See* Ratio, height-to-width
Hiding, 153-154, 166, 198-199
High/Low/Close charts, 10-11, 140, 170-179
Horizontal bar chart, paired, 125-128
Horizontal flip, an object, 269
Horizontal orientation (organization charts), 228-229
Horizontal scroll bar, 74
HyperShow, 277, 288-296. *See also* Links

I

Icons, 362
    active window, 372
    application, 367, 372
    from Slide Editor, 242
    justification, 76
    organization chart, 218
    organization chart detail, 232
    Slide Editor, 242
    view options, 30-31
Importing data, 17, 321-322
    ASCII files, 332-334, 349
    entire worksheet, 324-327
    part of a worksheet, 327-328
Importing graphics, 131-132
Inserting
    bar chart rows/columns, 104-105
    new topics in outline, 45
    table chart rows/columns, 73
    text in bar chart, 98-100
Installing
    Harvard Graphics, 359-362
    Windows, 366

International symbols and characters, 68-69, 163, 349
Intersection, row and column, 70
Italic to text, 84-85

J

Justification, 85, 231, 295
    in organization charts, 231

K

Key assignments
    default, 279, 291-292, 299-401
    HyperShow link, 289-292
Key combination commands, 101
    lists, 279, 395-397, 399-401
    speed, 20-21, 101, 395-396
    Windows shortcut, 20, 352, 354-355
Keyboard keys, 20, 396-397
Keywords in formulas, 180, 183-187

L

Labels
    adding pie chart, 199-200
    entering X-Axis, 111
    pie, 191
    pie chart percent, 214-215
    shared pie chart, 201-203
    vertical, 86
Labels format button, 162
Legends, 9, 95, 100-102, 124, 135
    changing, 156-160
    for pie charts, 212-213
Line attributes, graphics, 86, 146-147, 149-150, 242, 304-305, 309
Line attributes tool, 242
Line charts, 10-12, 139
    adding data labels to, 166-167
    creating, 140-142
    default settings, 143-145
    line thickness, 145-147
    mixed bar and, 152-153
    with overlap and 3D features, 154-155
    showing cumulative values, 156-157
    shown as data points, 151-152
Line style, line chart, 149-150
Line tool, 146, 243, 249-250, 251-252
Line width settings, 253-254
Line-fitting options, line chart, 150-151
Linear scaling (line chart), 161
Lines
    background border, 305, 309
    chart grid format, 165-166

Index **407**

grid, 86
linking two pie charts, 204-205
in table chart, 86
Linked 100% bar charts, 118
Linked stack bar charts, 116-118
Linking, 203-205, 321-322
Links. *See also* Hypershow
hot (DDE), 334-335
to worksheet data, 17, 312
warm, 323, 328-330
Lotus 1-2-3, 322-331

M

Macros. *See* Windows, macros
Margins, changing, 114-115
Marker styles, line chart series, 147-149
Maximize button (Windows), 367-368, 373
Maximize the display, 67
Memory
clipboard, 43
printer, 115
Menu bar, 21-22, 367-368
Minimize button (Windows), 367-368, 373
Monitors, 25
Monospace text font, 231
Months axis labels, alternate, 165
Mouse pointer, 41-42, 195
actions, 20-22, 279, 365-366
moving objects with, 195, 270
selecting tools with, 241
using keyboard or, 19-21
Movement keys, 399-401
Moving. *See also* Positioning; Rotating
application windows, 372-374
chart legends, 157-159
entries in an organization chart, 235-236
from slide to slide, 74-75, 278-279
objects, 256-258
objects using the mouse pointer, 195, 270
one slide at a time, 74-75
pie charts, 210-211
a row or column, 105-106
text with the Selection Tool, 77-78
windows as icons, 373
Multiple charts, displaying, 276
Multiple objects, 255, 259-260

N

New Presentation (File menu), 53, 140, 190, 237, 304, 325, 348
Numbered lists, creating, 65-67

O

Object attributes, changing, 259-260
Objects, 241. *See also* Symbols
adding, 248-254
alignment of, 271-272
copying, 263-265
deleting, 262-263
flipping, 268-272
grouping, 255-256, 257-258
moving, 256-258
positioning, 249-250
rotating, 268-272
selecting, 255, 265
sizing, 259-260
100% bar charts, 116, 122-123
Open presentation default view, 348
Opening
a file, 278
Symbol Library, 244
Windows, 366
Order (of series), 102, 106-107
Organization chart radio button, 219
Organization charts, 13-14, 217-221
adding levels to, 223-227
appearance options, 226-232
conversion to bullet chart, 237-239
view options for, 231-234
Outliner, 4-5, 22, 29-35
creating presentation with, 34-41
export ASCII text from, 338-339
import ASCII text into, 332
speed keys for, 397
Outliner icon, 31, 32, 221
Output devices, 25, 277
specific color palettes for, 81, 342-343
supplemental drivers for, 299-300, 362-363
Output options, 10-11, 114-115, 299-301
Overlap bar charts, 116-120
Overlapping
charts, 154-155, 296-298
windows, 373-374

P

Paired bar charts, 116-119, 125-128
Pasting. *See* Copy and Paste; Copying
Pathnames, directory, 26, 335, 378
Pencil tool. *See* Freehand tool
PERT charts, 15
Pie charts, 9, 11-12
adding labels below, 199-200
colors for, 193-194
creating, 189-193
display in column format, 206-207, 208
exploding slices, 196

legends for, 212-213
linked to a column chart, 11-13
linking, 203-205
moving, 210-211
multiple, 196-205
with shared labels, 201-203
size changes, 202-204, 210-211
tools for, 190
Placeholders, 37-38, 89, 308
Plotters, using, 299-300, 342
Point charts, 151-152
Point size, 78-80, 253, 265
   line thickness, 145-146
   titles or footnotes, 79-80, 135, 231
Polycurve tool, 249
Polygon tool, 242, 249
Polyline tool, 242, 249
Port, COM, 299-300
Positioning. *See also* Alignment; Moving
   application windows, 372-374
   line chart data labels, 166-167
   objects, 243, 249-250, 271-272
Postscript, 300, 320, 362-363
Preference settings. *See* File Preferences
Presentation styles, 277, 303, 318, 347-348
Presentations
   closing, opening, saving, 38-41
   editing, 41-49, 277-282
   menus for, 293-296
Preview print (Slide Editor), 305, 308, 397
Print command, 39
Print devices, setting up, 114-115
Print Manager (Windows), 378-379
Print speed keys, 397
Printers, 115, 300, 362-363
Printing
   charts, 113-116
   color palettes, 81-82
   data charts, 116
   handouts of slides, 11, 299
   one slide per page, 11
   the presentation, 38-40, 299-301
   1-2-3 worksheet file, 325
Program Manager. *See* Windows, Program Manager
Prompt to update data links, 349
Pull-down menu, 370

Q

Quattro Pro data, 323
Queue, print, 378-379
Quotation marks, string, 332

R

Radio buttons, 9, 23-24, 58, 275
Range of cells, 182,
   1-2-3 names for, 323-324
Ratio, height-to-width object size, 259
Recovery, file, 376
Rectangle, 305-306, 327
Rectangle tool, 242, 249, 264, 305
Redo, 248
Removing. *See* Deleting
Reorganization
   data series, 108-113
   organization chart, 223-227
   slides on the Slide Sorter, 279-280
Replace option, 61
Restoring
   icon to maximum size, 373
   with Undo, 236, 262-263, 281
Ribbon line chart, 154-155
Rotate handle, 268, 270
Rotate tool, 243
Rotating. *See also* Flipping objects
   linked pie charts, 205
   objects, 268-272
Rows
   bar chart, 104-105
   table chart, 73
   transposing columns with, 330-331
   1-2-3 worksheet data, 323-324
Ruler, text box, 76

S

Sample icons (toolbox palette), 246
Save as dialog box, 25-26
Save as option, 38, 41, 73, 103, 354
Save option, 103
Saving
   charts as symbols, 276
   data changes, 102-103
   files, 25-26
   1-2-3 worksheet file, 325
   presentation, 38-39, 190
   presentation styles, 318-319
Scaling, 115, 124, 164-165
Scatter charts, 151-152
Scientific Notation format, 162, 215
ScreenShow, 16, 277-278, 282-288, 293-296, 397
Scroll bar (Outliner), 30, 74, 273
Scrolling slide off screen, 286
Select all (Edit menu), 85
Selection tool, 75, 242, 248, 250
Series (chart data)
   by product name, 108-113
   hiding, 153-154

Index **409**

markers, 147-149
mixed chart types, 177-179
Overlap option, 170-171
Series of charts, creating, 233-234
Set fill, background, 305
Setup device button, 114-115
Shadows, creating, 175, 273-275
Shortcut keys (Windows), 352, 354-355
Show series option for series, 153-154
Show subtitle and footnote, 221
Show text ruler, 76
Size
    character, 64
    delimited text line, 332
    lines in line charts, 145-147
    organization charts, 217, 221
    pie chart slices, 192
    pie charts, 202-211
    spreadsheet forms, 70
    text, 78-80, 135, 231
    tool, 199
Sizing
    application windows, 372-374
    objects, 259-260
Slices, pie. *See* pie charts
Slide. *See individual functions*
Slide Editor, 4-6, 32, 244-248
    as default view, 49-50
    options, 267-276
    preview, 305
    tools, 14-15
Slide Editor icon, 31
Slide Sorter, 5-7, 22, 49, 279-280, 295
    summary view, 233-234
Slide Sorter icon, 31, 279
Sorting pie slices, 207-208
Spacing, characters and lines, 64, 78
Special effects (Graphics), 273-276
Special symbols, 67
Speed keys, 20-21, 101, 395-397
Spelling check, 59-63, 137
Splitting windows. *See* Windows, tiling
Spreadsheet programs, 70, 179, 323-331. *See also*
    names of programs
Stack style bar charts, 116, 121-122
Stacked bar charts, 9, 168-169
Stamp, date (background), 308
Starting
    Harvard Graphics, 18
    Windows, 361, 366
Statistics line chart data series, 150-151
Step bar chart, 119-120, 122-125
Subtitle text, 99, 183, 219
Swap rows/columns, 330-331
Sweep effect (Graphics), 273-276
Switching
    between Slide Editor and Outliner, 32-34

    between windows, 371-372, 376
Symbol Library, 15, 244, 266, 270, 313
Symbol tool, 243-244
Symbols. *See also* Objects
    adding, 265-267, 313-314
    for bullets, 87-88
    in chart labels, 162-163
    line chart marker, 147-149
    mathematic, 180
    moving objects within, 256-257
    in pie chart labels, 214-216
    slides as, 276
System disk, 377

T

Table charts, 55, 68-73, 86-87
Templates, 16-17, 303
    applying, 315-317, 319-320
    creating, 310-320
    default, 312, 317-318
    for title charts, 312-314
Text attributes
    Eyedropper tool, 81
    speed keys for, 397
Text attributes tool screen icon, 242
Text boxes, 76-77
Text charts, 51-56
    fonts, 83-84, 230-232
    types of, 55-56
Text sample screen icon, 243
Text slides, 11-13
Text styles, 84-85, 229-232
Text tool, 76-77, 246, 249, 253-254, 265, 308
    screen icon, 242
35mm film, output to, 300-301
Thousands Separator, 162, 215-216
Three-column table charts, 70-73
3D charts
    area charts as, 170-171
    changing, 133-134
    field, 24
    line chart object depth, 154-155
    overlapped bar, 119-120
3D pie charts, 211-213
Thumbnail sketch, 49
Tick marks, 8
    adding, 124
    Error Bar, 176-177
    in HLC charts, 171-172, 174
    on the X and Y axes, 163
Time
    and date file was saved, 376
    slide display duration, 283, 286-287
    stamp (background), 308
Title bar (Windows), 367-368

Title charts, 34-36, 63-66, 312-314
Title radio button, 32, 58
Titles
    above pie charts, 196-197
    axes, 9
    bar chart, 98-100
    faded text for, 244-245, 311-313
    job, 232
    organization chart, 219, 221, 234-235
    Outliner, 30
    pie, 191
    ScreenShow menu, 295
    subtitle or footnote, 65, 79-80, 135, 231
Tool Lock (Graphics menu), 77, 248, 250
Topics (outline), ordering, 30, 41-46
Tracing tool. *See* Freehand tool
Transposing rows and columns, 330-331
Trend chart displaying straight lines, 150-151
Trend line fitting option, 150
2D display of a 3D chart, 205
2-dimensional overlapped bar charts, 119-120

U

Underlining text, 84-85, 351-355
Undo, 248, 262-263, 281
Ungroup, Graphics, 256, 336
Updating
    automatic file, 101-102
    warm links, 328-330, 349
User menus, ScreenShow, 293-296

V

Value labels pie chart, 214-216
Vertical bar (|), 71
Vertical bar chart, 325-326, 327-328
Vertical flip of an object, 269
Vertical labels, table chart, 86
Vertical orientation, organization charts, 225, 228-229
View
    Collapsing and Expanding, 47-48, 232
    Outliner, 4-5, 22, 221
    Slide Editor preview, 305
    Slide Sorter, 49, 233-234
View icons, 244-245
Viewing
    default presentation, 237, 348
    organization charts, 231-234
    presentation style, 320

print preview, 305, 308, 397
slide template, 315
symbols as names, 244

W

Warm link to worksheet data, 323, 328-330
Window border (Windows), 367-368
Windows, 350, 365
    Accessories dialog box, 352, 369
    cascading, 373-374
    Clipboard, 43, 264, 281
    Control Panel, 215, 299-300
    File Manager, 375-378
    Interface, 367-374
    macros, 341, 355
    Main group, 369-370, 375
    Print Manager, 378-379
    Program Manager, 352, 362-363, 367, 369
    shortcuts, 20, 352, 354-355
    speed keys, 397
    Task List, 266, 335, 352, 354, 371
    tiling, 373-374
Wordprocessing files, 321-322, 337

X

X-axis bar charts, 8, 92
X-axis data points, 104-107
X-axis labels, 108, 110, 181
X data types, 108-113
XY-bar charts, 51-52
XY charts, 9
XY-line charts, 142-167

Y

Y-axis bar chart, 52
Y-axis charts, 8
Y-axis range
    in HLC charts, 173, 175
    narrowing the, 173, 175
Year entries, reversing order of, 106-107

Z

Zero, 182, 208-210
Zoom-in/out tools, 242-243, 273

Command Card

Slide Editor Toolbox Icons

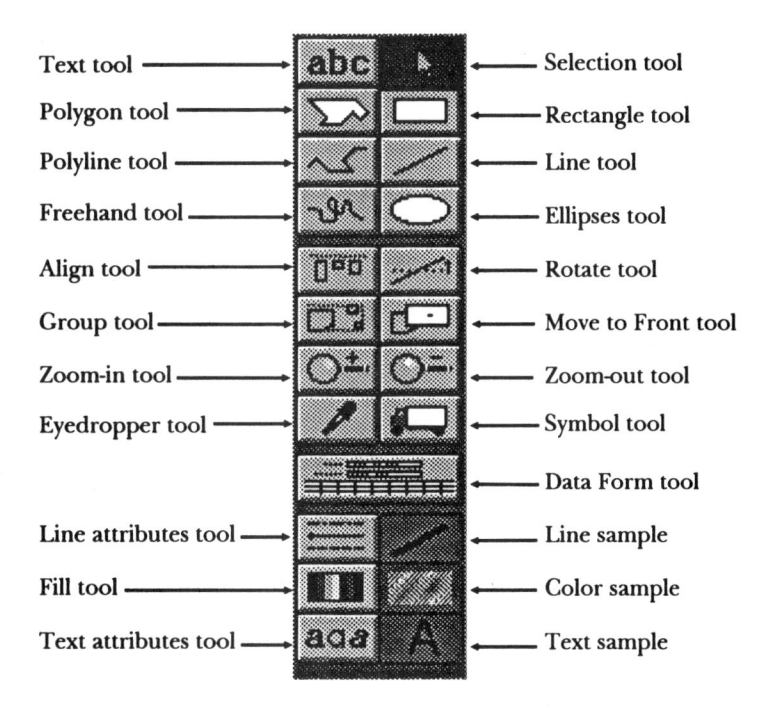

Text tool		Selection tool
Polygon tool		Rectangle tool
Polyline tool		Line tool
Freehand tool		Ellipses tool
Align tool		Rotate tool
Group tool		Move to Front tool
Zoom-in tool		Zoom-out tool
Eyedropper tool		Symbol tool
		Data Form tool
Line attributes tool		Line sample
Fill tool		Color sample
Text attributes tool		Text sample

View Icons

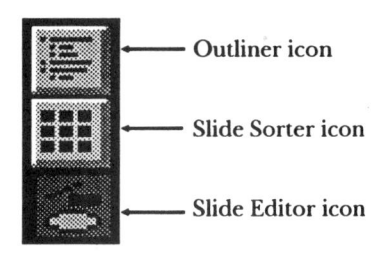

- Outliner icon
- Slide Sorter icon
- Slide Editor icon

Selected Main Menu Pull-Down Options

FILE
New presentation
Open
Save
Save as
Close
Setup
Print
ScreenShow
Symbol Library
Import
Export
Preferences
Exit

SLIDE
Add slide
Delete slide
Go to slide
Background
Slide template
Presentation style
Color pallette
Change presentation font
Edit handouts master
Add titles/footnote

CHART
Edit data
Chart options
Series
Legend
Frame
Grid
Axis
Labels
Organization Charts
Add chart to slide
Change chart type
Chart to image
Series statistics

EDIT
Undo
Redo
Cut
Copy
Paste
Paste link
Clear
Select all
Check spelling
Personal dictionary

TEXT
Font
Size
Style
Color
All attributes
Set bullet attributes
Justify
Set anchor point
Show text ruler
Add stamp

GRAPHICS
Fill
Line attributes
Special effects
Button attributes
Ruler/grid
Tool lock
Group
Ungroup
Move to front
Move to back
Rotate
Flip
Align
Center on slide
Edit object

©1992 Osborne **McGraw-Hill**   Harvard Graphics for Windows Made Easy

Osborne McGraw-Hill

You're important to us...

We'd like to know what you're interested in, what kinds of books you're looking for, and what you thought about this book in particular.

Please fill out the attached card and mail it in. We'll do our best to keep you informed about Osborne's newest books and special offers.

▶ YES, Send Me a FREE Color Catalog of all Osborne computer books
To Receive Catalog, Fill in Last 4 Digits of ISBN Number from Back of Book (see below bar code) 0-07-881_ _ _ _ _

Name: _____ Title: _____

Company: _____

Address: _____

City: _____ State: _____ Zip: _____

I'M PARTICULARLY INTERESTED IN THE FOLLOWING *(Check all that apply)*

I use this software
- ☐ WordPerfect
- ☐ Microsoft Word
- ☐ WordStar
- ☐ Lotus 1-2-3
- ☐ Quattro
- ☐ Others _____

I use this operating system
- ☐ DOS
- ☐ Windows
- ☐ UNIX
- ☐ Macintosh
- ☐ Others _____

I program in
- ☐ C or C++
- ☐ Pascal
- ☐ BASIC
- ☐ Others _____

I chose this book because
- ☐ Recognized author's name
- ☐ Osborne/McGraw-Hill's reputation
- ☐ Read book review
- ☐ Read Osborne catalog
- ☐ Saw advertisement in store
- ☐ Found/recommended in library
- ☐ Required textbook
- ☐ Price
- ☐ Other _____

I rate this book:
- ☐ Excellent   ☐ Good   ☐ Poor

Comments _____

Topics I would like to see covered in future books by Osborne/McGraw-Hill include:

IMPORTANT REMINDER
To get your FREE catalog, write in the last 4 digits of the ISBN number printed on the back cover (see below bar code) 0-07-881 _ _ _ _

Computer Books

(800) 227-0900

Bookmarker Design — Lance Ravella

← Tear off for Bookmark

Osborne McGraw-Hill

Computer Books

(800) 227-0900

NO POSTAGE
NECESSARY
IF MAILED
IN THE
UNITED STATES

BUSINESS REPLY MAIL
First Class   Permit NO. 3111   Berkeley, CA

Postage will be paid by addressee

Osborne McGraw-Hill
2600 Tenth Street
Berkeley, California 94710-9938